THE FEDERAL IDEA

A significant part of the world's population lives under some sort of federal arrangement. And yet, the concepts of federalism and federation remain under-theorised. Federalist theorists have, for the most part, defined their object by opposition to the unitary state. As a result, they have not developed public law theories that capture the specificity of this type of polity.

Bringing together contributions from leading public law theorists and intellectual historians, this volume explores the foundations of federalism. It develops novel perspectives on the core problems of traditional federalist theory and charts new departures in federalist theory and federal power-sharing. At a time when we look for more inclusive ways of ordering public life, the volume fills an urgent theoretical and political need.

Volume 18 in the series Hart Studies in Comparative Public Law

Hart Studies in Comparative Public Law

Recent titles in this series:

Parliaments and Human Rights
Redressing the Democratic Deficit
Edited by Murray Hunt, Hayley Hooper and Paul Yowell

The Right to Freedom of Assembly
A Comparative Study
Orsolya Salát

An Inquiry into the Existence of Global Values
Through the Lens of Comparative Constitutional Law
Edited by Dennis Davis, Alan Richter and Cheryl Saunders

The Scope and Intensity of Substantive Review
Traversing Taggart's Rainbow
Edited by Hanna Wilberg and Mark Elliott

Entick v Carrington
250 Years of the Rule of Law
Edited by Adam Tomkins and Paul Scott

Administrative Law and Judicial Deference
Matthew Lewans

Soft Law and Public Authorities
Remedies and Reform
Greg Weeks

Legitimate Expectations in the Common Law World
Edited by Matthew Groves and Greg Weeks

The Dynamics of Exclusionary Constitutionalism
Mazen Masri

Constitutional Courts, Gay Rights and Sexual Orientation Equality
Angioletta Sperti

Principled Reasoning in Human Rights Adjudication
Se-Shauna Wheatle

Human Rights and Judicial Review in Australia and Canada
Janina Boughey

The Foundations and Traditions of Constitutional Amendment
Edited by Richard Albert, Xenophon Contiades and Alkmene Fotiadou

The Federal Idea

Public Law Between Governance and Political Life

Edited by
Amnon Lev

·HART·
PUBLISHING
OXFORD AND PORTLAND, OREGON
2017

Hart Publishing
An imprint of Bloomsbury Publishing Plc

Hart Publishing Ltd
Kemp House
Chawley Park
Cumnor Hill
Oxford OX2 9PH
UK

Bloomsbury Publishing Plc
50 Bedford Square
London
WC1B 3DP
UK

www.hartpub.co.uk
www.bloomsbury.com

Published in North America (US and Canada) by
Hart Publishing
c/o International Specialized Book Services
920 NE 58th Avenue, Suite 300
Portland, OR 97213-3786
USA

www.isbs.com

HART PUBLISHING, the Hart/Stag logo, BLOOMSBURY and the Diana logo are trademarks of Bloomsbury Publishing Plc

First published 2017

British Library Cataloguing-in-Publication Data
A catalogue record for this book is available from the British Library.

ISBN: HB: 978-1-50990-711-3
ePDF: 978-1-50990-713-7
ePub: 978-1-50990-712-0

Library of Congress Cataloging-in-Publication Data

Names: Lev, Amnon, editor.

Title: The federal idea : public law between governance and political life / edited by Amnon Lev.

Description: Oxford ; Portland, Oregon : Hart Publishing, An imprint of Bloomsbury Publishing Plc, 2017. | Series: Hart studies in comparative public law ; volume 18 | Includes bibliographical references and index. | Description based on print version record and CIP data provided by publisher; resource not viewed.

Identifiers: LCCN 2017012594 (print) | LCCN 2017015466 (ebook) | ISBN 9781509907120 (Epub) | ISBN 9781509907113 (hardback : alk. paper)

Subjects: LCSH: Federal government.

Classification: LCC K3185 (ebook) | LCC K3185 .F427 2017 (print) | DDC 342/.042—dc23

LC record available at https://lccn.loc.gov/2017012594

Typeset by Compuscript Ltd, Shannon
Printed and bound in Great Britain by CPI Group (UK) Ltd, Croydon CR0 4YY

Contents

Part III: Federal Trajectories

Contributors

Nicholas Aroney is Professor of Constitutional Law, School of Law, The University of Queensland

Olivier Beaud is Professor of Constitutional Law, Université Panthéon-Assas, member of *Institut Universitaire de France*

Jessica Bulman-Pozen is Professor of Law, Columbia Law School

Jean-François Gaudreault-DesBiens is Associate Dean, Research and Communications, and Canada Research Chair in North American and Comparative Juridical and Cultural Identities, Faculty of Law, Université de Montréal

Duncan Kelly is Reader in Political Thought at the Department of Politics and International Studies, University of Cambridge, and fellow of Jesus College, Cambridge

Amnon Lev is Associate Professor (law and philosophy), Faculty of Law, University of Copenhagen

Dwight Newman is Professor of Law & Canada Research Chair in Indigenous Rights in Constitutional and International Law, University of Saskatchewan

Edward L Rubin is University Professor of Law and Political Science, Vanderbilt Law School

Cheryl Saunders is Laureate Professor Emeritus of Law, Melbourne Law School, and John Kincaid, Robert B and Helen S Meyner Professor of Government and Public Service and Director of the Meyner Center, Lafayette College

Stephen Tierney is Professor of Constitutional Theory, School of Law, University of Edinburgh, and Director of the Edinburgh Centre for Constitutional Law

Introduction: Federalism and Public Law Theory

AMNON LEV*

THE SURGE OF interest in the foundations of public law has yet to extend to federalism, despite the fact that a significant part of the world's population lives under some sort of federal arrangement.[1] Notwithstanding an extensive literature on the constitutions of specific federations, federalism as such remains under-theorised. As a result, we know very little about the intellectual foundations of the federation; what the values and ideas are that underpin this type of polity, inform its government and shape the normative expectations of the governed. The present collection of essays is an attempt to remedy this lacuna. Whether or not it succeeds depends on the individual contributions. Still, it might not be without interest, as a preliminary, to develop the intuition that informed the work of assembling them. It concerns sovereignty. Other differences aside, theorists of federalism agree that the doctrine of sovereignty is the main obstacle to federalism's development.[2] But this cannot be the whole story. Despite the exorbitant claim sovereignty makes to be the sole source and form of power, belief in it did not

* My thanks go to Professor Denis Baranger for his always incisive comments to this introduction.

[1] To take but one, albeit prominent, example, federalism does not feature at all in Martin Loughlin's explorations of the idea and foundations of public law. If Loughlin recognises the pivotal importance of the American political experience for the development of modern public law, what retains his attention is not its federal nature. To Loughlin, the interest of the system of government articulated by Hamilton and Madison is that it demonstrates that republican government can co-exist with a strong executive (see Martin Loughlin, *The Idea of Public Law* (Oxford, Oxford University Press, 2003); *The Foundations of Public Law* (Oxford, Oxford University Press, 2010)).

[2] Olivier Beaud, *Théorie de la Fédération* (Paris, Presses Universitaires de France, 2009) 58–65; Michael Burgess, *Federalism and European Union: The Building of Europe 1950–2000* (Abingdon, Routledge, 2000) 12–13; Guiseppe Duso, 'Pensare il federalismo: tra categorie e costituzione' in Guiseppe Duso and Antonino Scalone (eds), *Come pensare il federalismo? Nouve categorie e trasformazioni costituzionali* (Monza, Polimetrica, 2010) 77–78; Daniel J Elazar, 'The United States and Europe: Models for Their Epochs' in Kalypso Nicolaidis and Robert Howse (eds), *The Federal Vision: Legitimacy and Levels of Governance in the United States and the European Union* (Oxford, Oxford University Press, 2001) 34; Murray Forsyth, *Union of States: The Theory and Practice of Confederation* (New York, Leicester University Press, 1981) 79–80; Carl J Friedrich, *Trends of Federalism in Theory and Practice* (London, Pall Mall Press, 1968) 12–13; Anton R Greber, *Die vorpositiven Grundlagen des Bundesstaates* (Bâle, Helbing & Lichtenhahn, 2000) 65–69; Neil MacCormick, *Questioning Sovereignty: Law, State, and Nation in the European Commonwealth* (Oxford, Oxford University Press, 2002) 126–132; Robert Schütze, *From Dual to Cooperative Federalism: The Changing Structure of European Law* (Oxford, Oxford University Press, 2009) 31–32, 69; Christoph Schönberger, 'Die Europäische Union als Bund. Zugleich ein Beitrag zur Verabschiedung des Staatenbund-Bundesstaat-Schemas' (2004) 129 *Archiv des öffentlichen Rechts* 105–109.

prevent the emergence and comprehensive theorisation of constitutionalism which, after all, is a practice of how to distribute sovereign power between different, and often competing, actors, each of which holds power by right. Consequently, we are left to wonder what exactly it is about a *federal* distribution of power that renders it intractable to public law theorisation.[3] The intuition we shall develop here is that what obstructs the theorisation of federalism is not the idea of sovereignty but the basic structures of public law theory.

All this might seem very subtle and scholastic, and consequently ill-suited for an introduction. However, the failure to understand why public law theory has been so inhospitable to federalism has important implications for how we think about federal phenomena and for how, by what methods, we put our conceptions of federalism into practice. To this we might add another, essential consideration. As the degree to which sovereignty has left its imprint on constitutional orders varies considerably, defining federalism mainly by its opposition to sovereignty as federalism theorists are wont to do leaves unanswered the question of what the commonality of federal constitutions is. What is it that unites these constitutional trajectories that have the quality of being federal but which are, in other respects, very different? And what is the appropriate conceptual context within which we should consider them?

In order to shed light on these key questions, we shall take a somewhat unconventional approach to federalism. Traditionally, the theorisation of federalism proceeds from a consideration of the actual polities that we define as federal. We move in the opposite direction, from public law theory to federalism. This is not to suggest that there is a Platonic idea of federalism that exists independently of its instantiation in particular institutions. What it entails is the weaker, although still controversial, claim that the body of public law theory, as it has developed through time, determines the federal articulation of power in specific ways that recur across very diverse constitutional trajectories.

Understanding how public law theory conditions the way we theorise federalism will not give us a unitary notion of federalism. It will, however, enable us to delineate the conceptual space of federalism. We are, in a sense, shifting focus from federalism, as the account of specific polities, to the background against which federalisms appear. One might say that we are proposing something like a *peinture en négatif* of federalism as a category of public law theory. Taking this approach entails relinquishing what is perhaps the most fundamental ambition of theory—that of defining its object—but at the same time, it enables us to show that federalism moves within a determinate, if not unitary, format.

The hypothesis we advance is that federalisms are articulated from within or, as the case may be, between two determinations of the space of public law theory found in, respectively, Locke's treatises of government and Kant's article on

[3] The emphasis here is on *theory*. As Sergio Ortino notes, sovereignty and federalism will often be compatible in fact; many political entities only become sovereign by federating (Sergio Ortino, *Introduzione al diritto costituzionale federativo* (Turin, G Giappichelli Editore, 1993) 31).

perpetual peace. We shall use the two texts as a sort of modal template for federalism. What this means in more simple terms is that we shall look to the two texts to see how a shared conception of political community constrains the theorisation of federalism both within and between polities. The determinations we are looking for concern the ontology of political community. If Locke and, following him, Kant excludes the federal from the government of the polity, it is because a federal polity would represent *a lesser form* of community. As we shall see when we consider the contributions to this volume, the idea that a federation is not, or not yet, a real polity continues to inform public law theory in different ways.

This introdution, and the approach it takes, is likely to strike some as overly abstract. The conceptual space we delimit is not yet the space of actual federations. Furthermore, the transition between the two texts we consider is likely to seem arbitrary, as they belong within universes that are, in many respects, dissimilar, in some respects even opposed. The abstract nature of the exercise is the price we have to pay for bringing to light the intricate implication of federalism and public law theory.

I. MAKING PUBLIC LAW WORK AS THEORY

The first, and in many ways definitive, problem of public law theory is how to get beyond its beginning; how to move theory beyond the limiting case of society—the state of nature—from which Hobbes had shown the necessity of the passage into civil society in a demonstration premised on conditions of generalised violence that allowed him to subordinate all other considerations to the imperative of self-preservation, creating a unitary format of obligation. If this move allowed him to hold that subjection was freely entered into, it also had the effect of rendering singularly fragile the entire edifice of public law. Predicating the sovereignty of sovereign power on the free choice of the individual meant that the alienation of liberty from (prospective) subject to sovereign could be revoked at any moment. Even if, on the terms of Hobbes' theory of commonwealth, the recovery of agency would engage only the individual and, as such, have no *political* import, founding subjection in liberty had the effect of suspending the ties of community. As articulated by Hobbes, these ties are coterminous with political obligation. In deciding whether to commit to the social contract or not, the individual was faced with the sovereign, not with the community into which he is about to compact, the existence of which remains suspended on his decision. It is to this state of affairs that Locke refers, albeit somewhat obliquely, when he notes that a constitution where each would be 'under no other ties, than he was in before in the State of Nature' would dissolve the community it sought to create, thus making 'the mighty *Leviathan* of a shorter duration than the feeblest Creatures, and not let it outlast the day it was born in.'[4]

[4] John Locke, *Second Treatise* in Peter Laslett, *John Locke. Two Treatises of Government* (Cambridge, Cambridge University Press, 1960) §§ 97–98, pp 332–333.

What ailed sovereignty from the beginning was the weak symbolic presence of the community it purported to ground. This weakness manifested itself in yet another way that would be central to the project of theorising public law. The precarious existence of the commonwealth had an epistemological corollary. Inasmuch as commitment extended only so far forth in time as it was borne by an act of individual will, and therefore needed to be constantly re-affirmed, the object of commitment could never be anything other than the formal existence of a constitution. But to Locke, the conviction, however firm, that the rule of law must replace force—the foundation on which Hobbes would establish civil order—cannot in itself put an end to the ills to which the state of nature exposes man. He who is to subject himself to the sovereign must be told more than that he will have a master:

> [It is] vain then to talk of Subjection and Obedience, without telling us whom we are to obey. For were I never so fully perswaded, that there ought to be Magistracy and Rule in the World, yet I am nevertheless at Liberty still, till it appears who is the Person that hath right to my Obedience: since if there be no Marks to know him by, and distinguish him, that hath Right to Rule from other Men, it may be my self, as well as any other.[5]

Not only must we be assured of the existence of sovereign power; we must also have certified ways of telling how power is distributed within the commonwealth. Locke's insistence on this point is clearly an implicit critique of Hobbes but crucially, the need for signs or marks of sovereignty is predicated on the absence of constraints that made Hobbes' state of nature a state of war. In this respect, man is where Hobbes left him. He is (still) judge of whether or not to give up his freedom and, absent a constitutional articulation of power to indicate the rightful holder of it, deciding to do so would not be rational:

> [A] Man can never be oblig'd in Conscience to submit to any Power, unless he can be satisfied who is the Person, who has a Right to Exercise that Power over him. If this were not so, there would be no distinction between Pirates and Lawful Princes, he that has Force is without any more ado to be obey'd ...[6]

At the level of Locke's text, the (partial) remedy for the problems we have detailed above is the principle of majority rule; that the consent of the majority be 'received as the act of the whole, and conclude every individual.'[7] The reason for introducing majority rule is obvious. By shifting the burden of community from the individual to (a part of) the collective, Locke interposes an entity between subject and sovereign to stand in for the people. The significance of this is most readily apparent where the individual chooses to step back from the social contract but more importantly, the interposition of the majority between subject and sovereign is also

[5] Locke, *First Treatise* in Peter Laslett, *John Locke. Two Treatises of Government* (Cambridge, Cambridge University Press, 1960) § 81, p 202; *cf* II, § 225, p 415. On the semiosis of sovereignty in Locke, see Denis Baranger, 'The apparition of sovereignty' in Hent Kalmo and Quentin Skinner (eds), *Sovereignty in Fragments: The Past, Present, and Future of a Contested Concept* (Cambridge, Cambridge University Press, 2010) 59–61.

[6] Locke, *First Treatise* § 81, p 203.

[7] Locke, *Second Treatise* § 98, p 332.

operative where the former does not question his initial commitment. The existence of a functioning majority can therefore serve as a warrant of the constant existence of the community which, in turn, means that the existence of the community no longer appears as a function of individual consent, except in the limiting case of revolution.[8]

In moving theory beyond the moment of foundation, majority rule addresses both the problems that afflicted public law theory. It secures the object of public law theory *existentially* and *epistemologically*. Constancy entails identity, and with identity comes the possibility of analysing a community as an object with a determinate structure—a constitution. The importance of the introduction of majority rule can therefore not be overstated, which makes it all the more essential to understand how, by what operations, Locke makes the principle work. He justifies its introduction by two standard arguments: (1) majority rule is a procedural requirement if men are to join together in society; and (2) the laws of motion dictate that the majority should decide what course of action to pursue:

> For that which acts any Community, being only the consent of the individuals of it, and it being necessary to that which is one body to move one way; it is necessary the Body should move that way whither the greater force carries it, which is the *consent of the majority*; or else it is impossible it should act or continue one Body, *one Community* ...[9]

The arguments used by Locke are logical in nature, which would seem to imply that the use of majority rule was somehow self-evident.[10] Introducing the principle of majority rule in this manner belies the complexity of what Locke is doing. It is in fact far from given that the principle of majority rule will work *as theory*. For it to do so, political theory must have taken the first crucial step beyond the moment of foundation. The existence of the commonwealth, that is to say, the existence of sovereign power, can no longer be in question. Pufendorf makes the point very succinctly in his analysis of federations: 'The greater draws the less only in Bodies already constituted, not in those which are still to be established.'[11] As long as foundation continues to

[8] On the limited extent of the right of resistance in Locke, see Maurizio Merlo, 'Potere naturale, proprietà e potere politico in John Locke' in Giuseppe Duso (ed), *Il Potere. Per la storie della filosofia politica moderna* (Rome, Carocci editore, 1999) 170–74; Jacqueline Stevens, 'The Reasonableness of John Locke's Majority: Property rights, Consent, and Resistance in the Second Treatise' (1996) 24 *Political Theory* 443–47.

[9] Locke, *Second Treatise* § 96, pp 331–32.

[10] John Dunn notes that the institutions or practices of the time did not rely on majority rule and that the actual putting into practice of it would have seemed an absurdity to any seventeenth-century Englishman, including Locke (see John Dunn, *The Political Thought of John Locke: An Historical Account of the Argument of the 'Two Treatises of Government'* (Cambridge, Cambridge University Press, 1969) 128–129). He argues that it still made sense for Locke to champion majority rule as his concern was with the 'logical prerequisites' for political legitimacy. Even if we leave aside the question of whether, on the terms of Locke's theory, majority rule is in fact a logical prerequisite of political legitimacy, Dunn's reading underestimates just how fundamentally the problem that majority rule is introduced to solve implicates the possibility of theorising political community.

[11] Samuel Pufendorf, *Of the Law of Nature and Nations* (London, J Walthoe, R Wilkin, J and J Bonwicke, S Birt, T Ward, and T Osborne, 1729) VII, v, p 684.

be a problem *in theory*, the move from the requirement of unanimity to majority rule, away from the stand-off between the subject and the sovereign, remains a dead letter. This is clear from Hobbes' work. He argues that the designation of the sovereign, perhaps the most fundamental public law question of his entire theory of commonwealth, should be made by majority decision, but unsurprisingly, he does not develop the implications of this idea further. At no point is commitment to sovereign power so firmly entrenched that the identity of the person carrying it could credibly be raised as a separate question.[12]

Locke's method, if you will, is to replace Hobbes' question of how to adjudicate mutually exclusive rights claim with the question of how men interact in the absence of legitimate governmental authority.[13] Focus thus shifts from a situation in which the irresolution of law precludes the establishment of authority to a situation in which pre-political authority that is grounded in care, ultimately in fatherly love, is present and conditions social interaction. The move is made in and through a montage whereby the characteristics of pre-political authority are transposed onto the relationship of subject and prince. Habituation allows familial forms of authority to carry over into political society:

> Thus 'twas easie, and almost natural for Children by a tacit, and scarce avoidable consent to make for the *Father's Authority and Government*. They had been accustomed in their Childhood to follow his Direction, and to refer their little differences to him, and when they were Men, who fitter to rule them?[14]

In this way, fathers, 'by an insensible change,' came to be also '*politick Monarchs*' of their family and, with successive generations continuing their work, eventually laid the foundations of kingdoms, both hereditary and elective.[15]

Trust, the key concept in Locke's political theory, refers back to this first relationship of care. Locke devotes the entire first treatise to refuting Filmer's claim that monarchic power is an inheritance, in the final instance from Adam,[16] but as we have seen, he too models power on paternal authority. The extent to which power is a trust is a function of the capacity of the ruler to look after society as if it were a child left to his care. In 'the Infancies of Commonwealths,' Locke tells us, those entrusted with

[12] Thomas Hobbes, *Leviathan* (Indianapolis, Hackett Publishing Company, 1994) II, xviii, 5, p 112: 'For if he voluntarily entered into the congregation of them that were assembled, he sufficiently declared thereby his will (and therefore tacitly covenanted) to stand to what the major part should ordain …'

[13] See John Dunn, 'The Concept of "Trust" in the Politics of John Locke' in Richard Rorty, Jerome B Schneewind and Quentin Skinner (eds), *Philosophy in History: Essays in the Historiography of Philosophy* (Cambridge, Cambridge University Press, 1984) 290. For a brilliant analysis of the pivotal role Locke played in moving political theory from Hobbes' 'anti-constitutionalism' to what would become the format of public law theory in Britain, see Denis Baranger, *Écrire la constitution non-écrite. Une introduction au droit politique britannique* (Paris, Presses Universitaires de France, 2008) 80–93.

[14] Locke, *Second Treatise* § 75, p 317; *cf* § 107, p 338.

[15] ibid § 76, p 318.

[16] Peter Laslett saw the choice between Filmer and Hobbes as mutually exclusive; it was the former who set the terms of the argument, 'not Locke himself, and decidedly not Hobbes' (Peter Laslett, *John Locke. Two Treatises of Government* introduction, 67–68). However, if Locke needs to engage with Filmer, it is because of the aporetic situation in which Hobbes had left public law theory. Locke needs to naturalise power; to confer upon it something of the aura of fatherly authority, without making power a divine right. Trust enables this balancing act and in turn marks its success.

rule 'commonly' used their power so. Had they failed in their paternal duties, their offspring would not have grown to maturity:

> ... young Societies could not have subsisted: without such nursing Fathers tender and carefull of the publick weale, all Governments would have sunk under the Weakness and Infirmities of their Infancy; and the Prince and the People had soon perished together.[17]

The idea of trust derives its force from its hybrid nature: it is, at the same time, natural and moral. As a quasi-filial duty, it is something of which we can presume the existence *and* censure the absence. Trust permits the oscillation between description and prescription in Locke's text. But as society grows, it becomes less and less credible that familial forms of authority grounded in care can rein in power. This is a function of size, obviously, but it is also a function of a more general change in the nature of social relations that grows out of social development. In the 'poor but vertuous Age' in which governments were begun, the familial analogy could still be relied upon, but ambition and luxury would subsequently drive a wedge between princes and their people, teaching the former to have 'distinct and separate interests' and impressing upon the latter the need to 'examine more carefully the *Original* and Rights of *Government*.'[18]

In other words, the motive forces that disaggregate political society, placing ever-greater demands on trust, also render trust more fragile. What we might call Locke's *moral conservatism* consists in his belief that trust is a non-renewable stock that is left over from before the beginnings of political order. Given the thrust of social development, the question becomes how to preserve what is left of trust. This conservative intuition underpins and informs Locke's attempt to set limits *in law* to the power of the prince. His preoccupation with the forms of power in government is borne out of a desire to locate the point at which the exercise of government ceases to aim at the common good that should always be its lodestar.

Underlying Locke's exposition is a conception of power that revolves around legislative power. Legislative power is elevated to the position of supreme power on the supposition that it is, by nature, incapable of being completely arbitrary. Arising out of the transfer to the legislator of the joint power of every member of society, legislative power cannot have more power than a person in the state of nature could have in himself; hence, the legislative could never have the power to destroy life or take away property.[19]

[17] Locke, *Second Treatise* § 110, p 342.

[18] ibid § 111, p 343. In focusing on trust we are leaving out several essential aspects of Locke's political theory, most importantly the question of property. Knowing that Locke argues from the existence of the commons system, according to which individual property rights arise only through labour-induced individuation of what was owned in common, allows us to understand why the distinction of *mine* and *thine*, even in the absence of a sovereign, does not set off the destructive dynamics that defines Hobbes' state of nature (see James Tully, *A Discourse on Property: John Locke and his Adversaries* (Cambridge, Cambridge University Press, 1980) 135–147, 153–154). However, as the introduction of money, and the *amor sceleratus habendi* to which it gives rise, disrupts the primordial alignment of the interests of princes and their people, it is essentially left to trust to hold together the polity.

[19] Locke, *Second Treatise* § 135, p 357.

Our modern sensibilities may not allow us to share Locke's confidence in legislative power, but we can nevertheless appreciate that the point of his exercise is to indicate a format of power that can lay claim to our trust because it is disposed to act in our best interest. Legislative power, as it is conceived by Locke, must overcome (its) nature to act against the best interests of those subject to it. This is not an absolute guarantee but it is a guarantee of sorts. On that supposition, the fact that government is made by law is a prima facie indication that a power given in trust is being exercised with respect of that condition, and it can therefore serve as a warrant that trust is both intact and in force.

Opposed to legislative power is a form of power that is not constrained by nature. Locke introduces *executive* power as a concession to practical political life: the laws, being 'at once, and in a short time, made,' require the existence of a power to attend to their application if they are to have 'constant and lasting force.'[20] This definition ties executive power to the operation of the laws which, in view of the status of legislative power, is just as we would expect. Proceeding further in Locke's analysis of government, we find that the compass of executive power stretches to include the exercise of power 'without the prescription of Law, and sometimes even against it,' if demanded by the public weal.[21]

Following on the heels of the distinction between legislative and executive power Locke introduces a subdivision of the latter. From executive power properly understood, he excludes a set of functions that relate to the exterior of the commonwealth. If the members of the commonwealth are distinct in relation to each other, they constitute one body in relation to the rest of the world. The power of joint external action Locke calls *federative* power. It 'contains the Power of War and Peace, Leagues and Alliances, and all the Transactions, with all Persons and Communities without the Commonwealth …'[22]

This is the trinity of powers—legislative, executive, federative—from which Locke fashions his constitutional theory. Before we unpack his determination of federative power and its position in the economy of government, a preliminary remark might be in order. It is clear that Locke's federative power does not correspond to what we today understand by federal government. There is nothing inherently federal about external action or about the specific activities that Locke groups together under the rubric of federative power. Indeed, what is of interest to us here is not how he defines federative power, but that it serves as the semantic placeholder of the aspects of government that are extraneous to the commonwealth, both in the sense of being externally directed but also, as we shall see, in the sense of not being referable back to the pre-political relations out of which political society grows. Locke may not define federal government as we do today, but in defining and closing off the domain of 'ordinary,' that is, political government, he lays the groundwork for the public law conceptions of federalism; a point we shall return to.

[20] ibid § 144, p 365.
[21] ibid § 160, p 375.
[22] ibid § 146, p 365.

Of all the conceptual operations that go into articulating the restricted economy of functions that shall henceforth define government, distinguishing between executive and federative power is perhaps the most important. Locke is breaking new ground in proposing to single out the power of external action. The novelty of his démarche is reflected in his comment that he is 'indifferent' to the name chosen as long as the thing be understood.[23] To justify his neologism, Locke tells us that a difference in kind exists between the two forms of power; a difference that is reflected in the constraints on the exercise of power. Action taken in relation to subjects 'one amongst another' is to be taken according to 'antecedent, positive, standing' laws whereas it is left to the prudence of those who have federative power to decide what is to be done in relation to foreigners. The 'variation of designs and interests' renders their actions less apt to be directed by law.

Locke's insistence that executive and federative power be 'really distinct in themselves' is puzzling given that they serve much the same interests and inhere in the same person. In fact, he himself tells us that they are 'hardly to be separated, and placed, at the same time, in the hands of distinct persons.' Doing so would be ruinous for the commonwealth as it would place its force under different commands.[24] The argument that they are distinct powers is compelling for war and for the conclusion of treaties; what we might loosely refer to as high politics. However, the question remains whether Locke has succeeded in showing that a state's external action is essentially different to the business of 'ordinary,' internal government. After all, federative power is also concerned with other less symbolically charged matters than those of high politics. Its remit extends to 'all Transactions, with all Persons and Communities without the Commonwealth.' We would be wrong to suppose this to be nothing but a residual category, added on so as to allow for all eventualities, even the least likely. On the terms of Locke's theory, we would expect such mundane matters, including the booming colonial trade in which he was actively involved throughout his life, to constitute a weighty concern to both the public and the state.

We have, therefore, good reason to doubt that the importance Locke attaches to the distinction between executive and federative power is just a function of the kinds of action that power is called to react to, as he would have us believe. Something else is going on that we cannot get a handle on unless we also take into consideration the political context within which power is exercised. Ultimately, what makes sense of Locke's insistence that action taken in relation to subjects 'one amongst another' is apt to be determined by antecedent laws, unlike action taken in relation to foreigners, is not the nature of the action but the fact that government by settled,

[23] On the afterlife, or lack of same, of Locke's neologism, see David Armitage, *Foundations of Modern International Thought* (New York, Cambridge University Press, 2013) 84.

[24] Unsurprisingly, scholars have, for the most part, ignored the distinction between executive and federative power, collapsing the two powers into a general conception of executive power (see, eg, Loughlin, *Foundations of Public Law* 384; Pasquale Pasquino, 'Locke on King's Prerogative' (1998) 26 *Political Theory* 199). Where they acknowledge its systematic import, it is seen as extraneous to Locke's philosophical argument (see MCJ Vile, *Constitutionalism and the Separation of Powers* (Indianapolis, Liberty Fund, 1998) 65–66, where the distinction is taken to reflect a prescient intuition of the different challenges facing governments of early modern Europe at home and abroad).

standing laws is a condition of trust, a precondition of giving up the natural power that accrues to every man before he enters political society.[25]

By spatially mapping power, Locke proffers a demonstration that a difference in kind obtains between executive and federative power; something he could not have shown from a consideration of their respective objects. As their domains do not overlap, federative and executive power must, by implication, be different. Locke underpins this claim by the analogy he proposes for federative power. Executive power and federative power are both natural, but where executive power is construed on analogy with the authority of the father, federative power 'answers to the Power every Man naturally had before he entred into Society.'[26] Given the personal identity of the holder of executive and federative power, we might well question whether the analogy can shoulder the burden that Locke seems intent on charging it with. He could, without doing damage to the integrity of his system, have argued that protecting the nation/household has been always one of the tasks of paternal authority. If he does not, it is, we would argue, because his concerns extend beyond the determination of a function of government. The different provenances that Locke suggests for executive and federative power might not map onto the person of the sovereign, but that is not their real purpose. The point of his argument is to situate political power within a closed domain which, in turn, re-establishes the possibility of aligning government on natural sentiment that was lost as society outgrew familial modes of organisation. The existence of an outside confirms, and entrenches, the reality of what is inside. Thus, the existence of a common frontier beyond which power is freed from the strictures of constitutional law comes to confirm the political nature of internal government; in other words, it confirms trust.[27]

Again, it might be objected that all this concerns federalism only in a very general sense, inasmuch as it falls under the rubric of public law theory and draws on (some of) the same sources. Indeed, Locke has nothing to say about federalism as we know it today. Nonetheless, his determination of the domain and the function of public law theory effectively configures how what we know as federalism operates. In excluding federative power from the remit of 'ordinary' government, he places it outside the reach of trust. It operates in a domain where relations are inherently conflictual. Given that it is non-political, its scope cannot extend beyond what is needed to sustain the polity. This is not to say that Locke's treatises already contain Montesquieu's theory of federalism. Rather, the claim is that in seeing federalism as an instrument to service the most basic considerations in a polity, above all self-preservation, Montesquieu was acting on a determination that was constitutive of public law theory and within a domain that was already in place.

Assigning distinct domains to internal and external state action was required to solve the problem of how to make public law work as theory. Seen in this light,

[25] Locke, *Second Treatise* §§ 136–37, pp 359–360.

[26] ibid § 145, p 365.

[27] Re-aligning government on trust requires the spatialisation of governmental power, but that which is generated in and through this operation—the hierarchical ordering of 'ordinary,' political government and its auxiliary functions (of which federalism shall be one)—involves space only in a minimal way, as position, which is why it is so easily transposed from the interstate sphere to the sphere of the state.

Locke's distribution/demarcation of the domains of government action is the terminus of the quest to establish the foundations of public law theory.[28] As we hope to have shown, this exercise entails a configuration of the domain of public law theory that had profound consequences for federalism. To become operative, public law theory had to achieve closure. What ultimately tied it to the notion of a perfectly constituted, and therefore closed, polity was not an obsession with the indivisibility of sovereign power but rather the baggage of implicit assurances and invitations—trust—that fuels constitutionalism. Public law theory confined its regard to that which is underwritten by trust. By that token public law theory disqualified federalism as non-political because its ambition is, and has always been, to justify government by working out and substantiating the formal relations of subjection on which sovereignty rests.

II. MODES OF FEDERALISM

Our analysis of how Locke's treatises of government configured the domain of public law theory focused on the spatial distribution of government action and on the implicit ontological determination of political community that motivated it. In order to understand how the ontology of political community conditions the way we think about the federation, we need to consider more closely what the configuration of the space of public law theory entails about agency at the level of the polity.

A first point: on the account that Locke gives, federative power is of an essentially personal nature. Where executive power grows out of paternal authority and is held to its standards of care, both in relation to his own family and to the extended family that is political society, federative power attaches directly to the person of the holder and is therefore not saddled with any normative expectations. This might seem trivial, but belief that the external exercise of power attaches to the *person* of the sovereign has structured the way foreign affairs are conducted, constitutionally as well as professionally. To give but one example, the conventional belief that the full range of constitutional controls do not apply to the conduct of foreign affairs has its origin in the disaggregation of the realm of paternal authority into distinct domains of governmental action. Equally, if we consider the means by which foreign affairs were conducted—the agents and instruments of early modern diplomacy—we find that, for both instructions and remuneration, they depended directly on the person of the monarch rather than on the collective he represented. Indeed, the institution of a diplomatic system reflected a belief that the monarch was not supposed to leave the territory of his kingdom, except to go to war or into exile.[29]

[28] One might fault Locke for inconsistency inasmuch as the spatial distribution of executive power leaves us without a moral criterion with which to judge the external action of the state. But if there is incoherence, as John Dunn tells us there is (Dunn, *The Political Thought of John Locke* 162–164), it might not reflect a muddled mind as he supposed, but the contradictory demands that must be met in order to carve a domain of action where power can be coded by law.

[29] Lucien Bély, *L'art de la paix en Europe. Naissance de la diplomatie moderne XVIe–XVIIIe siècle* (Paris, Presses Universitaires de France, 2007) 296–311; Heinz Schilling, *Konfessionalisierung und Staatsinteressen 1559–1660* (Paderborn, Ferdinand Schöningh, 2007) 120–129.

Closer to our topic, the belief that the agent of federative power is the person of the sovereign, not the collective of which he is the representative, also explains why Pufendorf, as he analyses the different forms of government, should place federations on a par with the personal union of monarchies, these being the only two systems of government he considers.[30] The belief in the personal nature of external action also entails that even if an external exercise of power can commit the commonwealth, it is not an immediate expression of, and cannot therefore compromise, its capacity for agency. Federative ties might bind the commonwealth, but they do not alter its fundamental status as a political society. Locke is thus at pains to point out that a government does not cease to be independent for being in league with another community.[31] Despite being less than compelling in logic, the argument shall go on to become a commonplace in European public law theory.[32]

The implication is that agency, real, full agency, is the province of proper political societies. That is not to say that the federation is a chimera; Pufendorf, it will be remembered, recognises it as a distinct form of government. But if a federation is a government, what it orders is not a society in the full sense of the term. This intuition underlies Montesquieu's definition of the federation, according to which its concerns do not extend beyond common defence.[33] Security is obviously a requirement for political society to flourish but it remains that, on this definition, the *federal* dimension of a polity does not include any of the determinations that constitute it as a *political* entity. The lesser being of the federation is reflected in its reduced agency; an agency that is non-political in the sense of not ranging over the full dimensions of a polity and in the sense of being tied so intimately to the person of the sovereign as to seem almost private.

We see how this nexus of agency and ontology conditions the theory of federation in the famous pages that Kant devotes to the federation. At first blush, there would seem to be little to connect his enquiry into perpetual peace to Locke's treatises of government. For one, the scope of Kant's enterprise is universal, in contrast to the avowed particularity of Locke's theory of government. However, a closer reading reveals that Kant's theory of universal federation is predicated on the ontological hierarchy of state and federation that falls into place in Locke's text. Kant relies on federalism to get beyond the international state of nature which is a function of the perfection of the state. Being already legally ordered internally, the state satisfies the

[30] Pufendorf, *Of the Law of Nature and Nations* VII, vi, pp 681–82.

[31] Locke, *Second Treatise* § 14, pp 276–77. The distinction between inner and outer has not yet fallen into place in the work of Hugo Grotius who notes that leagues established on unequal terms, requiring a more onerous performance from one party, lessen its sovereign jurisdiction (*imperium*) (see Grotius, *The Rights of War and Peace* (Indianapolis, Liberty Fund, 2005) II, xv, xii, 21, p 826). Correspondingly, Grotius argues that the determination of whether or not the acts of the king can be overridden by civil law should be made according to whether he acts in a public or private capacity (II, xiv, i, 2, p 803).

[32] See, eg, Georg Friedrich von Martens, *Précis du Droit des Gens Moderne de l'Europe* (Paris, Guillaumin et Cie, Libraires, 1858 (third edition, first edition 1788)) I, i, § 16, p 78; Emer de Vattel, *The Law of Nations* (Indianapolis, Liberty Fund, 2008) I, i, § 10, p 84. Samuel Pufendorf questions whether one can in fact distinguish between (unitary) polity and federation (see Pufendorf, *Of the Law of Nature and Nations* VII, v, p 683).

[33] Charles-Louis de Secondat Montesquieu, *The Spirit of the Laws* (Cambridge, Cambridge University Press, 1989) II, 9, 1, pp 131–32.

requirements of practical reason and cannot therefore be coerced into subjecting itself to a power capable of enforcing the law, which was, of course, how individuals were made to exit the state of nature. But at the same time, Kant is adamant that the contest of state power—war—must not be allowed to stand as a judicial means of resolving disputes. States must join together in a pacific union or league (*Friedensbund*) that will 'gradually' extend to include them all, although this league cannot, or cannot be allowed to, develop into a global republic.[34]

The federation has to be universal because its agency is not such that it can moderate the relations of states on the standard terms of state interaction. If only a fundamental transformation of the mode of state interaction will allow the federation to emerge, it is because the federation is in itself not real enough to contest the primacy of the state (which is, of course, the primacy of the states). This explains the oft-noted oscillation in Kant's text between his commitment to leave behind the international state of nature and his repudiation of the unitary universal polity that would be required to accomplish that goal.[35] To most, this indeterminacy is a failure of Kant the thinker, guilty of contradicting himself or of allowing considerations of what is practicable to dissuade him from carrying his theory to its logical conclusion.[36] We would argue that it is precisely because Kant conceives of the federation on the format put in place by modern public law that he cannot commit to either of the two alternatives.

The ontological underpinnings of Kant's theory of federation also condition his exposition of the trajectory that mankind must follow on its way to perpetual peace. Most take him to mean that the pacific league will come about in increments as more and more states are brought on board. Kant does sometimes seem to conceive of the future political trajectory of mankind after this fashion. There are, however, good reasons to suppose that matters may be more complicated than that. On the terms of Kant's philosophy, it is an open question whether a global federation could actually come about in this way. He gives no indication of what ties would bind together the parties to the union or how they would organise themselves in relation to non-members.

[34] Immanuel Kant, *Perpetual Peace* in HS Reiss (ed), *Immanuel Kant. Political Writings* (Cambridge, Cambridge University Press, 2005) 104. Similarly, Johann Gottlieb Fichte, *Grundlagen des Naturrechts* in Johann Gottlieb Fichte, *Sämtliche Werke* (Berlin, Walter de Gruyter, 1965) III, pp 379–82.

[35] Paul Guyer, *Kant on Freedom, Law, and Happiness* (Cambridge, Cambridge University Press, 2000) 416; Jürgen Habermas, 'Kant's Idea of Perpetual Peace with the Benefit of Two Hundred Years' Hindsight' in James Bohman and Matthias Lutz-Bachmann (eds), *Perpetual Peace: Essays on Kant's Cosmopolitan Ideal* (Cambridge, Massachusetts, MIT Press, 1997) 117–18; Thomas Pogge, 'Kant's Vision, Europe, and a Global Federation' in Jean-Christophe Merle (ed), *Globale Gerechtigkeit* (Stuttgart, Frommann-Holzboog, 2005) 502–504, 507.

[36] Pauline Kleingeld argues that it was neither unreasonable nor self-contradictory for Kant not to commit to a global republic; on the terms of his theory, he was justified in making international association voluntary as only free association would respect the autonomy of each polity (see Pauline Kleingeld, 'Approaching Perpetual Peace: Kant's Defence of a League of States and his Ideal of a World Federation' (2004) 12 *European Journal of Philosophy* 309–11). This would make sense of Kant's text without having to rely on overly strong ontological assumptions. The claim that Kant was right to tie self-determination to non-universal polities trades off our belief that universal bodies do not, or not to the same extent, allow for self-determination. On the terms of Kant's theory, it is not clear, however, that self-determination involves space in anything but a trivial sense. If it does not, there is no reason why the given configuration of the loci of self-determination should count as an argument against realising a requirement of reason.

It is not clear that a less-than-universal federation could avoid being drawn into the international state of nature. It might of course elect to use its power to advance the general cause of federalism but this move would not be admissible to Kant. He would not allow that power could be used to rid the world of power, and he has nothing but scorn for the tradition of European public law theory that relied on the unceasing opposition of forces to uphold the equilibrium between states.[37]

This should make us wary of supposing that Kant conceives of the federal trajectory as the gradual process of traversing a finite series, in the process changing the institutional make-up of the world. Indeed, if we look to the text, we find that what spreads gradually is not the union or league but the 'idea of federality' (*Föderalität*). It is surely not without significance that Kant should have chosen to designate that which is at work in history as an idea, and that he opted to designate its object as federality, a term that is unfamiliar even in the German language. We would argue that this choice reflects the nature of agency in federations, which suggests that history will not follow a linear trajectory towards its designated end goal. On this view, the advent of universal federation will be the result of a momentous historical change that occurs at the point where the idea of federality has so saturated being as to bring about its transformation.

We are not looking to decide this question or to establish what intention is most plausibly attributed to Kant. The interest of his text is precisely that its view of the federation's nature and future trajectory is indeterminate, and that the indeterminacy is structural, as it were, in that his theory is predicated on the suspension of the federation between the state and the global republic. We should not view this as a failure on Kant's part. For our purposes, it is in fact a boon in that it sheds light on how federalism operates as theory. It reveals that it oscillates between two modes: a first, and fundamental, mode in which agency is strictly limited to what is necessary for the perpetuation of the polity, and a mode in which federalisation generates, and proceeds from, a utopian, non-violent mode of social interaction. Again, this might seem to be too theoretical to be of relevance to the study of federations, but the implication of these two modes, and the oscillation between them, resurfaces as public law theory attempts to establish a criterion to distinguish between unions of states that are held together by violence (empire) and those that are not (federation).[38]

Both modes of federalism are predicated on the primacy of the state as the natural, exclusive locus of political life. Unlike the first mode, this is perhaps not immediately clear for federalism's second mode, but if federalism is utopian, it is, first and foremost, in the very literal sense of not possessing enough reality to contest the primacy of the state, any state, which is why it must aim at the complete transformation of the mode of state interaction. Federalism's ethical utopianism is a sublimation of a prior incapacity to take up position anywhere within the state system. The bifurcation of federalism theory into instrumental and normative approaches merely repeats

[37] Kant, *Perpetual Peace* 103. For an analysis of the systematic function of the principle of equilibrium in European public law theory, see Amnon Lev, 'The Transformation of International Law in the 19th Century' in Alexander Orakhelashvili (ed), *Research Handbook on the Theory and History of International Law* (Cheltenham, Edward Elgar Press, 2011) 122–28.

[38] On this point, see the contributions of Olivier Beaud and Cheryl Saunders to this volume.

this dichotomy of modes. The oscillation between them is an exact structural parallel to the dialectic generated by the antinomies of pure reason in Kant's critique of pure reason. In both instances, normativity arises as reason ventures beyond its designated domain, and in both instances, tension is resolved by transforming a claim of reason into a regulative ideal. In federalism's case, this resolution takes the form of values that are subsidiary to the material ends of the polity and can therefore only condition the exercise of government.[39] Thus, we might say that federalism operates as an *idea* of public law theory.

For our purposes, the interest of the modal structure of federalism is that it gives us some purchase on the way federalism is situated, and situates itself, in time. With this question we touch on one of the most fundamental differences between the public law theory of the federation and of the state. For reasons that are tied to the constitution of its domain, the public law theory of the state needed to find a way to neutralise historical time. If Hobbes' theory of commonwealth came to define its horizon, if not its actual domain, it is arguably because his theory offered a way to justify power that did not rely on, indeed excluded reference to, the past possession of it. The terms on which he articulates the alienation of liberty by the individual bar the road to any attempt to contest the legitimacy of power by reference to the means by which it was got. In situating the institution of power at a level of extreme violence, Hobbes appropriates for his theory the terrain from which contestation would be articulated. Whatever the level of violence used in the actual institution/creation of a commonwealth, the account of what *really* happened was sure to remain within the bounds of what had been imagined in theory. History would thus invariably confirm theory (which is why Hobbes could collapse the difference between acquisition and institution, the two modes of erecting a commonwealth. On the view of history that he propagates, the attendant differences in how man came to be in society are of no relevance to his obligation of obedience).[40]

Locke proceeds along the path initiated by Hobbes, even if his approach is more subtle. Rather than place sovereign power outside history, in a *nunc stans* that can be instantiated at any point in time, Locke recognises the historical nature of both government and society. The purpose of his theory is to persuade us that government and society will stay in sync as they move through time. This is the function of trust. As we have seen, it supervenes on relations of care that originate below the level of social action is precisely to serve as a warrant that neither sovereign nor citizen will exercise his freedom in ways that would necessitate a reset of the relationship of government. Public law theory proceeds on this supposition of a good enough fit between people and government, which has the effect of rendering the contingency of social action trivial and, as such, irrelevant for the purposes of theory. It would take us too far afield to trace the process of acculturation/sedimentation by which the idea of fit passed from modern political philosophy into public law theory. Suffice to say that it plays a pivotal role even in public law theories that have

[39] On this point, see the contribution of Jean-François Gaudreault-DesBiens to this volume.

[40] Hobbes, *Leviathan*, II, xx, 2, p 127. On this point, see Amnon Lev, *Sovereignty and Liberty: A Study of the Foundations of Power* (Abingdon, Routledge, 2014) 53–63, 98–99.

distanced themselves from natural law, an example being Georg Jellinek's theory of state where the assumption of fit is what makes the definition of the state as a subjective synthesis stick.[41]

States, as constructs of public law theory, are in history the way an object is in a container, its nature unaffected by the element in which it finds itself. Matters are more complicated in a federation. Time is not equally operative in federalism's two modes. The first mode, as it is articulated by Locke, aligns federalism on the presentism of the state, neutralising history by reducing it to a sequence of events that impact the polity without affecting its being. The second, Kantian mode embeds federalism theory in time. It entails that the way time is traversed *as history* is constitutive of the federal polity. This would suggest that not all forms of federalism are equally, and essentially, historical. However, history is operative at a more fundamental level that concerns both modes in equal measure. The modal determination of federalism is already historical. In its first mode, federalism might, seen from the outside, be indistinguishable from the public law theory of the state, but its disregard for history has other motives. It does not blank out history as irrelevant, or indeed pernicious, to the study of its object; its disregard for history is a function of how a specific polity has developed through time.[42] What this means is that contingency affects federal polities at the level of form, unlike the state where it is cabined off within the stream of history that the state purports to channel and direct.[43] To theorise a federal polity, public law theory cannot therefore rely on the presupposition of alignment/synchronicity as it has done in relation to the state. It must embrace the element of the particular which has important methodological implications for the study of federalism.

It is not without irony that the embeddedness of federalism in history—traditionally a metaphysical marker of insubstantiality—is the source of its protean ability, amply demonstrated in this volume, to invest new political contexts. Federalism is inherently *iterable*, unlike the public law theory of the state which, despite its formality, is tied to its given context. Only by supposing political relations to be based on complete subjection (Hobbes/Rousseau), or on paternal care (Locke), did it succeed in neutralising history. As a result, constitutional transition appeared to it as the irruption of violence within an ordered space, a *catastrophe*. The ease with which federalism negotiates transitions across differences of time, territory, and theory would seem to belie the semantic dependence on public law theory that we have argued for. Still, the question remains whether this protean liberty is not tied to, and contingent on the existence of, a finite domain of theory which would, by default, be that of the state. Could federalism ever exit the conceptual orbit in which public law theory moves? Could there be an *original* federalism?

[41] See Georg Jellinek, *Allgemeine Staatslehre* (Berlin, Verlag von O Häring, 1900) 159–61. For a recent example of how the idea of fit continues to inform public law theory, see Loughlin, *Foundations of Public Law* 202–205.

[42] For an example, see Malcolm M Feeley and Edward L Rubin, *Federalism: Political Identity and Tragic Compromise* (Ann Arbor, University of Michigan Press, 2008) 100–115.

[43] On this point, and for a particularly striking example of how contingency is involved in the development of a federal polity, see the contribution of Dwight Newman to this volume.

III. ASPECTS OF THE FEDERAL IDEA: AN OVERVIEW OF THE VOLUME

For reasons that should now be clear, public law theorists are loath to entertain the question of origins. However, it invariably comes up as we consider how best to study federalism and federations. At the level of methodology, the idea of origins simply translates the attempt to disengage theory from the concepts and categories of traditional public law theory. If most contributions in this volume do not go as far as that, they all test the boundaries of public law theory. In doing so, they reveal how it operates to constrain reflection on federalism and federations and by what strategies these constraints may be negotiated. The contributions have been grouped around three themes: (1) theorising federalism; (2) governing the federation; and (3) federal trajectories. Situating federalism in the context of public law theory obviously opens up a very wide field of enquiry. It hardly needs saying that many other themes could, and should, have been chosen.

The first contribution, Nicholas Aroney's account of the federal condition, presents a formidable challenge to conventional federalism theory and, it must be said, to the approach we have taken here. Against the conventional view that modern federalism dates back to the work of Alexander Hamilton and James Madison, he argues that their most enduring legacy was to replace an older, 'real' federalism, expressed most clearly by Johannes Althusius, by a generalised account of the human condition where federalism featured only as a means to ensure just and limited government. It is this 'real' federalism that Aroney wants to recover. In fixing that objective, he reintroduces the question of the *originality* of federalism as an account of man's social condition.

From Althusius Aroney takes two connected ideas: the notion that man is a social animal and that man's sociability is refracted across a spectrum of communities of varying scope into which man is born but which are, at the same time, a result of choice and agreement. On the strength of these two ideas, he counters the methodological individualism that public law theory inherited from Hobbes and Locke. Man is never out of society and, more importantly, the society in which he finds himself is always plural, which means that there is no foundation for the primacy of the state argued for by Hobbes and Locke.

Aroney is well aware that the Althusian account of social life cannot be recovered wholesale. He subtly, and convincingly, reconceptualises it by replacing its intricate social architecture of guilds, colleges, churches, cities, and provinces with an account of social organisation that takes the family as the centre of all social life. The family is the nucleus from which the social world proceeds in a natural, unforced manner, a stark contrast to the violence of the Hobbesian account. On this view, proximity, physical and then social, is an indicator of meaningfulness and, by extension, legitimacy, which grounds a priority of the local that is both historical and normative.

The force of Aroney's account rests on his ability to articulate the social world from its most intimate, and immediately meaningful, forms. Given the wealth of the dimension that his enterprise engages, it is not surprising that his text is also a protreptic, an invitation to push further the work of theory. It is not the least of its merits to indicate where theory is needed, perhaps most urgently in relation to the question of political relations. In the brief but dense remarks Aroney dedicates to this question, a subtle inflection of his approach takes place. He acknowledges that government may in fact be legitimate even where it is not underpinned by ties of proximity. In those instances, the foundation of its legitimacy is its capacity for 'authoritative coordination of persons within a particular jurisdiction,' in other words, the state's monopoly on the legitimate use of force. In bringing into his account a structure that does not originate within, and cannot be reduced to, the dimension of meaningfulness that is the federal condition, Aroney reproduces, albeit on a much smaller scale, the distension of political life found in traditional conceptions of federalism. It is no coincidence that it is the status of political relations that causes the inflection of Aroney's theory. Belief in the primacy of the political is, after all, one of the fundamental tenets of public law theory, and it is therefore not surprising that it should be the string that keeps federalism theory attached to the body of public law theory.

With Olivier Beaud's contribution on federation and empire, we find ourselves at the other end of the spectrum. Where Nicholas Aroney theorises the federal condition from its existential foundations, Beaud determines his object from its formal characteristics. The intuition that informs Beaud's analysis is that to define the federation, one must compare it to the empire with which it is, at the same time, similar (in terms of structure) and dissimilar (in terms of the relationship of the parts). The question he raises concerns the nature of that which holds a union of states together: force or freedom. As such, it goes right to the heart of the indeterminacy that we touched on in our analysis of Kant's article on perpetual peace. Ultimately, the aim of Beaud's work, here as in earlier work, is to liberate federalism theory from the assimilation of federation and state that has been standard since Georg Jellinek proposed his classic classification of federal-type polities into federal states and confederations. Still, it is very much to Jellinek's *œuvre* that Beaud's work hearkens back, both by its methodology—the use of ideal types—and by its insistence on taking political form as the real object of public law theory.

The hypothesis on which Beaud's analysis proceeds is that legal form tracks the nature of political life; that the difference between a federation and an empire, which concerns the nature of the relationship between the parts of the polity (hierarchical/non-hierarchical), is reflected in the law that establishes the polity. To that end Beaud distinguishes between a federative compact and a federal treaty; only the former is an expression of self-determination and, as such, generative of federation, which he shows from an analysis of Napoleon's 1806 imposition of a Helvetic union where the 'federal' content of the constitution was undercut by the non-autonomous manner of its creation.

Beaud goes on to consider what determines a trajectory as federal or imperial, this time drawing on a more recent example, namely the re-conquest of the occupied territories of France by the forces of General de Gaulle. The campaign departed from the colonial dominions of France, but only once the territory of the motherland had been taken back was de Gaulle's claim to represent France seen, and felt, to be compelling. In trying to account for the 'imperial' bias that orders the parts of the polity around a centre, Beaud is led to consider the socio-cultural determinants that militate against domination, thus favouring the federal over the imperial. If his contribution continues the efforts of European public law theory to find ways to bridge the gap between the institutional and the existential dimension of law, it also points to a new set of topics with which theorists of European public law have traditionally been unwilling to engage; perhaps most importantly the question of the importance of political practice for the realisation of constitutional order.

Concluding the first section is Jean-François Gaudreault-DesBiens's contribution, which proposes a theory of federal adjudication that is, at the same time, a theory of the 'federal' constraints on the exercise of constitutional power. Gaudreault-DesBiens advances two claims: that there are such constraints and that, in some federal trajectories, federalism can become an end in itself, a constitutional good. It is left to the courts to uphold and protect this good, both in adjudicating federalism-related disputes and by fostering a genuine federal culture. In placing the courts at the centre of his theory, Gaudreault-DesBiens is consciously reclaiming the judicial branch for federalism, pushing back against a devaluation of federalism that has meant that the judiciary has come to be seen rather as a means to overcome or circumvent federalism.

The idea that federalism is a constitutional good situates Gaudreault-DesBiens's work in opposition to institutionalist and functionalist accounts of federalism. However, the interest of his account is that while he is unwavering in his commitment to this idea, he also recognises the importance, indeed the primacy, of institutionalism and functionalism. Steering a course between these two claims commits him to anchor his conception of the federal in principles rather than rules. Thus, he distinguishes between three categories of principles that are operative in the adjudication of federalism-related disputes: (1) deontic-axiomatic principles that enshrine the essence of federalism; (2) suppletive principles that form part of a particular federative context but are intimately bound to their given context that they cannot be generalised and therefore fall short of axiomatic status; and (3) agonistic principles that govern the actual resolution of federalism-related disputes.

The tripartite typology of principles, and the reflection on the role they could, and should, play in the adjudication of federalism-related disputes, provides important tools for future research into how federalism operates to inform the exercise of power. At the level of jurisprudence, the focus on principles recalls the work of Ronald Dworkin; an affiliation that Gaudreault-DesBiens assumes. However, more so than the ontology and hermeneutics of law, it might be around the underlying conceptions of constitutional politics that the convergence is most pronounced. Like Dworkin, Gaudreault-DesBiens sees the courts as loci of informed political debate, on condition that they reframe the substantive questions so as to bring into focus, and into adjudication, the values of federalism. Federalism may play no substantive part in Dworkin's theory, but a strong affinity obtains between the values that guide his and Gaudreault-DesBiens's theory of adjudication. In both, the values by reference to which the courts adjudicate are procedural or, at least, subordinate to other, material ends. The values that underpin federations on Gaudreault-DesBiens's reading—loyalty, solidarity, equality—are as centrally placed in a polity, and as essential to its survival, as are the values of justice and fairness identified by Dworkin. In fact, they might even be purer expressions of the impersonal concern for polity, which lends weight to Gaudreault-DesBiens's claim that the law of federalism is the archetypical form of political law.

Gaudreault-DesBiens's reflections on federal values get right to the heart of the subsidiarity of federalism in relation to both the material ends of the polity and considerations of institutional design. Equally, they also address the all-important question of how federalism can contribute to broadening the temporal scope of government action beyond the *presentism* of public law theory. In so doing, Gaudreault-DesBiens provides precious insight into the singular nature of this power within power that is federalism, suggesting, paradoxically, that it is by not dominating the present that federalism opens up to the future.

The theme of power carries over into the contributions of the next section that deal with different aspects of the *government of a federation*. In her contribution Jessica Bulman-Pozen considers the implication of federalism and separation of powers, an essential question not only because it sits at the intersection of governmental practice and constitutional law, but also because it raises the question of the iterability of federalism. Her account is premised on the demise of classic dual federalism, as a result of the expansion of the federal executive's range of action that has chipped away at domains formerly reserved for the states.

If the concept of federalism is sufficiently elastic to accommodate this shift away from its original format, the question remains in what sense the scheme of cooperation between federal executive and states that replaced it is federal. Bulman-Pozen's answer is that the cooperative scheme reproduces the dynamics of federalism in and through a triangulation involving the federal executive, Congress, and the states. She convincingly shows how the latter, charged by Congress with implementing federal law, are enlisted by the legislative branch against the federal executive and thus come to serve as guardians of federal law. As surprising as this may be, the states are in fact, as Bulman-Pozen points out, very well placed to fill that role; not only do they have the resources and the leverage to successfully pursue their aims, but to the extent that they are executors of federal regulatory schemes, they also have standing to sue the federal executive for non-respect of the scheme.

Introducing state governments into the execution of federal law creates a competition between government actors, reproducing, if only within the context of the specific regulatory scheme, a situation of checks and balances; not between branches of government but within the executive branch—hence the qualification of this dissemination or separation of powers as *fractal*. The separation of powers argument comes to stand in for federalism in a way that calls to mind Madison's work where the principle of the separation of powers defines the particular structure of government, as opposed to its general form, while federalism is the only means of safeguarding the other branches of government against the encroachment of the legislature. Bulman-Pozen thus offers a powerful illustration of how federalism is iterated in governmental practice; how specific dynamics relocate within constitutional orders to attach themselves to other constitutional practices.

The next contribution, Edward L Rubin's account of federalism as a means of governance, carries on the enquiry into the iteration of federalism, albeit in a very different perspective. Rubin boldly asks what uses federalism might serve today in governing a polity; under what conditions a federal ordering of the polity is called for. To that end, he compares federalism to other modes of governance—consociation, decentralisation, and local democracy—and concludes that it is useful only in a limited number of situations, especially where there are competing political identities within a polity, and that competition aligns with the distribution of the population within the territory.

Unsurprisingly, this instrumental conception of federalism goes hand in hand with a minimalist, even deflationist, account of what we can expect federalism to do for us. Rubin emphatically denies that federalism has any substantive normative import. There are no federal values and, contrary to conventional wisdom, federalism is not necessarily and at all times protective of rights. Whether or not the use of federalism will protect rights depends entirely on the context within which it is put to use. Where a majority within a sub-unit is refusing to acknowledge minority rights, opting for a federal configuration of the polity is likely to enable or even facilitate that practice which means that federalism in turn becomes another means of oppression. Rubin allows that group rights are organically linked to federalism. However, the recognition of what would be a rather minimalist normative basis for federalism is subject to important caveats concerning the possibility of conflict between, on the one hand, rights of the dominant group within the sub-unit and, on the other hand, individual rights of non-members or rights of minoritarian groups living within the area.

Quite understandably, reactions to Rubin's theory of federalism, and to the work he has previously done with Malcolm F Feeley, have focused on the substantive issues he raises. For our purposes, the presuppositions on which his account of federalism rests are of equal interest. It thus bears noting that if Rubin holds that federalism is devoid of substantive content, its valence simply a function of the situations in which it is employed, his description of those situations in which a federal ordering of the polity is called for nevertheless points to a specific understanding, if not a definition, of federalism. Federalism, he tells us, is concerned with the management of competing political identities within a polity, but the crucial point here is that federalism is indicated when the tension that results from this competition is irresolvable (which is why federalism, to Rubin and Feeley, necessarily involves a tragic choice between the expression of self and the commitment to the polity). The use of federalism is really only called for where tension is such as to pose a threat to the existence, or cohesion, of the polity; where the alternative to federalism would be the alternative between 'secession and oppression.'

We might say that what Rubin develops, or adapts to present-day conditions, is federalism's first mode in which it serves as a basic condition of the polity's existence, a remedy not against external threat as in Montesquieu's federalism, but against internal disaggregation. Rubin's critique of mainstream federalism theory raises the question of how federalism and history are implicated. He does not deny that federalism is historical. On the contrary, he stresses the contingency, and hence the historicity, of federalism. The belief that federalism does not have an inherent normative content has as its corollary that only history, the element of the given, will tell us whether federalism is called for. What Rubin denies is that the history that led up to the choice to order the polity along federal lines can be construed as a destinal trajectory, a movement towards an end goal that was preordained and therefore colours a people's history, marking it as a *federal* history. His work is a forceful reminder that if federalism's inscription in history is inevitable, its theory must constantly subject itself to critique so as to separate historical narrative from edifying myth.

Closing out the section on government is Cheryl Saunders' contribution on executive power; a topic that is of special interest to us for the prominence it has within the genealogy of federalism we propose. Saunders proposes a dual axial format around which we should think about how executive power operates, and the space it claims for itself in a federal polity. The first axis concerns the design of the federation. Saunders shows how different approaches to federal design give rise to different conceptions of what can be done in the exercise of executive power. The second axis concerns the way the provisions for federalism sit within, and interact with, the wider constitutional setting of the polity. As it was in Jessica Bulman-Pozen's contribution, the question is how federalism and separation of powers combine and interact, but the approach taken in the two chapters is very different. Bulman-Pozen shows how federalism's dynamics are re-enacted in the competition between government actors, separation of powers taking over from federalism. Saunders shows how, in the process of metabolising the legacy of the constitutional tradition of which the polity used to be a part, federalism operates as an additional consideration in, and a backstop to, the exercise of executive power in the general economy of public law that has grown up around the separation of powers.

With Saunders' account, we plunge into the conversion from empire to federation that we have touched on already. She brings out one of its fascinating implications: that the retreat of imperial authority has the effect of expanding the scope of executive power within the polity. The executive power formerly held at the level of the empire devolves to the new polity that must integrate it into its constitution in a process that runs Locke's dissociation of federative power in reverse. Saunders shows how the implications of this re-appropriation of power, now seen as flowing from a federal compact, are worked through in the seminal *Williams* cases, noting that this re-appropriation confirms the no-longer applicable British constitutional law as the relevant reference for the effort to indicate the limits to executive power. Out of this emerges a compound concept of executive power in which understanding of what the executive branch can do without legislative authority is shaped by considerations of both separation of powers and federalism.

Saunders stresses that hers is an Australian story, but as with all federal trajectories, its implications can be generalised. We knew that, for being created from pre-formed matter, federations have to take on and process a political history in which they were not agents; what her account suggest is that for reasons that are not essential but may very well be ideal-typical, they have to do so *in* and *as* law. Establishing whether there is an ideal-type and what range of federations it covers would surely be one of the tasks of the comparative work that Saunders invites in conclusion.

Before we consider the remaining contributions, a few preliminary remarks might be in order concerning the heading of *federal trajectories* under which we have grouped them. In analysing the operation of federalism within public law theory, we have been sensitive to the way philosophemes of public law theory perform as they become disembedded from the relatively self-contained circuits of theory in which they were set. The uncontroversial intuition that informs our account is that federalism is constituted in and through the inscription of its theory in time. This inscription has the effect of obliterating the principled distinction between theory and context to the point where we might say that federalism *is* its context. The remaining four contributions all enquire into the drivers of this inscription: what determines whether or not the philosophemes of federalism find uptake and, if so, what gets taken up and so forms part of the determinants of the trajectory of the federal polity?

In the first contribution, Duncan Kelly takes a closer look at how ideas of federalism influenced Woodrow Wilson's conception of the ends and means of political action leading up to and during World War One. As he notes, Wilson's conception of federalism has been somewhat overlooked by students of political theory, which is equally true of students of federalism. Yet, as the chapter shows very clearly, Wilson was the conduit through which ideas of federalism came to inform the actions of the United States of America at a time when the geopolitical order of the twentieth century, and America's place in it, was being decided.

Kelly works on several levels to draw together the many layers of meaning that come together in this federal trajectory, perhaps the grandest of the last century. At the individual level, he shows how Wilson absorbed nineteenth-century European public law theory, most notably the hugely influential federalist state theory of Johan Kaspar Bluntschli, and how that theory, on his reading of it, eventually hardened into a manual for action. At the level of politics, Kelly carefully situates Wilson's federalism between the challenges that he believed were facing the United States of America: on the one hand, its implication in the conflict between Europe's powers that Wilson increasingly came to see in terms of a war for democracy and against autocracy and, on the other hand, the need to rein in an inherently unruly democracy at home. The chapter shows how these two dimensions of Wilson's action conditioned and constrained each other. Finally, Kelly tracks the affinities between Wilson's federalism and the political projects it came into contact with (nationalism/globalism/imperialism) and between which he sought to steer a course: from the inconvenient affinity between the pan-Germanism that Wilson denounced as a cancer at the heart of Germany and his own idea of pan-regionalism over the strategic recovery of his federalist ideology in pan-nationalisms that turned it against Western imperialism, and reaching down to the domestic context where Kelly shows how federalism, in Wilson's mind, became the bedrock of the nation's exceptionalism.

Kelly presents us with something like a topology of federalism at a critical juncture in modern history. Equally important for our purposes, Wilson, as he appears here, is a fascinating lens through which to view the challenges and pitfalls that present themselves if we try to realise the federalist's dream of elevating federalism from an auxiliary to government to a programme for political action. As Kelly notes in conclusion with reference to the European Union, this lesson has lost none of its topicality.

European federalism is the topic of the next chapter—the editor's contribution—that considers how this form of federalism sits within the history of public law theory, which is of course also a *European* history, a commonality that is essential. The chapter proposes a broadly dialectical account of how the ideology of federal integration emerged out of, and carried forward, traditional European public law theory. Perhaps more importantly, it also brings to light some of the mechanisms by which public law theory of the eighteenth century managed to reconcile a commitment to unconditional, unlimited power with the need for co-operation with other sovereigns, obviating the need to develop a theory of federalism.

Moving on to the federalism of the nineteenth century, the insuccess of federalism is used as a key to understand how, by what semantic means, public law theory conditioned reflection on federal polities to the point where it could see the federation only as a subspecies of the unitary state. The chapter argues that the inability to grasp the specificity of the federation was tied to the semantic dependence of public law theory on sovereignty. This would seem to confirm the conventional readings that point to sovereignty as the primary conceptual obstacle to the development of federalism theory. However, what the analysis of Jellinek's seminal theory of federation suggests is that the commitment of public law theory that renders it incapable of grasping the federation is not to the indivisibility of power—that is, to sovereignty—but to the possibility of justifying power, the perennial ambition of public law theory.

Finally, the chapter considers what changes to public law theory were needed for a process of federal integration to get underway in Europe. Against a prevalent view that this process could only begin once sovereignty had run its fateful course in the Second World War, it suggests another, perhaps even more disconcerting genealogy that looks back to the First World War as the locus of a transformation of public law theory that eliminated its traditional reference to man and posited existential crisis as a permanent social condition. Against this backdrop, and in the context of the immediate post-Cold War period, the chapter analyses the sense of destiny that underpins the integration of Europe. It argues that the belief that federation is the inevitable endpoint of Europe's history is a result of a conjuncture of contingent circumstance and philosophical theory that allowed earlier strata of public law theory to be superimposed on the present.

The next contribution, Dwight Newman's analysis of the far-reaching dynamism of democratic federations, asks how federalism relates to democracy, perhaps the most potent determinant of a polity's development. Enquiring into the implication of federalism and democracy raises a number of methodological challenges, perhaps most importantly how to free up space for federalism. Acting on the almost instinctive association of democracy and popular sovereignty would posit federalism as a constraint on democracy, and ultimately confine it within a unitary horizon that it precisely puts into question. As a preliminary to the analysis, Newman therefore briefly considers, and discards, conceptions of federalism that are tethered to the idea of popular sovereignty. Instead, he opts for what is, at first glance, an uneasy combination of methodological individualism and collective identity, which allows him to keep federalism from being cannibalised by democracy and, in conclusion, to point to a different, more vibrant conception of democracy in which it is not constrained but invigorated by federalism.

Like Rubin, Newman defines federalism in terms of identity but where Rubin, in accordance with the mode of federalism he is developing, sees identities as terms of opposition, Newman sees them as the elements of the dynamic construction of the demos. He accepts that federalism is a function of pre-ordained differences within the polity but adds a reflexive component. Federalism responds to *and* constructs (or entrenches) divisions within democratic identities. On this view, federalism is the process by which a federal polity works itself out. One might almost say that it is the process by which a polity, any polity, works itself out, seeing that identities within modern democratic societies are invariably going to be divided. The point is not to make federalism into a master concept of political theory but to integrate the element of contingency, of which we have emphasised the constitutive importance for federalism. Federalism, Newman tells us, cannot offer a complete explanation for the path that a federal polity takes. What it can do is to open up a venue through which contingency, including completely random shocks, can impact the polity's development.

To Newman, the infusion of contingency invigorates the polity. Underlying his account is a conception of democracy that, even if it is couched in the consequentialist language of preference satisfaction, revolves around the willingness to constantly question the shape of the polity as it exists at any given time, 'providing,' as he poignantly puts it, 'the seeds for its own dynamism.' This openness to what may arrive is the operative part of his conception of democracy, which is why he can hold that federalism was designed precisely as a fulfilment of the democratic principle and that the federal idea may embody a more dynamic form of democracy than anyone has thus far assumed. In drawing our attention to *federal democracy*, which is, in a sense, prior to popular sovereignty, Newman shows us another way in which federalism, this form of government that public law theory has traditionally defined in purely functional terms, deploys a normative power that operates discretely, within our institutions but fundamentally modifying their meaning.

The concluding contribution, Stephen Tierney's analysis of plurinationalism, also treats of the democratic foundation of public law theory. Tierney questions an implicit, yet essential presupposition of federalism that it shares with liberal constitutionalism: that whatever other 'peoples' inhabit the territory of a state, be it federal or unitary, they are conceived in a categorically different way from 'the people' of the territorial state. There can be only one 'people' in a state. In pointing to this presupposition—the demotic premise—Tierney shows one of the forms in which the idea of the federation as a *lesser community* continues to inform public law theory. As it did already in Kant's doctrine of right, the notion of the people as an extended family takes over from the idea of paternal authority and care that underpinned the invention of public law theory in Locke's work.

The emergence of sub-state territorial polities such as Catalonia, Quebec and Scotland challenges the demotic premise. These polities describe themselves as distinct *demoi*, and they relate as such to the state on whose territory they find themselves; not as minorities but as polities that are equal to the state inasmuch as they fulfil, or have the potential to do so, the many roles it plays in the life of a citizen. Tierney notes that the normative claims that these sub-state national societies make on the citizens do not give rise to a politics of difference but rather to what he intriguingly calls a politics of similarity. Interestingly, he argues that plurinationalism poses an even more insidious threat to the unitary state than the prospect of secession. If secession entails the loss of control over territory, it does not put into the sovereignty of the state. Plurinationalism, on the other hand, 'seeks to reorientate the very meaning of statehood itself by pluralising the monistic assumptions which underpin the traditional statism, assaulting the very implicit normative self-understanding of the state.'

Tierney argues forcefully that plurinationalism's rise signals a failure of liberalism which does not offer the resources needed to respond to the challenge it poses. Liberalism's failure implicates statism and federalism in equal measure as both operate on the demotic premise. However, where statism openly assumes it as the setting of its commitment to liberty and equality, its most fundamental normative values, the premise remains implicit in federalism. Federalism, on Tierney's reading, is thus caught between statism and plurinationalism. The challenge he leaves us with is to construct a federalism that does not rely on a monistic approach to the demos. The success of that project might liberate federalism from its dependence on public law theory; failure, on the other hand, might show that the community between them concerns not only their rise but also their decline.

Part I

Theorising Federalism

1

The Federal Condition

NICHOLAS ARONEY*

WHAT ACCOUNT OF the human condition—of human goods and of human sociality—would furnish the kinds of understandings and principles that would explain and justify a federal ordering of society and politics? Very little political philosophy and legal theory is directed to this particular question. Most of the work in these fields has been directed to questions about the historical development, normative justification and legal description of the post-Westphalian nation-state. That which theorises federalism has often proceeded on a view of human sociality and politics associated with that conception, contributing to an incomplete and one-sided account of federalism. However, there is evidence of a recent growing interest in the theory of federalism as such, rather than the theory of the federal-state as a type of state-organisation.[1] This chapter, drawing on several threads and themes in the literature, will propose an account of the human condition which, it will be argued, has the potential to provide a more complete context from which to understand, and a more coherent set of reasons for favouring, a federal ordering of society and politics.

Such a chapter necessarily negotiates much contested terrain. The chapter is therefore split into two quite different parts. The first part surveys some of the terrain, and attempts to clear a path through it. It examines several highly influential accounts of the human condition and politics, assessing their capacity to make an explanatory understanding and normative justification of federalism possible. The second part changes tack; it is more constructive. It seeks to sketch a positive account of the human condition which might explain and justify a federal ordering of society and politics. The mode of this part of the argument is transcendental, in the sense that it endeavours to articulate the conditions of a normative federal theory, premised on a descriptive and explanatory account of what federalism is in practice. While directed to a set of normative propositions about federalism that will ultimately be framed within the context of a moral discourse of goods and oughts, the paper does not purport to articulate such a moral theory, but only to explore and describe the conditions of its existence. To do so, as will be seen, it is necessary to question several assumptions about the human condition and human politics which underlie

* The support of Australian Research Council grant FT100100469 is gratefully acknowledged.

[1] See, eg, Olivier Beaud, *Théorie de la Féderation* (Paris, Presses Universitaires de France, 2009).

accounts of the unitary nation state and to articulate an alternative set of fundamental understandings.

I. THE LIBERAL CONDITION

A. Hobbes and Locke

Thomas Hobbes and John Locke proposed two highly influential descriptions of the human condition contributing significantly to the conceptualisation and justification of the modern unitary state.[2] It is a commonplace of political philosophy to highlight the very significant differences between their accounts of the state of nature, the law of nature, the social contract, and the grounds, purposes and extent of political authority. But when their two theories are compared with that of Johannes Althusius,[3] an earlier and less well-known figure in the social contract tradition,[4] a very different picture emerges.

For both Locke and Hobbes, the state of nature is not only a condition of equality in liberty, but also an essentially solitary state of being. The two publicists differed in their accounts of that condition, particularly in relation to the nature and content of the laws of nature that pertain to and shape the terms of the social contract by which such individuals form themselves into a political society. But they were agreed in starting, conceptually, with the individual and building their account of the formation of the state on that basis. Both acknowledged, conceptually, the existence of non-state social groupings in the state of nature, especially 'families' or 'households',[5] but they denied that such 'concord' as might exist in them could supply the kind of security these needed; and they certainly did not conceive, as Aristotle had done, of the political community being essentially composed of combinations of such households and villages.[6] The social contract, for both Hobbes and Locke, is an agreement among individuals directed to the establishment of a political society that is fundamentally unitary in nature. This is especially evident in Hobbes, who wrote of a 'Leviathan' or 'Mortall God' in which all of the powers of government are concentrated. This singular authority, he said, may be constituted as '*one* Man or *one* Assembly of men', but it must necessarily possess '*one* Will' in order to provide an effective 'common Power' to which the many and diverse wills of all individuals can effectively be subjected.[7] In order to guarantee this, he continued, all potentially competing groups and authorities must be absolutely subject to the unitary authority of the sovereign,[8] just as all potentially competing undertakings, agreements or

[2] Thomas Hobbes, *Leviathan* (London, Dent, 1973); John Locke, *Two Treatises of Government* (Cambridge, Cambridge University Press, 1960).

[3] Johannes Althusius, *Politica: An Abridged Translation* (Indianapolis, Liberty Fund, 1995).

[4] Otto Van Gierke, *The Development of Political Theory* (London, Allen & Unwin, 1939).

[5] Hobbes, *Leviathan* I, 3; Locke, *Second Treatise* §§ 77–87.

[6] Aristotle, *Politics* I, ii.

[7] Hobbes, *Leviathan* II, 17.

[8] ibid II, 20.

covenants must be absolutely inferior to the social contract.[9] A political society will contain various towns, provinces, universities, colleges and churches, each with their distinct laws and customs, but Hobbes insisted they all must ultimately be subject to the superior will of the sovereign.[10] For competing leagues or covenants among the subjects of the sovereign are in fact dangerous, and must be unlawful.[11] Such 'things that weaken or tend to the dissolution of a commonwealth' include, he said, not only the opinion that the sovereign is subject to civil law and that the sovereign is divided,[12] but also 'the immoderate greatness of a Town' or a 'great number of corporations; which are as it were many lesser Commonwealths in the bowels of a greater, like wormes in the entrayles of a naturall man.'[13]

Hobbes' position was of course extreme, but the same unitary conception of political society and authority was also there in Locke's thought. For although Locke's scheme very clearly allowed a diversity of associations and institutions to operate freely within a political society, these associations were justified as expressions of the autonomous rights of individuals, just as it was on the foundation of a social contract between individuals, exercising their rights, that the political society would be based.[14] Thus, as his discussion of self-governing cities and subordinate magistrates makes clear,[15] Locke considered that political society is in its essential nature unified, and that the legislative power in each society must be supreme over all such subordinate institutions, expressing its will by majority vote.[16] It is true that Locke envisaged the possibility of a league, and even a confederation, created by the exercise of the 'federative power' of the commonwealth;[17] and his theory is also consistent with a form of political decentralisation through the exercise of the community's primordial power to decide what 'form' of government 'they think good.'[18] But for Locke, because the two essential and highest locations of sovereignty are in either the individual or the political society as a whole, the only expressions of 'federalism' that his theory can admit are forms that are premised on this sovereignty. Thus, on one hand, his theory left room for individuals to form various kinds of private associations as an exercise of their personal rights, and on the other hand, it allowed space for the development of a 'confederation' in which the constituent political societies must always retain their unique status as 'sovereign' states. But it provided no ground for theorising about 'federations' in the sense that James Bryce used the term when he described the early United States as 'a Commonwealth of commonwealths, a Republic

[9] ibid II, 18.
[10] ibid II, 20.
[11] ibid II, 20.
[12] ibid II, 1. Conversely, relations between separate sovereigns are a kind of state of nature, regularised only by treaties between sovereign states.
[13] ibid II, 19. For a discussion of the role of associations within Hobbes' thought, see DB Robertson, 'Hobbes's Theory of Associations in the Seventeenth-Century Milieu' in DB Robertson (ed), *Voluntary Association: A Study of Groups in Free Societies* (Richmond, John Knox Press, 1966).
[14] Locke, *Second Treatise* § 4.
[15] ibid § 133, § 210.
[16] ibid § 96, § 134.
[17] ibid § 145.
[18] ibid § 132. Thus Locke distinguished between the formation and dissolution of society and the formation and dissolution of the government (see § 221).

of republics, a State which, while one, is nevertheless composed of other States even more essential to its existence than it is to theirs'.[19]

B. Althusius

The account of the human condition presented by Johannes Althusius in the *Politica Methodice Digesta* is very different from that of Hobbes and Locke in several respects. Part of the difference concerns the way in which his theory combines certain Aristotelian ideas with the concept of a founding contract or covenant. At the beginning of the *Politics*, Aristotle had presented the political community of the *polis* as a composition of households, clans and villages.[20] Adapting Aristotle's account to the more complex social and political institutions of the high middle ages, Thomas Aquinas extended this picture to include a much greater variety of groups and institutions of a social, economic, religious and political character, including neighbourhoods, guilds, colleges, confraternities, religious orders, kingdoms and provinces, and including the most universal of institutions: the empire and the church.[21] Following Aristotle and Aquinas, and unlike Hobbes and Locke, Althusius also emphasised the idea that human beings are born naturally into forms of community and authority, such as families and local communities, but he added that all such social and communal forms come about through deliberate choice and agreement. Community life, for Althusius, is thus both 'symbiotic' and 'covenanted'; it depends on a common commitment to a harmonious participation in community life.[22] On his view, families and colleges (ie, guilds) are formed by 'a special covenant' (*pactum*),[23] and these 'simple and private associations' are, in turn, the constituent parts of wider 'public' associations, such as towns, cities, provinces and commonwealths. Public associations are therefore necessarily derived from the primary associations, for 'without [the] primary association others are able neither to arise nor to endure.'[24] Moreover, said Althusius, the various collegia are customarily distributed into the three estates (clergy, nobility and people),[25] and it is through the three estates that 'the people of a provincial city, realm, or polity' consent to and ultimately control its affairs.

Families, vocational associations, communes and provinces are accordingly necessary and constitutive links between the individual and the commonwealth for Althusius.[26] As he put it:

> [H]uman society develops from private to public association by the definite steps and progressions of small societies. The public association exists when many private associations

[19] James Bryce, *The American Commonwealth* (London, Macmillan, 1893) I, pp 12–15, 332.

[20] Aristotle, *Politics* I, 1–2, *cf* III, 9.

[21] Nicholas Aroney, 'Subsidiarity, Federalism and the Best Constitution: Thomas Aquinas on City, Province and Empire' (2007) 26 *Law and Philosophy* 161.

[22] Althusius, *Politica* I, 1–2, 17.

[23] ibid II, 2–5; see also IV, 1–5, 8, 12, 17, 22. Despite its grounding in nature and necessity, even the family is initiated by covenant; the collegium, a 'spontaneous and merely voluntary society', is emphatically formed by covenanted agreement (*pacta conventum*) and common consent.

[24] ibid II, 2. The city is thus grounded in 'the common consent and covenant of each and all' (VI, 7).

[25] ibid IV, 30.

[26] ibid I, 6; II, 2–5; IV, 1–5, 7–8, 12, 17, 22; V, 8, 10; VIII, 2; IX, 1–5.

> are linked together for the purpose of establishing an inclusive political order. It can be called a community, an associated body, or the pre-eminent political association.[27]

A local community (a village, town or city) is a kind of public association 'composed of many families and collegia living in the same place'—it is not composed simply of 'the individual members of private associations.'[28] Likewise, the province consists of its orders and estates, or the larger collegia,[29] and the universal association arises when 'many cities and provinces obligate themselves to hold, organise, use, and defend ... the right of the realm.'[30] Finally, the most universal of all these associations is:

> [A]n imperium, realm, commonwealth, and people united in one body by the agreement of many symbiotic associations and particular bodies, and brought together under one right. For families, cities and provinces existed by nature prior to realms, and gave birth to them.[31]

The members of the commonwealth therefore are 'not ... individuals, families and collegia, but cities, provinces and regions agreeing among themselves on a single body constituted by mutual union and communication.'[32]

The bond of the commonwealth, Althusius said, is a kind of 'consensus', 'trust', and a 'tacit or expressed promise' among these members.[33] The commonwealth is therefore more of a 'matrix' than a hierarchy; a *consociatio consociationum* or a 'commonwealth of commonwealths',[34] in which every smaller society is a true and original community, with its own communal life and sphere of rights.[35] As such, 'every constituting body is prior and superior to what is constituted by it.'[36] As Sobei Mogi observed:

> [T]here is a natural law structure of society in which families, vocational associations, communes and provinces all exist as necessary and organic members intermediate between the individuals and the state and in which the wider union is consolidated from the corporative unities of the narrower unions and thereby obtains its members. These narrower unions as real and organic communities create by themselves a distinct common life and a legal sphere of their own, and at the same time give up to the larger union so much as it needs in order to fulfil its specific purposes.[37]

Political society for Althusius thus rests on a covenant between its constitutive members. These members are not simply individuals, but include towns, cities and

[27] ibid V, 1.
[28] ibid V, 8, 10.
[29] ibid VIII, 2, 40.
[30] ibid IX, 1.
[31] ibid IX, 3.
[32] ibid IX, 5.
[33] ibid IX, 7.
[34] See Daniel Elazar, *Exploring Federalism* (Tuscaloosa, University of Alabama Press, 1991) ch 1; Thomas Hueglin, 'Johannes Althusius: Medieval Constitutionalist or Modern Federalist?' (1979) 9(4) *Publius: The Journal of Federalism* 9, 28.
[35] Althusius, *Politica* VI, 16, 41–45, 52; VII, 1–2; VIII, 3, 40, 53–54; IX, 7.
[36] ibid XVIII, 8.
[37] Sobei Mogi, *The Problem of Federalism: A Study in the History of Political Theory* (London, Allen & Unwin, 1931) I, 29–30.

provinces. When members such as these agree to form a larger political community, the terms of that agreement include both a reservation of a certain degree of autonomy over their internal affairs and the grant of particular powers to the wider community. The terms of such agreements also involve the special representation of the constituent members in the governing institutions of the wider community and, because the whole scheme rests on their consent, the members retain a special capacity to influence decisions concerning changes to the entire arrangement.[38] A federal pact in the form of a 'covenant' is therefore the foundation of all forms of association for Althusius. In particular, the universal community is created by a covenant or federal pact between the constituent communities; and the supreme magistrate is likewise instituted 'by covenant or constitution'.[39] Indeed, Althusius uses the terms constitution and covenant interchangeably, for the *lex fundamentalis* 'is nothing other than certain covenants by which many cities and provinces come together and agree to establish ... one and the same commonwealth.'[40]

Althusius did not discard the concept of *maiestas* or sovereignty altogether.[41] But against the views of Jean Bodin (and Hobbes), he ascribed it to the 'the total people associated in one organic, symbiotic body from many smaller associations', that is, the 'entire associated body of the realm' in the 'consent and concord of the associated bodies',[42] and he insisted that even with this qualification, sovereignty is 'neither supreme and perpetual, nor above the law'.[43] As Otto von Gierke put it, the constitutive status of the provinces and cities, and their reserved sphere of rights presented 'an insuperable barrier' of fundamental law to the exercise of any particular right of sovereignty within the commonwealth.[44]

C. Madison

Something of the tension between these differing accounts of the human condition is reflected in the thought of James Madison, one of the key figures behind the drafting of the United States Constitution, a document which is widely regarded as setting forth an archetypical model of federalism that has shaped ideas and practices of federalism ever since. The tension in Madison's thought can be illustrated by an examination of two of his most important *Federalist Papers*, written with Alexander Hamilton and John Jay in an effort to convince the voters of the State of New York to ratify the proposed new constitution for the United States of America.

[38] See Thomas O Hueglin, *Early Modern Concepts for a Late Modern World: Althusius on Community and Federalism* (Waterloo, Wilfred Laurier University Press, 1999) 3, 63, 65.
[39] Althusius, *Politica* XIX, 23.
[40] ibid XIX, 49.
[41] ibid IX, 20–21.
[42] ibid IX, 18–19.
[43] ibid XI, 21.
[44] Gierke, *Development of Political Theory* 266; see Althusius, *Politica* IX, 3–4, 7, 13, 15–24; XVIII, 69, 85, 105; XIX, 7–8, 49; XXXVIII, 7, 53, 71–73, 76, 110–114.

In *Federalist* No 51, Madison drew especially on the ideas of Locke, Montesquieu and Hume to show how the proposed constitution would provide an appropriate range of protective devices by which the 'rights of the people' would be secured. Like Locke, Madison presented the power of government as something that is deliberately surrendered by 'the people' solely for the purpose of better protecting their inherent natural rights. Like both Locke and Montesquieu, the first of Madison's protective devices, written into the design of the proposed system of government, was an institutional separation of powers: a division of the government into distinct and separate departments, each responsible for a different government function. Locke's departments and functions of government (legislative, executive and federative) were different from those of Madison and Montesquieu (legislative, executive and judicial), but the idea of controlling and limiting the government by dividing it into separate departments was much the same. Unlike the apparently hypothetical nature of Locke's social contract and contract of government, however, Madison seemed to suggest that the proposed constitution, if ratified, would embody an actual historical contract entered into by the people. Madison had some good reason to suggest this; the proposed constitution was about to be the subject of a deliberate vote in the ratifying conventions being held in each of the original 13 states. Moreover, in anticipation of its ratification, the proposed constitution ventured to speak in the name of 'We the people of the United States', an expression to which the Antifederalists objected most strongly, on the basis that a genuinely 'federal' constitution must rest upon the consent of 'We the States', not 'We the people'.[45]

The reality lay somewhere between these two views. While the proposed constitution certainly appealed to the 'the people', it stood to be ratified, not in a national convention in which all of the people of the United States would be represented together, but in separate conventions held in each of the American States. Moreover, on its own terms the proposed constitution would only bind those States that in fact ratified it.[46] This suggested that the constitution would more properly rest on the consent of the *peoples* of the States understood as a plurality, rather than some imaginary consolidated and singular national *people*.[47] This latter point was something that Madison plainly acknowledged and very capably analysed in *Federalist*

[45] Patrick Henry, for example, had thundered: '[What] right had they to say, We, the People … who authorised them to speak the language of, We, the People, instead of We, the States? States are the characteristics, and the soul of confederation. If the States be not the agents of this compact, it must be one great consolidated National Government of the people of all the States' (see Patrick Henry, 'Speech in the Virginia Ratifying Convention, 4 June 1788' in Herbert J Storing (ed), *The Anti-Federalist: Writings by the Opponents of the Constitution* (Chicago, University of Chicago Press, 1985) 296–97). Samuel Adams likewise objected: 'I stumble at the threshold. I meet with a National Government instead of a foederal Union of Sovereign States' (see Bernard Bailyn (ed), *The Debate on the Constitution: Federalist and Antifederalist Speeches, Articles, and Letters During the Struggle over Ratification* (New York, Library of America, 1993) I, 446).

[46] United States Constitution, art VII.

[47] *McCulloch v Maryland* 17 US (4 Wheat) 316, 403 (1819) (Marshall CJ): 'It is true, they assembled in their several states—and where else should they have assembled? No political dreamer was ever wild enough to think of breaking down the lines which separate the states, and of compounding the American people into one common mass. Of consequence, when they act, they act in their states. But the measures they adopt do not, on that account, cease to be the measures of the people themselves, or become the measures of the state governments.'

No 39. In that essay, Madison pointed out that the 'foundation' and 'ratification' of the constitution, although done in the name of 'the people of America', would actually be given 'by the people, not as individuals composing one entire nation, but as composing the distinct and independent States to which they respectively belong'. The constitution would rest, in other words, upon 'the assent and ratification of the several States, derived from the supreme authority in each State, the authority of the people themselves'. The act establishing the constitution would, therefore, 'not be a *national*, but a *federal* act', he concluded. Moreover, this founding of the federal constitution by the peoples of the states considered as a plurality,[48] Madison further demonstrated, shaped the entire logic and structure of the constitution, especially when considered in relation to the composition of the representative institutions of the federal government, the extent and operation of the powers of the federal government, and the authority by which future changes in the constitution could be introduced.

In *Federalist* No 51, however, Madison elided much of this. There he presented the proposed constitution in more unitary terms; and the merits of the constitution were now more instrumental than contractarian. Madison put it this way: while in an ordinary republic administered by a single government the people depend upon a separation of powers to safeguard their rights, in a 'compound' republic they enjoy a 'double security' through both a separation of powers among departments of government and a division of power between two distinct governments. While Madison's argument acknowledged and emphasised that the form of government was federal, the people from whom the federal government would derive its authority was now presented as a unitary *demos*, not a federal plurality of *demoi*. The rights of the people to be protected were therefore uniform across the entire federation: they were the natural rights that individuals possess in the state of nature which governments at all levels are obligated to respect and secure. Certainly, these rights may be more than merely liberties to act and immunities from governmental interference: for both Locke and Madison, they included civil or civic rights to participate in self-government. But Madison's account of the democratic process treated the merits of the federal division of power as something that is of only instrumental value, and not something that is defended in contractarian terms.

To see the point more clearly, we need to recall Montesquieu's influential argument for what he called the *république fédérative*.[49] Montesquieu argued that the twofold virtue of a federal republic is that it enables citizens in their respective constituent republics to continue to participate in their own local self-government while enjoying the benefit of collecting the resources and military capabilities of the entire body of federated republics to defend themselves against external enemies. Montesquieu's picture was of several originally independent small political societies agreeing through a federal compact to form a larger society while preserving to themselves a full capacity to exercise their own self-government. Although Alexander Hamilton would make much the same argument (albeit turning it to his own ends) in

[48] Note, however, that Madison continued to refer to 'the people' in the singular.

[49] Charles-Louis de Secondat Montesquieu, *Spirit of The Laws* (New York, Hafner, 1949) IX, 1.

Federalist No 9,[50] and while Madison was plainly drawing upon Montesquieu's defence of the separation of powers in *Federalist* No 51, Madison said nothing there of the federal republic in this specific sense. For Montesquieu's picture was of a plurality of small republics contracting together to form a federal republic, while in *Federalist* No 51 Madison's picture was of a single people devising a system of separated powers and divided governments as a means of preserving and protecting their common rights. As a consequence, the federal character of the republic in *Federalist* No 51 was exhausted by the existence of a plurality of *governments*; whereas for Montesquieu, the federal character of the republic was grounded in the plurality of the constituent *republics* or *peoples* out of which it was constructed and upon the basis of whose consent it would come into being.

The third aspect of Madison's argument in *Federalist* No 51, inspired by David Hume,[51] was also thoroughly instrumental. Hume had argued—contrary to Montesquieu—that a republic formed at the scale of an entire country would have better prospects of avoiding 'tumult and faction' than those formed on the scale of a city or a local community.[52] The very size of the republic, Hume argued, would have a tendency to 'refine' the politics and make it difficult for factions to conspire together against the public interest. Madison's third argument in *Federalist* No 51 was similar: an extended or federal republic would not only protect the society against the oppression of its rulers, but would also help to prevent one part or faction within the society from interfering with the rights of another. It would have this effect, he argued, because the society is itself 'broken into so many parts, interests, and classes of citizens, that the rights of individuals, or of the minority, will be in little danger from interested combinations of the majority'.[53] This kind of solution to the problem of the tyranny of the majority was something that Locke, reasoning on the basis of unitary conception of the state, could never have imagined. In that respect, Madison's third argument, like his second, was clearly about a compound or extended republic, and not a unitary one. But the divergence from Locke was even more radical than this. For Madison's reasoning was no longer about the powers surrendered by the people to the government and the problem of limiting the government to the exercise of its powers in a way that respects the rights of the people. It was now about factions among 'the people' themselves and it involved a far-reaching criticism of Montesquieu's much more sanguine account of the virtues of the small republic as an arena of participatory self-government. Indeed, Madison, borrowing from Hume, effectively turned Montesquieu on his head: small republics are actually vice-ridden, and it is the extended or compound republic that provides the appropriate remedy. By mixing up the various political arenas in which all of the

[50] *The Federalist Papers*, No 9 (Alexander Hamilton) (London, Penguin Books, 1987); *cf* Thomas O Hueglin, 'Federalism at the Crossroads: Old Meanings, New Significance' (2003) 36(2) *Canadian Journal of Political Science* 275.

[51] Mark G Spencer, 'Hume and Madison on Faction' (2002) 59(4) *The William and Mary Quarterly* 869.

[52] David Hume, 'Idea of Perfect Commonwealth' in David Hume, *Essays: Moral, Political and Literary* (Oxford, Oxford University Press, 1963) 499, 512–13.

[53] *The Federalist Papers*, No 51 (James Madison).

different sectional interests must operate (interests which, significantly, cut across state and district boundaries) a compound republic helps to prevent them from forming oppressive majority coalitions that can extract government policies that favour private preferences instead of the common good. The break with Montesquieu was thus radical indeed. Madison said that 'the larger the society ... the more duly capable it will be of self-government'. By suggesting that the various factions extend beyond state and district borders and constitute the real vice of all popular governments, Madison undercut the proposition that each state or locality might have coherent interests of its own and that federalism might enable the people of each state or locality to pursue their own legitimate interests and values, and to protect their distinct identities, substantially free from external interference.

What was the result of Madison's approach? In sum, it constituted a partial break with the contractualism of Locke and a complete upending of the federal republicanism of Montesquieu. Federalism was no longer a negotiated agreement among states; it now appeared as a form of government designed by wise, aristocratic statesmen as an instrumental means to an end. Like master architects formulating a grand design for good and limited government, the founders of the constitution aimed to create an ideal republic in which power is balanced against power, government is balanced against government, and faction is balanced against faction. As Madison put it, the best republic is one in which there is a 'judicious modification and mixture of the federal principle.'[54] The federal principle is no longer centred on a set of premises about the proper rights, prerogatives and legitimate purposes of the federating states, but is rather one tool of constitutional design among others. More fundamentally, there is no longer a federal condition which makes federalism necessary and desirable, but rather a generalised human condition which calls for constitutional devices to ensure just and limited government, in the context of which federalism is nothing more than one possible means to that greater end.

D. Arendt

In the face of a modernity that presupposes much of this, Hannah Arendt proposed a recovery of what she understood to be an Aristotelian account of the human condition. Embedded also in her many works is an advocacy of a republican federal principle that is sharply opposed to theories of national state sovereignty associated with figures such as Bodin and Hobbes.[55] Arendt well recognised the way in which the American colonies had, by the time of the revolution, become fully 'articulated' countries, constituted and constructed from the bottom up, first in their respective villages, townships and cities, then in their counties and their districts, and lastly into entire states—that is, the 13 original states that eventually federated to form the United States of America—much in the same way that Althusius had proposed in his federative

[54] *The Federalist Papers*, No 51.

[55] Douglas Klusmayer, 'Hannah Arendt's Case for Federalism' (2009) 40 *Publius: The Journal of Federalism* 31.

account of politics.[56] Arendt likewise drew attention to the fact that this plurality of political communities had constituted themselves by 'covenant', 'combination', 'consociation', 'compact' and 'confederation': terms that had been used in essentially the same sense by Althusius some decades before they were first uttered in the Americas.[57] She also insightfully observed that the American practice of covenanting contained within itself both the republican principle of deriving the authority of government from the people and the federative principle 'according to which constituted bodies can combine and enter into lasting alliances without losing their identity.'[58]

However, Arendt's understanding of Locke, while properly contrasted with Hobbes' absolutism,[59] failed to take full stock of the unitary presuppositions and direction of Locke's thought. Arendt was, it is true, a critic of the eventual design of the United States Constitution in its emphasis on representative institutions and its failure to provide opportunity for direct popular participation in self-governance, such as through the 'ward system' of 'elementary republics' that Thomas Jefferson had advocated.[60] But she did not fully consider the instrumentalist turn in Madison's arguments in *Federalist* No 51 as the source of this movement from participation to representation, involving as it did a turn from a plurality of peoples into a plurality of governments.[61] But it was precisely *this* move that militated against Arendt's own preference for a multiplicity of discrete political communities, in which citizens can participate in their local self-government.[62]

Arendt located the demise of the Aristotelian participatory ideal in a movement from the 'active' life of political engagement to the 'contemplative' life of philosophical-theological meditation.[63] Intrinsic to this shift, she argued, was the substitution of the Greek 'political' with the Roman 'social', which she saw exemplified in Thomas Aquinas's translation of the Aristotelian concept of 'man as a political animal' into a concept of 'man as social and political'.[64] Aquinas's adaptation of Aristotle to the much wider diversity of social, religious and political forms and grades of community that constituted high medieval society as a whole was indeed significant. However, it was significant not only for according the 'political' a place among many other manifestations of social life, but also for opening the way to a conception of the universal political community as a thing constructed out of many smaller, constituent communities. In Aquinas, this did not quite mean 'federalism', but in Althusius, it virtually did.

For these reasons, Arendt's account of the human condition is not quite sufficient to support the kind of republican federative ideal that she so plainly favoured in her writings. An alternative account, which is more appreciative of human sociality in its

[56] Hannah Arendt, *On Revolution* (London, Penguin, 1990) 176.
[57] ibid 167–72.
[58] ibid 171.
[59] See Klusmayer, 'Hannah Arendt's Case for Federalism' 41.
[60] Arendt, *On Revolution* 127, 248–55.
[61] ibid 147, 152–54.
[62] Klusmayer, 'Hannah Arendt's Case for Federalism' 49.
[63] Hannah Arendt, *The Human Condition* (Chicago, University of Chicago Press, 1998) 20–21.
[64] ibid 22–27, citing Thomas Aquinas, *Summa Theologica* I, 96.4.

non-political forms and expressions, seems to be necessary. To that task this chapter now turns. The account must begin at the beginning.

II. THE FEDERAL CONDITION

A. Personal Relations

We human beings are born out of the wombs of our mothers. Our first human relationship is intensely personal, corporal and intimate. For most of us, our birth delivers us into the care of parents, and a life lived together with siblings, within a family of some description or other.[65] These are relationships we do not choose but find ourselves born into. As infants we make demands for certain desirable things (food, comfort, contentment) and the elimination of others (hunger, pain, distress), and we also find ourselves to be objects of the demands and expectations of others (such as those of our parents and our siblings). We learn quickly—before we are able to express it clearly in words or conceptualise it in abstract terms—that our condition is one of living in relationship with other human beings. On mature reflection, we are able to describe these relationships as involving many different forms and modes of human relationship, which we might distinguish as involving combinations of self-directed action, negotiated cooperation and authoritative coordination among human beings, rationally calculated to secure certain things that are apprehended as good and desirable, as well as to avoid things that are bad and undesirable. We are thus dependent creatures born into nurturing families.[66]

Many other kinds of relationship develop at an early time. Some are due primarily to kinship—grandparents, uncles and aunts, cousins. Others are a consequence of proximity and of common interests and projects—neighbours, friends, colleagues, and so on. The existence, regularity, quality and structure of these relationships vary among persons and cultures, but something along these lines is the experience of most if not all human beings. To these relationships we attribute all sorts of characteristics, purposes and goals, which we again conceive to be good or desirable: basic goods such as friendship, play, learning and health, and various instrumental goods which we apprehend as rational means to these ends (such as the use or possession of houses, vehicles, tools, toys, and so on).[67]

[65] See Jean Bethke Elshtain, *Public Man, Private Woman: Women in Social and Political Thoughts* (Princeton, Princeton University Press, 1981) 326–27: 'familial ties and modes of child bearing are essential to establish the minimal foundation of human social existence. ... [T]he family's status as a moral imperative derives from its universal, pan-cultural existence in all known past and present societies. ... Aristotle and all the other political theorists ... who asserted the primacy of politics ... were guilty of a serious distortion. It is the family which "pervades all our perceptions of social reality". ... This makes the family "the universal basis of human culture". ...'

[66] Alasdair Macintyre, *Dependent Rational Animals: Why Human Beings Need the Virtues* (Chicago, Open Court, 1999) 123: 'Families at their best are forms of association in which children are first nurtured, and then educated for and initiated into the activities of an adult world in which their parents' participatory activities provide them both with resources and models.'

[67] On the distinction between basic and instrumental goods, see John Finnis, *Natural Law and Natural Rights* (Oxford, Oxford University Press, 1980) chs 3–5.

Some of these relationships and forms of sociality are experienced as mostly obligatory and necessary, while others are more voluntary and contingent. Some are intensely personal and local, while others are more diffuse, impersonal and distant.[68] John Finnis offers three helpful illustrations of these kinds of 'associating or coming together' in human relationships.[69] This first might be called a kind of cooperation: it is that of two students, without formal agreement, behaving in a cooperative manner in the classroom so as to secure a good that they share in common—an effective learning environment.[70] Finnis's second example is also of cooperation, this time with formal agreement, as when two students each individually contract with a tutor to teach them.[71] Finnis remarks that Aristotle classified both of these as relationships of utility: there is no common good involved, but rather each is involved 'in the service of each attaining his own objective'. Finnis observes that these are different from a third and much more intense degree of relationship, which he calls 'friendship'. Friendship, he says, is a relation of human beings where the relationship is an end in itself, which one pursues for the sake of both oneself and one's friend.[72] As Finnis puts it, friendship is therefore 'the most communal although not the most extended or elaborated form of human community'.[73] Thus described, the epitome of friendship is intensely personal and local, for this personal intensity of relationship cannot be extended very far. Relations that are more extended are by necessity less personal, therefore, and less intense and demanding.[74] For these reasons, we have an inclination to treat familial, personal and local relationships as not only autobiographically prior, but also as morally prior—as binding us with ties that are richer, deeper and stronger than the more distant relationships that we have with persons whom we regard as mere acquaintances, let alone those whom we do not know personally and yet regard as fellow human beings entitled to concern and respect.[75] This suggests that we are—legitimately I think—bound essentially by local attachments; and yet we also aspire to the universality of the human race.[76]

[68] The related distinction between 'association' and 'community' (*Gemeinschaft* and *Gesellschaft*) is important analytically, but blurred in practice. Analytically, the bonds of association are voluntary and contingent while the bonds of community are obligatory and necessary. The bonds of community are thicker and more intensive on a local scale (eg the bonds of love and care within a family), thinner on an extended scale (eg the duties of mutual respect owed among all human beings, the duties of mutual assistance in grave emergencies). In practice, wider associations, although usually voluntary and contingent, are formed on the presupposition of the underlying communal bonds that exist on an extended scale.

[69] Finnis, *Natural Law and Natural Rights* 135.

[70] ibid 139.

[71] ibid 139–40.

[72] ibid 140–44.

[73] ibid 143.

[74] This insight underwrites Finnis's insistence that Plato overreached when he called for the communal sharing of women, children and possessions. That sort of sharing is highly personal and necessarily domestic, and cannot be extended, humanly, beyond the household, as Aristotle argued (see Finnis, *Natural Law and Natural Rights* 144–45).

[75] Local attachments are constituted by an array of related affections, practices and duties. Wider, universal aspirations are constituted by an array of thinner, but fundamental, duties grounded in the common dignity of all human beings.

[76] This aspiration to the universality of human dignity appears to be historically more recent than our local attachments. In the Western tradition, at least, there is a story that can be told of a movement from the mostly bounded and localised to the more extended and general, when it comes to conceptions

While we thus tend to experience our most intensely personal relationships of family and kinship as historically necessary and morally obligatory, and while most of our more distant relationships (such as those in market places and common spaces) tend to be voluntary and contingent, there are some distant relationships that we experience as also obligatory and necessary, for which we use the adjectives 'political' or 'governmental'. The political and governmental relationship, especially under liberal-democratic conditions, has elements of self-directed action, negotiated cooperation and authoritative coordination, but it is the modern state's assertion of a monopoly over the legitimate use of force that decisively sets it apart.[77] As such, the liberal-democratic state is concerned with public deliberation about the authoritative coordination of persons within a particular jurisdiction.[78] Much of contemporary political philosophy and constitutional theory revolves around questions of public deliberation, political authority and territorial jurisdiction. In a politically stable environment the authority and jurisdiction of the most local and effective government is experienced by us as necessary and obligatory, whereas the influence of other governments, which lack effective jurisdiction over us (because they are weaker or more distant), is experienced as at most voluntary and contingent. The relationships between these governments, their jurisdictions over us, and our political participation in their deliberations constitute the subject matter of federalism, broadly conceived.

B. Social Relations

These factors and principles are illustrated in many forms of human sociality, even though there is great diversity in the specific embodiment of them from one social setting to another, and there are significant disagreements about the determination of those specifics. Thus, for example, the close communal ties constituted by family and kinship are characteristically the most intense in spousal, parent-child and sibling relationships, and become progressively less intense as the degrees of consanguinity decrease, such that they are at their weakest (although still existing) in the biology that unites all human beings together. Likewise, local neighbourhoods and villages frequently share a sense of association and community born of the fact that individuals and families are living in close proximity to one another. Although the degree of 'community spirit' varies considerably from place to place, as a general rule, the closer the proximity, the stronger the ties of mutual responsibility, care and assistance tend

of human nature and dignity, public good and sociality. This extension of the frontiers from the local to the universal is one of the important threads, for example, in Charles Taylor's account of our modern identity: Charles Taylor, *Sources of the Self: The Making of Modern Identity* (Cambridge, Mass, Harvard University Press, 1989). See also Finnis, *Natural Law and Natural Rights* 106–109 on the problems of egoistic or group bias.

[77] Max Weber, 'Politics as a Vocation' in Hans H Gerth and Charles Wright Mills (eds), *From Max Weber: Essays in Sociology* (Oxford, Oxford University Press, 1946) 77.

[78] From the Latin *iuris dictio:* to say or declare the law.

to be. Significant degrees of reciprocal cooperation and authoritative coordination frequently develop in these contexts, although the degree to which this is the case depends on judgements of the necessity, convenience and efficiency of having such cooperation and coordination regulated on various scales ('municipal', 'provincial', 'continental').[79] Associational relationships, such as those of social clubs and sporting associations, are similarly characteristically formed at a local level but also have a tendency to develop into wider associations on a regional, continental and even global scale, and are typically organised on a federalistic basis that preserves the identity and autonomy of the local clubs and associations, qualified by duties of membership and submission to general rules promulgated by federal authorities. Religious communities are likewise characteristically formed and nurtured most deeply at a local level, while often aspiring to universality in organisation and outreach; indeed, while there is great diversity in religious beliefs and organisational structures, all of the 'universal' religions aspire to local and global expressions of community. Similar observations can be made about the organisation of workers' unions, employers' associations, political parties and special interest groups, which are often organised in federalistic ways, especially when the political system is itself federal.

The bonds that unite each of these many different forms of human association are diverse; each such association has its own characteristic set of purposes which it pursues. For largely 'personal' reasons we live with our families, we associate with our friends, we worship with our co-religionists, and we work, study and play with various colleagues and acquaintances in all sorts of ways. For largely 'locational' reasons of proximity and accessibility we live with our neighbours, we play in our local parks, we trade in local market places, and we gather in local public spaces. Relationships of belonging and membership, of voluntary cooperation and of authoritative coordination occur in all of these settings in different ways, including the political and governmental.

Governmental authority, especially after the Peace of Westphalia, is predominantly locational (ie jurisdiction is territorially defined), although there are also extensions of authority exercised by modern states over persons (eg citizens) wherever they may happen to be located.[80] The defining mark of the modern state, in other words, is standardly said to be its claim to sovereignty over all that occurs within a particular territory. Relationships between states, and the demarcations of their authority over persons, are organised around these claims to territorial sovereignty. In addition, the

[79] Although contemporary political theory has tended to overlook this due to its focus on the nation-state as the locus of political authority, there is a real sense in which cooperation and coordination existing at a neighbourly and local scale provide the foundations for its existence on a wider scale. The electoral systems in modern democracies refer to this connection, for example in the use of 'wards' for the election of local or municipal governments, in the use of local districts for the election of state governments, in the use of local districts and entire states for the election of federal governments, and likewise in the formation of inter-national organisations (such as the European Union). See Nicholas Aroney, 'Democracy, Community and Federalism in Electoral Apportionment Cases: The United States, Canada and Australia in Comparative Perspective' (2008) 58(4) *University of Toronto Law Journal* 421.

[80] It is possible for it to be otherwise. Before the rise of the modern nation-state, the predominant basis of governing authority, at least in Europe, was through personal relationships of fealty and allegiance; and yet, oaths of allegiance (or the like) are still required of those who hold political or legal office within modern states.

modern 'constitutional' state seeks to give effect to the principles of the rule of law and the separation of powers, especially the authority of courts to determine the law pursuant to which the executive and legislative power of government must be exercised. Under the rule of law, modern states distinguish a special kind of 'legal' power, which is the lawful power of government as authorised by the constitution and affirmed by the courts. This legal power, although associated with political power, is at once something more specific, justiciable and authoritative than general political power (understood as effective influence or control).

The result is a paradoxical concept of the modern state as both 'sovereign' and 'constitutional'. Contemporary federalism, in its 'state' form, is typically conceptualised in these terms. According to the standard definition, a federation exists when there is a division of sovereignty among levels or orders of government set out in a written constitution that is enforced by the courts.[81] However, federalism poses a fundamental challenge to the underlying theory of state sovereignty, particularly in its 'strong', 'extra-constitutional' form.[82] Part of the reason for this is that, in the standard theory, the sovereignty of the state has a tendency to absoluteness: it tends to assert a claim to authority over persons which supervenes on any competing loyalty or allegiance and it purports, in its strong form, to possess the power and authority to reconstruct the entire ensemble of human relationships if it so wishes. The assertion of this kind of sovereignty is incompatible with the normative priority claimed by the many more basic forms of association and community that have been described in this essay. It is also incompatible with federalism, because federalism involves the effective assertion of two (or more) political authorities over the same (ie overlapping) territory. Some argue that the idea of sovereignty can preserved within a federation through its ascription to 'the people'. However, every such attempt to do so encounters the continuing question of not only 'We, the people', but also 'We, the peoples'.[83] Federations routinely recognise multiple political identities not only in their 'distributions of power' between 'federal' and 'state' institutions of government, but also in the composition and construction of those institutions so that they represent 'the people of the federation' and 'the peoples of the states', as well as in the very formation or establishment of the federation in a 'compact' between constituent states.[84] As Carl Schmitt argued, in a federation, the question of sovereignty 'always remains open'.[85]

[81] Albert V Dicey, *Introduction to the Study of the Law of the Constitution* (London, Macmillan, 1915) 134–67; Kenneth C Wheare, *Federal Government* (Oxford, Oxford University Press, 1963) ch 1.

[82] For the distinction between the 'strong' and the 'weak' form of Westphalian sovereignty, see Peter Stirk, 'The Westphalian Model, Sovereignty and Law in *Fin-de-siècle* German International Theory' (2005) 19 *International Relations* 153.

[83] Henry Paul Monaghan, 'We the People[s], Original Understanding, and Constitutional Amendment' (1996) 96(1) *Columbia Law Review* 121; Kalypso Nicolaïdis, 'We, the Peoples of Europe …' (2004) 83(6) *Foreign Affairs* 97; Stephen Tierney, '"We the Peoples": Constituent Power and Constitutionalism in Plurinational States' in Martin Loughlin and Neil Walker (eds), *The Paradox of Constitutionalism* (Oxford, Oxford University Press, 2008) 229.

[84] Nicholas Aroney, 'Formation, Representation and Amendment in Federal Constitutions' (2006) 54 *American Journal of Comparative Law* 277.

[85] Carl Schmitt, *Constitutional Theory* (Durham, Duke University Press, 2008) § 29, III.1, p 390.

There is a deep presuppositional question about whether federal systems are to be understood as deriving their form and nature from a 'negotiated process of federating' or are the result of a 'deliberate legislative plan'. When federations are formed by human agents, there necessarily are elements of both planning and negotiation, but there are important differences between the two ways of understanding what is at stake that contribute to different practices, theories and evaluations of the phenomenon of federalism. In *Federalist* No 51, as has been seen, Madison approached the question of federalism from a planning perspective, treating it as a tool to be used by the wise constitutional law-maker when trying to solve coordination problems within a society. In *Federalist* No 39, however, he recognised that federations are the result of negotiated agreements between independent states. Madison and Hamilton had their preferred plans for the design of the new constitution, but they had to make compromises to secure the agreement of those who had other plans for the federation.[86] In *Federalist* No 39, Madison accordingly demonstrated how the proposed constitution could be regarded as consistent with republican and federal principles. But why would we find such principles attractive? Only if we assume that it is legitimate for localised political communities to exercise powers of constitutional self-determination when negotiating the terms of a proposed federal constitution. However, this makes sense only if we accept that local political communities are *normatively prior* to the larger political communities of which they might become constituent members. On this view, local political communities come into being as a result of legitimate attachments to locality and personal relationship, while relatively extended associations arise out of our desire for goods that can only be secured effectively on a wider scale. For it is an intrinsic feature of the human condition that the relatively personal and local is not only historically prior to the relatively more impersonal and distant, but is ordinarily accorded a normative priority in our affections, orientations and concerns.

C. Political Relations

Much inter-human cooperation and coordination is thus secured through familial, neighbourly, social, religious and economic associations of varying kinds and forms, enabling many human goods to be secured both more richly and more widely than would otherwise be the case. Mainstream political philosophy has tended to overlook the relationship between these forms of cooperation and coordination and the formal institutions of the state. However, contemporary states themselves routinely display comparable patterns of local, provincial and general organisation (whether 'federal' or not). All of this gives rise to issues associated with the claims of states to a monopoly of ultimate coordinating authority and coercive force over a particular territory. The tension lies in the fact that local forms of association and community are generally prior in time to the state, and modern states come into being through

[86] Michael Zuckert, 'Federalism and the Founding: Toward a Reinterpretation of the Constitutional Convention' (1986) 48 *Review of Politics* 166.

the gradual consolidation and deepening of central authority over increasingly larger territorial domains.[87] Even the most 'artificial' of state systems of governance, rapidly imposed through techniques of military expansion, colonisation or post-colonial 'state-building', have to grapple with pre-existing local attachments and the various layers of personal and communal authority that are invested in them.

Federalism arises in these contexts, sometimes as an 'aggregative' agreement among formerly autonomous political communities,[88] and sometimes as the 'devolutionary' response of a relatively unified political community to demands or claims from within for local autonomy. Such claims to autonomy by nascent political communities within a unitary state are typically associated with assertions of a kind of 'priority', both historical and normative, such as the claims for autonomy made by the Scots in the United Kingdom, the Catalans in Spain, and the Quebecers in Canada.[89] The distinction between aggregation and devolution is therefore important, but must not be exaggerated. *Whether* a federation is formed by integrative or devolutionary processes, the *extent* to which this is the case, and exactly *how* it occurs, determines the legal assumptions and formative conditions under which a federation comes into being. These legal assumptions and formative conditions operate like legitimising premises that shape and in some respects determine the form and structure of the institutions and governing processes that are ultimately adopted in a federal constitution.[90] As such, the form and structure of a federation is shaped by both the legally-acknowledged rights to constitutional self-determination of its constituent members and their politically-effective capacities to influence the constitutional negotiations. There is thus a distinctively 'federal' account of the nature of and the relationship between constituent power and constituted power within federal systems. Not all federations rest upon 'We, the people'; many rest upon 'We, the peoples'.

Conceived as an ideal type, a federation that is 'purely' aggregative will be constructed on the basis of the legally-required agreement of every one of its constituent states, which agreement functions as the 'constitution' of the federal arrangement, as Althusius recognised. An aggregative federal system will be based, in other words, on the *negotiated cooperation* of several political communities, rather than the *authoritative coordination* of one government over others. The decision to form a federation (a 'state consisting of states')[91] in such circumstances involves an agreement to create a federal government with authority over the combined territories of the constituent states. The fundamental, formative decision-making rule of a fully aggregative federation is thus unanimity among its constituent states. The authority, composition, and decision-making rules of the proposed federal government are accordingly of great interest to the constituent states. For it is in: (1) the defined

[87] Joseph Strayer, *On the Medieval Origins of the Modern State* (Princeton, Princeton University Press, 1970).

[88] Hence the derivation of 'federal' from the Latin *foedus:* treaty, covenant, compact.

[89] Stephen Tierney, *Constitutional Law and National Pluralism* (Oxford, Oxford University Press, 2004).

[90] I seek to show this in Aroney, 'Formation, Representation and Amendment in Federal Constitutions'.

[91] See Bryce, *The American Commonwealth* I, pp 12–15, 332.

limits of federal authority; (2) the composition of the institutions of the federal government; and (3) the decision-making rules of those institutions, that the continuing capacity of the constituent states to exercise local self-government and to participate in the governance of the federation as a whole is preserved. Each of these three institutional devices is frequently used to secure these objectives, and specific combinations of them produce different constitutional 'balances' between the federation and the states.

The constituent states preserve to themselves the highest level of autonomy when they each retain individual control over the disposition of the collective affairs of the federated states. This can be achieved in various ways, such as: (a) by ensuring that the decisions of the federation are not binding or not enforceable without the confirming or enforcing action of each state within its territory; and/or (b) by insisting that the governing institutions of the federation consist of delegates of the states themselves and that decisions must be taken by unanimous vote. When federal systems use either or both of these methods of state control, they guarantee so much constituent state autonomy that they are commonly called 'alliances' or, at most, 'confederations of states'. Relatively more centralised federal systems, usually called 'federations', 'federal states' or even 'union states', occur when: (c) the jurisdiction of the federal government is defined to include particular matters concerning which its decisions will overrule those of the states; and/or (d) the composition of the federal government and its decision-making rules are defined in a manner that reduces or (in some respects) eliminates the distinct voice of the states. For example, the composition of the institutions of the federal government can be organised such that they consist of representatives of groups other than the constituent states, such as local electoral districts within the states or, in some sense, the people of the federation as a whole. Similarly, the decision-making rules of federation may depend on majority rule rather than unanimity among the states. There are numerous possible variations on (c) and (d): the competences of the federation can be more or less extensive and the representation of the states and the voting rules can be more or less distant from the principle of unanimity. Indeed, there is a trade-off between what is sometimes called 'exit' and 'voice'. For example, if extensive competences are conferred upon the federation they can, from a state point of view, be kept in check through state representation and decision-making rules that are closer to unanimity, while if very limited competences are conferred the states may be willing to relinquish direct control or influence over federal decisions in relation to those matters.[92] However, federations also have to operate within an international order in which political authority is exercised by other nation-states, many of which have no similar limitations on their international personality and capacity, and so there is strong incentive for constituent states to confer sufficiently effective capacities on their federal governments in relation to international affairs and international law.[93]

[92] See Koen Lenaerts, 'Constitutionalism and the Many Faces of Federalism' (1990) 38 *American Journal of Comparative Law* 205.

[93] The 'international' capacities of the federal and state governments is thus another important mark of distinction between federal systems lying at the 'confederation' and 'federation' ends of the spectrum.

In addition, there is the important question of how the whole federal arrangement is to be formally altered in the future. In systems that are at the 'confederation' end of the spectrum, the principle of unanimity is likely to be retained for constitutional amendments, whereas in systems at the 'federation' end of the spectrum the constituent states are likely to have relinquished individual control over the constitutional destiny of the federation as a whole. Nonetheless, because the very terms of the federal agreement are in play, the decision-making rule for constitutional amendment is likely to lie somewhere between unanimity and majority. Moreover, different amendment procedures can be adopted for different kinds of change: those of most concern to the constituent states will be more carefully guarded, while other matters of less concern will not. Again, the possible variations on these themes are numerous and diverse.

In a modern constitutional environment, all three branches of government are actively involved in the daily operation of a federal system. The political branches of government (legislature and executive) often seek to exercise their constitutional powers to the widest extent politically and legally possible and the judicial branch interprets its constitutional role as one of adjudicating disputes over the precise demarcations of governmental power. Once a federal system comes into being, it thus develops a political and juridical life of its own, and it will evolve constitutionally in response to the interplay of the executive, legislative and judicial branches of the federal and state governments, each operating in the context of the country as a whole. Depending on the constitutional, political, social and economic settings and circumstances of the federation, this evolution may be in the general direction of centralisation, decentralisation or the maintenance of a relatively stable 'balance'.[94] Nonetheless, the text and structure of the federal constitution, read in the light of its juridical assumptions and motivating purposes, normally continues to play a fundamental role in the normative order of the federation. The evolution of the federal system is not open-ended, as if the negotiated terms of the constitution can be manipulated to mean anything. Text, structure, history, purpose and context all influence the way in which a federal constitution is interpreted and applied.

D. Coercive Relations

The analysis so far has tended to assume that federal systems are typically aggregative and thus rest on the individual consent of every constituent state. But, as noted, some federal systems emerge and develop under conditions in which the constituent states are not recognised as entirely independent self-governing political communities that are fully in control of their constitutional destinies. For example, they may be colonies or former colonies that remain subject to some form of imperial control (eg Canada and Australia until the 1980s) or they may be states under military supervision after having lost a war (eg Germany and Austria after the Second World War).

[94] See the chapters in Nicholas Aroney and John Kincaid (eds), *Courts in Federal Countries: Federalists or Unitarists?* (Toronto, University of Toronto Press, 2017).

Moreover, in comparison with each other, the constituent states may not be equal in their respective capacities for independent self-government and constitutional self-determination. Under such conditions, the capacity of the states to bargain as independent equals is qualified, and this shapes the kinds of federal arrangements each of them is able to secure. If the states enter as constitutive non-equals, unless some strong reason or other factor intervenes, they are likely to remain unequal within the federation. If they are dependent on some external political authority, whether imperial or supervisory, this external authority will have a role in the formation of any federative arrangement, the level of its involvement being determined by the extent of its recognised authority and effective influence.[95] Fully devolutionary arrangements—in which the emergent constituent states are officially understood by the central authority to be no more than historic ethno-cultural identities or subordinate administrative units—lie at the far end of the spectrum of such federative schemes. However, as noted, even in these cases the movement towards a federal form of government is typically premised upon political claims by the emergent states to rights of constitutional recognition and self-determination.

Devolutionary arrangements can themselves vary considerably. At one end of the spectrum, unitary states with strongly centralised systems of governance ordinarily have to delegate powers of administration and adjudication to officials in order to ensure that central policy is applied and enforced in outlying areas. A unitary state may, however, choose also to institute a policy of administrative decentralisation allowing degrees of discretion in the application of central policy at the peripheries of the state. This decentralisation can be more or less extensive, and it may include the grant of delegated law-making powers, such as the kinds of limited self-governing powers that are conferred upon local or municipal governments in many unitary states. Moreover, the degree to which such devolutionary arrangements are constitutionalised can vary. In some cases the devolutionary arrangement remains, at least formally, within the power of the central government to amend and repeal; in other cases the arrangement is constitutionalised, and can only be altered by a formal constitutional amendment processes that lies beyond the ordinary governing powers of the central authority. Because these latter arrangements are constitutionally entrenched, it has become customary to describe them as genuinely 'federal', although the juridical foundation of the constitutional settlement is devolutionary rather than aggregative. There is no need to quibble with the label, provided the underlying distinction between devolution and integration is kept in mind, for there remain important differences between to the two types of federal system, especially in relation to their ultimate juridical presuppositions—that is, unless those presuppositions are themselves challenged and overthrown through legally effective revolution, a possibility that need not involve armed insurrection, although it sometimes does.

[95] For example, the Canadian colonies in the 1860s enjoyed relatively less constitutional autonomy than did the Australian colonies in the 1890s, and this distinction accounts for several important differences between the two constitutions as enacted in 1867 and 1900 respectively. Scotland, Wales and Northern Ireland enjoyed even less autonomy within the United Kingdom in the 1990s and the British Acts which established devolution reflect this as well. See Nicholas Aroney, 'Devolutionary Federalism within a Westminster-Derived Context' in Aileen McHarg et al (eds), *The Scottish Independence Referendum: Constitutional and Political Implications* (Oxford, Oxford University Press, 2016).

Beyond this, it is possible to venture even more detailed generalisations about relationships between the formative conditions under which a federal system comes into being and the kinds of federative arrangements that eventually emerge. Differences in the initial construction of political authority can be very significant. For example, federative arrangements that are formally established by international treaties between the executive governments of the constituent states tend to privilege executive authority within the federative arrangement itself (eg the European Union). Those that are established on the basis of deliberative assemblies and legislatures tend to favour the same kinds of institutions for political and constitutional decision-making within the federation (eg the United States). And those that are established on the basis of direct appeals to the peoples of the states tend to adopt systems of direct election and referendums for political and constitutional decision-making (eg Australia). When one digs deeply into the formation of any particular constitution, the story is even more complex, but rather like a fractal image, discernibly similar patterns tend to repeat themselves in the detail, as I found in my analysis of the making of the Australian Constitution and the way in which the Australians made use of the American, Canadian, Swiss and Germany models in their debates and deliberations.[96]

Why do such patterns tend to emerge? Some may say that there is a kind of path-dependency in play, driven primarily by the rational self-interest of the parties in the negotiations. The reasoning will be something like this: 'if the constitution will *have* to be approved by the elected politicians of each state, then we will *need* to give those politicians an effective say in the governance of the federation in the future'. Others may say that normative values are at play, the reasoning being: 'if the constitution *ought* to be ratified by the peoples of the states, then the peoples of the states *should* also determine whether to amend the constitution'. In my reading of the convention debates in Australia, and elsewhere, there is ample evidence of both kinds of arguments.

Whatever the formative conditions, assumptions, expectations and aspirations under which a federal system comes into being, these will tend to shape the kind of federal arrangement that is adopted, whether the system is initially aggregative or devolutionary. That said, there is much to be said in favour of the view that the aggregative model is normatively preferable and most consistent with the underlying account of the human condition outlined in this chapter. For, as noted, even in federal systems that are formally devolutionary, the pressure to move towards such a system of government is usually generated by regional claims to local self-governance that are premised upon rights to constitutional self-determination. This suggests that all federative systems presuppose a set of political and constitutional values that build from the local outwards because they treat the local as in some sense historically, logically *and* normatively prior.

[96] Nicholas Aroney, *The Constitution of a Federal Commonwealth: The Making and Meaning of the Australian Constitution* (Cambridge, Cambridge University Press, 2009).

I venture that something like this is the ordinary condition of federalism. From a 'realist' perspective, federalism consists of a set of uneasy and not necessarily stable compromises between divergent social, economic and political interests oriented respectively to locality/particularity on one hand and generality/universality on the other. From a more 'normative' perspective, however, federalism is a means by which our legitimate orientations to *both* locality and universality—each of them characteristics of the human condition generally—can best be accommodated.

2

Federation and Empire: About a Conceptual Distinction of Political Forms

OLIVIER BEAUD

IN *ON REVOLUTION* Hannah Arendt compares the genesis of the French and American Republics, noting that the primary challenge that faced the Founding Fathers was:

> [H]ow to establish union out of thirteen 'sovereign,' duly constituted republics; their task was the foundations of a 'confederate republic' which (…) would reconcile the advantages of monarchy in foreign affairs with those of republicanism in domestic policy. And in this task of the Constitution there was no longer any question of constitutionalism in the sense of civil rights (…) but of erecting a system of powers that would check and balance in such a way that the power neither of the union nor of its parts, the duly constituted States, would decrease or destroy one another.[1]

The problem which the German philosopher points to in relation to the United States of America is inherent in any act of federation. How to conceive of a *non-hierarchical duality of powers* of Federation and member states within a single territory is the challenge that federal constitutions and theories of Federation have to take up. This marks the profound difference between the Federation[2] and an empire, which, in all its forms, revolves around the subordination of a peripheral territory to a dominant centre. And yet, in what follows, it is by reference to the empire that I shall attempt to elucidate the nature of the Federation. The reasons for this, seemingly counterintuitive, choice will become clearer as we proceed. At present, suffice to note that my analysis proceeds on a two-fold intuition: (1) to grasp the nature of the Federation, we must understand it as a political form in its own right with its own internal logic and its own set of values; and (2) the specificity of the Federation appears only when placed in juxtaposition to the empire. I shall try to unpack this first intuition by showing what it entails to understand the Federation as a political form and how this attempt implicates Federation and empire (I). I shall then go on

[1] Hannah Arendt, *On Revolution* (London, Penguin Books, 1963) 152.

[2] By Federation I mean the whole of the federal polity, made up of the member states and the federal government, which I shall refer to as the 'federation'.

to present a legal reconstruction of the structural opposition between the notions of Federation and empire (II). Drawing on an example from French political history, I shall map that opposition onto a distinction between federative compact and federal treaty on the basis of which I shall consider the limiting case of federations that were established as part of an imperial regime (III). Finally, I consider how the relationship between centre and periphery conditions our conception of the relationship between Federation and empire and of how they deal with diversity (IV).

I. THE FEDERATION AS A POLITICAL FORM AND ITS RELATION TO EMPIRE

It is a well-known fact that publicists have always regarded the Federation with considerable suspicion, the reason being that the concepts of public law theory are predicated on the unitary nature of power or, more precisely, on the imperative need for unitary power. This is why that most radical philosopher of the state, Thomas Hobbes, denied the viability of federal institutions: an *imperium in imperio* is, he tells us, inconceivable. However, the theoretical impossibility of the Federation has not stopped jurists from studying their history and from theorising those *respublica composita*. In previous work I have tried to show that the Federation can—and should be—understood as a political form, or, more precisely, as a legal and political form.[3] In what follows I shall briefly recapitulate the most salient points of that theory so as to frame the exposition:

(1) The choice of the word 'Federation'. First, this is obviously not a neutral choice, and it serves as the pivot of several arguments in my earlier work on federations. It implies a rejection of the classical distinction between federal state and confederacy (or federation and confederation). Despite its porous nature, this distinction has held theorising on federalism in a stranglehold, distorting the reality it is supposed to describe with deleterious effects for scholarship.

By choosing the word 'Federation' I also wanted to signal that this political form should be placed on a par with the state and the empire. In other words, the Federation is conceived in this book as a legal and political form on an equal footing with the state, even though in doctrine and in practice the former is usually overshadowed by the latter.

Last, but not least, I opted for a study of the Federation *in itself and for itself*, without paying attention to its various species. This is not to deny that there are different kinds of federation and that they can be classified in a rigorous manner. In the last part of *Théorie de la Fédération*, devoted to the relationships between the political form and the governmental form, I refer to the ideal kind of opposition between two types of Federations: the republican Federation—the *federal republic* or the federative republic—on the one hand, and the federation of monarchies on the other hand. Other typologies are of course possible. Following William Riker,[4] one might have opposed centralised and

[3] Olivier Beaud, *Théorie de la Fédération* (Paris, Presses Universitaires de France, 2007) 434.
[4] William Riker, *Federalism: Origin, Operation, Significance* (Boston, Little Brown, 1964) 169.

peripheralised federalism. Ultimately, classification is of secondary importance. The primary consideration is to move theory beyond the distinction between federal state and confederacy.

(2) My theory of federation is structured around two moments, each of which must be emphasised, a negative moment and a positive one. The negative moment, which could be called a 'negative' constitutional law of the Federation, consists in the realisation that neither the notion of sovereignty, nor the *summa divisio* between confederacy and federal state, can capture the legal and political peculiarities of the federal phenomenon. As a corollary to this negative moment, there is a 'positive' constitutional law of the Federation. The main idea that I defend is that the Federation is both a union of states and an institution, which makes possible the coexistence of two public powers, the federal power and the federated (or member states') powers. This leads to the rather paradoxical statement that the Federation rests upon an explicitly assumed structural duality of public powers, a duality that must be protected by legal and political processes, respecting the equality between the federal and the federated orders, and organising the plurality. To put it in another way, *political dualism* means that there is, on the one hand, a political unity that flows from the association of member units—the Federation—and, on the other hand, a plurality or a multitude of political units—the member states. In creating a federation, the member states have not forsaken their legal status of 'states' and they are not willing to be treated as mere provinces. In this description, the federation is not simply a type of state or a form of government. It is a political entity, a federal polity, which can accommodate different systems of government. The double and contradictory aspects of the *telos* prove this: driven by common ends such as safety and welfare to form a Federation, the states are also driven by their particular ends to protect their independence and autonomy.

(3) To conclude, the Federation, as I describe it, is *a federal union of states, and not a federal state*. Here is the true novelty of my approach: while the dominant legal doctrine endeavours to expound the differences between the two federative forms (confederacy/federal state, confederation/federation), I try to bring out their common features which commits me to positing the existence of a federative law (*droit commun fédératif*) which should not be confused with *federal law* that includes only the law of federal states. This is the hypothesis of the *constitutional autonomy of the Federation*, which means that the public law of the Federation and the public law of the state are two different things, and that the Federation must be recognised as a political and legal form in its own right.

One might well ask why I have chosen to come back to the relationship between federalism and imperialism. My interest in federalism dates back to a paper entitled '*The Federation, between the State and the Empire*,' written for a conference on state, Europe and social issues organised in 1994 by the French economist Bruno Théret. I had two intuitions: first of all, the Federation is a political form that cannot be reduced to the form of the state and, at the same time, it is also more than an international organisation; second, the Federation is in part similar to an empire inasmuch as it involves the aggregation of states, but different insofar as it is a union based on the will and free consent of the states. Here, I would like to unpack further the distinction between Federation and empire, or federalism and imperialism. In *Théorie de la Fédération* I did not go beyond a sketch of this ideal-typical distinction, as my primary focus was on the opposition of state and Federation. The intuition that guides the present work is that it is worth revisiting the opposition between Federation and empire, because it enables us to give a larger picture of the *three great political forms*: state (or city, *polis* in antiquity), Federation and empire.

In other words, my hypothesis is the following: whoever tries to shed light on the Federation as a political and legal form can only do so adequately by contrasting it with its symmetrical concept, that of empire. *These two notions represent the ideal-types of modern unions of states*. Therefore, it is important to highlight their common features and similarities which, incidentally, are what make possible a conceptual comparison. If their opposition were complete and absolute, comparing them would be pointless.

The first and most important similarity is that both Federation and empire are types of unions or associations of states, or more precisely of political entities (polities). Did not Raymond Aron, in reflecting on the manner in which the world could be organised in the future, ask how federation and empire would differ, 'if they included all humanity'?[5] His question implied that the two models, federal and imperial, represent the two only conceivable forms for organising international community. Another author observed that 'an empire is a specific form of international organisation, and that imperialism is an integral part of the process of organising the international community.'[6] However, merely pointing out that the empire, like the Federation, can be understood as a form of international organisation does not yet tell us about the structural cause of this similarity. One must add, this time from the vantage point of the jurist, that, as political units, empire and Federation are both composed by other political entities. Thus, the main feature that Federation and empire share is structural, a structure one might qualify as *ternary*. In the same way as the Federation is, in my opinion, composed of two units, the federal power and the member states, the empire consists of an imperial centre—in modern parlance, the metropolis—and the periphery composed of colonies or dependencies.

The second similarity between Federation and empire, which flows from this ternary structure, relates to nationality or citizenship. In both, nationality is multiple, given that the empire is a structure with two hierarchically organised components, the metropolis and the colonies. In an imperial regime, nationality law merely reflects this ternary structure and its complexity is no different from that of the objective law of the imperial political form. Seen from this perspective, the analogy between the ternary structure of the empire and the ternary structure of the Federation is rather strong, so much so in fact that in modern (colonial) empires and from the perspective of structure, colonies are, *mutatis mutandis*, the conceptual equivalent of the federated

[5] Raymond Aron, *Peace and War: A Theory of International Relations* (New York, Doubleday & Co, 1966).

[6] Karl Magyar, *The Foreign Policy of Hegemony: Imperial Politics in Historical Perspective* (PhD, Baltimore, John Hopkins University, 1972) 116.

states (member states). Therefore, as Christoph Schönberger has demonstrated in a groundbreaking work on federal citizenship,[7] the status of the indigenous nationality greatly resembles that of a member state's citizen in a Federation which German scholarship then designated as *Indigenat*. Thus, the indigenous in French colonial law, as an intermediary category, has certain points in common with the *Indigenat* status in German public law under the Second Reich. Understanding both requires that we abandon the notion that nationality is a unidimensional thing and take seriously the idea that all nationalities are pluralist; that nationalities always interweave and are always superimposed one on the other. Obviously, here too there are differences, but the structural analogy remains striking.[8]

Finally, the third similarity between Federation and empire pertains to their political nature. Like the State, both can accommodate different forms of government. At least, this idea holds for modern empires, those of the colonial era,[9] which are called colonial empires. Traditionally, the empire is matched with an autocratic form: on this view, the empire is the emperor who has power over all citizens under his domination. In this regard, Shmuel Eisenstadt wrote that '"Empire" (...) has normally been used to designate a political system encompassing wide, relatively highly centralised territories, in which the centre, as embodied both in the person of an emperor and in the central political institutions, constituted an autonomous entity.'[10] However, by defining the empire as a political form, identical to state and Federation, I want to argue that the imperial form is indifferent to the issue of who holds the central power. The empire is more than the emperor, much in the same way as the state is more than the sovereign. In the same way that there are authoritarian states or authoritarian Federations, so there are 'liberal' empires, in the sense that the imperial centre can have a liberal form of government. The French colonial empire was a republic, while the form of government of the British Empire was that of a constitutional monarchy.

One must be careful not to be misled by these similarities into forgetting the differences between Federation and empire, which emerge clearly from Michael Doyle's classic definition of empire as 'a system of interaction between two political entities, one of which, the dominant metropolis, exerts political control over the internal and external policy—the effective sovereignty—of the other, the subordinate periphery.'[11] Or, to put the point in more general terms, 'Empires are relationships of political control imposed by some political societies over the effective sovereignty of other political societies.'[12]

[7] Christoph Schönberger, *Unionsbürger: Europas föderales Bürgerrecht in vergleichender Sicht* (Tubingen, Mohr Siebeck, 2005). For a French summary, see Christoph Schönberger, 'La citoyenneté européenne comme citoyenneté fédérale' (2009) 1 *Annuaire de l'Institut Michel Villey* 252ff.

[8] On this point, *cf* Yerri Urban, *L'indigène dans le droit colonial français* (Paris, LGDJ, 2010).

[9] Here, I appropriate a distinction proposed by French political scientist, Jean Leca (personal correspondence, on file with author).

[10] Shmuel N Eisenstadt, 'Empires' in *International Encyclopedia of the Social Sciences* (New York, Macmillan and Free Press, 1972) vol IV, p 41.

[11] Michael W Doyle, *Empires* (Ithaca, Cornell University Press, 1986) 12.

[12] ibid 19.

In an empire there is no real equality between the members of the imperial body, quite the opposite: the relationship is one of domination and subordination between a centre and its periphery in which the latter has lost its 'effective sovereignty'. In other words, the concept of empire denies the principle of sovereign equality of states that is at the modern system of international law as well as all modern federations. The aim of the present discussion is to bring out the nature of this profound opposition between empire and Federation. This requires that we clarify an additional three points.

First, it should be understood that I deal less with federalism and imperialism than with Federation and empire. My analysis proceeds on the, by now conventional, distinction between 'empire' (which refers to the notion of polity) and 'imperialism' (which refers to policy).[13] Imperialism is dynamic whereas empire is static. This dynamism of imperialism is captured both in the definition given by Moritz Julius Bonn—'a policy which aims at creating, organising and maintaining an empire; that is, a state of vast size composed of various more or less distinct national units and subject to a single centralised will'[14]—and in the more famous definition of Joseph Schumpeter: '[I]mperialism is the objectless disposition on the part of a state to unlimited forcible expansion.'[15] In my view, it is, however, best summarised by Michael Doyle who defines imperialism as 'the process of establishing and maintaining an empire.'[16]

Furthermore, there is a strong tendency to link imperialism to a certain political ideology, a tendency I oppose. For the study of empire and imperialism I appropriate the distinction introduced by Preston King between Federation and federalism. 'Federalism' is employed where the interest is primarily ideological, while 'federation' is applied to designate a more descriptive, institutional arrangement.[17]

The second clarification relates to the historical dimension of the inquiry. It would be a mistake to consider the concepts of empire and Federation to be atemporal and universal. It is crucial that we take account of history. There are ancient empires and modern empires, much in the same way as there are ancient federations and modern ones; the dividing line, to me, seems to be the emergence of the modern state in the fifteenth and sixteenth centuries. Yet, a comparison between the federations of ancient Greek cities and ancient imperialism can be useful in order to grasp the different political rationales that drive each of these institutions.

[13] Jacques Rupnik, 'L'Europe centrale et les Balkans á la recherche d'un substitut d'empire' in Anne-Marie Le Gloannec and Aleksander Smolar (eds), *Entre Kant et Kosovo. Etudes offertes á Pierre Hassner* (Paris, Presses de Sciences Po, 2003) 340.

[14] Moritz Julius Bonn, 'Imperialism' in *Encyclopedia of the Social Sciences* (New York, MacMillan and Free Press, 1965) vol VII, p 605.

[15] Joseph Schumpeter, 'Zur Soziologie der Imperialismen' (1918–1919) VI *Archiv für Sozialwissenschaften und Sozialpolitik* 3.

[16] Doyle, *Empires* 19.

[17] Preston King, *Federalism and Federation* (London, Croom Helm, 1982) 20–21.

II. THE IDEAL TYPICAL OPPOSITION BETWEEN FEDERATION AND EMPIRE

In the following I shall attempt to bring out the difference between Federation and empire by working through the analysis of great historian of federalism, Edward Freeman. At a time when British domination in Ireland was being questioned and attempts to liberalise the empire were made, Freeman felt called to analyse the idea of an 'Imperial Federation' which had emerged at the end of the nineteenth century.[18] He criticises the use of this expression by William E Forster, a founder member of the Imperial Federation League (which militated in favour of federalisation of the British Empire), who had given this title to a review article.[19] Freeman argues that federation and empire do not mix; the mere concatenation of the words does not mean that an entity which combines the features of a federation and an empire has come into being. He refutes this possibility by posing a sort of axiom: 'The simple truth is that the phrase "Imperial Federation" is a contradiction in terms, that what is imperial cannot be federal, and what is federal cannot be imperial.'[20]

To prove the existence of this radical opposition, Freeman uses, among others, a history of linguistic usages. He notes that the word 'empire' has lost its original meaning which, he says, dates back to the Roman Empire. Not without irony, he observes that in contemporary political speeches (of Victorian times),

> [i]t seems to have taken its place quite naturally as the highest term in an ascending scale. As the county is greater than the parish, and the kingdom greater than the county, so the empire is greater than the kingdom. The word 'empire' is used as one that comes as naturally to the lips as 'parish,' 'county,' or 'kingdom'.[21]

He further observes that only recently has notion of empire come to mean something beyond the kingdom, and that the adjective imperial still carries only a vague reference.[22] In his view, this extended usage of the word empire and its cognates is an abuse of language. It matters little, for our purposes, whether the semantic history of the word empire is correct or whether his demonstration is biased against Disraeli.[23] What matters is the conceptual issue that Freeman raises by focusing discussion on the concept of Federation.

He returns to the thesis defended by William Forster, who, paradoxically, relies on the canonical definition of a federal government given by Freeman—'a federal government in its perfect form is one which forms a single state with regard to other nations, but which consists of many states with regard to its internal government'—and

[18] The article originally appeared in *McMillan's Magazine* (1884–1885). I thank Mr Thibault Guilluy for having pointed it out to me. I have since discovered that it is referenced in Richard Koebner, *Empire* (Cambridge, Cambridge University Press, 1961) 296 and was republished in Freeman's book *Greater Greece and Greater Britain and George Washington the Expander of England* (London, Macmillan, 1886) 107ff.

[19] William E Forster, 'Imperial Federation' (1885) 306/LI *Nineteenth Century*.

[20] Edward Augustus Freeman, 'Imperial Federation' 430.

[21] ibid 431.

[22] ibid 432.

[23] Koebner, *Empire* 296.

applies it to the United Kingdom on the grounds that the dominions allegedly have self-government and therefore meet the two conditions for being considered a Federation: 'They are many states as regards their internal government, and they are also one state as regards other nations.' However, Freeman contests this interpretation on the ground that there is an irreducible ideal-typical opposition between the federative and imperial forms and notes the misleading use which Forster makes of his definition of federalism. Against Forster's attempt to run together federation and empire, he focuses on the legal reality of the relationship between the dominions and the British Empire, which Forster glosses over by claiming that the colonies have self-government as regards their internal affairs and that they are subjects, 'not merely of the Queen, but of our Parliament' as regards foreign affairs.[24]

The essential legal question is whether the colonies are 'subjects' of the Queen or the Parliament in Westminster, in other words, wherein this 'subjection' to the empire actually consists. It is here that the disagreement between Forster and Freeman becomes manifest:

> But the colonies can exercise no influence at all on foreign affairs; therefore they are in some sort 'subjects' in the way that Mr Forster describes. That is, they are not only subjects in the sense in which any man in a monarchy is a 'subject' of the Emperor, King, or Grand-duke; they are subjects in the sense of being a society of men which is subject to another society. They are, in short, what a (...) Swiss would have called *Unterthanen*.[25]

Thus, the central issue is whether it can be deduced, from the British colonies' right to self-government alone, that they are not subjected or subordinated to the United Kingdom, and therefore, as states, whether they can be considered as members of a federation. Freeman thinks not.

In his view, it is impossible to claim that the British colonies can be likened to the states of the Union (the United States) or the cantons of the Swiss Confederation, or to elude the problem, as Forster does, by arguing that the United Kingdom is an 'incomplete or one-sided Federation'. Such a political entity would not qualify as a federation.

> All the elements of a federation are wanting. There is no voluntary union of independent states, keeping some powers to themselves and granting other powers to a central authority of their own creation. There is instead a number of dependent bodies to which a central authority older than themselves has been graciously pleased to grant certain powers. *This state of things is not federation, but, as Mr Forster truly says, subjection.* It is perfectly true that an American state, as such, has no more direct voice in the foreign affairs of the American Union than a British colony has in the foreign affairs of the British 'empire.' But why? The colony has no such voice, because *it is a subject community* and never had a voice in such matters. The American state has no such voice, because the direction of foreign affairs is one of the powers which the States have ceded to the Federal authority. But, more than this, not only has the colony no direct voice in ordering foreign affairs, itself and its citizens have no voice, direct or indirect, in choosing those who have the ordering of them. But the American state and its citizens have a direct voice in choosing those who have the

[24] Quoted by Freeman, 'Imperial Federation' 434.
[25] ibid 434.

> ordering of the foreign affairs of the Union. [...]. Here are two very different stories: *[T]he difference between the position of the American State and the position of the British colony is nothing short of the difference between federation, and as Mr Forster truly says, subjection.* (emphasis added)[26]

By using this implicit definition of the Federation as a voluntary union of states placing powers in common the better to protect themselves, Freeman highlights the raison d'être of the opposition between empire and Federation: the federative freedom to unite and place the member states and the federal power (or 'federation' without a capital letter) on an equal footing once the Federation has been constituted. The concrete consequence of this difference can be seen in the status of the member bodies of these complex units: the member states of a Federation are political bodies, that is to say, states, inside another political body, while colonies are administrative bodies subject to imperial power and characterised by their state of subjection.[27]

This is why Freeman does not believe that an empire could easily be turned into a Federation. If some politicians or essayists like Forster believe otherwise, it is because they have an incorrect understanding of what a Federation is.

> Federation means something quite different. To establish a real federation, a federation on the American or Swiss model, certain states must agree to give up certain independent defined powers, foreign relations pre-eminently among them, to a central authority. The states which consent to this agreement, remaining independent states for certain purposes, cease to be independent states for certain other purposes. For these last purposes each state is merged in the larger body formed by the whole Union. A federal union therefore involves a certain loss of power and position on the part of the states which unite to form it. But, as federations have been formed hitherto, that loss of power and position has either been merely nominal or else has been fully made up in other ways. The most successful federal unions have been made by small states threatened by enemies whom none of them could resist singly, but whom they might hope to resist if united. (...) In each of the great federal unions some of the members, in some of them all the members, distinctly gained in political position by entering the Union. Federation is a check on independence; but many of the states had never known separate independence.[28]

This, perhaps, is the federal idea in all its conceptual purity. This understanding of a Federation also presupposes that all the citizens in the Federation have equal rights and that no people dominates the others. Yet in the case of the United Kingdom, it is clear that the British people decides for the other peoples, who are in some cases—like India—far more numerous than they. If an empire like this became a Federation, the people of Great Britain would have to admit they could be placed in the minority by the non-European inhabitants of the Federation.[29]

[26] ibid 435.

[27] ibid 435.

[28] ibid 439–40.

[29] ibid 444: 'The words "Imperial Federation," "Federation of the Empire," either mean nothing or they mean that on all "imperial" questions, the people of the English-speaking parts of the Empire shall be liable to be outvoted by the Hindoos and Muslims of India. A federation which does not give them equal federal rights with their European fellow-subjects is not a "Federation of the Empire," but only of a small part of the "Empire." Such a federation would be, as regards India, simply an enlargement of the

Other texts could have been used here to illustrate this opposition between Federation and empire—such as those by Carl Friedrich[30]—but in my view, Freeman's work has the advantage of underlining the great disparity in spirit and approach between these two political forms, the fact that while the empire uses force to integrate the periphery into the centre, the Federation is based on the free consent of the parties, as expressed in the federative constitutional pact. The empire sets up a hierarchy between the centre and the periphery and makes the dominated entities subjects, while the Federation aims at maintaining balance a between the member states and the federal power, thus maintaining the founding states as political units within the new federal entity.

III. AN ILLUSTRATION IN LAW: FEDERATIVE COMPACT AND FEDERAL TREATY

We are well aware that this opposition of two ideal-types could be criticised as being too vague or abstract. Jurists require more: they would bring out this difference by means of legal notions. This is what we will do by using the notion of federative compact (instead of federal constitution)[31] to account for the way a Federation is founded. The purpose of a compact, made by many separate units wishing to unite, is not to constitute (or re-constitute) a political centre designed to dominate the member states that created it. It illustrates the rationale of decentring, the legal expression of which is the founding document. It supposes a free choice of political self-determination by each entity and free will on the part of the monadic states that confederate. This is the opposite of the federal treaty and serves to illustrate the possibility of an imposed, but undesired, federative union, a phenomenon that has already occurred in the past. In fact, in certain cases, the federal founding act might result from an act of political hetero-determination, that is, it stems from the intervention of a third party unconnected to the real contracting parties (the future member states). In this particular case the so-called compact or constitution should, in our view, be described as a federal treaty, ie an international treaty under which

dominant "we," an admission of more members to "we"-ship and its privileges. The people of India have now for their masters the people of the United Kingdom only. They would then have for their masters the people of the United Kingdom and those of the British colonies also. Such an outcome might be highly imperial, but it would not be at all federal, at least not federal for the vast majority of the inhabitants of the Federal Empire.'

[30] Carl Friedrich defines the Empire as 'a coercive world order' and the Federation as a 'consensual world order' (Carl J Friedrich, *Man and His Government: An Empirical Theory of Politics* (New York, MacGraw Hill, 1963) 569ff), telling us that federalism 'holds out the prospect of organising the world at large as the alternative to imperial domination' (60).

[31] For a first account of the distinction between federal constitution and federative compact, see Olivier Beaud, 'La notion de pacte fédératif. Contribution à une théorie constitutionnelle de la Fédération' in Heinz Mohnhaupt and Jean-François Kervégan (eds), *Liberté sociale et contrat dans l'histoire du droit et de la philosophie* (Frankfurt, Vittorio Klostermann, 1997) 197–270. I rely on the notion of a *Bundesvertrag* as elaborated by Carl Schmitt, *Constitutional Theory* (Durham, Duke University Press, 2008) § 7–II, pp 112–66.

a dominant power agrees with the monadic states that federate, to 'contractually' arrogate to itself a right of oversight in respect of the Federation born from the said federal treaty. To illustrate this idea, a single example will suffice, namely the 'grant' of federalism to the Helvetic Republic by the French Republic, under Napoleon Bonaparte.[32] This federal treaty has a name that is well known in Swiss history: the Act of Mediation of February 19, 1803.

It should be recalled here that the first Article of the Constitution of the Helvetic Republic dated 12 April 1798, largely based on the Constitution of the Directory, at a period when 'Swiss dependency on France was (...) extraordinarily great'[33] is of great symbolic and political significance. Its first paragraph provides that 'the Helvetic Republic is one and indivisible'—a true unitary manifesto—and the second which abolishes the frontiers between the cantons is even more anti-federalist in spirit. Thus the political area is unified, homogenised, despite the fact that any self-respecting federal constitution maintains and guarantees the territorial integrity of the federated entities.[34] This constitution, Jacobin in many respects, was so contrary to Swiss history and traditions that it was found unsatisfactory, even though certain progressive social measures were greeted with enthusiasm by many. However, when the French army withdrew in summer 1802, domestic uprisings broke out because the counter-revolutionary forces, favourable to the old federalism and hostile to the recent Jacobinism, tried to force a highly 'federalist' constitution onto the other cantons (favourable to canton autonomy). When the counter-revolutionaries were on the point of winning, with the support of England, Napoleon responded to the appeal from the Helvetic executive by his offer of mediation.[35]

On 30 September 1802, he drew up a proclamation in which he proposed himself as mediator, threatening military intervention if the offer was not accepted. Thus began a negotiation process between France and the Swiss authorities. The Senate, a body set up by the Helvetic Constitution, promised to send Swiss representatives to Paris where the discussions between the group, composed of some 60 delegates (named the *Consulta*), and Napoleon and his advisers took place.[36] The Swiss

[32] The other example is the Rhine Confederation (Compact of 12 July 1806).

[33] Alfred Kölz, *Neuere Schweizerische Verfassungsgeschichte: Ihre Grundlinien in Bund und Kantonen* (Bern, Stämpfli Verlag, 1992) vol I, 104.

[34] *Helvetic Constitution*, art 1, al 2: 'Il n'y a plus de frontières entre les cantons et les pays sujets, ni de canton à canton. L'unité de patrie et d'intérêt succède au faible lien qui rassemblait et guidait au hasard des parties hétérogènes, inégales, disproportionnées et asservies à de petites localités et des préjugés domestiques. On était faible de toute sa faiblesse individuelle, on sera fort de la force de tous.' (Alfred Kölz, *Quellenbuch zur neuren schweizerischen Verfassungsgeschichte* (Bern, Stämpfli Verlag, 1992) vol I, 126).

[35] Alfred Dufour, 'D'une Médiation à l'autre' in Alfred Dufour, Till Hanisch and Victor Monnier (eds) *Bonaparte, la Suisse et l'Europe: Actes du colloque européen d'histoire constitutionnelle pour le bicentenaire de l'Acte de Médiation (1803–2003)* (Zürich/Bâle/Genève, Schulthess, 2003) 33–35. Victor Monnier underlines that it is at the request of the Swiss that Bonaparte intervenes as a Mediator (see Victor Monnier, 'L'acte de Médiation de 1803 et sa dimension contractuelle' in *L'idée contractuelle dans l'histoire de la pensée politique* (Presses Universitaires d'Aix-Marseille, 2008) 396).

[36] For a detailed analysis, see Victor Monnier, 'Les travaux préparatoires de la *Consulta* et l'Acte fédéral de 1803' in Dufour, Hanisch and Monnier (eds), *Bonaparte, la Suisse et l'Europe* 63–72.

representatives did not discuss the federal constitution, only the canton constitutions. The document drawn up after these negotiations, the Act of Mediation, was signed on 19 February 1803 by Napoleon and the Swiss representatives. On 5 March 1803, it was then adopted by the Senate of the Helvetic Republic, which thanked Napoleon for restoring law and order in Switzerland, and it entered into force on 10 March.[37] The circumstances of how the Act of Mediation came about show that, in formal terms, it was granted by France,[38] thus in violation of the principle of federative freedom. What interests us here is this contradiction between the manner of its inception, reflective of a situation of hetero-determination, and its federal content.

All observers agree as to Napoleon Bonaparte's great political wisdom in giving the Swiss a constitution that was far better suited to their history and political mores. The expression 'political masterpiece' is often used to qualify this Act of Mediation which he imposed on the Swiss. In a letter addressed to the deputies of the 18 cantons dated 10 December 1802, he underlined the federative nature of Switzerland which needed to be upheld,[39] and thus contradicted the clumsy Jacobin policy of the Directory. In a way, he returned to the diplomatic tradition of the Ancien Régime in its relations with Switzerland.[40] He modernised the old Confederation by bolstering the role of the federal Diet and adding a new executive body, the *Landamann*, which for the first time gave a role to the executive power, and he exported to Switzerland a few revolutionary seeds (equality for all citizens and abolition of privilege) that took root and flourished.

The Act of Mediation was ultimately beneficial to the Swiss people.[41] It was, however, adopted at a time when Switzerland was under French occupation. As such, it was more the fruit of imperial intervention than of a process of self-determination. The document is, indeed, oddly constructed for a supposedly federal act as it includes all the constitutions—that is, the 19 canton constitutions—in alphabetical order as well as the federal constitution. It is as if Bonaparte had wanted to exert control over the canton constitutions as well. The Act also contains transitional provisions giving Bonaparte the right to appoint the Swiss *Landamann*. The meaning of all this becomes clearer when we realise that Napoleon's political aim was not so much to emancipate Switzerland as to use it for the purposes of French foreign policy.[42]

[37] I am following the account given by Kölz, *Neuere Schweizerische Verfassungsgeschichte* vol I, pp 143–44.

[38] ibid vol I, 144.

[39] Napoleon Bonaparte, letter of 19 frimaire An XI (10 December 1802): 'La Suisse ne ressemble à aucun autre état, soit par les événements qui s'y sont succédé depuis plusieurs siècles, soit par sa situation géographique et topographique, soit par les différentes langues, les différentes religions et cette extrême différence de mœurs qui existe entre ses diverses parties. La nature a fait votre état fédératif; vouloir la vaincre ne peut pas être d'un homme sage.' (*Correspondance de Napoléon Ier* (Paris, 1861) 158–61; quoted by Jean Tulard, 'Le Premier Consul et l'Acte de Médiation' in Dufour, Hanisch and Monnier (eds), *Bonaparte, la Suisse et l'Europe* 4.

[40] Alfred Dufour points to the parallel between this Mediation and the one carried out in 1737–38 (see Dufour, 'D'une Médiation à l'autre' 11ff).

[41] *cf* the assessment in Pellegrino Rossi, *Cours d'histoire suisse* (Bâle, Schulthess, 2000) 332.

[42] Napoleon Bonaparte, letter of 19 frimaire An XI (10 December 1802): 'La politique de la Suisse a toujours été considérée, en Europe, comme faisant partie de la politique de la France, de la Savoie, et du Milanais, parce que la manière d'exister de la Suisse est entièrement liée à la sûreté de ces états. Le premier

In other words, anxious to ensure that France was surrounded by peaceful neighbours, Bonaparte showed great interest in Switzerland because of its geographical location. His political goal was the security of France. This did not pass unnoticed. One of the Swiss representatives at the negotiations of the Act thus noted with great lucidity: 'The purpose of the First Consul is undoubtedly to annihilate Switzerland politically, while procuring the greatest happiness possible for the Swiss.'[43]

The status of Switzerland as a vassal can clearly be seen in the Act of Mediation. In fact, it was 'laid down by the First Consul of the French Republic between the parties that divide Switzerland'. Far from freely uniting, the cantons were 'declared confederated' by Napoleon.[44] Thus they played the passive role of subjects to which the 'protecting' power granted not only the various canton constitutions but also 'their' federal constitution (Federal Act, ch XX) which it guaranteed.[45] The closing provisions of the Act perfectly highlight the meaning of a text drafted by a Protector intending to grant and guarantee to its protectorate a peace they would be incapable of establishing alone.

> This Act, the result of patient conferring between wise minds and friends of good, in our view appears to contain the provisions the most propitious to the pacification and happiness of Switzerland. Once they are executed, the French troops shall be withdrawn.
>
> We hereby *acknowledge* Helvetia, constituted in conformity herewith, as an independent power.
>
> We hereby *guarantee* the federal constitution [*constitution fédérale*] and that of each canton against the enemies of Helvetian peace, whoever they might be, and undertake to continue the peaceable relationships that have united our two nations for several centuries.

This text enables us better to understand the distinction between a federative compact, which entails constitutional self-determination, and the federal treaty, a pseudo-pact that results from an act of hetero-determination. The Act of Mediation politically restructured Switzerland as a federation, but in doing so, it made Switzerland a subject of France that set itself up as its sovereign protector. The ultimate proof of this protectorate can be found in history: once freed from French

devoir, le devoir le plus essentiel du Gouvernement français, sera toujours de veiller à ce qu'un système hostile ne prévale point parmi vous, et que des hommes dévoués à ses ennemis ne parviennent pas à se mettre à la tête de vos affaires. Il convient non seulement qu'il n'existe aucun motif d'inquiétude pour la portion de notre frontière qui est ouverte et que vous couvrez, mais que tout nous assure encore que si votre neutralité était forcée, le bon esprit de notre gouvernement ainsi que l'intérêt de votre nation vous rangeraient plutôt du côté des intérêts de la France que contre eux.' (quoted in Jean Tulard, 'Le Premier Consul et l'Acte de Médiation' 4).

[43] Letter of the Minister Stapfer to the Secretary of State Mohr (18 January 1803), quoted in William E Rappard, *La constitution fédérale de la Suisse* (Neuchatel, La Baconnière, 1948) 21.

[44] Acte féderal, ch XX, art 1: 'Les dix neuf cantons de la Suisse, savoir (…) sont confédérés entre eux conformément aux principes établis dans leurs constitutions respectives' (in Kölz, *Quellenbuch* vol I, 175).

[45] The last article of the Acte de Médiation reads as follows: 'Nous *garantissons* la constitution fédérale, et celle de chaque canton, contre les ennemis de la tranquillité de l'Helvétie, quels qu'ils puissent être, et nous promettons de continuer les relations de bienveillance qui, depuis plusieurs siècles, ont uni les deux nations' (in Kölz, *Quellenbuch* vol I, 188).

control, some cantons did not hesitate to say that this Act of Mediation had been 'imposed by a foreign power and (...) repealed by the resolute determination of the High Allied Powers.'[46] It is therefore difficult to qualify this Act as a federal constitutional compact because it is not an act of political self-determination but an unequal treaty imposed by the protecting power upon its protected power. In spite of its intrinsic qualities, the Act did not outlast Napoleon's reign.[47] Even if the political artist's performance merits applause, it is nevertheless the case that Bonaparte wanted to control Switzerland by granting this Act of Mediation, and deliberately transgressed the principle of self-determination of peoples of which the French Revolution had been the carrier.[48] It is easier to understand why the most recent historical research suggests that we consider this Act of Mediation as a 'unilateral act for which Bonaparte alone was responsible.'[49]

Without exaggerating the freedom to re-found their Confederation enjoyed by the Swiss cantons in 1813–1815, it must be said that the federative compact of 1815 is of a different nature. As was the case for the German Confederation, this new Federation would not have come into being but for the assistance of foreign tutelary powers,[50] but this time, the midwife did not reserve the possibility of intervening once the new political body had grown to maturity. A closer reading of the text confirms the idea that the genesis of this new political entity did in fact spring from the free federative wish of the member states of the Swiss Confederation. The title indicates the difference with the unilateral Act of 1803, since this founding text is called 'Federal Compact (*Bundesvertrag*) between the twenty-two cantons of Switzerland.'[51] Already in the Preamble, it is clearly indicated that this compact was formed by the wish of the signatories to 'unite' to form a confederation.[52] The provision that best expresses the idea of the act of federal self-foundation, that is, the idea according to which the creation of a Helvetic federation is the business of the Swiss cantons, and theirs alone, is the final provision of Article 12. A criticism of the previous system of 1803, based on constraint, comes through in the text:

> The XXII Cantons shall constitute the Swiss Confederation; they hereby declare that they have freely and in of their own wish entered into this federal union (*Bund*), that they shall

[46] Letter of the government of Bern sent on 30 December 1813, to the canton of de Zürich (quoted in Rappard, *La constitution fédérale de la Suisse* 32).

[47] *cf* the assessment of William E Rappard: 'On le sait, ce ne furent nullement des défauts inhérents à l'Acte de Médiation qui firent abroger. Ce fut bien plutôt, la chute de son auteur qui entraîna celle d'une œuvre dont le seul vice grave résidait dans sa paternité' (ibid 27).

[48] *cf* Kölz, *Neuere Schweizerische Verfassungsgeschichte* vol I, 144.

[49] Monnier, 'L'acte de Médiation de 1803 et sa dimension contractuelle' 416–17. Monnier discusses the formula of Charles Borgeaud who described the Acte de Médiation as 'treaty and a constitution.'

[50] Rappard goes even further, arguing that the compact of 1815 'n'en était guère moins imposé par l'étranger pour avoir été négocié en Suisse' (Rappard, *La constitution fédérale de la Suisse* 34).

[51] *Bundesvertrag zwischen den XXII Kantonen der Schweiz* (17 August 1815); quoted in Kölz, *Quellenbuch* vol I, 193.

[52] *Bundesvertrag zwischen den XXII Kantonen der Schweiz* (17 August 1815): 'Les XXII cantons souverains de la Suisse, savoir: Zurich, Berne, Lucerne, Uri, Schwyz, Unterwalden, Glaris, Zug, Fribourg, Soleure, Bâle, Schaffhouse, Appenzell des deux Rhodes; St.-Gall, Grisons, Argovie, Thurgovie, Tessin, Vaud, Valais, Neuchâtel et Genève, se réunissent (*vereinigen sich*), par le présent Pacte fédéral, pour le maintien de leur liberté et de leur indépendance contre toute attaque de la part de l'étranger, ainsi que pour la conservation de l'ordre et de la tranquillité dans l'intérieur'.

> abide by it as brothers and confederates in all circumstances, and in particular, that they shall fulfill mutually, and as of this day, all the duties and obligations that shall arise therefrom; and so that an act of such importance for the security of the common fatherland receives, following the tradition of our fathers, a religious sanction, this Federal compact shall be not only signed by the deputies of each State authorised therefore, and sealed with the new seal of the Confederation, but it shall also be confirmed and corroborated by a solemn oath to God Almighty (§12, Compact of 1815).

Leaving to one side the pathos of this text and the reservations which certain cantons had about a text mainly imposed by the Diet, one would have to say that a clearer expression of the principle of self-determination could not be found. Undoubtedly, this transactional document was a work of 'untimely and brutal reaction' whereas the Act of Mediation was a 'work of intelligent and moderate reaction.'[53] In analysing the federative compact, what matters is that there is no longer an external guarantor of the federal constitution. On the contrary, the 1815 pact consecrates the identification between the authors and recipients of the federative compact.

To sum up, the example of the Act of Mediation reveals that it is possible in legal terms to distinguish between the federal treaty and the federative compact. In the case of the federal treaty, an alliance is made between, on the one hand, a protector of the Federation and, on the other hand, the monadic states by which only the latter became member states of the Federation that has been created. The outside protector or guarantor denies the principle of political self-determination by obliging the states to unite and form a confederation. This is a pseudo-federative compact but not a genuine federal treaty.

The Act of Mediation teaches jurists that the absence of identification between the contracting parties and the future members of the Federation should call into question the sincerity of the federal compact. In other words, one of the contracting parties—the French State, also the *protector*—did not intend to become a member of the Federation but to remain the guarantor of the treaty. Under the treaty, the dominant state positioned itself outside the Federation as a third party. It contracted a federative treaty without wishing to become a member state of the future Federation. It was, thus, an interloper in this Federation. This particular case highlights an essential point, which is a condition *sine qua non* of any true federative compact: the monadic states and the member states must be one and the same in a Federation. In other words, those uniting in a Federation must be the same as those who will become the parties thereto, its member states. This argument confirms the importance of the parties to the contract in a federative compact, since we are in presence of a statutory compact (*Statusvertrag*).[54]

The advantage of this opposition between two legal concepts (federative compact and federal treaty) is that it better describes the domination exercised by a State or imperial power over countries forced to confederate. The analogy with the contractual concept leads us to another analogy with private law, the idea of vitiated consent, one cause of which is duress. It is this, indeed, that the German jurists objected

[53] Rappard, *La Constitution fédérale de la Suisse* 28.

[54] *cf* the important book by Anton Greber, *Die vorpositiven Grundlagen des Bundesstaates* (Bâle, Helbing & Lichtenhahn, 2000) ch 6, especially 175–84.

to the Confederation of the Rhine: it was 'not created by a compact (*Vertrag*), but by duress,' and the goals and objectives of this Confederation were not those of its German members. It was intended to further Napoleon's project, the aim of which was to stabilise his dominion across Europe.[55] Of course, there can be no real federative compact in the absence of a free exchange of consents, what we call federative freedom.

IV. SOME REMARKS ON UNITY AND DIVERSITY

Having set out these differences between Federation and empire, we are naturally led to ask what it is that decides between the two. Recently, we have had the opportunity of exploring this question in the context of an analysis of a special episode in French history: the civil war during the Second World War between the Vichy regime of Petain against '*France Libre*' of General de Gaulle. The battle extended to the colonial dominions and it was in the overseas territories of French African colonies that the fate of de Gaulle was decided. After their initial defeat in Dakar, the Free French Forces achieved success in Chad and Cameroon, which began the conquest of the territories of the colonies.

In this situation, France was a divided country. On the one hand, the metropolis was controlled by the Vichy regime (the other half was occupied by the Germans) and on the other hand, the colonial territory was also divided with one part still under the control of the Vichy regime and another, growing in size, under the control of forces loyal to de Gaulle. This situation of extreme tension opens up a context within which we can ask whether it still makes sense to refer to an empire where the centre has been cut off from the periphery. Or, in other words, should we accept the claim that *France Libre* became the official representative of the French Empire by virtue of controlling the majority of the colonies, although it was not in control of the metropolis? The fact is that the claim of *France Libre* to represent the rightful government of France remained conditional until the liberation of the metropolitan territory from June and especially August 1944. Only with the conquest of the 'continental' territory could *France Libre* pass the new republican statute laws.[56]

The defining characteristic of the empire is thus the hierarchised duality between, on the one hand, the centre (metropolis or motherland for colonial empire) and, on the other hand, its peripheral dominions. This hierarchy always favours the centre, that is, the metropolis. Liberating France meant first liberating its metropolitan territory. This crucial episode from French history confirms the domination of the centre over the periphery in an empire, not from the point of view of norms but of territories.

At this point, we might take stock of the similarities between empire and Federation, some of which have already been listed above: empire and Federation are both unions of states, they both have a ternary structure (as reflected in their laws on citizenship),

[55] Bodo Dennewitz, *Der Föderalismus* (Hamburg, Drei Türme Verlag, 1947) 52.

[56] See Olivier Beaud, 'La France libre, Vichy, l'Empire colonial' (2015) 14 *Jus Politicum* 11–12, 18–21 (subsequently in *Penser juridiquement l'Empire?* (Paris, Dalloz, 2017)).

and, as political forms, they both include different forms of government. In principle, there is such a thing as a liberal empire. To these similarities we should add another one which concerns the question of *diversity* or *plurality*. As political forms, Federation and empire are defined by their high tolerance of diversity.

This is a striking feature of the empire. One of the great lessons of the Roman Empire is its undeniable capacity to control a huge range of heterogeneous populations. As the historian Clifford Ando writes, 'the great challenge for the Roman government was to maintain the order within the groups of populations which were always and everywhere, legally, ethnically and linguistically, heterogeneous.'[57] Denis Baranger echoes this intuition as he analyses the history of the British Empire. Even if the empire, like the state, is always struggling to keep the peace in its dominions, it does not want uniformity between them. In the words of Baranger:

> [A]s it is not destined to become another self (to become standardised or homogeneous), a subject that is integrated in the empire can remain hostile, so long as it stays obedient. For England, Ireland remained the model of this inside enemy that would not let itself be incorporated and which never ceased to assert its own peculiarity.[58]

Arguably, the empire, unlike the state, is desirous of and even fosters diversity and pluralism. It is a fact of history that empires which have tried to impose uniformity, like the French colonial empire, failed miserably. The importance of diversity also makes sense of why some scholars try to apply the concept of empire to the European Union. However, federalism is also linked with diversity and pluralism. Everybody knows the famous motto of the American Republic '*E pluribus unum*'. It is probably less known that Albert Dicey wrote about federalism in his pioneering handbook of constitutional law, noting that there were two preconditions for building a Federation: one, objective, and the other, subjective. Taking the subjective condition first, it relates to the feelings of the peoples of each state: 'The existence of a very peculiar state of sentiment among the inhabitants of the countries which it is proposed to unite. *They must desire union, and must not desire unity*. If there be no desire to unite, there is clearly no basis for federalism.'[59] And Dicey concludes: 'The aim of federalism is to give effect as far as possible to both of these sentiments.'[60]

But the existence of this ideal of combining unity and diversity which Federation and empire share should not lead us into error. Also there is here an essential difference between these two political forms that can be brought out on the basis of Dicey's first, objective precondition of federalism that relates to the common features of the nations that have decided to share the same political future:

> There must exist, in the first place, a body of countries such as the Cantons of Switzerland, the Colonies of America, or the Provinces of Canada, so closely connected by locality,

[57] Clifford Ando, *L'Empire et le Droit. Invention juridique et réalités historiques à Rome* (Paris, Odile Jacob, 2013) 26–27.

[58] Denis Baranger, *Ecrire la constitution non-écrite. Une introduction au droit politique britannique* (Paris, Presses Universitaires de France, 2008) 271.

[59] Albert V Dicey, *Introduction to the study of the Law of the Constitution* (Indianapolis, Liberty Fund, 1982) 75.

[60] ibid 76.

> history, by race, or the like, as to be capable of bearing, in the eyes of their inhabitants, an impress of common nationality.[61]

As Dicey tells us, federalism requires that we strike a very precarious balance. On the one hand, too strong an impress, to borrow another phrase of his, inclines the Federation in the direction of a nation-state which one might define as 'the identification between nation and polity.'[62] On the other hand, a lack of homogeneity between the parts of a Federation would spell the end of this kind of federalism. In this respect, it appears that there is an essential difference between a Federation and an empire, the latter allowing for a much greater degree of differentiation in how states are brought together in union.

These observations lead us to raise two questions that are of pivotal importance for an understanding of federalism: what kind of homogeneity is required to build a Federation? And to which extent must the part of a Federation be homogenous? There are, in fact, different elements to this homogeneity. The primary requirement is *political homogeneity*. A Federation has better chances of surviving when the member states have the same political form of government. Montesquieu already noted that for a federation of republics, a 'république fédérative,' to survive, all its members would have to be a republic.[63] It therefore poses a great danger to the survival of the entire federation, should the government of one of its members become autocratic. This threat to the political unity of the Federation explains why most federations acknowledge a right of a federal intervention in case of regime change within a member state.

But political homogeneity also means economical homogeneity. Since the collapse of the communist system, the obstacles that stood in the way of uniting all of Europe have disappeared. It is well known, for instance, that the difference of the economy policies in USA in the nineteenth century between the North and the South were major sources of tension. Nowadays, the main threat to European Union would seem to be the pursuit of economic homogeneity through liberalisation which risks producing 'some kind of ethnic or nationalist backlash.'[64] Seen from this perspective, the greatest heterogeneity may spring from the enlargement and the discrepancy between the countries of Western and Eastern Europe.

Homogeneity might also have a *cultural* component, although this is controversial. This idea is perhaps most prominently associated with Alexis de Tocqueville. In one of his fascinating paragraphs on federalism, where he tries to answer the question of why the federal system is not a possibility in all nations, he compares the success of the American federal experience with the failure of the Mexican one, stressing

[61] ibid 75.

[62] Jean Baechler, 'Europe et Fédération' in Jean Baechler, *Contrepoints et commentaires* (Paris, Calmann-Lévy, 1996) 249.

[63] Charles-Louis de Secondat Montesquieu, *The Spirit of the Laws* (Cambridge, Cambridge University Press, 1989) 9, 2, 131–32.

[64] Murray Forsyth, 'The Political Theory of Federalism. The Relevance of Classical Approaches' in Joachim Jens Hesse and Vincent Wright (eds), *Federalizing Europe?: The costs, benefits and preconditions of federal political systems* (Oxford, Oxford University Press, 1996) 43.

that constitutional engineering cannot in and of itself explain the success or failure of a particular Federation:

> Thus, to succeed, the federal system not only needs good laws but circumstances must also favor it. All peoples who have been seen to confederate had a certain number of common interests that formed the intellectual bonds of the association. But beyond material interests man also has ideas and sentiments. In order that a confederation subsist for a long time, it is no less necessary that there be homogeneity in the civilization than in the needs of the various people that compose it.[65]

The requirement of cultural homogeneity (*homogénéité dans la civilisation*) leads Tocqueville to deny that the government of Switzerland is truly federal because of the difference between the Canton of Vaud and the Canton of Uri, an argument which he peculiarly supports by reference to the supposed impossibility of applying the same laws throughout the territory. According to Tocqueville, the citizens of the United States of America are a true people because they share not only the same religious and political ideas but also the same philosophical and moral conception. Famously, John Jay made the same point in the *Federalist Papers*:

> Providence has been pleased to give this one connected country to one united people—a people descending from the same ancestors, speaking the same language, professing the same religion, attached to the same principles of government, very similar in their manners and their customs.[66]

The requirement of strong sociological homogeneity is typical of the early federal union in Europe and America. But in the nineteenth century federal systems began to emerge in which the constituent members were ethnically and linguistically diverse, for example the reconstituted Swiss Confederation and the Canadian or British North American Confederation.[67] Comparing the American federal experience with the Canadian just after the Dartmouth Report, Tocqueville saw no future for such a non-homogeneous federal union. Canada was divided between two different peoples, each with a different language. He saw the difference in language as being reflective of more fundamental differences between two societies that had different laws, different mores, different religions etc. To Tocqueville, two 'enemy nations' were facing each other. The end would not be a federal solution but the assimilation from one people by another people—the French minority by the English majority. History has shown his diagnosis to be false. On the contrary, the Canadian Federation is an example of a (difficult) bi-national Federation with two ethnic groups who have learned to live together, even if it is difficult. As Charles Taylor aptly noted in the title of a book that deals with this particular topic, the Canadian experience has been about 'reconciling the solitudes.'

Tocqueville did not see that another kind of federation could exist, a heterogeneous Federation in which the power of the centre is constrained by this ethnical facto.[68]

[65] Alexis de Tocqueville, *Democracy in America* (Chicago, University of Chicago Press, 2000) 158.
[66] John Jay, *The Federalist Papers* (London, Penguin Books, 1989) No 3, p 91.
[67] Forsyth, 'The Political Theory of Federalism. The Relevance of Classical Approaches' 33.
[68] ibid.

As Murray Forsyth notes, modern federal systems are 'organized to accommodate ethnic groups by giving them political status within the system.'[69] The example of Canada illustrates this protection of ethnic groups through the protection of their language, extending to the right to use their native language, different prohibitions of using the majority language (even if we must also acknowledge the dangers that inhere in this policy).[70]

In conclusion, Federations are arguably more demanding than empires when it comes to the requirement of homogeneity. Also here, Federations stand between the empire, which tolerates and accepts the diversity of peoples that it unifies by force, and the state, which, in its national incarnation, has considerable difficulties in dealing with diversity.

***

I will conclude with three remarks on the differences between these two ideal types of Federation and empire:

(1) In legal terms, the difference between a Federation and an empire can be demonstrated by their different genesis. It is not merely the opposition between force and free will nor indeed the opposition between a federal treaty (or unilateral act) and a federative compact that are relevant. The institutional repercussions of these founding acts must also be taken into account. In a Federation, the federative compact maintains the political existence of the member bodies, that is to say, their identity, whereas in an empire, they no longer have an existence as political bodies. The founders of modern international law were well aware of this. Thus, Pufendorf noted two hypotheses: the creation of a new state by aggregation (federation) or by fusion (empire).[71]

He criticised Thomas Hobbes for having put in his category of composite states 'those which merely contain several subordinated bodies: (and) those which enlarged by swallowing up other states, that they incorporated into their former dominion.'[72] Now, what we have suggested here is that the method of forming each political entity is not without relevance to its nature. If the Federation can remain a union of states, it is because this union is deliberately decided, whereas in the case of the empire, union or unification results from a unilateral decision from the central power that decides to extend its domination over 'dependencies' or 'peripheries' that are merged into a new body against their will.

[69] Murray Forsyth, 'Introduction' in Murray Forsyth (ed), *Federalism and Nationalism* (Leicester, Leicester University Press, 1989) 1.

[70] See Colin H Williams, 'A Requiem for Canada' in Graham Smith (ed), *Federalism: the Multiethnic Challenge* (Abingdon, Routledge, 1995) 29.

[71] Samuel Pufendorf, *Droit naturel et des Gens* (Caen, Presses Universitaires de Caen, 1987) 504.

[72] ibid 282–83.

(2) This ideal-typical opposition between the Federation and the empire may also be formulated by describing their institutional structure, that is, the relationships between the parts and the whole, or the members of the empire with the empire and the members of the Federation with the federation. Hence, the empire results from the action of a political centre imposing its wishes on the other states or polities, consigning them to a peripheral position, as its periphery. On the contrary, the Federation does not stem from the action of a centre, but from decentred decisions taken by a plurality of states deciding to unite. The consequence is that the empire is a political entity dominated by a centre, a motherland or metropolis that constitutes the 'hard core which is irradiated by what was first characterised as an excess of State; and this polarising centre is constantly necessary to the operation and growth of empires.'[73] This difference is reflected, among other things, in their respective methods of enlargement (admission for a Federation, conquest for an empire).

(3) Finally, the third difference relates to citizenship. The characteristic of the imperial form is to treat people subject to imperial power unequally. There are the real citizens, those who dwell in the metropolis itself and those citizens of the metropolis that set out to found colonies), and then there are the others, the natives of the colonies who are first and foremost *subjects*, even if they may become members of the empire.

In conclusion, from the institutional viewpoint, an empire can only be conceived as a hierarchised duality between the centre (metropolis/motherland) and its peripheries, whereas the Federation must be conceived of as a *duality of equals* between the Federation and the member states.[74]

[73] Gérard Bergeron, *Petit traité sur l'Etat* (Paris, Presses Universitaires de France, 1990) 41. See also the profound remark of Denis Baranger: 'L'empire est défini par son centre, non (comme l'État) par ses limites. Dans l'empire, tout espace extérieur—terre dominée pour le moment par un Prince, mer environnante et bientôt l'ensemble des océans—est un intérieur potentiel mais le sort réservé à cet intérieur est d'une autre nature que ce qui arrive dans les limites de l'État' (Baranger, *Ecrire la constitution non écrite* 271).

[74] I would like to thank Mrs Andrea Hamann and Gabrielle Smart sincerely for having translated the French manuscript into English and Amnon Lev for supervising the work.

3

Towards a Deontic-Axiomatic Theory of Federal Adjudication

JEAN-FRANÇOIS GAUDREAULT-DESBIENS*

THIS PAPER ARGUES in favour of a principle-based, deontic approach to federalism. It emphasises the need to integrate such an approach both in the legal theoretical reflection on this particular type of political regime, and, most importantly, in the concrete adjudication of federal disputes.

It further challenges the dominant legal scholarship on this question, which unduly reduces federalism either to a set of institutional features or to a merely instrumental role, thereby tending to obscure the aspirations and values underlying federalism, as well as the need for a legally-sensitive normative theory of federalism. Indeed, in many federations, especially those belonging partly or entirely to the common law tradition, legal scholarship on federalism has generally overlooked the importance of anchoring this particular type of political regime within what could be called an 'interval of principles.' More often than not, federalism has been equated with, and reduced to, the formal constitutional division of powers applicable in a given federation, as understood and construed from a technical angle. The sole focus of such an approach was, and still is, the institutional design of the federation under study and the explicit norms that establish its federal structure; perspectives informed by this approach will hereafter be characterised as institutionalist. Such an institutional focus has predictably come at a price, as very little energy has been devoted to figuring out what the commonly-invoked 'federal principle' may entail, beyond ritual references to foundational interpretive doctrines, which can easily be instrumentalised with a view to promoting particular viewpoints on federalism, its nature, and the outcomes it should lead to. As far as legal scholarship is concerned, it is as if a principle-based reflection on federalism could be the domain of philosophers,[1] but not of

* Being part of a longstanding work-in-progress, this chapter summarises, expands on, and supplements a set of arguments, several of which were first made, in whole or in part, in the articles listed at nn 40 and 75. Readers who have consulted these previous contributions should thus not be surprised by some potential overlaps.

[1] See, among others, Daniel Weinstock, 'Towards a Normative Theory of Federalism' (2001) 53 *International Social Science Journal* 75; Wayne J. Norman, 'Towards a Philosophy of Federalism' in Judith Baker (ed), *Group Rights* (Toronto, University of Toronto Press, 1994) 79; William Ossipow, 'Architecture fédéraliste et exigence de justice' (1998) 9 *Philosophie politique* 113.

jurists, who, paradoxically, are often called upon to concretely resolve complex normative dilemmas without always having access to all the normative resources they might need in view of selecting the strongest interpretation possible amongst competing ones. In other words, little time has been spent in the legal field reflecting on a potential system of reasons underlying the federal idea.[2]

Regrettably, another intellectual hurdle has further slowed down the reflexive process. With the rise of functionalism in social sciences after World War II, many scholars, some of whom were already adhering to institutionalist paradigms, have adopted what could be characterised as a 'toolbox approach' to federalism, which envisages this constitutional regime as a mere tool that can be used to solve particular problems in certain institutional contexts. On that view, federalism is subservient to other political, social or, most often, economic values, turning it into a means by which these values can be fostered. This approach is captured in one of the influential books on federal government, where it is claimed that federalism 'is only at the most a means to good government, not a good in itself.'[3] One finds an interesting illustration of this conception in Barry Weingast's work. Weingast ascribes federalism the function of preserving markets, and identifies ideal institutional conditions in which this particular type of federalism may blossom.[4] Such an approach is forthright: it supports federalism to the extent that it can help promote other values, arguably external to it. By so doing, it somehow takes stock of federalism's relative indeterminacy as regards the fostering of external values. Indeed, as Davis pointed out more than 30 years ago, the 'federalness' of a system cannot *systematically* explain particular positive or negative socioeconomic outcomes, as these outcomes are inevitably influenced by other variables.[5] Yet, even though approaches such as that advocated by Weingast tend to instrumentalise federalism for purposes that are external to it, they still attribute some positive role to the specific type of federalism that they promote.[6]

This is not always the case, however. Indeed, other scholars, somehow deploring the salience of issues pertaining to political identity in discussions about federalism,[7] go as far as seeing in this regime a 'grim expedient that is adopted in grim circumstances, an acknowledgment that choices must be made among undesirable

[2] For an exception, see Kalypso Nicolaidis and Robert Howse (eds), *The Federal Vision: Legitimacy and Levels of Governance in the United States and the European Union* (Oxford, Oxford University Press, 2001).

[3] Kenneth C Wheare, *Federal Government* (Oxford, Oxford University Press, 1963) 34. See also Richard E Simeon, 'Criteria for Choice in Federal Systems' (1981–82) *Queen's Law Journal* 131.

[4] See, for example, Barry Weingast, 'The Economic Role of Political Institutions: Market-Preserving Federalism and Economic Development' (1995) 20 *Journal of Law, Economics, and Organization* 1.

[5] Solomon Rufus Davis, *The Federal Principle: A Journey Through Time in Quest of Meaning* (Berkeley, University of California Press, 1978) 211–12.

[6] In the same vein, Roberta Romano lauds the efficiency of the federal division of powers in the United States, arguing that vesting the states with jurisdiction over the incorporation of business associations creates a competitive economic environment that is favourable to entrepreneurship and corporate innovation. See Roberta Romano, *The Genius of American Corporate Law* (Washington, The AEI Press, 1993).

[7] Malcom N Feely and Edward Rubin, *Federalism: Political Identity and Tragic Compromise* (Ann Arbor, University of Michigan Press, 2008) 39.

alternatives.'[8] In other words, federalism would be a last resort solution. This lukewarm endorsement, to put it mildly, highlights a concern about the hurdles that this regime erects in the quest for establishing institutional mechanisms that optimise the *efficiency* of governance tools.[9] The question is whether the resources that can be mobilised in a federal framework are susceptible of leading to optimal outcomes, as evaluated from the standpoint of goals external to federalism itself—this line of questioning bears the imprint of public goods theory, which became very influential in political economy as of the late 1950s.[10] Although efficiency is only one viewpoint among others from which to evaluate federalism,[11] it has exerted an overwhelming influence on federalism scholarship as a result of the adoption by several authors, particularly in the Anglo-American world[12] and irrespective of their disciplinary perspective,[13] of a functionalist (or realist) grid used to grasp both federalism and its various manifestations.[14] Legal scholars have followed suit, and increasingly resort to efficiency-related arguments to make sense of the normative puzzles raised by disputes over federal divisions of powers. However, even if valuing efficiency may in some cases lead to the legitimation of the federated entities' jurisdiction over certain topics, notably through an explicit or implicit reliance on the principle of subsidiarity, it most of the time benefits central governments, particularly in an era of globalisation where economic, environmental, political or social challenges ignore national borders, and where it is often highest level decision-makers who are objectively in a better position to meet such challenges, be it alone or through collaborative processes. It is thus easy to see how efficiency-based arguments may end up undermining one of federalism's central values, ie respect for cultural, social and legal diversity.[15]

That being said, what must be noted for this chapter's purpose—bearing in mind that labels are always reductive or misleading to some extent—is that to institutionalists and functionalists alike, federalism cannot be understood or represented

[8] ibid 40.

[9] ibid 39.

[10] Lawrence H White, *The Clash of Economic Ideas: The Great Policy Debates and Experiments of the Last Hundred Years* (Cambridge, Cambridge University Press, 2012) 332ff.

[11] In addition to efficiency, Simeon identifies viewpoints on federalism stemming from two other perspectives: community and democracy (see Simeon, 'Criteria for Choice in Federal Systems').

[12] It is worth noting that the anchoring of this functionalist model in Anglo-American federations de facto makes it the predominant conceptualisation of federalism given, on the one hand, the broad influence of English-speaking scholarly literature (which, like any other form of scientific literature, tends to promote certain values rather than others bearing in mind the recognition criteria that predominate in its realm at some points in time), and, on the other, the political and historical significance of many federations associated to the Anglo-American tradition. Think, for instance, of the United States, but also of Canada, Australia or India.

[13] On the impact of disciplinary perspectives on how federalism is grasped, see Barry Friedman, 'Valuing Federalism' (1997) 82 *Minnesota Law Review* 317, 385 (observing, somewhat unsurprisingly, that economists tend to value efficiency).

[14] In the field of political science, a recent exception lies in Jenna Bednar's work, which noticeably seeks to find a balance between the various values susceptible of being mobilised within federations. See Jenna Bednar, *The Robust Federation: Principles of Design* (New York, Cambridge University Press, 2009).

[15] Jean Leclair, 'The Supreme Court's Understanding of Federalism: Efficiency at the Expense of Diversity' in Jean-François Gaudreault-DesBiens and Fabien Gélinas (eds), *Le fédéralisme dans tous ses états. Gouvernance, identité et méthodologie/The States and Moods of Federalism: Governance, Identity and Methodology* (Brussels, Bruylant & Éditions Yvon Blais, 2005) 395.

as a regime that *intrinsically* entails aspirations or values which need to be fostered and cultivated in the daily life of federations by political and legal actors. Thus, against solely institutionalist and/or functionalist approaches, this chapter argues that federalism is both a means to achieve external objectives *and* an end in itself, at least for certain specific purposes. While there is no point denying that federalism does have a toolbox dimension, we might surmise that it also enshrines core aspirations, which may be formulated as principles *and* given tangible legal clout. However, because of their very nature, and taking into account the intrinsic generality of principles, they are adaptable to various federal contexts and models. Indeed, beyond these differences, the *foedus*, which encompasses the essential dimensions of the federal compact,[16] remains an element common to all federations.[17] These principles, which are core to the federal idea, are by design 'internal' to federalism, which excludes those that enshrine values that have a merely contingent relation to this political regime.[18] Think, for example, of economic efficiency or social justice, which may be promoted in any type of political regime, federal or not, and which cannot plausibly be characterised as intrinsically flowing from federalism or from the political-constitutional dynamic inherent to a federation; in other words, their relation to federalism is contingent rather than necessary. Last, the identification of these principles also takes stock of the overlapping, and sometimes conflicting, political identities that citizens have to wrestle with in a federation, and of the consequences of such overlaps. The principles mirror the intellectual space within which citizens structure their political allegiances, when, for example, they question themselves about their primary locus of identification in the federation, or when they are called upon to evaluate the legitimacy of a public policy promoted by one level of government or the other.

So this chapter's main thesis can be put as follows: not only can federalism be envisaged as a constitutional principle, it can also be represented as underlying a bundle of foundational sub-principles, which may provide, both in the daily life of a federation and in times of crisis, a *deontic* interval within which constitutional powers can, and should, be exercised. These principles can be derived or extrapolated from both the federal idea itself and the fundamental structural characteristics common to all federations. Moreover, their identification can be inspired by the political-constitutional dynamic that results from the presence of such structural characteristics.

These principles first bring us back to the initial goals or values of the political community constituted as a federation, ie its *telos*;[19] those responsible for individuating them in particular cases assume an obligation of means to act in a manner

[16] On federal compacts, see Olivier Beaud, 'La notion de pacte fédératif. Contribution à une théorie constitutionnelle de la fédération' in Jean-François Kervégan and Heinz Mohnhaupt (eds), *Liberté sociale et lien contractuel dans l'histoire du droit et la philosophie* (Frankfurt, Vittorio Klosstermann, 1999) 197.

[17] Davis, *The Federal Principle* 215.

[18] Especially since the links between federalism and extrinsic normative values are tenuous at best and hardly demonstrable. See Simeon, 'Criteria for Choice in Federal Systems' 134.

[19] On the federation's *telos*, see Olivier Beaud, *Théorie de la fédération* (Paris, Presses Universitaires de France, 2007) 273ff.

that can reasonably be characterised as fostering these goals, or, to put it negatively, as not unduly undermining the possibility that they be achieved. In this respect, implementing such principles responds not to a zero-sum logic, but to one revolving around the notion of the 'possible';[20] in such a context, they serve as 'optimisation precepts.'[21] These principles, which could be characterised as 'substantive,' must be distinguished from other types of principles whose function is procedural, such as conflict principles, or suppletive. Although this chapter's emphasis will be on substantive principles, the latter types, which are also extremely important, will also be briefly addressed.

This chapter's thesis should not be assimilated to an anti-institutionalist manifesto, far from it. Institutions do matter, but reducing the legal representation of federalism to them is in my view myopic, as it wilfully blinds the analysis to federalism's inherently relational dynamic, from which normative consequences can be drawn and that the law must take stock of. Nor should the thesis be understood as a mere anti-functionalist manifesto, since it in no way denies the importance of functional considerations for our understanding of federalism. These considerations undeniably have a role to play, particularly as they may serve to counterbalance other types of political dynamics undermining some federations, such as the narcissism of small differences which systematically exalts diversity at the expense of any idea of federal citizenship,[22] thereby transforming into an identity issue any dispute concerning the division of powers, as technical as it may be. My main target thus lies in approaches that systematically value the *hegemony* of institutionalism or functionalism in federalism scholarship, since federal legality is, in my view, irreducible to institutional or functional legality.

In other words, federal legality cannot, and should not, be captured by any particular value magically destined to predominate all others. Nor should it be reduced to its explicit and institutional normative dimensions. I will often emphasise in this chapter the importance of developing and maintaining a federal culture; the foundational principles that the theory will highlight, which represent normative parameters that should systematically be taken into consideration in the adjudication of federal disputes, seek to ensure that such culture is fostered. These principles obviously do not guarantee any particular and constant outcome since their application is inherently contextual, but, if implemented, they could serve as stern signposts that federalism, as a constitutionally-protected political regime, is to be taken seriously, and that it should not too easily be tampered with for the sake of promoting any value external to it, be it efficiency or the nationalist aspirations of a federated entity.

Affirming the existence of a consubstantial link between the law of federalism and the presence of a federal culture draws the attention to one of this chapter's central

[20] Gustavo Zagrebelsky, 'Ronald Dworkin's principle based constitutionalism: An Italian point of view' (2003) 1 *I-CON* 621, 633.

[21] See Robert Alexy, *A Theory of Constitutional Rights* (Oxford, Oxford University Press, 2002).

[22] On the narcissism of small differences, see Sigmund Freud, 'Civilization and its Discontents' in Sigmund Freud, *Civilization, Society and Religion: Group Psychology, Civilization and its Discontents and Other Works* (London, Penguin Books, 1985) 251.

methodological and epistemological presuppositions, ie that the sources of the law of federalism cannot be confined to formal norms and institutions existing in a given federation. An urban metaphor, so to say, can be relied upon to illustrate this idea. When we look at the representation of our cities on official maps, we generally see, given the scale these maps adopt, highways, avenues, boulevards, and streets. Sometimes, arrows indicate one-way roads. In a way, the message that such maps convey is that residents of the city mapped out use these arteries to circulate. And they certainly do, but their circulation patterns are much more diverse; depending on how they circulate, they may not even use some of the roads indicated on the map: we all know that in most cities, there are roads that have no pavements, because they were conceived for car users rather than for pedestrians or cyclists, whose movements are restrained by the formal road networks but who may nevertheless circumvent these restrictions by other means. Indeed, they may use side roads, alleys, cross-cutting paths or unadopted roads. Thus, actual circulation patterns not only do not correspond to the idealised image projected by official maps, but reveal a much more complex, multi-layered, and less linear picture of entangled official and unofficial paths.

The law of federalism is hardly different. It can indeed be depicted as a normative web anchored in a given federation's particular history and culture, and composed of formal constitutional and infra-constitutional norms, judicial decisions, constitutional conventions and principles, as well as political practices that are more or less juridified. All these sources account for the complexity of that field of law, and point to the porosity of the law/politics distinction. In a way, the law of federalism is arguably the archetypical form of 'political law.' Political law presupposes a reflexive method which, not being solely centred on explicit legal sources, allows interpreters to take a reasoned and reasonable distance from such sources where appropriate.[23] Yet, the adjective 'political' should not obscure the fact that it is law nevertheless.

Given the limited size of this chapter, I will briefly present and justify the main propositions that give shape to my thesis. For the same reason, I will have to refrain from providing possibly illuminating concrete examples; as a result, my discourse will remain at a rather abstract level. The proposals expounded in this chapter range from the predictable to the controversial. Admittedly, they are all debatable at one level or another. In conclusion, I will sketch the interval of principles to which I am referring in the chapter. Elaborating on the potential content and scope of each of these principles shall take place elsewhere.

I. PRELIMINARY REMARKS

A. Thinking That What You Do Not See Does Not Exist Could Be Wrong

Echoing Shakespeare, novelist Vladimir Volkoff writes in his preface to a French translation of Lawrence Durrell's *Alexandria Quartet* that 'the world is made

[23] Michel Villey, *Philosophie du droit. Définitions et fins du droit* (Paris, Dalloz, 1984) II, 163–164.

of much more than its appearances.'[24] So is federalism, for reasons that will be expounded later. However, the dominant legal approach to federalism has focused on the external appearance of federalism—explicit law and formal institutions—and more specifically on divisions of powers enshrined in written federal constitutions, as construed by the relevant case law. Texts are undeniably important, and they are often determinative. But can they realistically pretend to entirely frame and determine interpretation? Nowadays, very few scholars beyond those adhering to originalist theories of interpretation would argue that they do.[25]

In that context, legal definitions of federalism, which are invariably institutional, have predictably been strongly influenced by formalism. On that view, federalism refers to a lasting union between different political communities constituted in legal orders for the purpose of forming a broader and distinct legal order which vertically comprises at least two levels of governments the existence and powers of which are constitutionally entrenched, and the exercise of which is susceptible of review by an independent and impartial arbitrator. Such a definition is not incorrect, far from it, but I shall argue later that it is incomplete, as it does not address the deontic parameters that are arguably core to federalism and that could, and in my view should, be included in a definition of this particular mode of government so as to grasp not only its institutional dimension but also its relational nature.

The formalist emphasis on texts and institutions predictably triggered alternative approaches, among which functionalist ones are the most prominent. But like their institutionalist counterparts, these functionalist reactions mostly ignored the possibility that a *deon-telos* inherent to federalism could exist and be operationalised in a federation's *logos*.[26] In essence, they sought to identify the optimal decision-maker for achieving particular tasks linked to the elaboration and implementation of public policies. Efficiency-related concerns became predominant, and were often justified by reference to the needs, real or alleged, of the citizens, thereby adding the latter to an equation that had originally been conceived of as involving only two variables: the federation as a whole and the federated units, both being envisaged from an institutional standpoint. This questioning of federalism itself in the name of the citizens' concrete needs or interests, which led to the creation of an opposition between these citizens and institutions depicted as being disconnected from them, proved to be a clever discursive strategy in view of reducing federalism to the status of a simple tool the role of which was to serve other values posited as more important. In some influential work, the very relevance, and even usefulness, of federalism was questioned.[27]

[24] Vladimir Volkoff, 'Préface' in Lawrence Durrell, *Le Quatuor d'Alexandrie* (Paris, La Pochotèque, 1992) 5: 'Le monde est fait de bien autre chose que de ses apparences.'

[25] Originalism is itself a radically historicist and in my view naive version of formalism, the literalism of which reveals the influence of religious puritanism. See Wendy Steiner, *The Scandal of Pleasure: Art in an Age of Fundamentalism* (Chicago, University of Chicago Press, 1995) 42.

[26] I borrow the expression 'deon-telos' from David J Lametti, 'The (Virtue) Ethics of Private Property: A Framework and Implications' in Alastair Hudson (ed), *New Perspectives on Property Law, Obligations, and Restitution* (London, Cavendish Publishing Ltd, 2004) 39, 43.

[27] William Riker, 'Six Books in Search of a Subject or Does Federalism Exist and Does It Matter?' (1969) 2(1) *Comparative Politics* 135.

Functionalism often gave short shrift to texts, historical conceptions of a federation's purposes or goals, or the values underlying federalism itself, whatever they may be. Through its adherence to what could be characterised as a 'presentist' logic, ie one that seeks to respond to needs perceived as most urgent in the short term, it heralded the instrumentalisation of constitutional norms and reasoning in view of furthering specific social, political or economic agendas deemed more relevant or appropriate, generally by majority interests, at a certain stage of a federation's evolution.

While functional concerns about which level of government is better equipped or positioned to deliver particular bundles of services to citizens must be taken seriously, the instrumentalisation of values external to federalism per se, or merely ancillary to it, such as economic efficiency, may in the end threaten federalism by delegitimising it.[28] Federalism, so the objections go, produces disproportionate systemic inefficiencies, creates negative externalities, or is simply misadapted to contemporary realities. Applied in a hegemonic manner, an efficiency-based perspective may lead one to conceive of federalism as a mere constitutional nuisance that must be overcome or, at least, circumvented. And given the often difficult process of amending a federal constitution, the branch of the state to which many will turn in view of achieving the objective of overcoming or circumventing federalism is the judiciary, which raises important questions about the normative interval within which courts decide federalism-related cases. In sum, the careful handling of functional arguments cannot, and should not, be taken for granted from the standpoint of federalism, especially given the various definitions that can be given to efficiency.[29]

For most of the twentieth century, legal discussions about federalism have thus oscillated between a formalistic Scylla and a functionalist Charybdis. Although proponents of both approaches may have occasionally invoked (or instrumentalised) the 'federal principle' to buttress a particular argument, they consistently refused to address federalism from the perspective of a virtue ethics, which would have forced them to look beyond explicit normative toolboxes, on the one hand, and normative assumptions hidden under empirically-grounded (sometimes shakily) efficiency-based claims, on the other.

As mentioned, this chapter's argument is that federalism is irreducible to the explicit normative expressions or structures found in various federations around the world. As important as they may be, they are appearances, no more, no less. But first

[28] Harold Laski was rather straightforward about that in the title of a famous article advancing his thesis that federalism was unable to cope with the pace of modern societies (Harold Laski, 'The Obsolescence of Federalism' (1939) XCVII *The New Republic* 367).

[29] See Noura Karazivan and Jean-François Gaudreault-DesBiens, 'On Polyphony and Paradoxes in the Regulation of Securities within the Canadian Federation' (2010) 49(1) *Canadian Business Law Journal* 1. Functionalism's consequentialism is also problematic, as it provides an impoverished account of individual decision-making. Critiquing both rational choice and irrationalist theories, Raymond Boudon has shown that in addition to instrumental rationality, individuals also refer to values or principles when making decisions, and that their adhesion to such values or principles may even override the negative consequences they may suffer as a result of a particular choice. In other words, a form of axiomatic rationality must also be taken into consideration when examining decision-making processes (see Raymond Boudon, *La rationalité* (Paris, Presses Universitaires de France, 2003) 30–31).

and foremost, federalism should not be reduced to a mere supportive role of values which are external to it.

Granted, scepticism is important whenever someone makes a claim that something exists that cannot be seen. It is therefore crucial to qualify my claim. I am not asking anyone to believe in the existence of any metaphysical entity; I am merely talking about giving a more precise meaning to an idea—a construct, that of federalism. Saying that federalism is reducible to the particular normative expressions or structures found here and there that purport to give it some materiality, expressions which sometimes appear incommensurable, is merely expressing an idea. So is my claim that federalism is not reducible to such expressions. We are in the realm of argumentative discourse, of persuasion, not empirical evidence. In that field, as Gaston Bachelard once wrote, 'nothing is given, everything is constructed.'[30]

B. Federalism is Not Merely Subservient to Other, More Fundamental, Values

I remember an exchange that I had some years ago with the late Richard Simeon, then my colleague at the University of Toronto. Richard was an eminent federalism scholar in the field of political science. I was expressing my dissatisfaction with the current state of the theorisation of federalism in legal scholarship, and regretting the lack of any substantial reflection on what the so-called 'federal principle' could imply from a normative standpoint. Although Richard admitted that it was difficult to find a balance between different viewpoints about federalism—and he had himself written a seminal article about those viewpoints[31]—he could not see how an appeal to the 'principles of federalism' or, alternatively, to an original intent somehow deemed to be discernable in a particular constitutional text, could help solve the political dilemmas facing contemporary federations. He was of the view that federalism, as any other institutional mechanism, is an instrument that serves other, *more fundamental*, values, and that its success should be evaluated in light of how well, or how badly, it actually serves such values in a given federation. In other words, under his view, federalism could not be regarded as an end in itself, but as a means of achieving other objectives.

Being skeptical about originalist conceptions of interpretation, I had to agree that appealing to a constitutional text's alleged 'original intent' could hardly be helpful in view of solving deep normative dilemmas related to federalism, if such dilemmas can ever be solved. I could not pretend either that a mere reliance on the principles of federalism would definitely solve such dilemmas, for example those raised by the tension between autonomy and solidarity. At the very least, they could certainly not solve them for all practical *political* purposes. But while law, and constitutional law in particular, is intrinsically related to politics, as it enshrines values that are often first and foremost political in nature, it is not entirely reducible to politics, and

[30] Gaston Bachelard, *La formation de l'esprit scientifique. Contribution à une psychanalyse de la connaissance objective* (Paris, Librairie Philosophique J VRIN, 1983) 14.

[31] Simeon, 'Criteria for Choice in Federal Systems'.

the task of its interpreters remains quite different from that of other public officers responsible for elaborating and implementing policies. Indeed, legal interpreters arguably assume a heavier burden of justification than other decision-makers, notably political actors, when making decisions susceptible of affecting a federation's evolution. This is particularly true of judges who, as explicit or implicit guardians of the constitution, are under the obligation to *impartially* provide *strong, constitutionally cognisable, reasons* in support of their normative choices. 'Strong' reasons must be distinguished from other types of reasons, which we may call 'good' or 'weak.' As Raymond Boudon argues:

> The notion of good reasons characterises situations where a subject accepts a conclusion because he is unable to find a system of reasons that is superior to that which leads him to the conclusion envisaged and, at the same time, where he intuitively feels doubt about this system's validity. In some cases, this may lead him to look for better reasons.[32]

A good reason is one to which an interpreter refers to persuade himself that the conclusion he has reached is the correct one; it is not first and foremost conceived as a tool of persuasion of external audiences. It remains possible, however, to expand its reach in a justification process that is public, which renders necessary the identification of the context in which this work must be performed. In a federation, the framework in which judges decide cases is that of the federal constitution, which provides them, explicitly or implicitly, with what Boudon calls a 'superior system of reasons.' Bearing that in mind, a strong reason in a federal context would be one that responds to the *internal* requirements of the applicable constitutional regime; hence the importance that the reasons invoked by the interpreter be recognisable in light of such requirements, ie that they be reasonably related to the values that can plausibly be found to lie at the core of the federal idea, or that they be perceptible within the federation's structures, institutions or interpretative tradition. Moreover, the interpreter must invoke them in a context where he is bound to address the constitutional text and the (sometimes contradictory) precedents, as well as to make sense of their gaps, silences and ambiguities. The interest of resorting to principles is that they might help circumscribe an interval of acceptable federalist discourse for the purpose of giving meaning to the often largely indeterminate provisions that govern formal divisions of powers, and in view of making choices between interpretations that all claim their fit with federalism as understood in a particular jurisdiction.

Granted, principles provide no panacea, given their rather vague formulation. However, identifying a small core of principles arguably inherent to federalism and trying to specify what they minimally imply, normatively speaking, may actually help

[32] Raymond Boudon, *Raisons, bonnes raisons* (Paris, Presses Universitaires de France, 2003) 139: 'La notion de *bonnes raisons* caractérise les situations où un sujet accepte une conclusion parce qu'il ne parvient pas à trouver un système de raisons supérieur à celui qui conduit à la conclusion en question et où il éprouve en même temps un sentiment intuitif de doute sur la validité de ce système. Dans certains cas, cela peut provoquer chez lui une attitude de recherche de raisons meilleures.' For a stinging critique of the belief in the existence of a single good answer, see Yves-Marie Morissette, 'Deux ou trois choses que je sais d'elle (la rationalité juridique)' (2000) 45 *McGill Law Journal* 591.

frame decision-makers' reasoning—judges being significantly important ones—in a manner that is more conducive to the preservation of a genuinely federative dynamic and culture, both in the judicial arena and in the political sphere.

Such principles may frame the action of decision-makers when they evaluate the burden of justification they must discharge when deciding cases involving federalism. Obviously, because we are talking of open-textured principles, their individuation would inevitably be informed by the structural considerations, the history, and the political climate of each federation at the time a particular decision is made. Yet, a framework would be in place that could possibly limit the discretion of such decision-makers when managing the tensions inherent to the life of a federation. In the analysis of the peculiarities of a given federal experience, these decision-makers could come to the conclusion that principle X, even if it is accepted to be at the core of federalism, does not weigh much in the context of their particular federation—think, for example, of a possible principle of 'federal solidarity' in the United States of America. However, they would be obliged not only to provide strong reasons explaining why their interpretive tradition empirically rejects that principle, but also why it should be rejected, beyond the mere weight exerted by that tradition in their country's legal interpretation of federalism. In other words, they would be required to speak to that principle, which would supplement their prior empirical finding (that principle X is of little weight in the context of their federation) with a normative reevaluation of that finding (to be performed *whenever* that principle can reasonably be brought to bear in a case). This hermeneutic approach emphasising the decision-maker's reflectiveness would also reduce the likelihood that a kind of value formalism be substituted to other predominant types of formalism.

Let me stress again that we are in the argumentative realm here. As HLA Hart observed about the use of principles, the very fact that a plurality of principles can be resorted to by a decision-maker entails that 'it cannot be *demonstrated* that a decision is uniquely correct: but it may be made acceptable as the reasoned product of informed impartial choice. In all this we have the "weighing" and "balancing" characteristic of the effort to do justice between competing interests.'[33] The 'interval of principles' contemplated in the theory proposed in this chapter, within which federalism-related disputes should be adjudicated, seeks to further circumscribe the spectrum of 'informed impartial choice' in view of ensuring that the competing interests brought to bear in the decision-making process do not obscure serious concerns pertaining to federalism.

Returning to the question as to whether institutions (federal ones or not) can be considered as ends in themselves, it must be acknowledged that no institution is ontologically an end in itself, no more than federalism can be characterised as being superior or inferior to other types of political regimes. One can however argue that they may become so in certain circumstances, especially when they bear witness to fundamental, and structuring, political choices made by a political community at a critical juncture of its history. Federations could present characteristics that would justify treating them as ends in themselves, at least to a certain degree and taking into consideration the values (susceptible of transformation into principles) that

[33] Herbert LA Hart, *The Concept of Law* (Oxford, Oxford University Press, 1961) 200.

inspire their creation and that their very structure seeks to protect or preserve. The caveat 'to a certain degree' is important here, as not all federations (or functional equivalents) may be equally apt at being elevated to the status of ends in themselves. A useful distinction can be made, in this respect, between federations overlapping with genuinely 'federal' societies, ie societies where political communities overlapping various territorialised ethno-cultural groups, often minority ones, coexist (such as in Canada, Belgium, Switzerland or Spain),[34] and federations that may be socially and regionally diverse but not to the point of constituting federal societies in and of themselves (one might think of the United States of America, for example). In the former, a federal structure may more easily become an end in itself, since it is likely to be envisaged and valued as a mediating tool between the citizens' multiple political identities (at least, a dual political identity) and as a guarantor of the perpetuation of these multiple political identities within the broader federal community. This last factor actually speaks to the dynamic of the federation, which, as mentioned, must remain genuinely federal. This means that it must remain engaged in a critical dialogue with the values underlying the creation of the broader polity as a federation, which sheds light on federalism's relational nature.

The elevation of the federal character of a polity as an end in itself is thus more probable in societies that are already 'federal,' as this term was defined above. Canada, where very salient regional differences are constitutive of asymmetrical relations to the federation, provides a telling example. Federalism is clearly more 'sacralised' in Quebec, Canada's only predominantly French-speaking province, than in other parts of the country. For most Quebecers, the perpetuation of this political regime, preferably in a much decentralised form, is a sine qua non condition of their sense of belonging to the broader political community and, thus, of the unity of the federation. This points to the resilience of the so-called 'community perspective'[35] within territorialised minority groups, which overrides in such groups other competing, more consequentialist or functionalist approaches to federalism, often preferred by majority groups. Faced with opposing views as to the intrinsic significance of federalism in a particular context, maintaining an authentic form of federalism arguably requires that none of these preconceptions systematically prevails over the other. Neither functionalist concerns nor communitarian ones, or any other approach for instance, should entirely occupy the mental space of federal actors or decision-makers. Nor should they allow for the functional obliteration of federalism through judicial *fiat*: even in federations where no genuine federal society is discernable, each federal actor has a right to the intangibility of its existence and of the federal structure.[36] Conversely, any change to that structure, and a fortiori, any attempt at eliminating a federal actor, should be made following procedures that these actors have previously accepted. Absent such procedure, their de jure equality within the federation arguably requires that they give their assent to such major changes, which

[34] William S Livingston, 'A Note on the Nature of Federalism' (1952) 67 *Political Science Quarterly* 81, 87.

[35] Simeon, 'Criteria for Choice in Federal Systems'.

[36] Beaud, *Théorie de la fédération* 328.

points, as will be expounded in the conclusion, to the existence of a suppletive principle of parity.

From this perspective, there is certainly a 'conservationist' impulse in the approach that I am advocating, but it would be mistaken to assimilate it to a form of 'conservatism.' Indeed, the idea of grasping federalism-related disputes from a principle-based standpoint does not seek to freeze the evolution of a federation to an alleged 'original' understanding or design on which its initiators would have hypothetically agreed. It seeks instead to ensure that such an evolution reasonably remains within the bounds of a truly federal alliance, taking into consideration, but not exclusively, this 'original understanding,' to the extent that it is ascertainable, which may not always be the case given the multiple and sometimes contradictory rationales that may have played a role at the time of the federation's creation. Thus, the proposed theory is not at all opposed to the idea of a 'living constitution,' as initially expounded by Justice OW Holmes in the American case of *Missouri v Holland*,[37] but it stresses the importance of remembering that while 'a living tree [is] capable of growth and expansion,' it must remain 'within its natural limits,' as Lord Sankey once wrote in the Canadian case of *Edwards v Canada*.[38]

It is precisely bearing in mind this moderately conservationist mission that the approach that I propose attributes to courts of law an important fiduciary role as regards federalism. This approach also posits that while *radical* transformations of a federation's structure and dynamic are better left to political actors, courts should ensure that political processes within a federation are not distorted in such a way that questions pertaining to the concrete and lasting existence of a genuine federal regime are not ignored or obscured under the guise of promoting other values, such as efficiency. It therefore seeks to provide a federation's judiciary with conceptual tools with which to monitor these processes and, if needed, to intervene so as to reframe political debates in such a way that crucial federalism-related issues are *seriously* addressed.

The purpose of such monitoring is to impose upon both political and judicial actors the duty to provide not only a specific justification for their actions but also a *valid federal one*, this justification having to be examined from the standpoint of the core requirements or principles identified in the theory. With their dual normative and interpretive mission, these requirements could play a significant role in cases where a court is being asked to construe an ambiguous constitutional provision, one that grants a discretionary power to a federal actor, or even a constitutional silence. Most importantly, the type of judicial review envisaged should take place both in respect of the validity of a particular legislation or action, by inducing the court to choose the interpretation of the applicable constitutional provisions that is the most congruent with the principles of federalism, on one hand, and in respect of the manner in which an otherwise valid action is performed, on the other. In other words, while referring to the *telos* of federalism, this principled-based legal theory of federalism would first and foremost seek to address the *deontos* of federalism.

[37] *Missouri v Holland* 252 US 416, 432 (1920).
[38] *Edwards v Canada (AG)* [1930] AC 124, 124.

What bears noting here is that this *deontic-axiomatic* conception envisages federalism not only as referring to a particular institutional structure and to the norms giving a legal foundation to this structure, but also to a web of *relations* and, to some extent, to a particular disposition of the mind irreducible to any particular structure;[39] hence my constant emphasis on the role of legal norms in the construction and sustenance of a genuine federal culture. From this perspective, federalism is primarily understood as giving rise to various relationships ensconced in a particular type of structure where norms emanating from more than one level of government interact.

Characterised as such, a federal regime implies a culture that legal norms, both written and lived, must sustain. The theory envisaged in this chapter attributes to the judiciary of a federation a special role in fostering and helping perpetuate, within certain limits of course, this particular federal culture, notably by erecting normative safeguards susceptible of maintaining a minimal capital of trust between federal actors. In other words, the theory assumes that federalism must be taken seriously. The *constitutional* structures which give shape to the federal idea evince the soundness of this assumption, precisely because they are constitutional in nature and the norms that allow them to evolve are generally judicially reviewable. In that sense, the theory promotes the tangible implementation of what I have elsewhere referred to as the federal rule of law,[40] or what Jean Leclair has called federal constitutionalism.[41]

C. A Legal Theory of Federalism is Possible

Legal scholarship, political philosophy, and the constitutional jurisprudence of several federations abound with references to the 'federal principle.' From a conceptual perspective, however, what this principle entails generally remains little theorised, besides some crucial insights, which are often unduly vague from a juridical standpoint. Such is the case, for example, of Elazar's representation of federalism as a means to reconcile self-rule and shared rule,[42] or of the even vaguer depiction of federalism as a means to reconcile unity (and the solidarity arguably flowing from it) with diversity.

In most cases, the federal principle is approached from the perspective of the technical consequences it is deemed to imply as regards the institutional organisation of a particular political entity.[43] In such a context, any putative discussion of this principle's normative content and implications will often be hidden behind a technical

[39] Roderick A Macdonald, 'Kaleidoscopic Federalism' in Jean-François Gaudreault-DesBiens and Fabien Gélinas (eds), *Le fédéralisme dans tous ses états/The States and Moods of Federalism* 261.

[40] Jean-François Gaudreault-DesBiens, 'The Irreducible Federal Necessity of Jurisdictional Autonomy, and the Irreducibility of Federalism to Jurisdictional Autonomy' in Sujit Choudhry, Jean-François Gaudreault-DesBiens and Lorne Sossin (eds), *Dilemmas of Solidarity: Redistribution in the Canadian Federation* (Toronto, University of Toronto Press, 2006) 185.

[41] Jean Leclair, 'Federal Constitutionalism and Aboriginal Difference' (2006) 31 *Queen's Law Journal* 521.

[42] Daniel J Elazar, *Exploring Federalism* (Tuscaloosa, University of Alabama Press, 1987) 5, 53.

[43] Classical doctrinal works tend to define the principle of federalism on the basis of a legal order's institutional features.

analysis of the legal consequences to be derived from the federative division of powers in force in a given jurisdiction. In fact, as Wayne Norman suggests from the standpoint of political philosophy, 'it is not overstatement to suggest that there does not exist in any detail an adequate political philosophy of federalism itself.'[44] Martin Papillon made a similar remark from the perspective of political science, calling for further explorations of the normative meaning and consequences of federalism.[45]

These observations are even more accurate in respect of the *legal* theory of federalism, but it must at the same time be acknowledged that theorising federalism from a legal standpoint raises particular problems.

The main one lies in the diversity of federal systems around the world and the plurality of constitutional expressions of the idea of federalism. Some believe that it is simply impossible to imagine a legal theory of federalism that would do justice to that diversity.[46] Others express skepticism about the viability of meta-theories of federalism on the ground that each particular federation reflects a political compromise informed by specific historical and socio-political circumstances. For example, Vicky Jackson's thesis emphasises that every federal system, being constructed as a 'package deal,' has a sort of systemic unity which forces observers to examine each part in light of the role it plays in the system and of the constraints the system places upon it. She further highlights the particular *historicity* of each federal system.[47] Her observations first and foremost deal with the methodology and epistemology of comparative law, rather than with the sustainability of meta-theories of federalism per se, but they obviously raise important warning signs about that sustainability as well. Any meta-theory of federalism must take stock, in one way or another, of the contextual variables influencing the shape and dynamic of federalism in a given jurisdiction.

From such a perspective, general theories about federalism are either perilous to elaborate or doomed to be easily falsified. These cautionary observations are critically important, as they point to some epistemological and methodological obstacles that should be avoided when elaborating a legal theory of federalism. At the very least, the existence of such obstacles, which constitute 'uncomfortable facts' in the Weberian sense,[48] should not be obscured when so doing.

However, it is one thing to acknowledge the existence of a set of potential obstacles in elaborating a legal theory of federalism, it is quite another to hold that their mere existence renders absolutely impossible or unsustainable any theory of federalism elaborated from a juridical perspective. The latter view would actually confuse the

[44] Norman, 'Towards a Philosophy of Federalism' 81.

[45] Martin Papillon, 'Is the Secret to Have a Good Dentist? Canadian Contributions to the Study of Federalism in Divided Societies' in Linda A White, Richard Simeon, Robert Vipond and Jennifer Wallner (eds), *The Comparative Turn in Canadian Political Science* (Vancouver, University of British Columbia Press, 2008) 123, 138.

[46] See Constance Grewe and Hélène Ruiz Fabri, *Droits constitutionnels européens* (Paris, Presses Universitaires de France, 1995) 297 n 223.

[47] See Vicky C Jackson, 'Comparative Constitutional Federalism: Its Strengths and Limits' in Gaudreault-DesBiens and Gélinas (eds), *Le fédéralisme dans tous ses états/The States and Moods of Federalism*, 135.

[48] Max Weber, *Le savant et le politique* (Paris, La Découverte, 2003) 96.

act of theorising—which boils down to providing an explanation of a particular phenomenon that is irreducible to that phenomenon in its material expressions—with the comparative analysis of a particular set of empirical data: both the ends and the methods involved in each of these two endeavours are different. Thus, the very existence of the above-mentioned obstacles points to the scope and objectives of theoretical projects that do not seek to hide their primordial purpose.

A theory is no less a theory if its scope and objectives are, all things being equal, relatively modest, or carefully tailored. As well, even if it is limited in scope, a *legal* theory may have both explanatory powers and normative strength. Moreover, it can still qualify as a general theory if, once the above-mentioned obstacles have been duly considered, it explicitly privileges a certain approach to the phenomenon theorised, discloses it, and acknowledges its limits. Under that view, a theory can be normative while being still open to variations in its implementation, the central question having more to do with the type of norms contemplated in the theory than with the very plausibility of a normative theory. The validity[49] of a general, normative theory does not depend on its ability to avoid facing uncomfortable facts.

Thus, while attempts to elaborate an all-encompassing theory purporting to explain the totality of federal systems in a hegemonic manner, or to propose a 'hard' normative theory of all aspects and dimensions of such systems, would probably be doomed to fail, it is arguable that (re)theorising the federal *principle* from a legal standpoint, as opposed to theorising federal *systems* in general, is not entirely out of reach.

The reference made here to federal systems is not coincidental. As observed earlier, objections heard in the fields of law and political science against the possibility of 'general' theories of federalism almost invariably stem from scholars who tend to focus on the institutional or structural expressions of federalism and on the particular political cultures informing, and informed by, these expressions. To the extent that this refusal to generalise is grounded upon an empirical conception of what theorising entails (in law or legal science), it is epistemologically plausible. However, if it is grounded upon a *belief* that this very diversity of expressions renders any type of general theory impossible, the claim then becomes overbroad, in addition to possibly reflecting a more or less explicit adherence to a relativist ideology, as opposed to an adherence to an empirical methodology which would compel observers to take stock of the diversity of expressions of federalism and, thus, of the relativity of federalism itself.

Therefore, provided they acknowledge their limits and they do not systematically blind themselves to the realm of factuality, thereby stumbling on the epistemological obstacle of ideological universalism, normative constitutional theories, be they dealing with federalism or any other topic, are as legitimate and, to some extent, as 'valid' as any other. Their nature and function are simply different from more descriptive, empirically-minded, ones. For instance, they incorporate moral or ethical dimensions which provide them with an evaluative function. This evaluative function

[49] The use of the concept of validity in relation to a theory echoes Popperian epistemology. However, it is by no means clear that the model proposed in this epistemology squarely applies to the humanities.

allows for the transformation of the precepts which are drawn from these theories into normative proposals vested with a juridical mission, even though the occurrence of such a mutation is contingent rather than necessary. From this perspective, such theories may usefully inform, and even frame, the decision-making processes in which legal actors, be they legislators, judges, or lawyers, are involved. This actually represents the stage where normative *legal* theories depart from other types of normative theories.

To the extent that there are several different legal expressions of federalism, the remarks above, and the methodological and epistemological caveats alluded to, must be borne in mind when elaborating a normative legal theory of federalism that somehow assumes what Elizabeth Zoller calls the deep unity of federal processes.[50] Hence this chapter's emphasis on the sustainability of a normative theory of federalism and, incidentally, on the identification of 'core' federal values which, once juridified, would qualify as principles. Focusing on principles seems inevitable given the diversity of federal expressions. Indeed, this diversity can only be plausibly accounted for in a legal theoretical project such as the one expounded in this chapter by tackling the *federal phenomenon*[51] under the lens of *principles*, as they are understood in legal theoretical literature. Ronald Dworkin correctly emphasises in this respect that the processes by which principles are individuated prevent any recourse to the notion of validity, which relies on an all-or-nothing logic.[52] If one examines these processes from perspective of the relations of imputations that may be 'established between a set of facts and legal consequences by the norm-creating act of the legislator or of a court of justice,' it means that principles are characterised by a weak relation of imputation, as opposed to rules which are characterised by a strong relation.[53] Actually, the operational value of a principle and therefore its usefulness is a function of the relative indeterminacy of its scope of application.[54] A principle never dictates in a conclusive manner the outcome of its individuation,[55] and, may I add, if it is said to dictate an outcome, that outcome cannot be envisaged as reflecting a binary logic grounded on the valid-invalid, or legal-illegal, dichotomy. Such logic is the province of rules. A rule commands the application of the couple legal/illegal. A principle would command an evaluation based on couples such as acceptable/unacceptable, reasonable/unreasonable, or compatible/incompatible, and it would therefore involve a weighting logic.[56]

[50] Elizabeth Zoller, 'Aspects internationaux du droit constitutionnel. Contribution à la théorie de la fédération d'États' (2002) 294 *Recueil de cours de l'Académie de droit international* 39, 51.

[51] Jean-François Gaudreault-DesBiens and Fabien Gélinas, 'Opening New Perspectives on Federalism' in Gaudreault-DesBiens and Gélinas (eds), *Le fédéralisme dans tous ses états/The States and Moods of Federalism* 51.

[52] This influential thesis was first put forward in Ronald Dworkin, 'The Model of Rules' (1967) 35 *University of Chicago Law Review* 14.

[53] Raimo Siltala, *A Theory of Precedent: From Analytical Positivism to a Post-Analytical Philosophy of Law* (Oxford, Hart Publishing, 2000) 42.

[54] Isabelle Pariente-Butterlin, 'Principes et politiques chez Dworkin' in Stefen Wesche and Véronique Zanetti (eds), *Dworkin. Un débat* (Brussels, Mentis, 1999) 319, 326.

[55] ibid.

[56] George P Fletcher, 'Two Modes of Legal Thought' (1981) 90 *Yale Law Journal* 970, 978; Pariente-Butterlin, 'Principes et politiques chez Dworkin' 327.

Although the influence of core federal principles can arguably be felt in the functioning of several federations, the origin of those identified is not dependent upon their prior and tangible recognition, be it formal or informal, in the law of a particular federation or of a set of federations. On the contrary, their identification first and foremost stems from an intellectual exercise of conceptualisation. This is to say that my theoretical project is *not* a comparative law one, although it may use contextualised comparative data as a springboard to explore, from a legal angle, the potential meanings and scope of the core federal values so identified. However, in no way should the meanings and scope empirically attributed to such values in a given jurisdiction determine the meaning and scope given in the theory to the same values. It must thus be very clear that I am not advocating any legal transplant from federation *X* to federation *Y*. On the other hand, it would be highly problematic to systematically ignore the comparative data, as it may provide useful information about the constraints potentially framing the concrete application of the bundle of normative principles highlighted in the theory. Moreover, the academic and, as the case may be, judicial theorisation of a core value viewed as stemming from the federal principle in one jurisdiction may certainly inform, without determining it, a generic theorisation of this particular value in the context of a more abstract theorisation of federalism itself. Sometimes, the *explicit* naming in one federation of a value that *implicitly* informs the understanding of federalism in another one, and that is deemed inherent to federalism in the former, may usefully inform a broader theorisation of federalism in the latter. This presupposes that the influence of the former federation's normative and institutional peculiarities on the conceptualisation of the said value has been acknowledged, and that this value is stripped of the normative scoria peculiar to the jurisdiction where it was initially named. Such an affirmation further assumes that it is possible to extirpate that value from its original context, which requires its prior abstraction and objectivisation. If it cannot be done, it will very likely mean that the value in question is not 'core' enough to be retained for the sake of the theory. As such, reliance on comparative data, where appropriate, can serve a most useful revelatory function in the context of the elaboration of a broader normative theory of federalism, but that function remains instrumental and limited, as the frequency of reference to comparative data will vary from one sub-principle of federalism to another.

Last, a normative theory of federalism that is relevant from a legal standpoint cannot rely on legal sources alone. 'Living' federalism offers a locus where law, politics, and economics intersect; it designates both a constitutional regime revealing institutional recurrences and a political ideology. Thus, a macroscopic theory such as that emanating from legal philosophy seems inevitable. The legal theory proposed will thus rely, where necessary, not only on political philosophy, but also on political science and economics.

II. AMBITIONS AND LIMITS OF A NORMATIVE, DEONTIC-AXIOMATIC THEORY OF FEDERALISM

The heuristic assumption upon which the project of a normative, deontic-axiomatic theory of federalism relies is that there is a space for such a theory, which can be elaborated from a legal standpoint in view of making it susceptible of appropriation and implementable by juridical actors, particularly judges. This highlights the need to further specify the theory's aspirations and assumptions.

A. Such a Theory is Both Modest and Ambitious

A deontic-axiomatic theory of federalism developed from a legal standpoint must paradoxically be both modest and ambitious.

It must be *modest* in that, given the empirical diversity of federative expressions and the difficulty of precisely delineating what lies at the core of the federal idea, it can only purport to identify a limited number of sub-principles arguably flowing from the overarching 'federal principle.' It is also condemned to modesty because taking stock of that diversity requires, first, adopting a hermeneutic approach which is by definition sensitive to the various contexts in which the interpretation of such sub-principles occurs,[57] second, acknowledging that there are developments in the evolution of federations that are merely contingent, ie neither necessary nor impossible, and, third, emphasising principles rather than focusing on rules as preferred tools of normative intervention.

Yet, such a theoretical project remains *ambitious* by simply alleging, against various iterations of what I previously described as 'toolbox approaches,' that there may exist a bundle of core sub-principles stemming from the federal principle. And while it is empirically accurate to say that the concrete legal implementation of these sub-principles will vary depending upon the federation concerned, the very purpose of this project is to demonstrate that despite these variations, federalism implies some consistencies which are all tied to the federal structure or dynamic shared by the political communities where these consistencies manifest themselves. These consistencies are not revealed by similar outcomes in equivalent circumstances, but by overlaps in terms of questioning and reasoning modes. In other words, the argument is that irrespective of a federation's specific political culture and of the specificities of its formal constitution, the sub-principles that give a normative consistence to the federal principle will always be mobilised, explicitly or implicitly, when it comes to construe that constitution. This observation applies to every constitutional actor, not only the judiciary, but since the judiciary plays in most federations a very significant role in the arbitration of federalism-related disputes,[58] it is on this branch that the theory's primary focus lies.

[57] Given the role that the theory attributes to the federal principle and to the sub-principles flowing from it, and given the relative adaptability of the theory because of its hermeneutic anchoring, the problem raised by the theory's potential essentialism is somewhat attenuated. To such an extent, it could be characterised as a form of strategic essentialism in the Spivakian sense (see Gayatri C Spivak, *Outside in the Teaching Machine* (London, Routledge, 1993) 5).

[58] That being said, it is probably true, while unsurprising, that the judiciary's role tends to remain more modest, all things being equal, in civil law federations, such as Belgium or Switzerland, than in common law ones.

Last, a deontic-axiomatic theory of federalism envisaged from a legal standpoint is *immodest*, because any attempt at identifying core normative principles susceptible of juridification, even if this juridification mostly takes place at the interpretive level, is somewhat unusual in today's scholarly environment, where most scholars seem to share the implicit postulate that the different expressions of federalism are incommensurable because of the various political, economic and cultural contexts in which they arise. It is as if the specific origins of each federation provided an 'exceptionalist' glaze to each and every manifestation or evolution of federalism in that federation, somehow predetermining from A to Z their interpretation and making it impossible to grasp them from a more generic and systemic perspective, particularly when that perspective entertains normative objectives. So envisaged, the profound immodesty of the proposed theory lies in the fact that it alleges, against such theses, that from every federal structure flow a certain number of normative imperatives that are susceptible of being universalised.

B. Such a Theory Seeks to Enhance the Constitutional Potential of Each Federal Actor

The identification of federalism's core principles purports to achieve the fundamental objective that all federal actors be concretely able to fully actualise their constitutional potential. Reflecting on how individuals access the status of legal subjects, philosopher Paul Ricoeur argues that each individual should ideally realise himself or herself in such a way that he or she could be characterised as a 'capable' subject. With this concept, Ricoeur seeks to capture the individual who is free while being at the same time constrained and situated. This individual is able to designate himself or herself as the author of his or her life and as equally deserving of 'moral respect and of recognition as a legal subject.'[59]

Such a concept can be adapted for the purpose of elaborating a legal theory of federalism, for this regime requires not only that the governments that share internal sovereignty be autonomous and equal, but that they be, as constrained and situated actors, accountable for their actions before their electorate, between themselves, but also, and most importantly, before the federal principle. This might lead to a shift from a dualist paradigm centred on the notion of autonomy to a relational one that emphasises federal actors' heteronomy, given the inevitable interplay between autonomy and loyalty in a federal setting.

Concerns for a genuinely capable federal subject, and inquiries into the legal means by which this ideal can be achieved, are central in any federation because they ultimately shed light on the importance for all federal actors to concretely enjoy the autonomy, albeit relative, that is supposedly guaranteed to them in that federation's constitution. I stress here that this applies to *all* federal actors. Although the principle of autonomy is more often than not referred to with respect to claims made by federated units, the federal legal order must also be able to enjoy its own

[59] Paul Ricoeur, *Le juste* (Paris, Éditions Esprit, 1995) 30.

normative autonomy; even if a federation was created as a result of a political process of aggregation, the federal legal order, once created, is not a mere 'creature' of the federated units.[60]

C. Such a Theory Assumes the Crucial Role of the Judiciary in a Federation

Every constitutional actor is responsible for upholding federal values, but the judiciary has a special role to play, as it is the decision-making body that is less likely to be in a conflict of interests or in a jurisdictional conflict. If one concurs with this chapter's thesis that federalism, being irreducible to a mere technique of allocating jurisdictions, expresses an ideal of equilibrium between several values, one of the most significant judicial roles is arguably to foster and sustain a genuine federal culture, and to maintain an acceptable level of constitutional civility between federal actors.

Admittedly, one cannot reduce the law of federalism to written law, be it found in constitutional texts or in the judicial pronouncements interpreting these texts. Indeed, the law of federalism comes as much from the way its norms are appropriated, implemented, and experienced by federal actors, sometimes in unusual ways, as it comes from constitutional texts and rulings construing them. But such actors must be provided with some basic guidance as to what they can do and cannot do. It is in their interest that the parameters providing such guidance do not merely revolve around formal constitutional provisions governing the division of powers, which are often ambiguous or contradictory. Bringing into the equation regulatory principles whose normative content transcends the technical dimension of federative disputes may usefully frame the resolution of such disputes. Rulings incorporating such principles are also advantageous in that they are more likely to serve a pedagogical role. Indeed, rulings addressing division of powers issues from a solely technical angle are often perceived as overly complicated normative hotchpotches by many, from law students to politicians responsible for the main constitutional orientations of the governments they lead. In contrast, rulings that anchor their technical reasoning in a principle-based framework more clearly reveal the rationales, logics and aspirations usually hidden by technical reasoning while irreducible to it. When they are revealed, these rationales, logics and aspirations may more easily reach out to various audiences in the sociopolitical sphere—politicians, public administrators, media, etc—and facilitate the emergence of a genuine federal culture,[61] which may eventually be internalised in the daily behaviour of various federal actors. In other words, a judicial discourse revolving around a principle-based framework is more likely to induce its audiences to adhere to it than a merely technical discourse that not only obscures federalism's normative potential, but that also trivialises federalism's role as a central pillar of the identity of a given political community. Such a trivialisation process makes it easier to envisage federalism as an uncomfortable fact

[60] The principle of non-subordination has a mutual application within the federation. On this point, see Carl Schmitt, *Théorie de la constitution* (Paris, Presses Universitaires de France, 1993) 518.

[61] The reference to a judicial discourse addressed at various audiences is borrowed from the work of Chaim Perelman. See Chaim Perelman, *Logique juridique. Nouvelle rhétorique* (Paris, Dalloz, 1999).

and to try to circumvent its plenary application. As is the case with human rights, federalism bears aspirations that must constantly be recalled to social actors, even in a federation's daily life where the pragmatic challenges arising from the federal structure could negatively taint this political regime as a source of unwanted complications rather than as a springboard offering tools to meet these challenges. Taking federalism seriously is thus an imperative, which sheds light on the need not to underestimate the law's pedagogical mission in achieving that objective.

Most importantly, and contrary to what some have argued invoking notably functionalist concerns,[62] there is no convincing reason to preclude the judiciary from playing a central, albeit well-tempered and non-exclusive, role in the resolution of federalism-related disputes. This role can be fulfilled through the use of the vast array of normative resources available in order to ensure that federalism, while evolving, remains faithful to the aspirations that it bears and that guarantee its resilience as a constitutional regime. Whether formalised or not, the judiciary's complete (or even significant) withdrawal from the resolution of federalism-related disputes would open the door wide to all sorts of pathologies characterising unmarked political processes. Examples of such pathologies abound; one can think of the systematic prevalence of one value over another one (for example, efficiency over diversity, or the reverse), the equally systematic affirmation of the primacy of a federalised national will over that of the federated units (or the reverse), a lack of sanction of federal actors' opportunistic behaviours, etc.

However, the nature and scope of judicial interventions may vary widely. In this respect, it would be a mistake to confine them to enforceable declarations of invalidity of actions running against the formal division of powers. Such declarations are but one example of possible remedies against actions undermining federalism in a more than trivial way. They are warranted, of course, when faced with a legislative provision that has been adopted outside its author's constitutional authority. But absent such a situation, alternatives may notably include judgments declaring that action *X* of federal actor *Y* is contrary to principle *Z*, with a sanction that may vary depending on the particular political-constitutional culture of the federation involved. It could very well be that in a given federation, a judicially-enforceable injunctive relief could be contemplated while a mere declaration of incompatibility would be deemed sufficient in another federation. Irrespective of their variable degree of formal enforceability, such declaratory judgments could serve as potent reminders, not only to federal actors but to citizens as well, that a breach of federalism has occurred and that this breach is constitutionally problematic. In the hypothesis of a non-enforceable declaratory judgment, the debate would in effect be sent back to the political arena while forcing actor *Y* to unpack the reasons justifying its actions in a context where the actual impact of such an action on federalism is taken seriously instead of being obscured because of the allegedly greater importance of other concerns, as legitimate as they may be. The theory proposed in this chapter thus relies on a clearly political conception of constitutional law, where the establishment

[62] See, in the Canadian context, Patrick Monahan, 'At Doctrine's Twilight: The Structure of Canadian Federalism' (1984) 34 *University of Toronto Law Journal* 47.

and maintaining of a dialectical relation between the judiciary and other branches of the state is envisaged as both inevitable and positive.

However, one could object that mere declaratory, formally unenforceable, decisions, notably grounded upon broad principles, would lack effectiveness, and would therefore be useless. In a way, this line of argument would assimilate that type of judicial intervention as a form of judicial chattering, which should be avoided in federal contexts as in other contexts. While judicial chattering must indeed be avoided, such an objection would in my view reflect an impoverished conception of legal effectiveness. Indeed, judicial pronouncements do not necessarily have to be formally enforceable to be effective. Effectiveness can be envisaged in many different ways; it can be direct or indirect, immediate or delayed, concrete or symbolic.[63] Thus, judicial pronouncements do not necessarily need to compel federal actors to do or not do something under the threat of an enforceable sanction. The normative strength of a norm and its enforceability are not synonyms,[64] and the former may be vested with variable intensity. From this perspective, the prospect of a political sanction to a legal obligation can easily be envisaged and can prove as effective as a formal legal sanction. It bears observing that, in a federation where the rule of law prevails—and these federations are the only ones targeted by the theory proposed in this chapter—court rulings in constitutional matters, even if they are not legally enforceable strictly speaking, may still be, and tend to be, respected by the federal actors concerned by them. Think, for instance, of judicial opinions based on unenforceable constitutional conventions in the British constitutional model:[65] the existence of such conventions can be acknowledged by courts of law, but judicial declarations acknowledging their existence and, as the case may be, that a particular action breaches them, are neither legally enforceable nor opposable. In other words, the impossibility of legally enforcing a ruling should not inevitably lead one to conclude that such a ruling is devoid of any effectiveness or performativity, particularly if it concerns the deeper aspirations of a constitutional regime.

D. Such a Theory Reflects a Dynamic Conception of Constitutional Interpretation

As mentioned, the deontic-axiomatic theory envisaged in this chapter rejects purely legalistic or formalistic approaches to constitutional interpretation. Moreover, it enshrines certain assumptions about the alleged 'clarity' of a norm, and the intellectual endeavour that theorising about federalism represents.

As to clarity, it observes that it is only exceptionally that a constitution, federal or not, is really clear about the solution to be found to many normative dilemmas,

[63] Valérie Demers, *Le contrôle des fumeurs. Une étude d'effectivité du droit* (Montréal, Éditions Thémis, 1996) 67–86.

[64] See Catherine Thibierge et al (eds), *La force normative. Naissance d'un concept* (Paris, LGDJ & Bruylant, 2009).

[65] For the canonical iteration of that idea, see *Re: Resolution to amend the Constitution* [1981] 1 SCR 753.

whatever their nature; it therefore takes stock of the relative indeterminacy of many constitutional norms, which, more often than not, enshrine notions with variable content.[66] It further notes that the determination of what is clear implies a prior intellectual construction, and that a declaration of clarity often reflects a rhetorical strategy that seeks to discard, if not discredit, other equally reasonable options. As such, the clarity argument, albeit plausible in some cases,[67] primarily reflects an act of authority seeking to prevent current and future legal actors from integrating into the text (understood here as a broader normative narrative) their own understanding of the constitution, which may vary depending on contexts and eras.[68] In a way, this argument presupposes an absence of discussion: The text is not, and cannot be, discussed.[69] Moreover, this argument elevates clarity as an objective quality of the text.[70] Granted, any argument about the lack of clarity of a text is also a construct, but that construct does not aim at the closure of the debate. The constructivist approach that I adopt here is intimately linked to a conception of interpretation that heavily draws on hermeneutics, as will become even clearer in the next paragraphs.

As to the proposed deontic-axiomatic theory's assumptions about theorising, let us first recall that the very idea of elaborating a normative theory of federalism, developed from a legal standpoint, is viewed by many as pointless and impossible given the diversity of federative expressions. As previously noted, this relativistic argument denies that one can identify 'core' and 'universal' federal principles. A weaker argument, but leading to the same conclusion, would hold that even assuming that it is possible to identify a bundle of core sub-principles inherent to federalism, these sub-principles would be essentially political; moreover, their normative strength would at best be ambiguous or equivocal.

Of course, if one equates a normative legal theory with a theory that always produces determined and specific outcomes irrespective of the political and constitutional context of a given federation, this type of objection is probably valid. But it fails if one adopts a more complex view of interpretation, and a slightly weaker view of what a normative theory entails, for the identification of a set of core federal principles that can be judicially implemented does not necessarily entail a strictly uniform interpretation or implementation of these principles.

The interpretive approach that can allow for the identification of federal principles posited as susceptible of being universalised, and for the acknowledgment of the impact of local constitutional cultures and of other formal and informal constraints on legal interpretation, is derived from hermeneutics. More precisely, Gadamerian

[66] See Chaim Perelman and Raymond Vander Elst (eds), *Les notions à contenu variable en droit* (Brussels, Bruylant, 1984).

[67] This argument is especially plausible when construing binary rules whose meaning is largely predetermined by their author. On the concept of predetermination, see Gérard Timsit, *Gouverner ou juger. Blasons de la légalité* (Paris, Presses Universitaires de France, 1995).

[68] Michel van de Kerchove, 'Le sens clair d'un texte: argument de raison ou d'autorité?' in Guy Haarsher, Laurent Ingber and Raymond Vander Elst (eds), *Arguments d'autorité et arguments de raison en droit* (Brussels, Éditions Némésis, 1988) 291.

[69] Chaim Perelman, *Logique juridique* (Paris, Dalloz, 1976) 36.

[70] In this way, as Goltzberg correctly points out, clarity is extrinsic to the text (see Stefan Goltzberg, *Chaim Perelman. L'argumentation juridique* (Paris, Michalon, 2013) 24).

hermeneutics expresses the view that these constraints would inevitably inform the judicial interpretation of the legal principles identified as core federal ones. The said constraints would serve as pre-understandings that interpreters would confront with principles and facts.[71] But instead of *presuming* that a particular context excludes the application of a given principle, interpreters would have to provide strong reasons justifying the non-application of this principle in that context, or the predominance of one principle over another, be it systemic or merely ad hoc.

But while these empirical peculiarities may very well inform the judicial reflection on the actual *implementation* of these principles, they should not play any determining role for the purpose of *identifying* them, at least those that can reasonably be characterised as consubstantial to federalism itself. Once these principles are identified, however, judges and political actors would inevitably approach them through the lens of their own preconceptions. Such preconceptions would themselves be informed by the political and legal cultures, as well as the specific circumstances of the federation in which interpreters have evolved. But reliance on these principles could enable them to distance themselves from the diktats of these preconceptions and to provide new meanings, arguably more in tune with the core legal values underlying federalism. Assuming that interpretation is a value-laden process,[72] and that choices made in the context of federative disputes and concerning the legal characterisation of issues raised in these disputes are no less value-laden,[73] informed as they are by preconceptions as to the nature and the objectives of the federal regime at stake, and as to how it should function, reliance on normative principles susceptible of legal recognition, be it through formal sanctions or otherwise, could possibly and usefully reduce the incidence of arbitrariness and presentist logics in the processes leading to these choices.

III. CONCLUSION

Near the city of Hamilton, New Zealand, there is a cave that visitors can tour and where they can see 'glowworms.' Visitors first embark on a boat and then, in absolute darkness, follow a subterranean river until they see luminous points on the ceiling and on the walls of the cave; the luminous points are glowworms. Visitors never get to see the ceiling and the walls of the cave. It is as if they did not exist. The complete picture consists of the glowworms.

Constitutional texts are like glowworms. The focal point that they offer to onlookers tends to prevent the latter from looking beyond explicit textual provisions. As such, constitutional texts give the illusion of completeness, but it is at best an illusion. Indeed, there are walls and ceilings beyond them: there is always a sub-text that supports or inspires a text; there is always a hidden structure that informs a language.

[71] See Hans Georg Gadamer, *Vérité et méthode. Les grandes lignes d'une herméneutique philosophique* (Paris, Seuil, 1996).

[72] See Andrée Lajoie, *Jugements de valeurs. Le discours judiciaire et le droit* (Paris, Presses Universitaires de France, 1997).

[73] This includes the values of the decision-makers themselves.

The text is a constraint, but it is not a vampire: it does not, and cannot, suck the lifeblood out of constitutional law. The deontic-axiomatic theory proposed in this chapter precisely seeks to take stock of the incompleteness of constitutional texts, and of the irreducibility of federalism to formal divisions of powers. The theory's emphasis on the idea that some core sub-principles are consubstantial to the broader and often invoked principle of federalism reflects these assumptions.

The theory further posits that judicial rulings that thoroughly address all the sub-principles relevant to a case can significantly influence the behaviour of political actors by identifying reasonably clear legal parameters beyond which they cannot venture, but within which they can evolve. Conversely, the absence of such judicial pronouncements may allow them to impose their own conception of what is 'right' as regards federalism, notably through actions that neglect the particular requirements stemming from this type of political regime, or that disproportionately impact on the prerogatives and interests of other actors. This ultimately undermines the rule of law, which requires political actors to act in a manner that reveals a concern for the proportionality of their actions.[74] Indeed, in a federative context, the validity of a law often depends on whether or not the otherwise constitutionally legitimate aims pursued by the enacting government disproportionately encroach upon the other level of government's constitutional authority. And irrespective of whether or not a question concerns the validity of a law *stricto sensu*, the prima facie constitutionally valid action of a government may still upset the equilibrium of federalism if it disproportionately affects the interests of other federal actors.

Thus, by requiring that all federal actors be mindful of the consequences of their actions on other parties and that they therefore show some level of self-restraint, this requirement of proportionality makes it possible to win legitimatisation of actions that, while affecting others, are less likely to be perceived as *unduly* affecting them. Such an intersubjective legitimisation may of course flow from the free will of the political actors involved, but it may also be achieved when a court of law fully and thoroughly addresses the deep theoretical background of the topic it is adjudicating upon, and speaks to the core values embedded in the legal structure it is dealing with. This goes for the rule of law in general, but this goes as well for the federal rule of law.

In this regard, I have argued elsewhere that these values must be found through a reflection on the core, inherent requirements of a federal alliance.[75] Once juridified, these values can be characterised as generic substantive principles the trace of which can be found in all federations, albeit to different degrees, and which *are* generally applicable. Since such principles seek to speak to federalism's *deontos* and *telos*,

[74] On the connection between proportionality and the rule of law, see David M Beatty, *The Ultimate Rule of Law* (Oxford, Oxford University Press, 2004).

[75] See Jean-François Gaudreault-DesBiens, 'Le fédéralisme et le législateur fédéral' (2009) 2 *Revue de droit parlementaire et politique* 427; Jean-François Gaudreault-DesBiens, 'The Irreducible Federal Necessity of Jurisdictional Autonomy, and the Irreducibility of Federalism to Jurisdictional Autonomy'; Jean-François Gaudreault-DesBiens, 'The Canadian Federal Experiment, or Legalism without Federalism? Toward a Legal Theory of Federalism' in Manuel Calvo-Garcia and William LF Felstiner (eds), *Federalismo/Federalism* (Madrid, Dyckinson, 2004) 81.

they can be labelled deontic-axiomatic. Other principles, which find an expression in many but not all federations, can for their part be called suppletive. This means that to the extent that these principles refer to ideas or practices that may arguably be valued in a federative context, they may 'supplement' the system of reasons without systematically playing a role in it. In practice, suppletive principles *could* be applicable absent any explicit provision to the contrary. A last bundle of principles consists of agonistic principles. Agonistic principles' function is to provide tools for ensuring both a certain level of systemic security in dispute-resolution processes, through conflict principles or rules, and the presence of trusted institutions responsible for the orderly resolution of federalism-related disputes.

That being said, what could be the substantive principles? In my view, a federal alliance necessarily implies a minimum level, first, of trust between the parties, which presupposes that they act in a spirit of *loyalty* toward each other and toward the federal principle itself (it minimally imposes upon them a duty of self-restraint), second, of *equality* between them, understood here in terms of status equality, which renders problematic the de jure as well as the de facto subordination of one to another and which thus presupposes the relative *autonomy* of federal actors[76] (and from the principles of equality and autonomy flow the sub-principles of anti-hegemony and non-subordination); third, of *solidarity* between the parties, which raises the questions of distributive justice between a federation's governmental actors. It may then indirectly raise issues pertaining to interpersonal equality and meaningful federal citizenship.

For their part, suppletive principles arguably lie in the principles of parity and cooperation. The principle of parity presupposes the relative autonomy of each constitutionally-recognised level of government (and thus the federal legal order's autonomy vis-à-vis the federal and federated levels of government), and the corollary co-dependence of federal and federated legal orders within that federation. From this logically flows that attempts at instrumentalising the federation for a particular level of government's egotistic ends should be viewed with suspicion. Thus, as a matter of principle, whenever a decision is susceptible of affecting more than trivially the federation's existence and structural evolution, both levels of government should have an equal say in the process, which is the essence what the principle of parity stands for. In this respect, parity can aptly be seen as an offspring of the substantive principle of equality. However, willingly-agreed constitutional amendment provisions may, and sometimes do, tamper with this equality, to such an extent that parity can hardly be characterised as inherent to federalism. Yet, absent any such provision, it is fair to surmise that parity should be treated as one of federalism's operating principles, but a suppletive one.

The principle of coordination should be accorded a similar status. Coordination is a fact of life in all federations, albeit to various degrees. Yet, it is rarely envisaged as giving rise to legal obligations. The substantive principle of loyalty surely encompasses

[76] Since both the federal and the federated legal orders are autonomous vis-à-vis each other, Olivier Beaud speaks of a double independence (see Beaud, *Théorie de la fédération* 185). On the principle of autonomy, see Lidija Basta-Fleiner and Jean-François Gaudreault-DesBiens, 'Federalism and Autonomy' in Thomas Fleiner, Cheryl Saunders and Mark Tushnet (eds), *Handbook of Constitutional Law* (Oxford, Routledge, 2013) 143.

obligations pertaining to cooperation, but at its core, the cooperation in question is rather passive, as it generally implies obligations not to do things hindering otherwise legal and legitimate actions of a given federal actor. What about active cooperation then? Here again, and although the competitive or cooperative dynamic of a federation should not affect the identification of deontic-axiomatic principles, one cannot escape noting that both the strong normative emphasis on autonomy implied by federalism and the very specific dynamics informing the evolution of federations preclude recognising active cooperation as a deontic-axiomatic principle. A mere rebuttable presumption of active cooperation should therefore be applied absent constitutional provisions to the contrary.

Last, agonistic principles are necessary because a federation's minimally dual structure renders intergovernmental conflicts inevitable. If one agrees with the proposed theory's assumptions that conflicts, even when formulated through highly technical legal language, often speak to a federation's values, or that their outcome is susceptible of affecting in depth the federation's functioning, how these conflicts are resolved is of the utmost importance for all federal actors concerned, and also, more broadly, for the fate of the federation. A first question is *who* resolves these conflicts? I have argued earlier, for a host of reasons, that an authority that is not under the control of any federal actor should have the final say. Put in more abstract terms, acknowledging the existence of a principle of *federative arbitration* is in order. Such a principle should be understood as requiring that all intergovernmental disputes *concretely* affecting the federal division of powers as well as governmental actions *potentially* threatening the equilibrium of the federation be susceptible of adjudication by an independent and impartial third party, most likely a judicial authority. A further variable that must be taken into consideration in this context is that this independent and impartial third party is *bound* to decide cases. This trite observation points to the question of the grounds upon which such a decision can be taken. Let us assume for the sake of the discussion that neither the explicit provisions of a constitution nor the substantive principles envisaged in this chapter provide a stronger reason for deciding a federalism case in one way rather than another, and that no federal primacy clause finds application in that case. Let us further assume that valuable arguments can plausibly support either position in the debate. Moreover, let us surmise that a federal alliance benefits from some level of transparency, flexibility, proximity, and efficiency in its functioning. Last, let us agree that adjudication in such an alliance must be made in a context where some level of systemic security is ensured. Systemic security is understood here as underlying two distinct, but interrelated, requirements. The first one is that a clear and predictable conflict rule must be recognised in any federation, and the second one emphasises that conflicts must not be resolved by a conflict rule the mechanical application of which would end up obliterating the substantive principles highlighted in this chapter. In other words, such a conflict rule must not undermine the integrity of the system of reasons within which the adjudication of federalism-related disputes takes place. These considerations point, in my view, to the recognition of the concept of *subsidiarity* as an agonistic principle. Of the numerous meanings it has been given, subsidiarity seems best understood as a conflict rule the application of which is eminently contextual and fact-sensitive.

At this stage, whether or not one agrees with the particular principles emphasised above is not what primarily counts. What is important to understand is that the gist of the thesis defended in this chapter is that federalism is more than the technical division of powers found in a given constitution: it is also, and maybe first and foremost, a mode of constitutional apprehension of the political dynamic at play in states sharing some core structural features characterising a federation, and from which stems a particular mode of constitutional justification that is conditioned by the above-mentioned normative principles that form federalism's *deontos* and that speak to its *telos*. Altogether, these principles form a discursive and deontic interval from which interpretive consequences must be drawn. Indeed, in spite of the great variety of federative structures and archetypal dynamics, some recurrent patterns of constitutional justification transcend differences between federations.

This is why the *reading* of federalism envisaged in this chapter treats this particular type of constitutional regime as an end in itself, that is, as a constitutional good. Granted, federalism can also be viewed as a tool for achieving other political, social or economic objectives. However, in cases raising the question of federalism, such objectives should be regarded as fundamentally external to federalism itself, and should only be brought to bear once the court has approached the case from the standpoint of federalism itself, that is, after having examined the text of the constitution and the precedents in light of the core normative, and often implicit, principles underlying federalism. This is to say that, from a juridical perspective, the very fact that this type of regime is entrenched in the constitution, rather than in a mere statute, should induce interpreters to accord it a preeminent normative status and to draw interpretive consequences from it. Hence the importance of treating federalism as a constitutional good in such a context, on a par with, say, a constitutional structure of rights protection. It is moreover arguable, from an instrumental perspective, that the appropriate balance between external objectives is more likely to be struck if core federalism-related arguments and arguments based on those objectives are, to the extent possible, consciously dissociated. Instead of allowing such external objectives to be hidden behind technical legal arguments, the proposed approach therefore seeks to make them as visible as possible and as debatable as possible in the open. It also demands from arguments promoting these external objectives that they fit within the context of federalism, by forcing them to address the core federalism-related issues that they raise, instead of forcing federalism to fit within the instrumental templates that these arguments put in place.

To do this, however, we have to go beyond any kind of toolbox approach to federalism.

Part II

Governing the Federation

4

Federalism and the Separation of Powers

JESSICA BULMAN-POZEN*

AMERICAN CONSTITUTIONAL LAWYERS widely recognise federalism and the separation of powers as analogous structural principles. Both diffuse government authority to prevent the accumulation of excessive power in any one actor and to encourage different representatives of the people to check exercises of power by the others.[1] Together, federalism and the separation of powers are understood to offer a 'double security' to 'the rights of the people.'[2]

Less noticed are the important ways in which federalism and the separation of powers interact.[3] In an era of executive power, the states play a critical role in constraining the federal executive. And they often do so in a very particular, if unexpected, way: as champions of Congress.

States shape the balance of power across the three branches of the federal government because they are not separate sovereigns, as much federalism doctrine and scholarship posit. Rather than regulate a domain entirely distinct from that regulated by the federal government, states are frequently charged by Congress with helping to carry out federal law. When cohabiting a statutory scheme with the federal executive in such 'cooperative federalism' programs, states that disagree with the executive's decisions contest not the raw exercise of federal power, as traditional accounts of federalism would have it, but instead the executive's fidelity to the statutory scheme. Relying on authority granted to them by Congress, they launch their challenges from within federal law rather than beyond it. Importantly, states need not actually be Congress's faithful agents for them to claim this mantle and to provoke the federal executive to respond. By assigning states a part in executing federal law, Congress has—often unwittingly—empowered them to provide the sort of check on executive power that it largely has been unable or unwilling to provide directly.

* Portions of this chapter originally appeared at (2012) 112 *Columbia Law Review* 459.

[1] See, eg, *Gregory v Ashcroft* 501 US 452, 458–59 (1991); Akhil Reed Amar, 'Of Sovereignty and Federalism' (1987) 96 *Yale Law Journal* 1425, 1495.

[2] *The Federalist Papers* (London, Penguin Books, 1989) No 51, p 321 (James Madison).

[3] One important exception is Bradford R Clark, 'Separation of Powers as a Safeguard of Federalism' (2001) 79 *Texas Law Review* 1321, which argues that the separation of powers safeguards federalism by limiting the number and kinds of federal laws that may displace state law. This chapter takes up the opposite question: How federalism may safeguard the separation of powers.

In addition to influencing the relative power of the federal legislative and executive branches, states carrying out federal law also reproduce separation of powers values within the realm of administration, a dynamic we might term *fractal separation of powers*.[4] Most notably, cooperative federalism schemes engender robust competition among government actors about federal law even when competition is lacking within the federal government, for instance because Congress and the presidency are held by a single political party. Such schemes also restore some of the actual separation between policymaking and execution that tends to be lost in the administrative state.

Cooperative federalism is an intriguing safeguard of the separation of powers for practical as well as theoretical reasons. Existing proposals to rein in the federal executive push against the vastness of the federal administrative state, the breadth of delegation to the executive branch, and the rise of polarised and cohesive political parties. Cooperative federalism schemes instead harness these realities. First, they provide a check on federal executive power not despite the expansion of such power but because of it. It is the very growth of the federal administrative apparatus that has swept states up as necessary administrators of federal law. The more the federal executive branch must accomplish, the more it must rely on the states, and this positions states to challenge the federal executive.

Second, cooperative federalism programs seize on the practice of legislative delegation to the federal executive as a means of checking executive power. Many scholars worry about broad delegations in the administrative state and, more generally, the federal executive's substantial discretion in interpreting and implementing the law. But the more room Congress leaves the federal executive to manoeuvre, the more room it may also leave for state resistance when it grants administrative authority to both the states and the federal executive. Here, too, cooperative federalism recasts a feature of the administrative state that is widely understood to undermine separation of powers values.

Third, state administration of federal law exploits partisanship to serve checks and balances. Because there will never be party unity between the federal government and all 50 states, partisan competition exists between the federal executive and the states even during periods of party-unified federal government. Rather than seek to mute partisanship, as many proposals to restore separation of powers

[4] A brief note on this chapter's understanding of the separation of powers is in order. The separation of powers is an essentially contested concept that embraces opposed policies: 'separated powers, yet shared and overlapping powers; independence of branch functions, yet functions that check and balance each other' (Paul Gewirtz, 'Realism in Separation of Powers Thinking' (1989) 30 *William and Mary Law Review* 343, 343). The ends it serves are similarly multiple and competing: 'promoting efficient specialization, but avoiding the tyranny of too much efficiency,' (ibid) to name just one tension. This chapter focuses on checks and balances, in the form of competition among government actors, and in the service of democratic responsiveness, deliberation, and governmental accountability. While most will agree this is a core constellation of separation of powers values, those who privilege distinct separation of powers values may understand state administration of federal law very differently. See Steven G Calabresi and Saikrishna B Prakash, 'The President's Power to Execute the Laws' (1994) 104 *Yale Law Journal* 541, 639–42 (expounding a unitary executive position, focused on the President's responsibility to execute federal law, and suggesting that state implementation of federal law may undermine the separation of powers).

values would have it, cooperative federalism schemes capitalise on the polarisation of political parties to generate a continual check on the federal executive. For all of these reasons, cooperative federalism is a realistic, even organic, response to some pressing separation of powers concerns.

I. COOPERATIVE AND UNCOOPERATIVE FEDERALISM

The federal government's move, particularly with the New Deal and Great Society, to regulate in areas traditionally occupied by the states has bound up states in the administration of federal law. The dynamic is one of mutual empowerment more than federal aggrandisement: as the fourth branch grows, so too does the states' role grow within it.

In federal statutory schemes, states often serve as administrators of national programs, a sort of second executive branch operating alongside the President and the Washington bureaucracy. Through its conditional spending and conditional preemption powers, Congress has brought states into the administration of the United States' most substantial regulatory programs. States exercise concurrent authority with the federal executive in social welfare programs like Medicaid and the Patient Protection and Affordable Care Act; environmental programs like the Clean Air Act and the Clean Water Act; and a host of other schemes from immigration to telecommunications to financial regulation.[5]

These programs typically travel under the label 'cooperative federalism', but state actors do not always play nicely with their federal counterparts; their actions can be decidedly uncooperative.[6] While states furnish administrative capacity and democratic legitimacy, bolstering the ability of the federal government to achieve its objectives, they also inject contestation into national governance. Importantly, such uncooperative behaviour is rarely framed in terms of state versus federal authority as such. Instead, states tend to fight with the federal executive branch about the meaning of the statute Congress has designed and the allocation of federal authority.

Consider two examples from recent years: state opposition to the Bush Administration's failure to regulate greenhouse gas emissions and to the Obama Administration's immigration policies. The Clean Air Act authorises both the Environmental Protection Agency (EPA) and California to adopt vehicle emissions standards.[7]

[5] See 8 USC § 1357(g) (2012) (immigration); 33 USC §§ 1251–1387 (2006) (Clean Water Act); 42 USC § 1396a (2006) (Medicaid); 42 USC §§ 7401–7642 (2006) (Clean Air Act); 47 USC § 252(e)(5) (2006) (telecommunications); Dodd-Frank Wall Street Reform and Consumer Protection Act, Pub L No 111-203, § 1042(a)(2), 124 Stat 1376, 2012–14 (2010) (codified at 12 USC § 5552 (2012)) (financial regulation); Patient Protection and Affordable Care Act, Pub L No 111-148, §§ 1101, 1311, 1321, 124 Stat 119, 141–43, 173–79, 186 (2010) (to be codified at 42 USC §§ 18001, 18031, 18041) (healthcare). See generally Jessica Bulman-Pozen, 'Federalism as a Safeguard of the Separation of Powers' (2012) 112 *Columbia Law Review* 459, 472–76.

[6] See generally Jessica Bulman-Pozen and Heather K Gerken, 'Uncooperative Federalism' (2009) 118 *Yale Law Journal* 1256.

[7] California may adopt more stringent vehicle emission standards than the federal EPA if the EPA grants a waiver, and the statutory scheme makes a waiver grant the default (42 USC § 7543 (2006); HR Rep No 95-294, at 23 (1977)).

Because the state's power to set policy is secured by a federal statute, this scheme frames regulatory disputes between the state and federal executive in terms of the congressional grant of power, not independent state authority. When the Bush EPA declined to regulate greenhouse gas emissions and also denied California the waiver that would have allowed the state to regulate such emissions, California insisted that it was attempting to faithfully implement the Clean Air Act while the federal executive branch disregarded the statute. Its argument had less to do with federalism than with the distribution of federal authority: state officials argued that the Bush Administration was abdicating its statutory duty to act and that the state was seeking to vindicate congressional intent.

Arizona's fight with the Obama Administration concerning immigration policy had much the same character. Arizona's SB 1070 would have, among other things, made it a crime to be in Arizona without carrying registration papers, required police to determine a person's immigration status during a stop upon reasonable suspicion that the person was unlawfully present, and allowed police to make warrantless arrests of persons they believed to have committed certain crimes.[8] In defending the state law, Arizona did not challenge federal authority over immigration or insist on independent state authority. Just the opposite: it claimed the mantle of Congress and argued that it, and not the federal executive branch, was seeking to execute federal immigration law as Congress intended. The problem, Arizona argued, was that the federal executive was not carrying out federal immigration law to its fullest extent. And, it continued, Congress had lent states authority to cooperate in immigration enforcement so as to avoid such laggardness.[9]

II. CHECKING THE FEDERAL EXECUTIVE ON BEHALF OF CONGRESS

As both the Clean Air Act and immigration examples suggest, when states want to carry out federal law differently from the federal executive, their most powerful objection sounds not in federalism, but rather in the separation of powers: they try to tar the federal executive's choices as inconsistent with the statute that governs state and federal action alike. Rather than challenge the raw exercise of federal power, states instead challenge the faithfulness of the executive to the statutory scheme. They rely on power granted to them by one part of the federal government to contest the decisions of another part, and, whether rightly or wrongly, they cast themselves as Congress's faithful agents, in contrast to a wayward executive branch.

[8] See *Arizona v United States* 132 S Ct 2492 (2012).

[9] See, eg, Appellants' Opening Brief at 1–2, *United States v Arizona* 641 F 3d 339 (9th Cir 2010) (No 10-16645) ('The Department of Homeland Security ('DHS') has demonstrated its inability (or unwillingness) to enforce the federal immigration laws effectively. The Act's primary purpose, therefore, is to enhance the assistance Arizona and its law enforcement officers provide in enforcing federal immigration laws. The Arizona Legislature carefully crafted the Act to ensure that Arizona's officers would do so in compliance with existing federal laws ... The fundamental premise of the United States' argument is that DHS has exclusive authority to determine whether and to what extent it may receive assistance from state and local authorities in the enforcement of federal immigration laws. The United States' position, however, is contradicted by express directives from Congress. ...').

Cooperative federalism schemes thus have important implications for the respective authority of the federal legislative and executive branches. Debates that may initially appear to be about federalism are often about the separation of powers.

A. Checking the Federal Executive

A leading narrative in the separation of powers literature of the past several decades is the rise of executive power. Calling the executive 'the most dangerous branch'[10] and declaring that the executive 'subsumes much of the tripartite structure of government',[11] commentators have suggested that the three branches have become unbalanced, with the executive exercising a predominant, and often unchecked, role. Central to this story is the emergence of the administrative state. Since the New Deal, administrative agencies have carried out vast amounts of highly discretionary policymaking under broad delegations from Congress. They make rules under open-ended directives, such as setting air quality standards 'requisite to protect the public health',[12] and conduct adjudications under equally open-ended directives, such as granting licences 'if public convenience, interest, or necessity will be served thereby'.[13] Even when Congress delineates agencies' substantive mandates more particularly, they retain significant enforcement discretion, effectively allowing them to shape the content of federal law.[14]

But the very expansion of federal executive responsibility has meant incorporating the states into the executive apparatus. Especially as federal administrative authority extends to areas traditionally regulated by the states, Congress has turned to the states to help implement and enforce federal law.[15] When states disagree with the executive branch about how to carry out the law, they therefore have substantial authority to further a distinct vision.

Sometimes, as with Clean Air Act waivers, states may diverge from executive branch policy within the limits set by Congress and instantiate a different version

[10] Martin Flaherty, 'The Most Dangerous Branch' (1996) 105 *Yale Law Journal* 1725; see also, eg, Abner S Greene, 'Checks and Balances in an Era of Presidential Lawmaking' (1994) 61 *University of Chicago Law Review* 123, 125 ('[T]he framers' factual assumptions have been displaced. Now it is the President whose power has expanded and who therefore needs to be checked').

[11] Neal Kumar Katyal, 'Internal Separation of Powers: Checking Today's Most Dangerous Branch from Within' (2006) 115 *Yale Law Journal* 2314, 2316; see also, eg, Bruce Ackerman, *The Decline and Fall of the American Republic* (Cambridge, Mass, Belknapp Press, 2010); Peter M Shane, *Madison's Nightmare. How Executive Power Threatens American Democracy* (Chicago, University of Chicago Press, 2009); Cynthia R Farina, 'Statutory Interpretation and the Balance of Power in the Administrative State' (1989) 89 *Columbia Law Review* 452, 523; William P Marshall, 'Eleven Reasons Why Presidential Power Inevitably Expands and Why It Matters' (2008) 88 *Boston University Law Review* 505, 506.

[12] 42 USC § 7409(b)(1) (2006). These rules dwarf the volume of traditional legislation. See Peter L Strauss, '*Overseer, or "The Decider"? The President in Administrative Law*' (2007) 75 *The George Washington Law Review* 696, 752 ('[A]gencies adopt roughly ten times as many rules each year as Congress adopts statutes').

[13] 47 USC § 307 (2006).

[14] See, eg, JR DeShazo and Jody Freeman, 'The Congressional Competition to Control Delegated Power' (2003) 81 *Texas Law Review* 1443, 1453.

[15] See, eg, above note 5 and accompanying text.

of federal law.[16] In such cases, there may not be a direct conflict between state and federal implementation. The very coexistence of state and federal variants of a single federal program, however, means the federal executive's control over the federal law is limited, and visibly so.

In other instances, states may interfere with the federal executive's ability to carry out federal law as it chooses. Whereas states' power to diverge from federal executive policy stems from their ability to regulate more or less independently of the executive, their power to curb the executive stems from its inability to regulate independently of them. For example, states were able to halt Social Security disability reviews when the Reagan Administration sought to terminate many individuals' benefits because states were tasked with making the initial disability determinations.[17]

Finally, states may use the authority granted to them in cooperative federalism schemes to push the federal executive to take certain actions it otherwise would not have. States may, for instance, goad the federal executive into bringing enforcement actions it had declined to pursue or to implement a program more aggressively.[18]

The check cooperative federalism schemes furnish on executive power operates even when Congress has delegated broadly. When Congress enacts an open-ended provision and grants administrative authority only to the federal executive, the latter's power is at its height. But when Congress grants administrative authority to both the states and the federal executive, an open-ended grant of authority may instead stimulate competition by empowering states to challenge the federal executive. The open-endedness of administrative authority, that is, may confer discretion not only on the federal executive but also on the states, and the states may use their discretion to advance a different version of federal policy than the executive branch. In fact, as discussed below,[19] the broader the delegation, or the more ambiguous the statute, the more room there may be for states to contest federal executive power.

B. Championing Congressional Authority

Cooperative federalism schemes do not affect the federal executive's power in isolation, but rather vis-à-vis Congress. In some sense, any challenge to the executive alters the balance of power across the branches of the federal government: simply by constraining federal executive power, state administration of federal law affects the relative power of the executive and Congress. But cooperative federalism schemes also influence the relationship between the federal legislative and executive branches

[16] See also, eg, State Occupational Safety and Health Plans, US Department of Labor, <www.osha.gov/dcsp/osp/index.html> (showing that in roughly half the states, a federal agency implements the Occupational Safety and Health Act, while in the other half, the states implement the Act).

[17] See Bulman-Pozen, 'Federalism as a Safeguard of the Separation of Powers' 482–83.

[18] See, eg, Margaret H Lemos, 'State Enforcement of Federal Law' (2011) 86 *New York University Law Review* 698, 743–44 (describing how New York's attorney general nudged the EPA to bring a suit against coal-burning power plants under a provision of the Clean Air Act that the EPA had not previously sought to use). See generally Bulman-Pozen, 'Federalism as a Safeguard of the Separation of Powers' 478–86.

[19] See below nn 40–48 and accompanying text.

more directly, as states challenging the federal executive champion congressional authority in two closely related respects.

First, states rely on their federal statutory authority to launch their challenges. Their role in checking federal executive power is thus surprising from the perspective of traditional accounts of federalism. Such accounts suggest that states' strongest claims follow from their status as separate sovereigns. Yet in cooperative federalism schemes, states effectively relinquish arguments from their position as autonomous entities and instead press arguments based on their congressionally conferred authority. Rather than rely on their sovereign status to challenge the federal government as a whole, states rely on the power granted to them by one part of the federal government, the legislature, to contest the power of another part, the executive. Their opposition comes from inside the federal scheme rather than purely outside it.

Second, when state and federal policies clash, states cast themselves as faithful agents of Congress, seeking to carry out a statute as Congress intended, in contrast to a rebellious federal executive branch. States therefore not only owe their ability to contest federal executive policy to Congress in the first instance, but also take up Congress's mantle as they spar with the federal executive, emphasising the primacy of the legislative branch.

When a state and the federal executive disagree about how to execute federal law, the state's strongest claim of right comes from an appeal to the underlying statute. It is immaterial what is actually driving state resistance. Just as Congress includes states in statutory schemes for many reasons not related to checking the federal executive,[20] so, too, state actors fight with the federal executive for many reasons not related to ensuring that the President is satisfying his obligation to 'take Care that the Laws be faithfully executed'[21]—appealing to voter interests in the state, safeguarding budgets, generating a name for themselves in national politics. But whatever the reason they challenge federal executive policy, it will be in state actors' interest to cast their resistance in terms of fidelity to the statute because as a legal matter states can only trump the federal executive by invoking Congress.[22]

When California has applied for waivers under the Clean Air Act, for example, it has frequently suggested that the Act requires stronger regulation than the EPA is providing. In seeking to regulate greenhouse gas emissions, it argued that the Bush Administration had abdicated its statutory duty to do so and the state was thus vindicating congressional intent. Arizona similarly presented its bid to aggressively enforce federal immigration law as vindicating congressional intent against an executive branch bent on underenforcing the law.

[20] While Congress may create cooperative federalism schemes because it trusts state administrators more than the federal executive branch, it more often turns to the states for practical reasons: because they have relevant expertise; because they have in place an administrative apparatus that the federal government lacks; because relying on states will be cheaper or will foster experimentation; because states can be 'force multipliers' that amplify enforcement of federal law; because congressional delegations fight to protect existing state programs from federal preemption; or because of a more diffuse interest in devolution.

[21] US Constitution, art II, § 3.

[22] To be sure, states may also challenge the underlying statute. See, eg, *National Federation of Independent Business v Sebelius* 132 S Ct 2566 (2012). But when states accept the constitutionality of federal regulation, as they more often do, they can only trump the federal executive by invoking Congress.

When a state argues that it is Congress's superior agent, this forces the federal executive to do the same. In any given case, either the state or the federal executive may in fact have a stronger claim of fidelity. In other words, the state does not actually need to be Congress's faithful agent. What matters is that, with two agents, each is pushed to claim Congress's mantle. Sometimes, a court will then decide which agent has the better argument.[23] But even in the absence of such judicial settlement, the dispute between a state and the federal executive forces both to attend to the underlying law. Counteracting the tendency of federal statutes to take on a life of their own in the executive branch, the resulting competition between Congress's two agents can restore the focus of administration to Congress and the initial grant of statutory authority.

The litigation concerning Arizona's immigration law offers a vivid example of how each of the legislature's two agents may strive to present itself as the superior agent. To stop Arizona's challenge, the federal executive branch sued, arguing that the state law was preempted. But this required the federal executive to justify its enforcement policy, and in particular the ways in which it does not enforce the immigration laws to their fullest extent, with reference to Congress's purposes. The resulting legal battle was a contest between the federal executive and Arizona to establish which was truer to congressional intent. The federal executive argued that its enforcement priorities were consistent with the legislature's purposes. Arizona, meanwhile, argued that the federal executive was betraying Congress by under-enforcing the federal immigration laws. Supported by some members of Congress and several other states as amici, the state insisted that its law advanced the congressional design and served as a needed corrective to a willful executive.[24]

As the Arizona litigation demonstrates, the states and federal executive need not be evenly matched to engage in meaningful contests. States are at best junior partners in enforcing federal immigration law.[25] And the Supreme Court in *Arizona v United States* sided with the federal executive branch over the state.[26] But the very fact that the federal executive had to sue and publicly defend its enforcement decisions was a notable departure from plenary executive discretion. Because Congress has given

[23] See below nn 36–38 and accompanying text.

[24] See, eg, Appellants' Opening Brief at 1–2, *United States v Arizona* 641 F 3d 339 (9th Cir 2010) (No 10-16645); see also Brief of Amici Curiae of Members of Congress Brian Bilbray et al at 3, *United States v Arizona* 641 F 3d 339 (9th Cir 2010) (No 10-16645) ('The heart of the Administration's claims against sections 2 and 3 of S.B. 1070 is that those provisions seek to enforce federal provisions that the Executive chooses either not to enforce, or to enforce selectively.'); Brief of Amici Curiae States of Michigan et al at 8, *Arizona*, 641 F 3d 339 (No 10-16645) ('[A] State enforcing Congress's intent too well cannot violate Congress's intent'). The Supreme Court vindicated the federal executive branch, though Justice Scalia's dissent embraced the state's argument. See *Arizona v United States* 132 S Ct 2492, 2521 (2012) (Scalia J dissenting) ('[T]o say, as the Court does, that Arizona *contradicts federal law* by enforcing applications of the Immigration Act that the President declines to enforce boggles the mind').

[25] See, eg, 8 USC § 1357(g)(3) (2006) (providing that state officers' performance of various immigration functions 'shall be subject to the direction and supervision of the Attorney General').

[26] The Court's decision holding most of the controversial provisions of Arizona's law rested on the view that Congress intended the federal executive to set enforcement priorities. See below n 43 and accompanying text.

states a role in enforcing immigration law, Arizona was in a privileged position to contest federal executive decisions and to force the executive to explain its actions in terms of the legislative grant of authority.

More generally, by giving two different actors some role in a statutory scheme, whether or not these roles are identical or commensurate, Congress bakes competition into the scheme. Each agent has the incentive and ability to monitor the other and, when they disagree, to claim that it is the superior agent of Congress. The virtues of empowering two agents are touted in the administrative law literature concerning overlapping delegations of power by Congress to multiple federal administrative agencies. Here, too, commentators argue, competition can help keep administration focused on the underlying statute.[27] But to the extent one is concerned about the eclipse of federal legislative authority by executive authority, states may be superior co-agents. When Congress divides authority across two or more federal agencies, these agencies answer to two principals, Congress and the President, and the President is usually the stronger principal. One of the President's greatest claims of authority over the administrative state is the responsibility to reconcile overlapping and interdependent provisions of federal law,[28] and when federal agencies are fighting, this authority is at its height. Granting two different executive branch agencies authority to administer a statute may therefore increase the likelihood that the President will drive federal policy.[29] Furnishing authority to the federal executive and the states does not similarly enhance presidential power because the states do not answer to the President. The only principal the states and the federal executive branch have in common in such schemes (besides the ultimate principal, the people) is Congress, so their competition revolves around Congress.

There may be something particularly fitting about the way cooperative federalism furthers congressional authority. Congress is the branch of the federal government designed to represent state interests.[30] When states rely on powers granted to them by Congress to champion congressional authority, the relationship comes full circle. We therefore see a variation on the classic political safeguards of federalism argument: if Herbert Wechsler and his followers suggest members of Congress use congressional authority to safeguard federalism, the argument here suggests members

[27] See, eg, Jacob E Gersen, 'Overlapping and Underlapping Jurisdiction in Administrative Law' (2006) *Supreme Court Review* 201, 212.

[28] See Terry M Moe and William G Howell, 'The Presidential Power of Unilateral Action' (1999) 15 *Journal of Law, Economics, and Organization* 132, 143 ('The president's proper role ... is to rise above a myopic focus on each statute in isolation ... and to resolve statutory conflicts by balancing their competing requirements. All of this affords him enormous discretion to impose his own priorities on government unilaterally ...').

[29] See Jody Freeman and Jim Rossi, 'Agency Coordination in Shared Regulatory Space' (2012) 125 *Harvard Law Review* 1131; *cf* Rachel E Barkow, 'Insulating Agencies: Avoiding Capture Through Institutional Design' (2010) 89 *Texas Law Review* 15, 52 (noting that Congress may grant an administrative role to multiple agencies to increase the costs of presidential coordination and control).

[30] See, eg, *McCulloch v Maryland* 17 US 316, 435 (1819); *The Federalist Papers* Nos 45, 46, pp 294, 298–99 (James Madison); Herbert Wechsler, 'The Political Safeguards of Federalism: The Role of the States in the Composition and Selection of the National Government' (1954) 54 *Columbia Law Review* 543, 546–52.

of Congress, whether deliberately or incidentally, may use federalism to safeguard congressional authority.

C. Reinvigorating Horizontal Checks

In addition to restoring the focus of administration to the underlying law, cooperative federalism schemes may also engage Congress and the courts in administrative oversight, thereby reinvigorating horizontal checks and balances within the federal government. As many have noted, Congress frequently oversees administrative action by relying on interested parties to bring concerns to its attention.[31] States charged with partially administering a federal scheme are in an especially good position to sound such 'fire alarms' because they have the incentive, opportunity, and expertise to monitor federal executive action and the ability to get Congress to listen to them.

States have a strong incentive to monitor the federal executive branch insofar as its actions affect their own ability to carry out desired policies. In many instances, such monitoring is simply the by-product of a state attempt to administer federal law as the state would like. No extra effort was required for California to notice that the Bush Administration was not regulating greenhouse gases or for Arizona to notice that the Obama Administration was not enforcing immigration laws to their fullest possible extent.

Because they are embedded in the statutory scheme, states also have a privileged opportunity to furnish Congress with information about the executive branch's administration of a statute. For instance, Arizona's officers who are deputised to help carry out federal immigration law have firsthand knowledge about how the executive enforces the law. A frequent obstacle to effective congressional oversight of executive branch action is a lack of information. In extreme cases, the President's control over information and assertions of privilege may limit the ability of Congress to engage in oversight at all.[32] But even when there is not a concerted effort by the executive to withhold information from Congress, it may be difficult for legislators to find a toehold that facilitates effective oversight or provides a basis for corrective legislation. When they are embedded within a statutory scheme, states have a good opportunity to collect such information. Closely related, states often have expertise that helps them to frame information about the administration of federal law for non-specialist legislators. When California adopted regulations for greenhouse gas emissions, for example, it could furnish specific, expert information about how such regulations would work.[33]

[31] See, eg, Mathew D McCubbins and Thomas Schwartz, 'Congressional Oversight Overlooked: Police Patrols Versus Fire Alarms' (1984) 28 *American Journal of Political Science* 165, 166–67.

[32] Marshall, 'Eleven Reasons Why Presidential Power Inevitably Expands and Why It Matters' 520.

[33] See, eg, State Agency Greenhouse Gas Reduction Report Card, <www.climatechange.ca.gov/climate_action_team/reports/2012_CalEPA_Report_Card.pdf>.

States are able not only to monitor federal executive action, but also to make persuasive appeals to Congress. One need not endorse the political safeguards of federalism theory with respect to judicial review[34] to appreciate that state actors may make especially strong entreaties to the members of Congress charged with representing their interests. Because of the ties that bind state actors and their congressional representatives, state actors are likely to have their concerns taken seriously. And when these ties are not enough, states' special ability to appeal to the public and the media helps them to get legislators' attention.

States may also be able to engage a different group of legislators than might pay attention to a particular agency's action in the normal course. A common concern about congressional oversight is that only one part of the legislature, a committee or sub-committee, will follow agency action, and this committee or sub-committee may have different views from Congress as a whole.[35] If state actors take issue with the federal executive's administration of the law, however, they may complain to their state representatives regardless of those representatives' committee assignments.

In addition to calling on Congress to mediate disputes between states and the federal executive, states may turn to the courts as external arbiters and, in so doing, spur judicial review of executive decisions. Because of their resources, political might, and access to information about the administration of a statutory scheme, states are more formidable opponents than most litigants suing the federal executive. They are also better positioned to overcome doctrinal hurdles. When they are included in federal statutory schemes, states have standing to sue—often an insurmountable barrier for would-be litigants.[36] So too, states seeking to regulate in the face of federal executive inaction can circumvent doctrinal limits on judicial review of agency inaction. California, for instance, brought suit challenging the EPA's denial of the state's ability to regulate greenhouse gas emissions pursuant to a Clean Air Act waiver. Even though resolving this question would necessarily implicate the federal agency's own refusal to regulate, judicial review was available because the court was asked to examine an action taken by the agency, its decision to deny the waiver.

The ability of states that are included in federal statutory schemes to effectively force judicial review of federal executive inaction is also apparent in the case of Arizona's immigration law. Here, it was the federal executive that sued to enjoin the state law. But as part of its preemption argument, the executive had to explain

34 See, eg, Wechsler, 'The Political Safeguards of Federalism: The Role of the States in the Composition and Selection of the National Government' (arguing that judicial review of federalism questions is largely unnecessary because the states are protected by Congress).

35 See, eg, DeShazo & Freeman, 'The Congressional Competition to Control Delegated Power'.

36 In *Massachusetts v EPA*, the Supreme Court recognised broad state standing, citing its 'special solicitude' for state interests: 549 US 497, 520 (2007). But even without a special doctrine of state standing, states that are suing to vindicate their role in a federal statutory scheme will necessarily have standing. For instance, when the EPA rejected California's request for a waiver to regulate greenhouse gas emissions, the state's standing to challenge that waiver denial was not questioned. (In the end, the dispute between the state and the federal agency was resolved outside the courts when the presidency changed hands.)

why its enforcement priorities were consistent with federal law. Typically, this sort of question is not justiciable; an agency's priorities and the manner in which it marshals its resources to carry out federal law are issues courts eschew.[37] These issues effectively become justiciable, however, when Congress gives the states a role in the federal scheme, thereby at least arguably depriving the executive branch of its monopoly over enforcement decisions.

III. FRACTAL SEPARATION OF POWERS

Beyond altering the relationship of the federal legislative and executive branches, cooperative federalism schemes also reproduce certain separation of powers dynamics within the realm of administration. The dramatic growth of the administrative state since the New Deal thus presents not only a separation of powers problem but also the seed of a solution: separation of powers values may be furthered within the domain of a single branch. The benefits of divided representation typically associated with the split of authority across several branches may be realised within the executive's domain alone precisely because it has expanded to include the states as well as the federal executive.[38] We might term this reproduction of separation of powers values within a single branch's domain *fractal separation of powers*.

A. Competition

The primary separation of powers principle that cooperative federalism reproduces in the realm of administration is competition among government actors. The Madisonian model of ambition counteracting ambition depends on the federal legislature and executive checking one another. But, as many have noted, we do not always see vigorous competition between these branches of government.[39] Broad delegations by Congress to the executive branch are a particular concern. As this chapter has argued, state administration of federal law may be salutary in the case of such delegations insofar as state and federal administrators keep each other focused on the underlying statute and Congress's purposes. But there are decided limits to this. Most notably, sometimes Congress's intent will simply be that its delegate, the

[37] See, eg, *Heckler v Chaney* 470 US 821, 827–35 (1985) (describing agency decisions not to pursue enforcement action as presumptively unreviewable).

[38] For arguments that separation of powers values may be furthered within the federal executive branch itself, see Katyal, 'Internal Separation of Powers: Checking Today's Most Dangerous Branch from Within'; Mary Elizabeth Magill, 'Beyond Powers and Branches in Separation of Powers Law' (2001) 150 *University of Pennsylvania Law Review* 603.

[39] See, eg, sources cited in nn 10–11; see also Daryl J Levinson and Richard H Pildes, 'Separation of Parties, Not Powers' (2006) 119 *Harvard Law Review* 2311 (arguing that whether competition exists between the federal executive and legislative branches depends on whether these branches are party-divided or party-unified).

federal executive, make the hard decisions. In these instances, the very feature that leads to executive aggrandisement also complicates efforts to bound executive power with reference to congressional intent.

The Clean Air Act, for example, confers substantial discretion on the executive branch, providing that regulation should ensue when in the EPA Administrator's 'judgment' emissions 'cause or contribute to air pollution which may reasonably be anticipated to endanger public health or welfare.'[40] Executive discretion is also pronounced in the realm of immigration given that enforcement questions are by default subject to the executive's policy choices, resource allocation, and case-by-case judgments.[41] Indeed, the Supreme Court's decision in *Arizona v United States* rests on the view that Congress intended the federal executive to set enforcement priorities so that federal legislative and executive choices cannot be parsed in the way the state argued.[42]

Coming up against the limits of traditional separation of powers analysis, state administration of federal law in these cases does not so much influence the relationship of the federal executive and legislative branches as generate, at one remove, the competition that is lacking between these branches. This competition is best understood as fractal because it occurs within the domain of the executive, not between the legislature and the executive, but it still concerns federal law. And, even though it plays out in the administrative realm, such competition is often highly visible. Media nationwide, for instance, reported on California's challenge to the federal executive's environmental policy and Arizona's challenge to its immigration policy. Seizing on the very open-endedness of the congressional grants with respect to air pollution and immigration, states showcased other plausible interpretations of federal law and forced the executive branch to defend its chosen course of action. Such state competition with the federal executive recreates the benefits of fractured representation posited for the three branches of government within the sphere of administration.[43]

If Congress cannot be counted on to contest exercises of federal executive power, however, why can the states? Not, as traditional federalism scholarship might

[40] 42 USC § 7408(a)(1)(A) (2006); see, eg, *Whitman v American Trucking Associations, Inc* 531 US 457, 472 (2001) (considering but rejecting a nondelegation challenge to the Clean Air Act). *Cf Massachusetts v EPA* 549 US 497 (2007) (holding that the EPA has authority under the Clean Air Act to regulate greenhouse gas emissions and must decide whether to regulate such emissions based on whether they contribute to climate change, not other prudential and policy considerations).

[41] See, eg, *Heckler v Chaney* 470 US 821, 827–35 (1985) (describing executive branch decisions not to pursue enforcement action as presumptively unreviewable). In such cases, power is not necessarily the result of a decision by Congress to delegate broadly, but often the absence of any decision by Congress to limit executive discretion. Ibid at 833 ('Congress may limit an agency's exercise of enforcement power if it wishes, either by setting substantive priorities, or by otherwise circumscribing an agency's power to discriminate among issues or cases it will pursue.').

[42] See *Arizona v United States* 132 S Ct 2492 (2012); see also Adam B Cox, 'Enforcement Redundancy and the Future of Immigration Law' (2012) *Supreme Court Review* 31, 33 (noting that the *Arizona* decision endorses 'the idea that immigration law is centrally the product of executive "lawmaking"').

[43] See generally Bruce Ackerman, *We The People. Foundations* (Cambridge, Mass, Belknap Press, 1993) 183–86 (arguing that each branch represents the people in a different and partial way and such fragmented representation ensures no single branch can unproblematically claim the mantle of the people).

suggest, because states reliably advance distinctive state interests against the federal government's national ones. Instead, the same phenomenon that has overwhelmed the branch affiliation of federal actors—partisanship—is key. If party politics sometimes amplifies and sometimes mutes competition within the federal government depending on whether the legislative and executive branches are party-divided or party-unified,[44] it reliably generates competition between state and federal actors. When Congress grants the states a role in administering federal law, it does not just empower one state, but, in most instances, all of the states, and because there will never be party unity among the federal government and 50 states, some states can always be counted on to disagree with federal policy.[45]

The central role of partisanship underscores that state challenges to the federal executive tend not to advance particularistic state interests against national interests but rather one set of national partisan interests against another set of national partisan interests. For this reason, states challenging the federal executive usually find supporters and detractors at both the state and federal levels. When California fought with the Bush Administration about the regulation of greenhouse gas emissions, for instance, the state advocated approaches to regulation that had previously been broached by Democrats in Congress; Senate and House Democrats, in turn, supported California's waiver application. The cleavage was primarily partisan—Democrats wanted to regulate greenhouse gas emissions and Republicans did not. But this partisan fight played out in federalist terms because California's role in the statutory scheme gave it a unique set of tools.

So too, the fight between Arizona and the Obama Administration was a partisan one. Republicans at both the state and federal level sided with Arizona, while Democrats at both the state and federal level sided with the Administration. But again, the state was a critical player because it could take actions that federal politicians could not. Arizona passed its own law and forced a confrontation with the federal executive branch instead of simply stating an opposing view on the floor of Congress.

State administration of federal law thus harnesses the power of partisanship to offer competing visions of national policy within the realm of administration. While separation of powers scholars concerned about partisanship's muting of intragovernmental competition have argued that we should try to prevent strong parties from taking hold,[46] cooperative federalism is a more realistic way of fostering competition because it follows from strong parties instead of resisting them. Focusing on administration as a locus for addressing the perils of party-unified government, this approach seeks not to reduce the power of parties but rather to fight partisanship with partisanship. In this sense, cooperative federalism schemes might be considered

[44] See Levinson and Pildes, 'Separation of Parties, Not Powers'.

[45] Some states can also be counted on to agree with federal policy. As partisanship trumps actors' state or federal affiliation, it generates both opponents and allies for the federal executive. See generally Jessica Bulman-Pozen, 'Partisan Federalism' (2014) 127 *Harvard Law Review* 1077 (exploring how political actors use state and federal governments to articulate, stage, and amplify competition between the political parties).

[46] See Levinson and Pildes, 'Separation of Parties, Not Powers' 2379–85.

a sort of merging of two proposed institutional responses to party-unified federal government: creating minority opposition rights within the bureaucracy.[47]

B. Separation

State administration of federal law may reproduce not only competition but also an actual separation of powers in the realm of administration. It is commonplace to assert that the power to make the law must be separated from the power to execute it,[48] but the rise of the administrative state poses a well-recognised challenge to this tenet. Much of the policymaking done by federal agencies looks a lot like lawmaking, and these same agencies then implement the law. There are, to be sure, administrative responses to this problem—for instance, separating functions within agencies or across agencies.[49] But the commingling of powers within the executive branch nonetheless raises important questions about how separate these separate powers really are.

Cooperative federalism reintroduces separation in some cases, generating a meaningful division between policymaking and execution within the administrative domain. In particular, certain schemes assign a policymaking function to the federal executive and an execution function to the states. The United States' major environmental statutes, for instance, charge the EPA with establishing pollution standards—a type of policymaking we might consider analogous to lawmaking—but states then craft implementation plans and administer these standards.[50] Similarly some conditional grant schemes contemplate that the states will distribute benefits pursuant to regulations issued by federal agencies.[51] While these divisions of authority generally

[47] ibid 2368–79 (proposing minority opposition rights and insulating the bureaucracy); see also Bulman-Pozen and Gerken, 'Uncooperative Federalism' 1286–87 (discussing the 'federalist safeguards of administration'); David Fontana, 'Government in Opposition' (2009) 119 *Yale Law Journal* 548 (exploring regimes in which substantial governance authority is granted to the losers of elections). The fractal metaphor may be especially appropriate when it comes to partisanship, moreover, because there often will not be party unity within states. In the sub-realm of state administration of federal law, there may be competition over which actor, say a Democratic legislature or a Republican governor, gets to set policy or control an agency responsible for carrying out federal law. There may also be competition within the state executive branch if a state agency is headed by an elected official rather than a gubernatorial appointee and this official is from a different party than the governor. Thus, competition may inflect not only administrative decisions made by both the states and federal executive branch, but also the subset of decisions made by the state. *Cf* Jim Rossi, 'Dual Constitutions and Constitutional Duels: Separation of Powers and State Implementation of Federally Inspired Regulatory Programs and Standards' (2005) 46 *William & Mary Law Review* 1343 (considering state separation of powers issues arising in cooperative federalism schemes).

[48] See, eg, Bruce Ackerman, 'The New Separation of Powers' (2000) 113 *Harvard Law Review* 633, 686 ('The power to make laws must be separated from the power to implement them. If politicians are allowed to breach this barrier, the result will be tyranny. Although we may pretty this conclusion up with a citation from Madison or Montesquieu, it is simple common sense').

[49] See, eg, 5 USC § 554(d); *Martin v Occupational Safety and Health Review Commission* 499 US 144, 155 (1991) ('It is clear that Congress adopted the split-enforcement structure in the OSH Act in order to achieve a greater separation of functions than exists in a conventional unitary agency.').

[50] See 33 USC §§ 1316, 1318(c), 1342 (2006); 42 USC §§ 7409–7411 (2006).

[51] See, eg, 42 USC § 1396a(a) (2006) (Medicaid).

do not reflect a perfect separation between the power to set policy and the power to execute it, they approximate it, and, from a separation of powers perspective, an approximation may still be valuable. Indeed, even in the ideal constitutional rendering, the division between legislative and executive power is not a clean one; the very basis for the checks and balances that lie at the heart of the American system of separation is granting each branch a small piece of another's authority.[52]

By establishing some basic separation between policymaking and execution, cooperative federalism may mitigate concerns about the consolidation of lawmaking and executive power within the federal executive branch. In this sense, the very capaciousness of the administrative state again generates its own solution to the consolidation of power: discrete powers that are merged in a single branch of the federal government may also be meaningfully divided if multiple actors, with different bases of authority, carry out that branch's functions.

In other instances, cooperative federalism schemes may further a distinct vision of the separation of powers by restoring the role of legislators as policymakers. Even if the intuition that separation guards against tyranny is sound, it does not dictate how powers should be separated.[53] One argument for a functional distribution is that certain types of powers are best matched with certain types of decisionmakers. Legislative power may be entrusted to Congress so that policy is set by a deliberative body whose members are subject to frequent yet staggered election cycles that make them responsive to the people; executive power may be vested in the President to further unified, efficient administration by an elected officer; and judicial power may be granted to judges who have lifetime tenure and salary protections to ensure their independence.[54]

Such normative matchmaking sits uneasily with the rise of the administrative state. And this is not only a concern if we regard bureaucrats as composing a fourth, headless branch. Even if the bureaucracy is squarely within the executive branch and under the President's control, the extent to which it engages in policymaking upsets the assignment of this function to legislators. In some cases, cooperative federalism may push against this mismatch by restoring legislative control over policymaking—in the form of state legislation. Although Congress sometimes attempts to cut state legislators out of the implementation of federal law—for instance by imposing a 'single agency' requirement that forces state governments to house responsibility for

[52] For example, the Constitution provides that the President may participate in lawmaking with his veto and that the House and Senate may exercise executive and judicial roles, respectively, in the impeachment process. See generally *The Federalist Papers*, No 47, 303–304 (James Madison) (arguing that the separation of powers concern is not that each branch have no 'partial agency' in the acts of the others but rather that the 'whole power' of one branch not be exercised by another).

[53] We can imagine, for instance, dividing authority not by function but by subject matter. See Jacob E Gersen, 'Unbundled Powers' (2010) 96 *Virginia Law Review* 301 (comparing the separation of functions with 'the unbundled powers alternative, multiple branches exercising combined functions in topically limited domains').

[54] See David P Currie, 'The Distribution of Powers After *Bowsher*' (1986) *Supreme Court Review* 19, 19; see also Magill, 'Beyond Powers and Branches in Separation of Powers Law' 624–25 (exploring, though ultimately rejecting, this approach).

administering the program in a specialist agency[55]—in many cases, state legislators retain substantial authority over the law's implementation, and they may wield this authority to make policy decisions. It was, for example, California's legislature that directed the state Air Resources Board to promulgate regulations concerning greenhouse gas emissions under the Clean Air Act,[56] precisely the sort of controversial, norm-setting type of decision that critics of the administrative state would argue should be made by deliberative, democratically responsive legislators.

As this example illustrates, cooperative federalism schemes do not rematch policymaking with Congress; rather, they may empower Congress's state-level counterparts to make policy decisions concerning federal law. But if one is concerned about certain kinds of decision makers making certain kinds of decisions, state legislators may stand in for members of Congress. They, too, are subject to frequent and staggered election cycles that make them democratically responsive; indeed, they arguably have the stronger claim to responsiveness given that each of them represents fewer individuals.[57] Especially inasmuch as one is focused on the relative power of the popular constituencies represented by each branch of the federal government,[58] then, state legislatures may serve as well as federal ones.

IV. CONCLUSION

In the United States, this chapter has argued, states check federal executive power in an era of expansive executive power, and they do so as champions of Congress, both relying on congressionally conferred authority and casting themselves as Congress's faithful agents. When they disagree with the federal executive about how to administer federal law, states force attention back to the underlying statute: contending that their approach is consistent with Congress's purposes, states compel the federal executive to respond in kind. Cooperative federalism schemes not only affect the relationship of the federal executive and legislative branches but also reproduce separation of powers values in the realm of administration. In particular, such

[55] See, eg, 42 USC § 1902(a)(5) (Medicaid); see also Roderick M Hills, Jr , 'Dissecting the State: The Use of Federal Law To Free State and Local Officials from State Legislatures' Control' (1999) 97 *Michigan Law Review* 1201 (considering the extent to which federal law may delegate power to state institutions against the will of the state legislature).

[56] Cal Assembly Bill No 1493 (2002).

[57] *cf* Christopher S Elmendorf and David Schleicher, 'Informing Consent: Voter Ignorance, Political Parties, and Election Law' (2013) *University of Illinois Law Review* 363, 393–408 (arguing that voters rely on their national partisan preferences in state elections and do not attend to state politics). Especially to the extent states are making decisions about the implementation of federal law, however, voters' focus on national politics may not be a concern. See generally Bulman-Pozen, 'Partisan Federalism' 1116–22 (suggesting that voters may reasonably express national political preferences in state elections).

[58] See *Clinton v New York* 524 US 417, 452 (1998) (Kennedy J concurring) ('Separation of powers operates on a vertical axis as well, between each branch and the citizens in whose interest powers must be exercised'); Victoria Nourse, 'The Vertical Separation of Powers' (1999) 49 *Duke Law Journal* 749, 766 (arguing that separation of powers questions must be understood in terms of the relative power of popular constituencies that create the three branches of government).

schemes reliably generate competition about federal law even when partisanship mutes disagreement within the federal government.

The account offered here describes a very different federal polity—and a very different federal idea—from the one evoked by classic conceptions of dual sovereignty. The key to appreciating contemporary American federalism, it suggests, is to recognise the integration of the state and federal governments, rather than to insist on the separation of one from the other. Such integration has significant consequences for the states and Washington alike.

First, states are frequently empowered by the federal government. In cooperative federalism schemes, state authority is not a pre-existing aspect of state sovereignty, nor is it threatened by the expansion of federal authority as such. Instead, state power is affirmatively granted by Congress. Departing from traditional understandings of federalism that posit state and federal authority as distinct and in tension, this account regards states not as independent sovereigns but as parts of an expansive system of national governance that incorporates both state and federal actors.

Second, and related, the federal government often lacks plenary control over federal law. In cooperative federalism schemes, the federal executive branch shares responsibility for implementing the law with the states. If the states are empowered by Congress in the first instance, so too do state actions shape the power of the branches of the federal government in turn. Departing from traditional understandings of the separation of powers that consider only the three branches of the federal government, this account maintains that checks and balances across the federal government are critically influenced by the states. The thoroughgoing integration of state and federal actors means that we cannot fully appreciate either federalism or the separation of powers in isolation. They have evolved to be not just analogous principles, but also deeply intertwined governance structures.

5

Federalism as a Mode of Governance: Autonomy, Identity, Power, and Rights

EDWARD L RUBIN

THE ENORMOUS INTEREST in federalism that both legal and political science scholarship have displayed in recent years can be said to border on obsession. People who are obsessed with a particular subject not only think about that subject frequently, but do so when they should be thinking about something else. Someone who is obsessed with food, for example, spends all of his or her time at sports events thinking about the snacks. The same is true of federalism. Federalism scholars not only discuss the subject when they are considering truly federal arrangements, but also when they are considering other, readily distinguished modes of governance.

Obsessions often lead to misfortune, and the federalism obsession is no exception. One obvious misfortune is conceptual confusion. If we use the term federalism to describe various types of unitary nations, we will have no way to distinguish between those nations and truly federal ones, and thus no convenient way of identifying a federal regime. A second misfortune is that we will exaggerate the advantages of federalism, ascribing to it benefits that flow from other sources. The third and converse misfortune is that we will tend to minimise the disadvantages and dangers of federalism, thereby recommending its implementation when there is no necessity to do so. These second and third types of misfortunes are political—not just conceptual—because federalism is not something that should be implemented casually or indiscriminately. It is akin to political surgery, and it is an inadvisable solution to ordinary problems of governance, just as brain surgery is an inadvisable solution for a headache.

We can free ourselves from the federalism obsession by recognising federalism's essential character. Despite contrary suggestions in the vast legal and political science literature on the subject, federalism is not an ideology, it is not a means of mobilisation, and it is not a path to political salvation. It is a particular mode of governance. Federalism is a grant of partial but permanent autonomy rights to geographically-defined sub-units of a nation-state. As such, it needs to be distinguished from other modes of governance that bear a superficial similarity to it because they also involve divisions or delegations of a nation's sovereign power. As Part I will describe, these other modes of governance that are frequently—and incorrectly—conflated with federalism include consociation, decentralisation and local democracy.

Once the nature of genuine federalism is identified, Part II will then discuss the reason why a nation might choose to adopt this particular modality. The litany of advantages that the scholarly literature ascribes to federalism would appear to make this discussion a mere statement of the obvious. Most of these advantages, however, are not actually attributable to federalism but to the other modes of governance with which federalism is conflated. Federalism itself is useful only in a limited number of situations, specifically those where the political identity of the nation's populace is divided, and divided along geographic lines.

Part III will explore the way power is actually shared in federal regimes. It first considers the structure of the regime, that is, the way the sub-units that are granted partial autonomy are identified. In doing so, it employs a distinction that is not generally used in the federalism literature: the distinction between particularised federalism, which grants autonomy to delimited regions in an otherwise unitary nation, and comprehensive federalism, where the entire nation is divided into sub-units that are granted partial autonomy. Part III then proceeds to consider the distribution of power within the regime, the specific subject matters that are allocated to the autonomous sub-units. Typically, the choice of subjects is determined by political identity, that is, those areas where the divergent political identity of the sub-units' inhabitants produce attitudes that differ from those of the nation in general.

The final section discusses the normative value of federalism. Having distinguished many of the usual arguments for federalism that in fact belong to other modes of governance, it considers the core claim that federalism protects liberty. Once again, the validity of this claim depends on the relationship between genuine federalism and political identity. Federalism can only serve to protect liberty in cases of divided political identity. In such cases, the rights it protects are not the ones that form the core of modern human rights theory, but rather the less well-established category of group, or third generation rights. Here again, federalism is revealed as a particular mode of governance with a particular and delimited role, not a salvation or a panacea.

I. THE ESSENCE OF FEDERALISM: PARTIAL POLITICAL AUTONOMY

Federalism, as Malcolm Feeley and I have previously noted, is a mode of governing a nation that grants partial autonomy to geographically defined sub-units or regions of the nation.[1] It thus represents an intermediate position between a unitary state and an alliance of separate ones. For this definition to apply, there must be some set of governmental decisions that are reserved to the sub-units and that the central government may not displace or countermand. As a result, federalism can be described by saying that the sub-units possess rights against the central government, provided that this emotionally charged discourse is employed with caution. In most contemporary regimes, it means that the sub-units can enforce the boundaries of

[1] Malcolm M Feeley and Edward L Rubin, *Federalism: Political Identity and Tragic Compromise* (Ann Arbor, Michigan University Press, 2008) 2–17; Edward L Rubin and Malcolm M Feeley, 'Federalism: Some Notes on a National Neurosis' (1994) 41 *University of California Law Review* 903.

their autonomy by bringing suit against the central government in independent courts. But characterising a sub-unit's autonomy in rights discourse does not necessarily imply that this autonomy is supported by the sorts of normative arguments that support the political rights of individuals. Any connection between federalism and individual rights must be determined by analysis, not declared by verbal fiat.

Once federalism is understood in this manner, it can be readily distinguished from several other modes of governance with which it is frequently conflated in scholarly discourse. These include consociation, managerial decentralisation and local democracy. Consociation, as that idea has been developed by Arend Lijphart, is a mode of governance that attempts to achieve stable democratic government in a heterogeneous and potentially fractious polity through power sharing and group autonomy.[2] Mechanisms of consociation include proportional representation, coalition government, and minority veto power. Although it bears some resemblance to federalism in its concern with a heterogeneous polity, consociation differs from federalism in at least two basic ways. First, the groups that consociation protects can be, and often are, geographically dispersed, like African-Americans and Hispanics in the US, Muslims in India, or Christians in Lebanon. Second, the types of protections that consociation features give these groups an increased voice in national institutions, rather than autonomy over their own institutions. In other words, consociation protects groups that federalism cannot recognise, and in ways that federalism does not provide.

Decentralisation is a managerial device that allocates certain decisions to subsidiary units of an entity.[3] While it involves a grant of authority or decision making responsibility to the sub-unit, it differs from federalism because it does not involve any grant of autonomy. In political entities, this means that the central government determines the extent of the authority it wishes to confer and may cancel that authority in the future or countermand a particular decision by the sub-unit. Unlike federalism, which is used by some nations and not others, decentralisation is a basic management technique, like hierarchy or record-keeping, that is almost universally employed in institutional design.[4] Every nation larger than Monaco is decentralised to some extent.[5] So are most significantly sized corporations or non-profit organisations, universities and colleges, athletic leagues, religious institutions, and criminal organisations.

[2] Arend Lijphart, *Democracy in Plural Societies: A Comparative Exploration* (New Haven, Yale University Press, 1977); *Patterns of Democracy. Government Forms and Performance in Thirty-six Countries* (New Haven, Yale University Press, 1999).

[3] Feeley and Rubin, *Federalism* 20–29; Rubin and Feeley, 'Federalism: Some Notes on a National Neurosis'.

[4] Kenneth Arrow and Leonid Hurweiz, 'Decentralization and Computation in Resource Allocation' in Ralph Pfouts (ed), *Essays in Economics and Econometrics: A Volume in Honor of Harold Hotelling* (Chapel Hill, University of North Carolina, 1960) 34; Ernest Dale, *Organization* (New York, American Management Association, 1967) 104–30; Manfred Kochen and Karl Deutsch, *Decentralization. Sketches toward a Rational Theory* (Cambridge, Mass, Oelgeschlanger, Gunn & Hain, 1980); John Tomaney, 'A New Paradigm of Work Organization and Technology?' in Ash Amin (ed), *Post-Fordism* (Oxford, Blackwell, 1994) 157; Richard F Vancil, *Decentralization: Managerial Ambiguity by Design* (Homewood, Dow, Jones-Irwin, 1979).

[5] The only nation smaller than Monaco, which has an area of 0.76 square miles, is Vatican City, with an area of 0.2 square miles. San Marino, which measures 24 square miles, is divided into nine districts, called castelli. Liechtenstein, at 62 square miles, is divided into two regions, one with six communes and the other with five. Luxembourg, a whopping 999 square miles, has two basic levels of government

The tendency to conflate federalism and decentralisation is in part inadvertent and in part intentional. The inadvertent conflation results from the fact that both modalities empower subordinate components of the overall organisation. The intentional part results from the desire to claim for federalism the notable advantages of decentralisation, such as creating more manageably-sized institutions, bringing government closer to the people, enabling experimentation with innovative programs in delimited areas, allowing jurisdictions within the nation to compete for resources, or allowing individuals to choose between competing jurisdictions.[6] In fact, these are all unified policies, established by the central government, that use decentralisation as a means of implementation. If the decentralisation fails to achieve centrally-determined purposes, it will be reversed or re-designed. In contrast, the grant of autonomy that is the defining feature of federalism means that the sub-units can determine their own purposes, independent of those that the central government desires.

Finally, federalism should not be equated with local democracy. Neither side of the equation is correct. First, many unitary regimes choose sub-national officials by election. If the polity in general is a democracy, or even if it is not, the election of local officials may have certain advantages, such as giving people a sense of participation, choosing officials with ties to the locality, or (in a democracy) providing a means to identify potential leaders who can win national elections. For these advantages to be applicable, the local leaders must be given at least a modicum of authority, but they do not need to be given autonomy; their decisions can still be commanded, or countermanded, by the centre. To give an extreme example, in many American high schools, the students in each year's cohort elect a class president, but that person rarely possesses any independence from the school administration.

Conversely, dictatorships that do not allow any real elections can be federal regimes. Those who want to argue that federalism is organically linked to liberty may want to deny this, but to do so they must conflate totalitarianism and authoritarianism. As Hannah Arendt has pointed out, however, many authoritarian

(cantons and communes), like the cities and states in the United States (Thomas M Eccardt, *Secrets of the Seven Smallest States of Europe* (New York, Hippocrene, 2005)).

[6] Lynn A Baker, 'Should Liberals Fear Federalism?' (2002) 70 *University of Cincinnati Law Review* 433; Samuel Beer, *To Make a Nation. The Rediscovery of American Federalism* (Cambridge, Mass, Bellknap, 1993) 386–88; Charles Fried, 'Why Should We Care?' (1982) 6 *Harvard Journal of Law and Public Policy* 1; Lewis Kaden, 'Politics, Money and State Sovereignty: The Judicial Role' (1979) 79 *Columbia Law Review* 847; William Livingston, *Federalism and Constitutional Change* (Oxford, Clarendon, 1956) 7–10; Geoffrey Miller, 'Rights and Structure in Constitutional Theory' (1991) 8 *Social Philosophy & Policy* 205–209; Wallace Oates, *Fiscal Federalism* (New York, Harcourt, Brace, Jovanovich, 1972); Charles Tiebout, 'A Pure Theory of Local Expenditure' (1956) 64 *Journal of Political Economy* 416; Barry Weingast, 'The Economic Role of Political Institutions: Market-Preserving Federalism and Economic Development' (1995) 11 *Journal of Law, Economics, and Organizations* 1. All of these advantages of decentralisation, with the exception of creating more manageably-sized institutions, are prominently featured in Justice O'Connor's opinion for the court in *Gregory v Ashcroft* 501 US 452 (1991). Although strictly a statutory interpretation case, not a constitutional one, the decision in fact articulated the argument for federalism that has served as the basis for the US Supreme Court's subsequent, and otherwise under-explained constitutional decisions such as *United States v Lopez*, *Printz v United States*, and *New York v United States*. O'Connor's opinion also comports with much of the scholarly literature that champions federalism on similar, and similarly weak theoretical grounds.

regimes, unlike totalitarian ones, are based on law.[7] The mere fact that the leaders are chosen by some method other than popular election, such as heredity or designation, does not make them absolute and unconstrained. Medieval and Early Modern European monarchies, for example, were legally-bound regimes, and many can be considered federal, with noblemen possessing enforceable rights to rule geographically defined sub-units of the country.

It might even be possible for a totalitarian regime to be considered federal. To be sure, no one in such a regime can assert any rights against the ruler, but the ruler can grant regional authorities enforceable rights against everyone else, including other agents of the central government. Stalin, for example, granted considerable autonomy to the Soviet Union's constituent republics[8] and so long as he continued this policy (he abandoned it in the late 1930s), the regime can reasonably be regarded as federalised.

In other words, the federalist principle grants autonomy, either total or partially constrained, to geographically defined sub-regions. It says nothing about the way the government of either the centre or the sub-region should be chosen.

II. THE MOTIVATION FOR FEDERALISM: DIVERGENT POLITICAL IDENTITY

Once federalism is distinguished from consociation, decentralisation and local democracy, a basic question arises. The motivations for these other modes of government seem reasonably apparent, but why would anyone want to create a polity where geographical sub-units have partial autonomy from the centre, that is, autonomy with respect to certain issues but not others? It is an excessively complex arrangement and challenges established ideas about sovereignty and government control. One answer might be that a grant of autonomy makes consociation, decentralisation or local democracy-based governance mechanisms permanent or irreversible. But why would any polity want to do this? These mechanisms are all designed to achieve important political advantages. To make them permanent is to create the risk that they will remain in place when the advantages that they were designed to achieve have ceased to apply.

As Malcolm Feeley and I have previously discussed, the meaning and purpose of federalism are derived from basic issues of political identity.[9] They involve the way people conceive themselves in relation to others, and specifically to larger groups. Do they see themselves primarily as members of the nation in which they reside, as members of another nation, or as members of a distinct group that either crosses national boundaries or exists as a minority within a single nation? Perceptions of this sort are, of course, socially constructed, as Benedict Anderson has noted.[10] There is no

[7] Hannah Arendt, *Between Past and Future* (New York, Penguin Books, 1993) 96–97.

[8] Martin McCauley, *The Soviet Union: 1917–1991* (London, Longman, 1993) 111–27; Philip G Roeder, 'Soviet Federalism and Ethnic Mobilization' (1991) 43 *World Politics* 196.

[9] Feeley and Rubin, *Federalism* 7–12, 43–60.

[10] Benedict Anderson, *Imagined Communities: Reflections on the Origins and Spread of Nationalism* (London, Verso, 1983).

single factor, apart from the perceptions themselves, that determine people's sense of political identity.[11] In some cases, language can be determinative, but many different nations, some of which adjoin each other, speak the same language, such as the US and Canada, Peru and Ecuador, Algeria and Tunisia, or Germany and Austria, while other nations, such as India, China, Cameroon and Papua New Guinea maintain a national identity despite a multiplicity of languages.[12] This is also true for religion; the same two religions that split Ireland into separate regimes[13] produce no major difference in political identification in modern Canada or the US.[14] Ethnic differences within African post-colonial regimes have produced separatist movements in Nigeria and the Sudan, but not in Senegal, Cameroon or Tanzania.[15]

The reason a central government would agree to permanently relinquish some of its authority to a subordinate governmental unit is to satisfy a group of citizens who have a separate political identity and demand some sort of autonomy for the subordinate government that rules their region. Under these circumstances, federalism offers a way for a nation whose people have divided political identities to remain intact or to function effectively. It provides a pragmatic alternative to secession, oppression, or deep and continuous dissatisfaction. The reason any group of people within the society would expend their energy and political capital on such a challenging demand is that they possess a separate identity of this sort. In fact, group identity is probably essential for the political will formation that fuels demands for

[11] Frank Bechhofer and David McCrone (eds), *National Identity, Nationalism and Constitutional Change* (New York, Palgrave Macmillan, 2009); Manuel Castells, *The Information Age: Economy, Society and Culture: The Power of Identity* (Malden, Blackwell, 1997); James Fentriss and Chris Wickham, *Social Memory: New Perspectives on the Past* (Oxford, Blackwell, 1992) 87–143; Amin Maalouf, *In the Name of Identity: Violence and the Need to Belong* (New York, Penguin Books, 2000); Bernard Yack, *Nationalism and the Moral Psychology of Community* (Chicago, University of Chicago, 2012).

[12] There are some 500 Indo-Aryan languages spoken in north India and about 20 Dravidian languages, belonging to an entirely different linguistic family, spoken in south India (see David Crystal, *The Cambridge Encyclopedia of Language* (Cambridge, Cambridge University Press, 1987) 301, 308). Apart from numerous Altaic, Tai, Tibetic and Miao-Yao languages spoken by ethnic minorities in China, the Han Chinese majority speaks eight different languages, which use the same written form but are mutually unintelligible when spoken (ibid 307, 310–13). Most sub-Saharan African nations have a number of different languages (see Joseph Greenberg, *The Languages of Africa* (Bloomington, Research Center for the Language Sciences, 1970). In Cameroon, which is the size of California and has a population of about 20 million, over 200 different languages are spoken (see John Mukum Mbaku, *Culture and Customs of Cameroon* (Westport, Greenwood, 2005) 5, 14–15). Papua New Guinea, roughly the same size but with only about 6 million people, has over 600 languages (Crystal, *The Cambridge Encyclopedia of Language* 317).

[13] David Fitzpatrick, 'Ireland Since 1870' in Robert F Foster (ed), *The Oxford History of Ireland* (Oxford, Oxford University Press, 1989) 180–229; David McKittrick and David McVea, *Making Sense of the Troubles: The Story of Conflict in Northern Ireland* (Chicago, New Amsterdam, 2002); Claire Mitchell, *Religion, Identity and Politics in Northern Ireland: Boundaries of Belonging and Belief* (Aldershot, Ashgate, 2002).

[14] Steve Bruce, *God is Dead* (Malden, Blackwell, 2002) 31–36, 219–20; Will Herberg, *Protestant, Catholic, Jew* (New York, Anchor Books, 1955); Mark A Noll, *The Old Religion in a New World: The History of North American Christianity* (Grand Rapids; Wm B Eerdmans Publishing Co, 2002) 113–85.

[15] Michel Gould and Frederick Forsyth, *The Biafran War: The Struggle for Modern Nigeria* (London, IB Tauris & Co, 2013); Robert D Kaplan, *Surrender or Starve: Travels in Ethiopia, Sudan, Somalia, and Eritrea* (New York, Vintage Books, 2003); Harold G Marcus, *A History of Ethiopia* (Berkeley, University of California, 1994) 181–284; Martin Meredith, Martin, *The Fate of Africa: A History of Fifty Years of Independence* (New York, Public Affairs, 2005) 193–217, 268–71, 249–59.

federalism. If a group of people, regardless of linguistic, religious or cultural similarity, does not possess a separate political identity, they probably could not even conceptualise a demand for federalism, and they certainly could not mobilise any significant political support for it.

Federalism's ability to maintain political unity among people with different identities, however, is no cause for the sort of adulation that many scholars have lavished on it. It is not an independent principle of government, like liberty, social equality or self-determination. There is no normative account that makes it desirable per se. Rather, it is a pragmatic strategy, a means of organising the internal structure of a nation in order to solve a specific problem or set of problems. It can thus be more accurately described as a tragic compromise.[16] Federalism achieves political unity by means of an incomplete accommodation of conflicting political desires. No one gets everything they want from it; the goal is that various groups with differing identities get enough so that violence is avoided and material welfare is advanced.

Determining whether federalism is a truly desirable or advantageous mode of governance is a complex matter because it calls into question the nature or identity of the actor whose interests are being evaluated. From the perspective of the central government, and of any groups who identify with the central government, it would be preferable if everyone in their nation possessed the same political identity, so that there was no problem to be resolved. This is not a Panglossian fantasy; rather, it is the situation that applies in many nations, such as France, Chile, Japan and, as Feeley and I have argued, the United States.[17] From this perspective, the persistence of conflicting political identities in other nations is a misfortune for those nations' central governments, and the necessity to maintain national unity through partial grants of autonomy represents a tragic compromise.

Those groups who have maintained a separate political identity will generally have a different perspective. For them, the misfortune may be that they are too small or too militarily or economically dependent to function effectively as an independent nation. Their tragic compromise is that they must relinquish the bulk of their authority to the central government and rely upon the remaining autonomy that federalism provides to support and defend their sense of separateness. Of course, that sense of separateness may vanish over time. During the High Middle Ages, European royal regimes that subsequently became nations were loosely-joined agglomerations of principalities with different cultures, mutually incomprehensible languages or dialects and distinct political identities. The nation-building process of the Early Modern era melded many of these principalities into a single nation with a single sense of identity.[18] That ended their tragic sense of separateness, and simultaneously obviated the need for federalism.

[16] Feeley and Rubin, *Federalism* 38–60.

[17] ibid 96–123; Edward L Rubin, 'Puppy Federalism and the Blessings of America' (2001) 574 The Annals of the American Academy of Political and Social Science 37.

[18] Thomas Ertman, *The Birth of Leviathan: Building States and Regimes in Medieval and Early Modern Europe* (Cambridge, Cambridge University Press, 1997); Samuel Huntington, *Political Order in Changing Societies* (New Haven, Yale University Press, 1968); Max Weber, *Economy and Society* (Berkeley, University of California, 1978) 1070–1109.

III. THE FEATURES OF FEDERALISM AS A MODALITY OF GOVERNMENT

Having defined genuine federalism as a partial grant of autonomy to sub-units of a nation, explicated its basis in political identity and characterised its operation as a tragic compromise, the way it functions as a mode of governance can now be delineated. There are at least two major issues to be discussed: first, the structure of the regime, that is, the way it identifies the sub-units that are granted partial autonomy; and second, the distribution of authority, the specific subject matters that are allocated to the autonomous sub-units.

To begin with structure, federalism can only be used for groups of people who are geographically concentrated.[19] More particularly, a significant portion of the group must be located in a limited region or regions, and they must constitute the majority population of that region. Since federalism, by definition, grants autonomy to geographic sub-units of the nation, it serves no value if the group in question is geographically dispersed. African-Americans and Hispanics in the US, Muslims in India, or Christians in Lebanon may have separate political identities, but since they do not dominate any specific region of their country, federalism cannot do them any good and they must turn to other mechanisms. Thus federalism, unlike normative political principles such as liberty or justice, cannot be described as something that should be provided to all people, or even all people of a given nation. It is a device that can be used to satisfy particular demands by groups of people who, due to accidents of history, are positioned to make use of it.

The combination of geographical concentration with divergent political identity means that the configuration of federalism, as a modality of governance, will vary from one nation to another. In some cases, a nation where most people share a single political identity will have delimited regions where the majority of people possess a separate identity, often but not always as a result of a distinctive history or culture. The federalism-based solution to this situation can be described as particularised federalism; it grants autonomy to the delimited regions where a distinct political identity prevails, while maintaining a unitary or non-federal regime in the remaining, and larger portion of the nation. Particularised federalism is a feature of modern Italy, an otherwise unitary nation that has designated several autonomous regions, such as Sicily,[20] modern Spain with the Basque Country and Catalonia,[21] and even more recently in the UK, which has granted increasing amounts of autonomy to Scotland.[22]

[19] James Blumstein, 'Federalism and Civil Rights: Complementary and Competing Paradigms' (1994) 47 *Vanderbilt Law Review* 1251; Ramesh Dikshit, *The Political Geography of Federalism: An Inquiry into Origins and Stability* (New York, John Wiley & Sons, 1975); Will Kymlicka, 'Is Federalism a Viable Alternative to Secession?' in Percy B Lehning (ed), *Theories of Secession* (London, Routledge, 1998) 109.

[20] Sandra Benjamin, *Sicily: Three Thousand Years of Human History* (Hanover, Steerforth, 2006); Christopher Duggan, *A Concise History of Italy* (Cambridge, Cambridge University Press, 1994).

[21] Michael Eaude, *Catalonia: A Cultural History* (Oxford, Oxford University Press, 2008); John Hooper, *The New Spaniards* (London, Penguin Books, 2006) 217–82; Robert Hughes, *Barcelona* (New York, Vintage Books, 1992); Michael Keating, *Nations Against the State: The New Politics of Nationalism in Quebec, Catalonia and Scotland* (New York, Palgrave Macmillan, 2001); Paddy Woodwoth, *The Basque Country: A Cultural History* (Oxford, Oxford University Press, 2007).

[22] Keating, *Nations Against the State*; Murray Pittock, *The Road to Independence?: Scotland in the Balance* (London, Reaktion Books, 2013).

Another version of particularised federalism occurs when the sub-unit that is granted federalist autonomy rights is not conceived as a region of the nation, but rather as the area inhabited by a particular group of people. Often, this approach is used for an aboriginal or indigenous population, like Indian tribes in the United States, the Sammi (Lapps) in Sweden, the Aborigines in Australia, and the Yakuts in Russia. In contrast to the regionally defined approach, where the area granted autonomy is typically the same size as the decentralised provinces in the unitary part of the nation, the group or tribally defined approach can involve areas that are quite small relative to decentralised provinces. Thus, while the Navaho Reservation in the US is larger than ten of the nation's states,[23] many of the reservations are less than ten square miles, and thus much too small to function as a state.[24] Perhaps because so many of the reservations are disproportionately small, these reservations are not often regarded as examples of federalism, but they are.

In other cases, the nation is entirely divided into provinces or states that all possess equivalent autonomy rights, as is the case with Belgium, Canada, Switzerland and India.[25] This approach can be described as comprehensive, as opposed to particularised federalism. It is often based on the idea that the different portions of the nation all vary significantly from one another, or at least that there are enough regional variations to merit granting every sub-unit autonomy rights. In this situation, the nation's capital city is often given independent status so that it does not belong to any one of the sub-units. Even more distinctively, since the capital cities of unitary regimes are nearly always separate provinces as well on account of their size, the capitals of comprehensive federal regimes are often specifically established as governance centres, apart from the cities that serve as the commercial or cultural centres of the nation. This is true, for example, in the US, Canada, Australia, India and, more recently, Brazil. It stands in marked contrast to the capital cities of unitary regimes, or regimes with only particularised federalism, such as London, Paris, Warsaw, Moscow, Beijing, Tokyo, Seoul, Bogota and Santiago. If a comprehensive federal regime becomes a unitary one, however, as I argue occurred in the case of the United States, the capital city is likely to remain in place, as a remnant of the nation's federalised past.

While both particularised and comprehensive federalism grant autonomy rights to sub-units of the nation, they often lead to different attitudes and different governmental practices. Particularised federalism is frequently employed as a means of granting special privileges to a minority group or peripheral region, perhaps because of some

[23] The Navajo Reservation measures 27,425 square miles. West Virginia, the tenth largest state, measures 24,230 square miles. This is an exception, however; the next largest reservation, the Uintah and Ouray, measures 6,825 square miles, and is only larger than three states. There are 20 reservations larger than the smallest state, Rhode Island, but Rhode Island is very small for a state.

[24] Klaus Frantz, *Indian Reservations in the United States: Territory, Sovereignty and Socioeconomic Change* (Chicago, University of Chicago, 1999); D'Arcy McNickle, *Native American Tribalism: Indian Survivals and Renewals* (New York, Oxford University Press, 1973).

[25] Marleen Brans, Lieven De Winter and Wilfried Swenden, *The Politics of Belgium: Institutions and Policy under Bipolar and Centrifugal Federalism* (London, Routledge, 2009); Kaplan, *Surrender or Starve*; Kenneth McRoberts, *Quebec: Social Change and Political Crisis* (Toronto, McClelland and Stewart, 1988); Jonathan Steinberg, *Why Switzerland?* (Cambridge, Cambridge University Press, 1996).

perceived social or economic disadvantage that the members or inhabitants suffer. In other words, the regime is likely to regard itself, and be regarded by its majority inhabitants, as a unitary one with some exceptions being made for special situations. In contrast, a comprehensive federal regime is more likely to regard federalism as a defining feature. Rather than being a unitary regime with exceptions, it sees itself as systematically dividing governance responsibilities between the central and sub-unit administrations. Conversely, with particularised federalism, the inhabitants of the sub-units that have been granted autonomy will tend to regard themselves as separate groups, ones whose political identity creates a sense of difference between themselves and the national majority. In a comprehensive federal system, people are more likely to regard themselves as full members of the nation, but with loyalty divided between the central and sub-unit governments.

Given the multiplicity of political situations, it is difficult to generalise about the origins of particularised and comprehensive federalism. Particularised federalism is often the result of conquest, that is, a dominant group expands and absorbs areas that include distinctly different groups. This is certainly the case when the groups given federal rights are aboriginal inhabitants. But particularised federalism can also provide a solution for differential rates of assimilation to a dominant culture, as in the cases of Sicily and Catalonia. Both provinces became part of their dominant nation at the same time as other provinces, but for various reasons have retained a more separate political identity and are now granted certain autonomy rights through particularised federalism.[26]

Comprehensive federalism is sometimes explained or justified on historical grounds by asserting that the nation began as an alliance among its separate components. This is certainly an intriguing account for European nations at the present time. The European Union, which unquestionably began as an alliance, now has many features we associate with a nation state, such as a unified executive body, an elected legislature able to enact binding law, a single currency, and free movement of people and goods within its boundaries.[27] It will almost certainly not become a unitary regime in the foreseeable future, but it may well develop into a comprehensively federal nation-state. In that case, it will be a leading example of the way in which an alliance can evolve into a nation of that sort

The intuitively appealing idea that comprehensive federalism develops from an alliance is not necessarily grounded in historical reality, however. Often it is a unitary nation, such as the Netherlands and Italy, that originates in an alliance among separate political entities, rather than a federal or quasi-federal nation such as the United States or Canada. A better explanation might be that comprehensive federalism develops when the administrative structure of the nation is primarily located in its sub-units, so that these sub-units carry out many of the day-to-day affairs of governance.

[26] Benjamin, *Sicily: Three Thousand Years of Human History*; Duggan, *A Concise History of Italy*; Eaude, *Catalonia: A Cultural History*; Hooper, *The New Spaniards* 217–82; Woodwoth, *The Basque Country: A Cultural History*.

[27] Mark Gilbert, *European Integration: A Concise History* (Lanham, Rowman & Littlefield, 2012); John McCormick and Jonathan Olsen, *The European Union: Politics and Policies* (Philadelphia, Westview Press, 2014).

This was a feature of British colonial administration, and may be responsible for the elements of federalism in the US, Australia, India, and Canada. Canada is an interesting case because it began as separately administered provinces with elements of comprehensive federalism and was gradually evolving into a unitary regime after achieving independence. It was then subjected to insistent demands for particularised federalism from one its provinces, Quebec, where people possessed a separate political identity because of their distinctive language and culture. Its response was not to establish Quebec as a separate sub-unit with special rights, however, but rather to draw on its colonial past and revive comprehensive federalism, with Quebec as one of the federalised provinces.[28]

As far as the distribution of authority is concerned, there are certain powers that the central government of a modern federal nation must possess. These include control of the military, control of the money supply, trade control, taxing authority and the management of the nation's transportation and communication systems. Functionally, the reasons for this are apparent; they involve areas where coordination and uniformity are crucial to the nation's political or economic effectiveness. In most cases, the sub-units can be granted parallel or subsidiary authority. The US provides an interesting example. American states have their own militias, extensive authority to tax, and responsibility for urban transit and subsidiary highways. But the need for the national government to exercise overarching authority in these areas is generally an insistent one. In the nineteenth century, extensive doubts were expressed about the national government's constitutional authority to develop transportation networks.[29] By the twentieth century, the need for this authority was irresistible, and it was necessary to concoct stratagems for avoiding the perceived constitutional limits. Authority to regulate passenger air travel was originally asserted by the Post Office (because the airplanes also carried mail),[30] while the national highway system was justified as a means of moving troops for military defence.[31]

The areas of governance that a federal system cedes to the autonomous control of particular or comprehensive sub-units are likely to depend on the nature of the political identities that provide the system's rationale. This will vary, of course, from one nation to another, but often include language use, subsidisation of religion, education, family law and aspects of criminal law. Some of these, such as education and family law, are also common subjects for decentralisation, and federalised sub-units are often convenient modalities for decentralising government functions. But to reiterate, the rationale is different; the decision to decentralise typically depends on the central government's judgment of effective management, rather than on the political identity of the sub-unit's populace.

[28] Kaplan, *Surrender or Starve*; Keating, *Nations Against the State*; McRoberts, *Quebec: Social Change and Political Crisis*.

[29] Daniel W Howe, *What God Hath Wrought: The Transformation of America, 1815–1848* (Oxford, Oxford University Press, 2007) 211–22, 357–66.

[30] Thomas A Heppenheimer, *Turbulent Skies: A History of Commercial Aviation* (Hoboken, John Wiley & Sons, 1995).

[31] Tom Lewis, *Divided Highways: Building the Interstate Highways, Transforming American Life* (Ithaca, Cornell University Press, 2013).

IV. THE NORMATIVE BASIS FOR FEDERALISM

Thus far, federalism has been defined as a distinctive mode of governance and its motivation and its operation explained from the perspective of both the central government and the federalised sub-units. It will now be possible to step back, adopt the perspective of a critical observer, and explore the normative basis for federalism. In other words, a normative analysis must be abstracted from the process of political will formation that occurs in the centre and the sub-units of the nation. That analysis will be pursued here in two stages: first by discussing what are called negative and positive, or first and second generation rights, and then by discussing group, or third generation rights. The reason for making this division, as will be further elaborated, is the organic relationship between this third type of rights and federalism as a mode of governance.

A. Negative and Positive Rights and Federalism

As discussed above, many of the virtues ascribed to federalism are in fact products of decentralisation or local government and are unrelated to the grant of autonomy that serves as the defining feature of a federal system. In addition, these virtues, such as bringing government closer to the people, enabling experimentation, allowing jurisdictions within the nation to compete for resources, or allowing individuals to choose between competing jurisdictions, are often asserted without any well-developed normative theory to support them. What remains, however, after federalism is defined more carefully, is the normative claim that it protects individual liberty, a crucial component of individual or human rights.

Liberty and human rights, of course, are themselves complex terms that also require careful definition, but their basic idea stands on firm normative grounding and requires no further justification in modern political theory. It is an open question whether we want jurisdictions within a polity to compete for desirable resources; such competition, for example, enables them to offer excessive tax breaks to factory owners, monopolise a locally-produced resource like petroleum or open land, and implement programs that attract wealthy residents and discourage the poor. Similarly, enabling people to choose among legal regimes may give particular groups the opportunity to cluster together to escape taxes or exclude racial and religious minorities. The question is not whether people can choose to live where they wish, which can be regarded as a basic human right, but rather whether doing so should also enable them to choose a particular set of laws that operate to their advantage and to the disadvantage of others. Even the seemingly benign goal of bringing government closer to the people is normatively questionable; it may permit local or regional elites to dominate the smaller governmental units that result because it is easier for a narrow group to influence these units and harder for the public to pay attention to them. But no one these days seriously questions the value of human liberty and human rights.

The idea that federalism protects liberty may seem to be an appealing argument, but it immediately confronts serious empirical difficulties. Some of the nations with the very best human rights records, such as Sweden, the Netherlands, France and, until recently, the UK, are unitary regimes.[32] There is simply no coherent definition of political liberty that would support the claim that these regimes provide less liberty to their citizens than federalised democracies such as Canada, India and Brazil. This empirical observation is grounded in theory. Federalism only protects the partial autonomy of a nation's geographical sub-units. The sub-units may use their autonomy to either enlarge or restrict the rights that its inhabitants would otherwise possess as citizens of the nation; nothing in the nature of federalism itself tells us which will be the case. Similarly, the central government of a nation that employs federalism as its means of internal organisation can be either solicitous or dismissive of individual rights. Again, there is nothing in the grant of autonomy to geographical sub-units that can tell us what its stance on this subject will be. It is possible that federalism would constitute an important protection of liberty, or democracy, under certain specific factual circumstances, but that can hardly be generalised into a general principle of political organisation.

To proceed beyond such generalised empirical and theoretical observations, and explore the interaction of federal and human rights, it is necessary to consider the concept of human rights in some detail. A standard approach is to distinguish between first generation or negative rights, which protect people against specific government oppressions, second generation, or positive rights, which grant people specific entitlements like subsistence, health care, or education, and third generation, or group rights, which grant communities protections or benefits that extend beyond those granted to any of their members as individuals. Negative rights are the best established, and virtually everyone these days agrees that they are essential to a just society (United Nations General Assembly 1948, arts 3–21).[33] Second generation rights are more controversial, but they appear prominently in the UN's Universal Declaration of Human Rights (United Nations General Assembly, 1948, arts 22–26) and its supplemental International Covenant on Economic, Social and Cultural Rights (ICESCR; United Nations 1976) to which most nations in the world—except a few rogue states such as the US—are signatory. They appear as well in most modern constitutions,[34] and are strongly endorsed by many scholars.[35]

[32] For background information on the human rights positions of various nations, visit Human Rights Watch at <www.hrw.org>.

[33] Akhil R Amar, *The Bill of Rights: Creation and Reconstruction* (New Haven, Yale University Press, 2000); Isiah Berlin, 'Two Concepts of Liberty' in Isaiah Berlin, *Four Essays on Liberty* (Oxford, Oxford University, 1969) 118; John Hart Ely, *Democracy and Distrust. A Theory of Judicial Review* (Cambridge, Mass, Harvard University Press, 1981); James W Nickel, *Making Sense of Human Rights* (Malden, Blackwell, 2007).

[34] David P Currie, 'Positive and Negative Constitutional Rights' (1986) 53 *University of Chicago Law Review* 868–72 (1986); Mary Ann Glendon, 'Rights in Twentieth-Century Constitutions' (1992) 59 *University of Chicago Law Review* 521–29; Samuel Huntington, *The Third Wave: Democratization in the Late Twentieth Century* (Norman, University of Oklahoma Press, 1991) 21–26; Mark S Kende, 'The South African Constitutional Court's Embrace of Socio-Economic Rights: A Comparative Perspective' (2003) 6 *Chapman Law Review* 137.

[35] Jack Donnelly (ed), *Universal Human Rights in Theory and Practice* (Ithaca, Cornell University Press, 2013); William F Felice, *Taking Suffering Seriously: The Importance of Collective Human Rights*

Any argument that federalism supports either negative or positive rights, however, is difficult to justify. One way of doing so is to assume that the central government is intent on denying these rights and then argue that the autonomy of the nation's sub-units will allow them to resist that effort. The problem with this argument is that it works the same way in reverse; if the sub-unit governments are intent on violating negative or positive rights, and the central government supports these rights, then federalism will facilitate the violation. This is certainly not a remote possibility; it is exactly what occurred in the US, where the Southern states retained and expanded slavery and then, after the Civil War abolished it, permitted lethal violence against African Americans and denied them voting rights, education, health care and access to commercial facilities for a period of one hundred years, in violation of prevailing national norms.[36] This is not a detail, an accident or an historical curiosity; it is the principal role that federalism, and then assertions of federalism, have played in American history, and a towering injustice that cast serious doubts on our claims to be a moral polity.

A possible response is that the central government is more likely to deny people negative or positive rights than the government of a sub-unit, but it is difficult to understand why this should be true. To begin with, it must be remembered that the essential ingredient of federalism is sub-unit autonomy. If we assume any given level of rights denial at the national level, the effect of federalism, all else being equal, will be that some sub-units will be more protective of human rights, some will be less protective, and their policies will average out at about the same level as the general culture of the nation will support. The idea that things are not equal, and that sub-units will be more protective, seems to rest on the idea that increased participation by individuals tends to combat rights violations or denials, at least in a democratic regime, and that the level of participation in the government of a sub-unit will thus be greater than in the nation as a whole.

Both assertions are highly questionable, however. First, increased participation can readily lead to a denial of rights. The idea that there can be a 'tyranny of the majority,' and that counter-majoritarian institutions such as the courts are necessary for rights protection is certainly a familiar one in modern political and legal thought.[37] In particular, localised popular resentments in democratic regimes, such as those that prevailed in Northern Ireland against Catholics, the Indian state

(Albany, State University of New York Press, 1996); James Griffin, *On Human Rights* (Oxford, Oxford University Press, 2008); Paul Gordon Lauren, *The Evolution of International Human Rights. Visions Seen* (Philadelphia, University of Pennsylvania, 2003); Nickel, *Making Sense of Human Rights*; Henry Shue, *Basic Rights: Subsistence, Affluence, and US Foreign Policy* (Princeton, Princeton University Press, 1996).

[36] Douglas A Blackmon, *Slavery by Another Name: The Re-Enslavement of Black Americans from the Civil War to World War II* (New York, Anchor Books, 2009); David M Chalmers, *Hooded Americans: The History of the Ku Klux Klan* (New York, F Watts, 1981); David Oshinsky, *'Worse Than Slavery': Parchman Farm and the Ordeal of Jim Crow Justice* (New York, Free Press, 1996); Heather Cox Richardson, *The Death of Reconstruction* (Cambridge, Mass, Harvard University Press, 2001).

[37] Alexander Bickel, *The Least Dangerous Branch: The Supreme Court at the Bar of Politics* (Indianapolis, Bobbs-Merrill, 1962); Amy Chua, *World on Fire: How Exporting Free Market Democracy Breeds Ethnic Hatred and Global Instability* (New York, Doubleday, 2003); Ely, *Democracy and Distrust.*

of Gujarat against Muslims, and of course the American South against African Americans, can lead to catastrophic denials of rights.

Second, while it is almost certainly true that people can physically travel to a nearby governmental headquarters more readily, and probably true that organising the smaller group of people in a sub-unit is less expensive than organising the same interest group on a national level, that is true for those who oppose granting negative or positive rights as well as for those who support them. Moreover, the observation sounds somewhat old-fashioned in the era of air travel, high speed rail and the internet. A countervailing factor, moreover, is that national politics are more salient to people than regional politics. It may well be easier to mobilise support on the national level. In addition, a national government is more likely to possess the resources necessary to enforce negative rights, and certainly more likely to possess the resources necessary to implement positive rights.

B. Group Rights and Federalism

Suppose, however, that the central government's inclination to deny people human rights is not a general one, but is directed toward a particular group of people. This group is necessarily a distinguishable minority; if not a minority, then we are back to general issues of rights deprivation, and if not distinguishable, then any governmental action would be difficult to understand as oppression. If the group is geographically dispersed, then federalism will generally work to its disadvantage. It would be better off mobilising on a national level and relying on consociative mechanisms. But if the group is concentrated in a specific geographic area, and particularly if it dominates that area, then federalism might well protect it against rights violations by the central government. There are numerous examples of this situation, such as China's treatment of Tibetans and Uighurs, Yugoslavia's treatment of the Bosnians, Turkey's treatment of the Kurds, and Mexico's treatment of the Maya.

The significance of groups in identifying the effects of federalism on potential rights violations directs attention to third generation rights, which attach to groups, rather than individuals. These include a group's right to preserve its culture, to transact business and provide education in its language, and to be protected against various efforts to assimilate it into a national majority. While such rights are unquestionably less well established than first or even second generation rights, a number of United Nations treaties and declarations have recognised group rights to some extent (United Nations 1945, arts 13, 55, 57, 73; United Nations 1951; United Nations 1976, art 27) and scholars have provided both theoretical justifications and pragmatic prescriptions in their favour.[38] But the contours of the rights that the UN

[38] Ronald R Garet, 'Communality and Existence: The Rights of Groups' (1983) 56 *Southern California Law Review* 1001; Owen Fiss, 'Groups and the Equal Protection Clause' (1976) 5 *Philosophy & Public Affairs* 107; Will Kymlicka, *Liberalism, Community and Culture* (Oxford, Clarendon, 1989); *Multicultural Citizenship: A Liberal Theory of Minority Rights* (Oxford, Clarendon, 1995); Michael McDonald, 'Collective Rights and Tyranny' (1985) 56 *University of Ottawa Quarterly* 115; Vernon Van Dyke, 'Human Rights and the Rights of Groups' (1974) 18 *American Journal of Political Science* 725; Vernon Van Dyke, 'Justice as Fairness for Groups?' (1975) 69 *American Political Science Review* 607.

has articulated remain decidedly unclear, and other scholars, viewing political rights as attached exclusively to individuals, argue that group rights are an incoherent or inadvisable idea.[39] For present purposes, it can be assumed that the argument for group rights is at least strong enough to pursue its implications for a discussion of federalism's normative implications.

Recognition of third generation rights through federalism should be distinguished from what is sometimes called a right of self-determination for one group within the nation. While the principle of self-determination played an important role in the decolonisation process,[40] it has been widely criticised as irretrievably vague, morally unjustified and pragmatically disastrous when applied to conflicts among groups within a single nation. One of the major criticisms is that, as a normative principle, it seems to imply a right to secede, and thus threatens the dismemberment of any nation containing populations with disparate political identities. This was in fact the way the principle was implemented by one of its strongest proponents, Woodrow Wilson.[41] The settlement he urged in the aftermath of World War I involved the dissolution of the Austro-Hungarian Empire into a collection of small, ethnically-defined new nations, each of which possessed ethnic minorities of their own that led to a reiteration of the problem that the dissolution was designed to solve.[42] What followed, during the next century, was a lugubrious history that fully justified the comment, widely attributed to Winston Churchill, that the Balkans have produced more history than they can consume.[43] Self-determination seems even more problematic if the group demanding it happens to occupy a resource-rich part of the nation. That represents a potential threat to the economic viability of the remainder, and induces the suspicion that the people, or at least the leaders, of the seceding region are motivated by greed as well as by political identity.

Recognising the third generation rights of people within a particular geographic region of the nation avoids the negative consequences of self-determination or a right to secede. These rights refer to the way people are treated within the general polity, since that is the context where such rights would be recognised. Consider, for example the right to speak one's own language. It seems unlikely that the issue

[39] John Danley, 'Liberalism, Aboriginal Rights and Cultural Minorities' (1991) 20 *Philosophy & Public Affairs* 169; Amy Gutmann, 'The Challenge of Multiculturalism to Political Ethics' (1993) 22 *Philosophy & Public Affairs* 171; Harry N Hirsch, 'The Threnody of Liberalism: Constitutional Liberty and the Renewal of Community' (1986) 14 *Political Theory* 423; Chandran Kukathas, 'Are There Any Cultural Rights?' (1992) 20 *Political Theory* 105; Jeremy Waldron, 'Minority Cultures and the Cosmopolitan Alternative' (1992) 25 *University of Michigan Law Review* 751.

[40] Basil Davidson, *Africa in History* (New York, Simon & Schuster, 1991) 325–71; John Hatch, *A History of Postwar Africa* (New York, Frederick A Praeger, 1965) 25–41; Martin Meredith, *The Fate of Africa: A History of Fifty Years of Independence* (New York, Public Affairs, 2005) 141–78.

[41] Thomas J Knock, *To End All Wars: Woodrow Wilson and the Quest for a New World Order* (Oxford, Oxford University Press, 1992); Erez Manela, *The Wilsonian Moment: Self-Determination and the International Origins of Anticolonial Nationalism* (Oxford, Oxford University Press, 2009).

[42] Misha Glenny, *The Balkans: Nationalism, War and the Great Powers, 1804–1999* (New York, Penguin Books, 2001) 307–544, 634–61; Tony Judt, *A History of Europe Since 1945* (New York, Penguin Books, 2005) 665–85; Robert Kahn, *A History of the Habsburg Empire, 1526–1918* (Berkeley, Cal, University of California Press, 1974) 497–520.

[43] The largest of the newly-created nations, Yugoslavia, broke apart into eight separate entities, in part as a result of further interventionist actions by the US (Gibbs, 2009).

would arise in a unilingual nation; it is relevant when the group that asserts this right lives within a larger nation, and expects to continue doing so. Moreover, the right does not apply to the language people speak in their own homes, or are allowed to speak or write in public. Every theory of first generation or negative rights fully protects these activities. The additional claim of a group right would refer to matters such as the language used in the public schools, the courts, and by administrative agencies. In other words, the claim refers to the way a government, whose ongoing authority is accepted, treats the members of the group in question.

The practical effect of adding third generation, or group rights, to the discussion of rights is to broaden the scope of normative concerns to include most Western democracies. These nations grant first and even second generation rights to all their citizens at reasonably high levels, probably sufficient to preclude any general condemnation of them for rights violation. But they have often systematically denied group rights in situations that have become quite controversial within their own political discourse and raise serious questions for a critical observer. Egregious examples include the treatment indigenous or aboriginal populations in what have been described as Western settler societies such as the United States, Canada, Australia and New Zealand.[44] While the United States has always granted due process protection to landowners, even those who rebelled against the government to maintain slavery, it displaced nearly all the Eastern Indian tribes. The most notorious case were the Cherokee who, despite assiduous efforts to conform to American culture, were forced from their remaining land and sent on a death march across the country.[45] Even when they are treated more decently, these indigenous groups, such as the Maoris of New Zeeland or the Saami of Sweden, find themselves under considerable pressure to abandon their culture and assimilate. Similar problems can afflict non-aboriginal minorities who are otherwise granted equality. French-speaking citizens of Quebec were not denied any negative or first generation rights and were provided with equal and reasonably extensive rights to subsistence, education and health. But they experienced considerable pressure to abandon their language and culture as a result of the English-speaking majority's control over their nation's educational system, media and career opportunities.[46]

There is an organic connection between group rights and federalism, which is not the case with individual rights of either the first or second generation. Federalism, after all, refers to groups, not individuals. Just as no individual can assert a right

[44] Richard Gott, 'Latin America as a White Settler Society' (2007) 26 *Bulletin of Latin American Research* 269; Anthony Dirk Moses, *Genocide and Settler Society: Frontier Violence and Stolen Indigenous Children in Australian History* (New York, Berghahn Books, 2004); Daiva Stasiulis and Nira Yuval-Davis (eds), *Unsettling Settler Societies: Articulations of Gender, Race, Ethnicity and Class* (London, Sage Books, 1995).

[45] John Ehle, *Trail of Tears: The Rise and Fall of the Cherokee Nation* (New York, Anchor Books, 1988); Howe, *What God Hath Wrought* 342–57; Theda Perdue and Michael D Green, *The Cherokee Nation and the Trail of Tears* (New York, Penguin Books, 2007).

[46] Richard Handler, *Nationalism and the Politics of Culture in Quebec* (Madison, University of Wisconsin, 1988); Kaplan, *Surrender or Starve*; Keating, *Nations Against the State*; McRoberts, *Quebec. Social Change and Political Crisis*; Garth Stevenson, *Union. Canadian Federalism and National Unity* (Montreal, McGill-Queens University Press, 2009).

to speak his or her own language,[47] no individual can assert a right to exercise governmental authority. In both cases, it is only a group or community of people that can coherently advance these claims. Thus, the connection between a federalist compromise and first or second generation rights is adventitious. If the central government happens to deny negative or positive rights to a particular group, as opposed to its citizens in general, and if that group happens to be geographically concentrated, then federalism can protect that group, again assuming that the autonomy rights granted by it relate to the particular violations. But group rights are essentially demands for autonomy over areas connected with the group's traditional culture—not foreign affairs or national finance, but language, education, family law and criminal law. In this context, federalism is an almost direct translation of the group's demands into the terminology of national politics.

In addition to this symmetry, there is an appealing minimalism to using federalism to protect group rights. Such rights are, not surprisingly, applicable only to delimited groups; the concept simply does not apply to the majority of the nation's population. Thus, the federalism that would protect them is particularised, rather than comprehensive. This means that a nation can grant federal rights to a minority group without disrupting its overall political arrangements. To be sure, protection for a group could fit into a comprehensive federalist structure that was adopted for reasons relating to the majority of the nation, rather than the group. This is essentially what has occurred in Canada, where the demands of the French-speaking minority have been met by granting all the nation's provinces a measure of autonomy.[48] But it also means that a unitary nation can grant federalist rights to a minority group as a self-contained response to a particular problem. This is the situation in New Zealand and Sweden, for example.

It can even be argued that it is this particularised solution that has been adopted in the United States. The US claims to be a federal nation, but it functions more like a unitary, decentralised regime. It has, however, granted true autonomy rights to the American Indian tribes that have retained sufficient territory. It has also granted true autonomy rights to overseas territories that have ethnic distributions that are distinctly different from the nation as a whole: Puerto Rico, Guam and the US Virgin Islands. Even if one wants to argue that the US is a comprehensive federal regime, there can be little doubt that it has granted more autonomy rights to these political entities than it has to its constituent states.

[47] Ruth R Marin, 'Exploring the Boundaries of Language Rights: Insiders, Newcomers and Natives' in Stephen Macedo and Allen Buchanan (eds), *Secession and Self-Determination* (2003) XLV *NOMOS* 136; Denise Réaume, 'The Constitutional Protection of Language: Survival or Security' in David Schneiderman (ed), *Language and the State* (Brussels, Bruylant & Éditions Yvon Blais, 1991) 37. Wittgenstein makes the more general point that there is no such thing as a private language; language is necessarily a means by which people agree upon the meaning of sounds and symbols so that they can communicate with each other (see Ludwig Wittgenstein, *Philosophical Investigations* (Englewood Cliffs, Prentice Hall, 1958) §§ 241–94).

[48] Canada's shift to comprehensive federalism also met some of the demands of the Native American population through the creation of Nunavut, a separate territory treated somewhat similarly to a province (see Natalia Loukacheva, *The Arctic Promise: Legal and Political Autonomy of Greenland and Nunavut* (Toronto, University of Toronto Press, 2007)).

This appealing symmetry between group rights and a federalist solution, and the appealing minimalism of that solution, are subject to some important caveats, however, beyond the limits of geographic concentration that was described above. To begin with, even if one is willing to accept the validity of group rights, it seems difficult to argue that they are essential components of liberty, that is, that they are equally important as individual rights of either the negative or positive variety. Considered by themselves, rather than as a supplement to individual rights, they relate mainly to induced, rather than compelled assimilation. A violation of group rights, by itself, would generally consist of non-coercive inducements to the group to abandon its culture, such as providing education only in the majority language, or failing to provide funding for the group's cultural activities, or encouraging young people to leave the group by offering them opportunities in the larger society. While members of the group may perceive such actions as threats to liberty, and even respond to them with violence, most observers would not regard these inducements as morally equivalent to the denial of first or even second generation rights.

Second, as Will Kymlicka has pointed out, group rights may not only seem somewhat flimsy when standing by themselves, but they may conflict with the liberty of group members whose preferences differ from those who want to assert the group's rights to cultural survival. A culture will only persist, after all, if its young people subscribe to it, but if the group is a small or remote minority within the nation, its young people may yearn for the bright lights and broader opportunities that the majority culture offers. The group's efforts to survive, and to resist assimilation, may thus involve restrictions on these young people's freedom. Central government policies that support those efforts may thus appear as a violation of the young people's rights, most notably their right to equal opportunity.

The third problem with using federalism to protect group rights involves the problem of minorities among minorities. This is essentially the same problem that is presented by the right of secession, albeit in less severe form. It is rare for any group that dominates a significant amount of territory within a nation to be the only group within that territory. Naturally occurring patterns of settlement and migration generally lead to the presence of other groups, very often a multiplicity of groups. Because the area in question is necessarily part of a larger nation, the entry of other people into the minority group's territory process will be amplified by the tendency of the national majority to occupy all parts of the nation. Thus, an area that is dominated by a group with a different political identity than the nation as a whole is likely to contain a number of people whose identify with the nation, rather than the group. Because the group is trying to assert itself against national control, it is likely to feel particularly resentful toward this minority of citizens among them who prefer national rule to sub-unit autonomy.

From the perspective of this minority, of course, federalism will be much superior to secession as a way to solve the problem of divergent identity. As long as the sub-unit remains a member of the nation, the central government will be available to protect their rights, and that government is likely to show special solicitude for those who identify with it, and perhaps represent the ethnic group that forms its core. Nonetheless, the difficulties for this minority, and for other minorities that the central government may be willing to sacrifice to assuage the sensibilities of the divergent section, should not be underestimated. Here again, federalism emerges as a tragic compromise, not as an ideal principle of governance.

V. CONCLUSION

Federalism is a means of dividing government authority between a nation's central government and one or more geographically-defined sub-units. Unlike decentralisation, however, which is a managerial strategy employed by every nation and many other organisations as well, federalism divides authority by granting partial autonomy to the sub-units in question. It is relevant in situations of divergent political identity, where the inhabitants of the sub-unit do not feel that they are fully members of the nation as a whole, or that they have some separate political membership in addition. As such, it is a compromise between unity and separation. From the perspective of both the central government and the sub-unit, it has tragic overtones. The central government, and its supporters, would generally prefer that everyone in the nation identify with the nation itself, while the sub-unit, whose members have a sense of separateness, must settle for only partial autonomy because of political, economic or historic circumstances.

The rather extensive scholarly literature that apotheosises federalism only succeeds in obscuring its features and its operation. First, it confuses federalism with other approaches, desirable for different reasons, such as consociation, decentralisation and local democracy. Second, it conceals the existence and value of particularised federalism by suggesting that federalism is good for everyone, and thus necessarily of the comprehensive variety. Third, it advances the unsupportable claim that federalism, as a general matter, protects liberty. This not only claims advantages for federalism that it does not necessarily achieve, but also obscures the one type of liberty, group rights, that federalism can protect, as well as the problems that occur in using it to achieve this purpose.

The reason why federalism has attracted so many proponents, who make such wide-ranging and unsupportable claims for it, would be a study in itself. One possible reason, worth noting in conclusion, is the more general hostility towards modern government that appears in so much of the scholarly literature. While this inclination can be a useful warning against the oppressive tendencies of government, if properly framed, much of it reflects a less coherent and less justifiable romanticism about bygone times. Those times, whatever their moral value—and it is highly questionable—will not return. Governance is serious and essential business in the modern world, demanding sustained attention and detailed analysis. This is particularly true for federalism, a specialised mode of governance that is useful in some situations, inapplicable or undesirable in others, and clearly not a universal principle of political organisation.

6

Executive Power in Federations

CHERYL SAUNDERS

THE NATURE AND scope of executive power tend to be elusive in any democratic constitutional system. Executive power typically has a residual character, defined by reference to what legislative and judicial power are not. The actions that can lawfully be undertaken in the exercise of executive power may be diverse and open-ended and defy neat categorisation. The executive branch itself is sprawling and amorphous, offering a catch-all for public bodies that do not neatly fit elsewhere under a tripartite separation of powers. Most executive decision-making takes place behind closed doors, often in conditions of confidentiality, in contrast to the relative openness of at least the formal processes of legislatures and courts.

In polities that are constitutionally organised to give effect to the federal idea the challenge of understanding executive power is greater still. In federal-type systems, executive power necessarily is shared between at least two orders of government, each with their own executive organs. Whatever complexities are inherent in the conception of executive power are thus augmented by its interdependence with federal arrangements. As neither the conception of executive power nor the form through which the federal idea is given effect can be assumed to be standard across polities, an appreciation of the nature and scope of executive power in federal-type systems depends on variations along at least two axes. Each of these axes offers a range of possibilities that have implications for the scope and operation of executive power, even in isolation from each other. The point at which they intersect in a particular federation is likely to produce results that are distinctive as well.

One axis concerns the design of the federation itself. Along this axis, there is a pronounced distinction between dualist federations, in which each sphere of government is expected to execute its own legislation, and integrated federations, in which a significant proportion of central legislation is executed by other spheres.[1] The United States and Germany can be regarded, respectively, as exemplars of these two approaches, with all other federal-type systems ranged somewhere between the two, each with variations on the theme of their own.

[1] Thomas O Hueglin and Alan Fenna, *Comparative Federalism: A Systematic Inquiry* (Toronto, University of Toronto Press, 2015) ch 2.

The second axis along which the nature and scope of executive power must be seen reflects the wider constitutional setting of which the provisions for federalism are part. This setting includes, critically, the relationship between the executive and the legislature within each of the orders of government and, potentially, between the executive and the courts as well.[2] For this reason, in this chapter, I characterise variations along this axis in terms of the separation of powers. In examining executive power from this perspective, I focus not only on the execution of legislation but also on the power of the executive to act without legislative authority. In addition, however, there may be other aspects of the constitutional context that affect the scope of executive power in federal-type systems. These include underlying ideas about the relative scope of legislative and executive power that the Constitution assumes and may reinforce and any other, specific, constitutional provisions that have interpretive value in understanding executive power.

In what follows, I examine variations along each of these axes to identify the similarities and differences to which they give rise, individually and collectively, and to demonstrate their relevance to the nature and scope of executive power. In a final substantive part I use Australia as an extended case study, to bring depth to the treatment of the subject and to illustrate the practical relevance of the variations along both axes in the experience of one federated state. The scope of federal executive power is a live question in Australia, the emergent answers to which are distinctive, from a comparative point of view. In closing, I draw some brief conclusions from this study for the federal idea.

I am conscious that in developing the arguments in this chapter I am influenced by an Australian frame of reference, which may well not reflect approaches to thinking about executive power in federal settings elsewhere. Achieving a satisfactory level of objectivity is a challenge in any comparative exercise and is particularly difficult in the present context, where so many variables stem from history, theory and practice and shared terms mask what may be underlying difference. Even to understand that frameworks of reference may differ, however, is to make some progress in comparative terms. I hope that this chapter prompts others to engage with similar questions about the nature and scope of executive power in federations from perspectives that are more familiar in a manner that contributes to a deeper common understanding.

I. FEDERAL DESIGN

At obvious risk of over-generalisation, it is possible to identify two distinct approaches to the division of governing authority for federal purposes. They are described below as dualist (or thematic) and integrated (or functional). Each involves a very different treatment of executive power. Each has different implications for the lines of

[2] I refer to the 'executive' throughout as encompassing the administration, although this practice also differs to a degree between states. For the distinction, see Eberhard Schmidt-Afsmann and Christoph Mollers, 'The Scope and Accountability of Executive Power in Germany' in Paul Craig and Adam Tomkins (eds), *The Executive and Public Law: Power and Accountability in Comparative Perspective* (Oxford, Oxford University Press, 2006) 268.

accountability for the exercise of executive power within and across jurisdictional lines. To complicate matters further, these two approaches are not necessarily mutually exclusive, even in design. And once the operation of federations in practice is taken into account, features become further intermixed in ways that may enhance the de facto exercise of executive power, without the corresponding provision for political or legal accountability likely to be associated with constitutional design.[3]

As the term is used here, a dualist approach to federal design divides power vertically, in the sense that areas of government are assigned thematically to one or other of the spheres of government on a basis that assumes that each sphere will administer (or execute) its own legislation. Each sphere has a full set of institutions for the purpose: hence the label of 'dualism'. The United States, Canada and Australia are examples. As these examples show, federations in this category also may differ in a host of other ways, including the manner of the vertical division of power and the form of separation of powers for which the rest of the constitutional setting provides.[4]

The division of legislative power, as the principal manifestation of sovereign authority, invariably is the most prominent under any federal model. In conditions of dualism, the legislative power allocated to each sphere is likely to include authority to raise revenues for its own purposes as well. By definition, however, consistently with this model, executive and, sometimes, judicial power also are divided between the respective spheres of government for federal purposes, implicitly if not explicitly. As a default position, these are likely generally to mirror the lines for the division of legislative power. In an extension of the logic of this model, there may be constitutional inhibitions on the extent to which one order of government can be required, or even invited, to exercise the executive power of another.[5]

For the purposes of democratic accountability, each order of government in a dualist federation tends to be conceived as broadly self-sufficient, subject to constitutional provision to the contrary. Arrangements that cut across this proposition frequently include representation of the federated units in central institutions including, typically, a second chamber of a bicameral central legislature. Such a chamber may have considerable power within the central legislature but need not otherwise play a distinctively federal role. Co-operation across jurisdictional lines is common in such federations in practice. The occasion for co-operation may be stimulated by the federal division of powers but will be shaped by the dynamics of representative or, where it exists, direct democracy, including the separation of powers. In most cases

[3] This phenomenon is explored in relation to 12 federations in Johanne Poirier and Cheryl Saunders, 'Comparative Experiences of Intergovernmental Relations in Federal Systems' in Johanne Poirier, Cheryl Saunders and John Kincaid (eds), *Intergovernmental Relations in Federal Systems: Comparative Structures and Dynamics* (Oxford, Oxford University Press, 2015).

[4] In relation to the first point, the Constitutions of the United States and Australia list only the legislative powers of the federation, leaving the unspecified residue to the States. By contrast, in Canada the Constitution Act 1867 lists the exclusive powers of both the federation and the provinces. On the second point, both Canada and Australia have parliamentary systems, while the United States has a presidential system in which both the heads of the executive branch and the legislatures are separately elected.

[5] *Printz v United States* 521 US 898 (1997); *R v Hughes* (2000) 202 CLR 535.

co-operation involves the executive branch, relies in significant degree on executive power and effectively extends executive authority.[6] Some forms of co-operation detract from democratic accountability for the exercise of executive power and may raise concerns for that reason.[7] A culture of co-operation may come less easily in dualist federations in any event, as they are inherently more competitive in design.

In sum, therefore, in a dualist federation executive power is divided between the spheres of government along thematic lines. Whether and to what extent the question of the scope of executive power within each sphere is distinct from the scope of legislative power depends on the concept of executive power itself including, critically, the power of the executive to act without legislative authority. This issue is taken up in the next part. Political accountability for the exercise of executive power lies primarily within each order of government, in accordance with the arrangements for democratic government. Intergovernmental co-operation is likely to rely largely, if not exclusively on executive action and may cut across the principles and procedures for democratic accountability.

By contrast, in an integrated approach to federal design, power may be divided horizontally, along functional lines, empowering the sub-national sphere of government including, in some cases, local government, to administer or execute much central legislation as a matter of constitutional right. This approach to the division of power does not preclude a vertical division of powers as well. Every integrated federation also divides power on thematic lines, empowers the centre to administer some of its own legislation, and assumes that the sub-national sphere also will administer its own. The characteristic feature of a functional division of powers nevertheless ensures that administrative institutions are concentrated in the sub-national sphere. Where the power to tax also is divided along functional lines, taxation may be raised centrally but collected locally, necessitating constitutional provision for the distribution of the proceeds between spheres.

Germany serves as a prototype for federations of this kind.[8] There are many other examples, however, including Austria, Switzerland, India and South Africa. In some cases, including Germany, the explanation for the adoption of a horizontal division of powers is historical reinforced, perhaps, by assumptions about the state-wide application of legislation.[9] In other cases, the explanation for the choice variously lies in the challenges of accomplishing transition from a unitary to a federated state, in the expected demands of development, in a desire for a more centralised federation, or combinations of these. In some federations, of which India is an example, a

[6] Poirier and Saunders, 'Comparative Experiences of Intergovernmental Relations in Federal Systems'.

[7] Cheryl Saunders, 'Co-operative arrangements in comparative perspective' in Gabrielle Appleby, Nicholas Aroney and Thomas John (eds), *The Future of Australian Federalism: Comparative and Interdisciplinary Perspectives* (Cambridge, Cambridge University Press, 2012) 414.

[8] Werner Heun, *The Constitution of Germany: A Contextual Analysis* (Oxford, Hart Publishing, 2011) 62–64. In describing the execution of central legislation by the *Länder*, Heun characterises the system as one of 'executive federalism.' As this term is used in several very different senses in comparative federalism, it is avoided here.

[9] Daniel Ziblatt, *Structuring the State: The Formation of Italy and Germany and the Puzzle of Federalism* (Princeton, Princeton University Press, 2006).

horizontal division of powers is equated with the categorisation of legislative powers as concurrent.[10] Federations that divide power along functional or horizontal lines typically are combined with parliamentary systems of government or, as in the case of Switzerland, a conciliar form of government. There may be a question about whether integration could work satisfactorily under a presidential system, with a more complete degree of separation between the legislature and the executive.

By definition, in an integrated approach to the federal division of power, the executive power exercisable by one sphere of government for the purposes of the federal division of power does not necessarily parallel its legislative power, even as a starting point for analysis. In lieu of, or in addition to, a question about the division of executive power for federal purposes is another, about what can be done by one order of government in executing the legislation of another.[11] By definition again, under an integrated approach, mechanisms for accountability potentially cross jurisdictional boundaries. Whether and to what extent sub-national institutions are accountable to the centre or to their own voters for the execution of central laws depends on constitutional prescription and varies between federations. Federations of this kind may recognise a principle of federal loyalty, or good faith in dealings with each other.[12] Some more recent federal type-systems, of which South Africa is an example, have equated this with a principle of co-operative government.[13] In such federations, a second chamber of the central legislature also may play an operative role. The German federation, again, is the principal case in point. The Federal Chamber, or Bundesrat, provides a vehicle through which the executive governments of the *Länder* play a role in considering and approving the central legislation that they will administer, in a form of intrastate co-operation.[14]

It follows that, in all federations, there is a federal dimension to questions about the scope of executive power. The questions, and therefore the answers differ, however, both between and within the principal categories that I have outlined here. In federations designed as dualist, the scope of executive power depends largely, although not necessarily exclusively, on a division of power for federal purposes along thematic lines. In integrated federations, this division may bear less weight. In any event, in federations of this latter kind, it is relevant also to ask what can be done under the executive power that is constitutionally assigned to the sub-national sphere to implement central legislation. The distinction has implications for the understanding of mechanisms for accountability for the exercise of executive power.

[10] Constitution of India, art 73(1)(a). For this use of concurrency more generally, see Anna Dziedzic and Cheryl Saunders, 'The Meanings of Concurrency' in Nico Steytler (ed) *Concurrent Powers in Federal Systems: Meaning, Making and Managing* (Leiden/Boston, Martinus Nijhoff Publishers, 2017).

[11] In relation to Germany, see Hans-Peter Schneider, 'Federal Republic of Germany' in Akhtar Majeed, Ronald L Watts and Douglas Brown (eds), *Distribution of Powers and Responsibilities in Federal Countries* (Montreal, McGill-Queen's University Press, 2005) 124, 146.

[12] Anna Gamper, 'On Loyalty and the Federal Constitution' (2010) 4 *Vienna Online Journal on Constitutional Law* 157. For regret about the (more general) absence of a good faith doctrine in constitutional law in the US, see David E Pozen, 'Constitutional Bad Faith' (2016) 129 *Harvard Law Review* 885.

[13] Constitution of the Republic of South Africa, ch 3.

[14] Schmitt-Afsmann and Mollers, 'The Scope and Accountability of Executive Power in Germany' 283 (also making the point that the Bundesrat is not a Parliament).

Whatever the federal design, however, what can be done in the exercise of executive power in either sphere will also depend on the general conception of executive power. This is determined primarily by considerations of the separation of powers, informed by the rest of the constitutional context, of which federalism is only part. The general conception of executive power, including the extent to which it can be exercised without legislative authority, in turn will feed into the significance of the question of the division of executive power from a federal point of view.

II. SEPARATION OF POWERS

In any democratic state, federated or not, there is a constitutional conception of what can be done in the exercise of executive power. Often, executive power is conferred by legislation or, more generally, subsumed in the authority to implement legislation. Even in this familiar context, questions may arise about what the executive can lawfully do. The dispute in the United States over the extent of presidential discretion in enforcing immigration legislation is a case in point.[15] In addition, however, there is an important sub-set of the conception of executive power that concerns the authority of the executive to act without legislative or specific constitutional authority. Executive power that is not derived from legislation but inheres in the executive *qua* executive presents an additional challenge for the division of power in federal-type systems and merits particular attention for this reason. The challenge is complicated further where inherent executive power comprehends a variety of matters with differing rationales. Thus, to take the example developed below, common law states may accept a conception of inherent executive power that combines powers in relation to the exercise of external sovereignty, of which treaty making and ratification and the commitment of troops to war are examples, with capacities of a kind ostensibly exercisable by ordinary persons, such as authority to contract and spend.

It may be that, in the twenty-first century, the core concept of executive power is broadly similar in all democratic states, precluding direct interference with rights and duties and authorising conduct of the day-to-day business of government.[16] There are significant differences at the considerable margins, however, some of which also have a bearing on the dynamics of federalism. In each state, the conception of executive power is framed by a range of factors that might loosely be described as constitutional context. An important dimension of this context is the relationship between the legislative, executive, and judicial branches of government and the powers that the Constitution authorises each to exercise, explicitly or implicitly. Another is the constitutional provision for fundamental rights.[17]

[15] *Texas v United States* 787 F 3d 733 (5th Cir 2015), subject to review in the Supreme Court of the United States in 2016, on grounds that potentially include consideration of the President's obligation to 'take care that the laws be faithfully executed' in Constitution, art 2, cl 5.

[16] A useful resource for a range of states is Craig and Tomkins (eds), *The Executive and Public Law*.

[17] Schmidt-Afsmann and Mollers, 'The Scope and Accountability of Executive Power in Germany' 269.

At a deeper level still, constitutions tend simply to assume a conception of executive power, as a product of the historical experience of the state and its people, including that of the constitutional tradition of which they are part. In most common law states, for example, an underlying conception of executive power can be traced to the long evolution of the relationship between the Crown and Parliament, culminating in the revolutionary settlement of 1688, which retained the monarch as the embodiment of the state and limited—but did not eradicate—the prerogative.[18] Outside the common law world, other formative influences have been at work: different historical experiences at different times and with different outcomes; different understandings of the sources of law, including the role of legislation in legitimising the exercise of public power.[19] Over time, at least in established constitutional systems, the implications of history for the conception of executive power are explored and developed by generations of theorists and jurists in ways that influence and are influenced by more formalised constitutional arrangements. The result, potentially, is a somewhat different understanding of the conception of executive power between states, masked by similarities in terminology.

The point may be illustrated by reference to the apparent homogeneity of the conception of executive power in common law states. Most obviously, there has been a degree of divergence between the British and United States constitutional traditions, stemming from the revolutionary break between the two at the end of the eighteenth century, differences in their constitutional arrangements in form and substance, and their different paths towards representative democracy, as parliamentary and presidential systems respectively. The initial point of divergence has been consolidated since by the intervening 200 years of the operation of the respective constitutional arrangements in practice, under different conditions, prompting different trajectories in judicial doctrines and different theoretical explanations. The claim could be substantiated by comparing many features of both traditions, but one aspect of institutional design serves the purpose. The respective dynamics of parliamentary and presidential systems inevitably shape the scope of executive power and the discourse associated with it. Relevant features for this purpose include the implications of direct, rather than indirect, election of the executive in the United States; the capacity of the Parliament to override executive power in conditions of parliamentary supremacy; the effective autonomy of Congress in comparison with Westminster Parliaments; and the substitution of express presidential powers for powers in the nature of the prerogative, not least in empowering the President as commander in chief.[20] Justice Jackson's tripartite test for determining the scope of executive power

[18] Bill of Rights 1689 (UK); see Adam Tomkins, 'The Struggle to Delimit Executive Power in Britain' in Craig and Tomkins (eds), *The Executive and Public Law* 16.

[19] In relation to Germany, for example, see Matthias Jestaedt, 'Democratic Legitimization of the Administrative Power—Exclusive versus Inclusive Democracy' in Hermann Punder and Christian Waldhoff (eds), *Debates in German Public Law* (Oxford, Hart Publishing, 2014) 181.

[20] United States Constitution, art 2, s 2. Debate on the scope of the general vesting clause in art 2, s 1 is affected by this context, whether a broad view is taken of the power or not (see Ernest A Young, 'The Scope and Accountability of Executive Power in the United States' in Craig and Tomkins (eds), *The Executive and Public Law* 161, 165–66).

in the *Steel Seizures* case[21] has no obvious counterpart in analysis of executive power in the British constitutional tradition, where the assumptions that it makes about the relationship between the executive and the legislature do not apply. Albert Venn Dicey's definition of the prerogative has no purchase in the United States where, indeed, Dicey is relatively unknown.[22]

Even within the range of states that arguably derive their conception of executive power from the British tradition through processes of colonisation there now are differences in understanding of it. Most retain parliamentary systems, which they may continue to describe as 'Westminster' in character. Explicitly or implicitly, these treat the settlement of 1688 as a definitive stage in the evolution of the scope of inherent executive power. Instinctively, all assume that the legislature can override general executive power. There has never been a clear and agreed analytical framework for the inherent executive power, however, nor for the rationale underpinning it.[23] Different states may take paths of their own in resolving these questions for themselves, as problems arise from local practice. Invariably, also, there are particular differences in the constitutional experience of states in this tradition that have the potential to encourage divergent understanding of the conception of executive power. States with written Constitutions have a text on which interpretation can focus, unlike the United Kingdom from which the tradition derived. States that now are republics have an even greater incentive to abandon old analyses that drew on the royal prerogative or the capacities of the Crown as a legal person.[24] In an interesting example of path-dependency, states in which power exercised by imperial authorities has been transferred to the executive under independence constitutions need to grapple with a broader conception of executive power than is accepted elsewhere.[25] In those states that are also federations, an additional range of factors drawn from the competing interests of the centre and the constituent units may affect understanding of the conception of executive power as well.

This potential for divergent development of the concept of executive power in states in the British common law tradition is all the greater at a time when the concept of inherent executive power is under pressure in any event and, in that sense, is in a state of flux. Executive power in the nature of the prerogative, including the power to commit troops to armed conflict and to ratify treaties, is out of step with contemporary democratic expectations in relation to accountability, transparency and public consultation. Other categories of executive power, including the

[21] *Youngstown Sheet & Tube Co v Sawyer* 343 US 579 (1952).

[22] Albert V Dicey, *Introduction to the Study of the Law of the Constitution* (London, Macmillan, 1959) 425.

[23] Sebastian Payne, 'The Royal Prerogative' in Maurice Sunkin and Sebastian Payne (eds), *The Nature of the Crown: A Legal and Political Analysis* (Oxford, Oxford University Press, 1999).

[24] For example, Constitution of the Republic of South Africa, s 84, detailing the powers and functions of the President (see Romano Orru, 'South African "Quasi-Parliamentarianism"' in Hugh Corder, Veronica Federico and Romano Orru (eds), *The Quest for Constitutionalism: South Africa since 1994* (Abingdon, Routledge, 2016) 28).

[25] India is an example (see Shubhankar Dam, *Presidential Legislation in India: The Law and Practice of Ordinances* (Cambridge, Cambridge University Press, 2014)).

power to contract, whether characterised as within the prerogative or not,[26] can be used to effect public policy goals binding future generations with limited parliamentary control. Whether through the evolution of convention, judicial interpretation or legislative change, different solutions to these problems are emerging from the experiences of these states, creating differences in the conception of executive power itself.[27]

Features of a constitutional system that are associated with the separation of powers are the most obvious influence on the conception of executive power along this axis, but they are not the only ones. Others that are more subtle are easier to miss, however, for this reason. The impact of the choice between a generalist and a specialist court system for the purposes of organising adjudication serves as an example. While there are myriad variations, the latter typically mirrors a sharper conceptual distinction, not only between public and private law, but also between ordinary legal claims and claims about the constitutional validity of legislation. An apex court in a state in which generalist courts are the norm can deal with any legal issue properly raised before it, applying all applicable sources of law, including the Constitution, legislation and the common law. In such a court, the constitutionality of executive action, even in the exercise of, say, a power to contract can be raised and resolved applying the full range of legal sources and tools. By contrast, a specialist constitutional court may be inhibited from dealing with a pure exercise of executive power at all which, in any event, may be characterised as an issue of administrative law or, in the case of contract, as private law. Of course, arrangements for adjudication along specialist lines may merely reflect an established categorisation of legal questions. It may also serve to reinforce them, however. By contrast, a generalist court has a greater degree of flexibility in determining the boundaries of a private/public distinction between forms of executive power or even in eroding the distinction altogether.

The argument so far has sought to establish that the nature and scope of executive power in any federation involves examination of constitutional arrangements along two axes. One deals with the manner of the division of federal power. The other deals with the general conception of executive power primarily, although not exclusively, from the standpoint of the separation of powers. It has been convenient for analytical purposes to present the two dimensions of the problem separately here, but in reality they overlap. In any federation, the prevailing conception of executive power informs the organisation of power, including executive power, for federal purposes. Equally, the federal organisation of the state is part of the constitutional context that shapes the conception of executive power. Over time, this interdependence may increase, as the operation of the federation in practice raises an additional range of issues with which the conception of executive power must deal, causing it to be seen in a different light. While federalism interrelates with the conception of

[26] The reference here is to the different formulations of William Blackstone and Albert V Dicey (see Cheryl Saunders, 'The concept of the Crown' (2015) 28 *Melbourne University Law Review* 873).

[27] For a comparative examination of one aspect of this phenomenon, see Campbell McLachlan, *Foreign Relations Law* (Cambridge, Cambridge University Press, 2014) ch 4.

executive power in all federations, how this occurs and with what results varies in some degree. The next part illustrates how this relationship has shaped and continues to shape executive power in the federation of Australia.

III. AUSTRALIA

A. Federal Design

The Australian federation was formed in 1901 as an agreed means of bringing together six established self-governing British colonies in a single polity. It thus had many, although not all, the characteristics of federation by aggregation.[28] In an important exception, colonial status within the British Empire at the time of federation meant that the colonies that became States never possessed full sovereignty and that the Commonwealth itself lacked powers associated with external sovereignty for decades after federation took place.[29] The continued, unbroken relationship with the United Kingdom also required incorporation of the monarchy in the new Constitution.[30] These factors have had implications for the executive power of both the Commonwealth and the States in the Australian federation, not the least of which has been the expansion of the scope of executive power in section 61 as imperial authority withdrew.[31] Otherwise, however, as in most cases of aggregation, the States retained their existing Constitutions, institutions and laws, subject to provisions to the contrary in the Commonwealth Constitution.[32] Apart from the inroads necessarily made by federation into the scope of State power, these were not onerous. The Constitution established only federal institutions, leaving those of the States largely untouched. The Constitution also left rights protection to the institutions of the several spheres of government, in the exercise of their respective powers.

The expectation that each order of government executes its own legislation is evident on the face of the Constitution.[33] Subject to the role of the High Court of Australia as the final court of appeal in both federal and state jurisdiction,[34] each order of government also provides for adjudication on matters arising in its own sphere of authority. The Constitution divides legislative, executive and judicial

[28] Ronald L Watts, 'Comparing Federal Political Systems' in Alain-G Gagnon, Soeren Keil and Sean Muller (eds), *Understanding Federalism and Federation* (Abingdon, Routledge, 2016) 15, 18.

[29] Cases that recognise these historical realities and attach doctrinal consequences to them include *New South Wales v Commonwealth (Seas and Submerged Lands case)* (1975) 135 CLR 337 and *R v Burgess, ex p Henry* (1936) 55 CLR 608.

[30] The Commonwealth of Australia Constitution Act 1900 (Imp) of which the Constitution is part recites the agreement of the people of the colonies to unite in a federation 'under the Crown', with institutional consequences throughout the Constitution.

[31] *Barton v Commonwealth* (1974) 131 CLR 433.

[32] Commonwealth Constitution, ss 106, 107, 108.

[33] See, eg, the transfer of departments from the States to the Commonwealth, following the division of legislative power (ibid s 69).

[34] ibid s 73.

power between the spheres of government to these ends, by specifying the powers of the Commonwealth, leaving the residue to the States. The division of legislative power is spelt out in some detail, in more than 40 heads of power that are made available to the Commonwealth Parliament. Most, although not all, of these are held concurrently with the States, subject to the paramountcy of Commonwealth law.[35] They include an incidental legislative power in section 51(xxxix) that enables supporting legislation with respect to 'matters incidental to the execution of any power vested by this Constitution ... in the Government of the Commonwealth.' The heads of federal jurisdiction also are relatively detailed.[36]

The treatment of executive power, on the other hand, is much less specific. Section 61 provides:

> The executive power of the Commonwealth is vested in the Queen and is exercisable by the Governor-General as the Queen's representative, and extends to the execution and maintenance of this Constitution, and of the laws of the Commonwealth.

Some implications of the section nevertheless are clear. The executive power of the Commonwealth is distinct from that of the States. In terms of content, it clearly involves the execution and maintenance of Commonwealth law. What else it involves depends on the significance of the word 'extends,' the ambit of authority to execute and maintain the Constitution, the consequences, if any, of the investiture of power in the Queen, and the very conception of 'executive' power.

The federal division of fiscal authority also is part of the story of the federal division of executive power in Australia.[37] The Constitution allocates extensive power to impose taxation to each of the spheres of government, on the dualist assumption that each government would tax for its own purposes.[38] In an important exception, however, the power to impose duties of customs and excise was conferred exclusively on the Commonwealth, depriving the new States at the moment of federation of one of their most significant sources of revenue.[39] As a result, from the outset, there was a degree of fiscal imbalance, for which the Constitution attempted to make remedial provision. One section, which became a dead-letter in the early years of federation, required the regular distribution of Commonwealth 'surplus' revenue to the States.[40] Another provided simply for the payment of financial assistance by the Commonwealth to any State on such terms and conditions 'as the Parliament thinks fit'.[41] Over time, the fiscal imbalance worsened, as the

[35] ibid ss 51, 109. A short list of express exclusive power is set out in s 52.

[36] ibid ss 73, 75, 76.

[37] Cheryl Saunders, *The Constitution of Australia: A Contextual Analysis* (Oxford, Hart Publishing, 2011) 229.

[38] The Commonwealth power to tax can be found in s 51(ii). The State taxation power follows from the general scheme for the federal division of power and in particular ss 106, 107.

[39] Australian Constitution, s 90.

[40] ibid s 94. An accounting arrangement that effectively precludes the existence of any surplus for the purposes of this provision was upheld by the High Court in *New South Wales v Commonwealth* (1908) 7 CLR 179.

[41] Australian Constitution, s 96.

Commonwealth acquired a de facto monopoly over income tax[42] and the High Court interpreted the exclusive Commonwealth power to impose duties of excise as encompassing, in effect, all taxes on goods.[43] From the mid-twentieth century at the latest the Commonwealth had very considerable sources of revenue at its disposal, while the States were dependent on transfers, pursuant to section 96. This mismatch of legislative power and resources encouraged Commonwealth reliance on executive power to unilaterally extend its authority into areas of State responsibility, creating a recurring flashpoint for litigation that has been significant in shaping the scope of the power.

One final aspect of Australian federal design that has affected both judicial doctrine and political practice in relation to executive power is the Senate.[44] The Senate is the second chamber of the bicameral Commonwealth Parliament. It represents all the original States equally, is directly elected and has almost co-equal authority with the House of Representatives. It is rare for a government to have a majority in the Senate, providing an additional incentive for governments to avoid legislation in favour of reliance on executive power where they can. On the other hand, avoidance of the legislature raises concerns for federalism as well as separation of powers when the Senate is the principal formal institution of shared rule.

B. Separation of Powers

The Australian Constitution does not define the concept of executive power that is divided between the Commonwealth and the States by section 61. While other constitutional provisions detail aspects of executive power for particular purposes, they provide almost no assistance with the meaning of the generic term.[45] Like the companion concepts of legislative and judicial power in sections 1 and 71 of the Constitution, the meaning of executive power is simply assumed, leaving uncertainties to be resolved through judicial interpretation.[46]

Given the provenance of the Australian Constitution, one source of insight into the meaning of the concept of executive power is British constitutional law and practice. The potential relevance of British experience is heightened by Australian adaptation of key British institutions including constitutional monarchy and parliamentary responsible government broadly, but by no means entirely, along Westminster lines. The British conception of executive power might add to understanding of section 61 in at least three ways. First, executive power in the United Kingdom

[42] *South Australia v Commonwealth* (1942) 65 CLR 373; *Victoria v Commonwealth* (1957) 99 CLR 575.

[43] *Ha v New South Wales* (1997) 189 CLR 465.

[44] Australian Constitution, ch 1, pt 2.

[45] The power to establish departments of state in s 64 is one example; the power to appoint judges in s 72 is another.

[46] From the voluminous case law on judicial power, in particular, see *Brandy v Human Rights and Equal Opportunity Commission* (1995) 183 CLR 245.

extends well beyond the execution of legislation to include prerogative power.[47] Second, the common law also recognises the inherent authority of the executive to carry out a range of other actions, broadly of a kind that might be performed by any legal person, as long as they are not contrary to law. This anthropomorphism assumes that the executive can be equated with a legal person for this purpose, sometimes by relying on the personhood of the Crown.[48] If either of these possibilities applies in Australia, the immediate result is to extend the concept of executive power to which section 61 refers beyond execution of the Constitution and statute law. Third, in a feature of a different kind, executive power in the British parliamentary tradition can always be overridden by Acts of the sovereign legislature so long, at least, as the intention to do so is sufficiently clear.

The relevance of the British conception of executive power in Australia is necessarily tempered by constitutional differences between the two states. Most obviously, in Australia the concept of executive power is embedded in an entrenched constitution enforced through judicial review. The Commonwealth Parliament is not sovereign in the sense generally accepted for the Parliament at Westminster and could not override specific powers conferred on the executive by the Constitution, whatever the relationship between legislation and section 61. Equally significantly, the Constitution in which executive power is embedded protects approaches to the organisation of public power that in some respects are quite different to those in the United Kingdom, not least of which is the federal system itself. Thus, for example, if the concept of executive power under section 61 includes significant inherent executive power, divorced from statute, it becomes necessary to determine the basis on which power of this kind is divided between the Commonwealth and the States.

An alternative source of insight into the concept of executive power is the Constitution of the United States, on which the Australian Constitution was loosely modelled.[49] The profound difference, for this purpose, between a presidential and a parliamentary system means that the United States offers no guide to the precise conception of executive power. Nevertheless, the similarities in organisation of the first three parts of each Constitution, dedicated to the legislature, executive and judicature respectively, suggests that the questions that arise in Australia might also be analysed through a separation of powers lens. This possibility has been realised to the extent that the Australian Constitution has been held to provide for a three-way separation of powers, albeit one that makes allowance for the exigencies of parliamentary government.[50] It follows that there are enforceable limits on what can be done by the Commonwealth in the exercise of executive power, the demarcation of

[47] Payne, 'The Royal Prerogative'.

[48] John Howell, 'What the Crown May Do' (2010) *Judicial Review* 36.

[49] For a nuanced account of the multiple influences on the making of the Australian Constitution see Nicholas Aroney, *The Constitution of a Federal Commonwealth: The Making and Meaning of the Australian Constitution* (Cambridge, Cambridge University Press, 2009).

[50] *Victorian Stevedoring and General Contracting Company Pty Ltd v Dignan* (1931) 46 CLR 73; *R v Kirby, ex p Boilermakers' Society of Australia* (1956) 94 CLR 254.

which falls to be determined by reference to the text and context of the Australian Constitution. The concept of State executive power requires a somewhat different analysis, involving the State as well as the Australian Constitutions.

C. Breadth and Depth

The scope of federal executive power under section 61 has been a familiar legal battleground since federation. Over time it became accepted that, the final words of the section notwithstanding, executive power was not necessarily dependent on legislative or express constitutional authority; that, in other words, the Commonwealth executive enjoyed some inherent executive power. The extent of inherent power has remained contested, however, from the standpoint of both federalism and separation of powers. Nor has it ever been entirely clear how this development relates to section 61. On one, now older, view, prerogative and/or general executive power derived from the common law and were merely subsumed by the section.[51] On another, the function of ideas about executive power derived from the common law constitutional tradition is to inform the meaning of section 61 in a constitutional context. On yet another, the references in section 61 to the Queen or to the 'execution and maintenance' of the Constitution might be interpreted to authorise much of the action that could be taken in the exercise of inherent executive power elsewhere.

Australian discourse has sometimes described the problem of determining the scope of the executive power of the Commonwealth in terms of breadth and depth, broadly reflecting the two axes of executive power in federations with which this chapter began.[52] Depth thus refers to the scope of executive vis-à-vis legislative power and breadth refers to the ambit of the executive power of the Commonwealth vis-à-vis that of the States. Most litigation has focused on one or the other, encouraging discrete treatment of the two dimensions of the problem. Thus in *Barton v Commonwealth*,[53] in which the plaintiff challenged an Australian request to extradite him from Brazil, the principal issue was the relationship between prerogative power and statute and the federalism dimension was, properly, assumed to be satisfied. Conversely, in the *Australian Assistance Plan (AAP)* case, argument focused on whether expenditure on Regional Councils for Social Development fell within the powers of the Commonwealth, without seriously questioning whether the executive could spend public funds to this end without substantive supporting legislation.[54]

The *AAP* case was complicated for present purposes because the Court was divided over whether the power of the Commonwealth to engage in spending

[51] *Farey v Burvett* (1916) 21 CLR 433, 452.

[52] George Winterton, 'The Relationship between Commonwealth Legislative and Executive Power' (2004) 25 *Adelaide Law Review* 21, 29–30.

[53] *Barton v Commonwealth* (1974) 131 CLR 477.

[54] *Victoria v Commonwealth & Hayden* (1975) 134 CLR 338.

programs of this kind was unlimited by federal considerations and whether, in any event, it derived from the requirement for appropriation in section 81 or relied, at least in part, on the executive power. The reasons of Mason J offered an influential middle ground. On this view, the executive power would support engagement in spending programs in areas of Commonwealth constitutional responsibilities, which could be ascertained from the distribution of legislative powers and from the 'existence and character of the Commonwealth as a national government.'[55] The latter gave the Commonwealth 'a capacity to engage in enterprises and activities peculiarly adapted to the government of a nation and which cannot otherwise be carried on for the benefit of the nation.'[56] Notably, the judge who took this view held that the Australian Assistance Plan was invalid.[57]

Questions about the nature and scope of executive power in Australia have been raised in other contexts as well, further complicating an already complex jurisprudence. The executive power to contract without adequate parliamentary authority has been challenged at the State level as well, with results that have a bearing on problems arising in the Commonwealth sphere, despite the more 'unitary' context.[58] Litigation challenging the outcomes of intergovernmental schemes has established that the Commonwealth executive has power to enter into agreements with the States, subject to constitutional limits that remain to be explored.[59] It should be noted in passing that this is an aspect of executive power peculiar to a federal setting. Long-running lines of authority about whether and when the respective spheres of government could enact legislation that applied to the executive branch of the other led to decisions that tended to assume inherent executive power to contract in the course of, for example, drawing a distinction between State legislation that affected the 'capacities and functions' of the Commonwealth, and legislation regulating the transactions in which the Commonwealth executive 'chose to engage.'[60] The former was precluded but the latter was not, subject to Commonwealth legislation to the contrary.

D. A Compound Conception of Federal Executive Power

As long as the breadth and depth of executive power were treated as discrete questions in Australian constitutional litigation, the latter drew primarily on modes of analysis derived from the British constitutional tradition, with outcomes that were broadly equivalent. From the turn of the twenty-first century, however, a wave of cases raising problems of executive power began what—with hindsight—can be seen

[55] ibid 398.

[56] ibid.

[57] The final orders of the Court upheld the validity of the Plan, however, for reasons that are not directly relevant for present purposes.

[58] *New South Wales v Bardolph* (1934) 52 CLR 455; considered by French CJ in *Williams v The Commonwealth* (2012) 248 CLR 156, 211–214.

[59] *R v Duncan, ex p Australian Iron & Steel Pty Ltd* (1983) 158 CLR 535, 559, Mason J.

[60] *Re Residential Tenancies Tribunal of New South Wales v Henderson, ex p Defence Housing Authority* (1997) 190 CLR 410.

as a new turning. Executive power in the Australian federation now is a compound conception in which considerations of federalism and separation of powers influence each other in ways that are determined by reference to the Australian Constitution as a whole.

Oddly, the starting point was a decision of the Full Court of the Federal Court of Australia in which federalism was not in issue at all.[61] Instead, the question for the Court in *Ruddock v Vadarlis* was the validity of actions of the Commonwealth executive in intercepting and expelling non-citizens arriving by boat in reliance on inherent executive power. British authority on the scope of the prerogative for this purpose was equivocal, as the dissenting reasons of Black CJ showed. For the majority judges, however, this was not determinative.[62] The executive power of the Commonwealth was not a 'species of the royal prerogative' but a 'power conferred as part of a negotiated federal compact expressed in a written Constitution distributing power between the three arms of government ... and ... as to legislative powers, between the polities that comprise the federation'.[63] Construed in context, section 61 authorised the action here, which was 'central to ... sovereignty' and thus attributable to 'maintenance of the Constitution'.[64] The reasoning by which this result was reached drew extensively on the notion of nationhood previously used primarily to delimit the federal dimensions of the power.[65]

Federalism was directly in issue in the three cases that followed, later in the decade. The first of these, *Pape v Federal Commissioner of Taxation*, narrowly upheld the validity of economic stimulus legislation in the wake of the global financial crisis, on the grounds that a short-term emergency of this kind attracted the nationhood component of the executive power, which could then be supported by an exercise of the incidental legislative power.[66] Importantly for present purposes *Pape* also confirmed, however, that any executive power to spend was limited by considerations of federalism; that its scope depended on the interpretation of section 61, in the context of the Constitution as a whole; and that the requirement for appropriation played no necessary role in the resolution of the problem, prescribing instead the technical procedure for the release of moneys from the Consolidated Revenue Fund. The reasoning in *Pape* made it likely that further challenges would follow as they did, in the two *Williams* cases.[67]

The issue in both cases involved spending pursuant to a contract. In pursuance of a National Schools Chaplaincy Program, the Commonwealth had entered into a Funding Agreement with the Scripture Union Queensland (SUQ) to provide funding for chaplaincy services in Queensland schools that expressed interest in a chaplaincy placement. Individual contracts were concluded between the Commonwealth and

61 *Ruddock v Vadarlis* (2001) 110 FCR 491.

62 ibid (French J, with whom Beaumont J agreed on these points).

63 ibid [183] (French J).

64 ibid [191].

65 ibid [180], citing *Victoria v Commonwealth & Hayden* (1975) 134 CLR 338, 406 and *Davis v Commonwealth* (1988) 166 CLR 79, 93.

66 *Pape v Federal Commissioner of Taxation* (2009) 238 CLR 1.

67 *Williams v Commonwealth* (2012) 248 CLR 156; *Williams v Commonwealth (No 2)* (2014) 252 CLR 416.

SUQ in relation to the placement of each chaplain. The plaintiff was the father of children at one of the schools in question, who objected to having a chaplain at the school. The Program was undertaken solely in exercise of the executive power, subject to a general appropriation in the budget legislation appropriating moneys for the 'ordinary annual services of government' that specified the 'outcome' as '[individuals] achieve high quality foundation skills and learning outcomes from schools and other providers'.[68] The regulatory framework for the program was provided by executive Guidelines, which were subject to frequently change.

In the first *Williams* case, the High Court held by a majority of 6-1 that the Funding Agreement was not a valid exercise of the executive power of the Commonwealth and was not supported by section 61.[69] In itself this was not a surprising outcome, although it was hard fought by the defendant Commonwealth. The case is significant for the reasoning of four of the majority Justices, who reached their decision on the basis that the contract and associated spending were unconstitutional because they were unsupported by legislation, rather than because they exceeded Commonwealth, as opposed to State, executive power.[70] In other words, the majority held that the contract did not fall within the constitutional conception of executive power at all. The other two majority Justices[71] avoided decision on this issue, holding instead that the contract fell outside the scope of Commonwealth executive power, measured by reference to the somewhat more orthodox considerations of the contours of legislative power augmented by the demands of nationhood.

There was no single majority opinion; a familiar situation in Australian practice. As a result, there are some significant differences between the majority reasonings. There was enough in common between the three sets of reasons, however, to draw the following conclusions from them for the nature and scope of Commonwealth executive power. The text of section 61, interpreted in constitutional, including historical, context, is the primary point of reference. The scope of Commonwealth executive power is not determined by the scope of the prerogative or common law executive power in the UK, although this may inform the understanding of section 61. Insofar as reasoning about the scope of inherent executive power in other common law states rests on an analogy with the capacities of a legal person, reinforced by the location of executive power in the Crown, it has been rejected for Australia. The Constitution creates the Commonwealth (and, by inference, each State) as a polity and distributes functions between its branches in a manner that, ultimately, falls for determination by the Court. Construed in context, Commonwealth executive power necessarily is a composite concept, in which understanding of what the executive branch can do without legislative authority is shaped by considerations of both separation of powers and federalism, in the light of constitutional text and structure. Federalism indicators that influenced the reasoning of the Justices in

[68] *Appropriation Act (No 3) 2006–2007* (Cth) sch 1, quoted in the reasons of Hayne J in *Williams* [227].

[69] French CJ, Gummow, Hayne, Crennan, Kiefel and Bell JJ, Heydon J dissenting.

[70] This line of reasoning was adopted by French CJ, Gummow and Bell JJ and Crennan J.

[71] Hayne J and Kiefel J.

Williams included the potential for a broad executive power, underpinned by the incidental legislative power, to undermine the constitutionally-entrenched division of legislative powers, especially on a matter that clearly lay within State authority and could not conceivably be a candidate for the 'nationhood' power; the presence in the Constitution of section 96, authorising Commonwealth spending in areas beyond its legislative powers through grants to the States on such conditions as the Parliament 'thinks fit'; and the potential for a program based solely on the executive power to avoid the need for Senate consideration and approval.

The sequel to the first *Williams* decision showed how the now compound conception of federal executive power might have benefits for representative democracy as well as federalism. The immediate response to *Williams* was legislation to provide a loose subordinate statutory base for the National Schools Chaplaincy Program and more than 400 other executive spending programs deemed to be at risk.[72] Despite the somewhat provocative nature of this solution, which remains to be tested, any legislative underpinning for the scheme was vulnerable to challenge by reference to the federal division of legislative power. In *Williams (No 2)*, a challenge to the validity of the legislation was upheld by a unanimous High Court on the ground that there was no head of legislative power to support it.[73] Insufficiently daunted, the government now gave the School Chaplains Program effect through conditional grants to the States pursuant to section 96. While this was a hollow victory for the plaintiff, it was at least consistent with the federal framework. The intergovernmental agreement setting out the terms of the grant also is more stable in policy terms, if only because it involves two parties, than the departmental guidelines had proved to be.[74] Further, the new subordinate legislative basis for federal spending programs exposes them to scrutiny by the Senate Standing Committee on Regulations and Ordinances, which now insists that Ministers identify the federal head of power on which they rely, when new spending regulations are made.[75] And in yet another twist, the attention aroused by the transformation of the program into a conditional grant to the States caused the Senate Standing Committee for Scrutiny of Bills to begin to take a belated interest in the way these arrangements work.[76]

E. Unfinished Business

It seems likely that understanding of the nature and scope of executive power in Australia will continue to build on the doctrinal framework laid down in the first

[72] Financial Framework Legislation Amendment Act No 3 2012 (Cth).

[73] Joint reasons were published by French CJ, Hayne, Kiefel, Bell and Keane JJ. Crennan J published separate reasons.

[74] Project Agreement for the National School Chaplaincy Programme, <www.federalfinancialrelations>. gov.au/content/npa/education/school_chaplaincy_programme/Project_Agreement.pdf (viewed 11 April 2016).

[75] Patrick Hodder, 'The *Williams* decisions and the implications for the Senate and its scrutiny committees', Papers on Parliament No 64 (2016) 143, 150–52.

[76] Senate Standing Committee for the Scrutiny of Bills, *Alert Digest 2/16*, 'Appropriation Bill (No 4) 2015–2016', 9.

Williams case. The Court rejected the Commonwealth's attempt to reopen these issues in *Williams (No 2)*. Political practice is beginning to adjust to a more limited ambit for inherent executive power. It may be that the doctrine is not entirely secure, however. The terms of the joint reasons in *Williams (No 2)* were sufficiently carefully phrased to preserve both the strands of reasoning over which the six-member majority divided in the earlier case.[77] And in a post-*Williams* decision, on a matter entirely within the federal sphere of responsibility, one more recent member of the Court went to some lengths to confine the authority for which the cases stand.[78]

The doctrine is vulnerable also, however, because aspects of it remain unclear. The existence of Commonwealth executive power in association with a valid Commonwealth statute or pursuant to particular provisions of the Constitution is straightforward enough. In these instances, also, questions about federalism are automatically resolved. Commonwealth claims to inherent executive power present a more complex case. *Williams* suggests several bases on which they might be resolved. In some cases the executive might exercise powers 'in the nature of the prerogative' that are properly attributable to the Commonwealth; in others executive action might be justified by 'the character and status of the Commonwealth as the national government'; in others again, the executive has power to act in the course of administering the Departments of State. The federal character of the Constitution plays a role of some kind in each of these categories. Nevertheless, their scope and the boundaries between them are by no means clear. In particular, it remains to be determined which contracts and spending programs require supporting legislation and which do not. This is an issue on which comparative experience might well assist.

In addition, it remains to be determined whether the same limits on the capacity of the Commonwealth executive to act without legislation affect the executive power of the States. At first glance, the dependence of the *Williams* reasoning on the context of the Australian Constitution, including its federal features, makes extension to the States unlikely. Separation of powers also is a much less prominent feature of the Constitutions of the States.[79] On the other hand, the Australian Constitution recognises both the Commonwealth and the States as polities, providing a basis on which anthropomorphic reasoning can dismissed for both.[80] And there are precedents in Australia for the extension to the States of the effect of doctrines governing the position of the Commonwealth under the Australian Constitution.[81] This can be expected to happen, in one way or another, in connection with executive power as well.[82]

[77] *Williams v Commonwealth (No 2)* (2014) 253 CLR 416, 469.

[78] *M68/2015 v Minister for Immigration and Border Protection* [2016] HCA 1, Gageler J.

[79] *Durham Holdings Pty Ltd v New South Wales* (2001) 205 CLR 399.

[80] Section 75(iv) refers to suits between 'States', just as s 75(iii) refers to suits in which the 'Commonwealth' is a party.

[81] The principal examples are the constitutional protection of judicial review on grounds of jurisdictional error and protection of the integrity of the judiciary: respectively, *Kirk v Industrial Relations Commission* (2010) 239 CLR 531; *Kable v Director of Public Prosecutions (NSW)* (1996) 189 CLR 51.

[82] Saunders, 'The concept of the Crown' 873.

IV. CONCLUSIONS

This study of executive power in federal systems suggests three points of particular interest for work on the federal idea.

First, the arrangements by which power is organised and limited to secure the federal idea in a working federation are interdependent with the rest of the constitutional system, which also may evolve over time to reflect the modalities of federalism. Thus, while legislative and executive powers inevitably are divided between the orders of government in any federation, how they are divided and the manner of their exercise depends on the constitutional and legal setting in which they are embedded. Whether executive power presents itself as a distinct issue may depend on the extent to which there is a conception of executive power independent of legislation or of the scope of legislative power. Where, on the other hand, the constitutional setting acknowledges substantial inherent executive power it presents an additional set of problems for federalism to resolve. The Australian case study shows how, in these conditions, the conception of executive power may adapt to the federal setting.

Reflection on these dynamics suggests the second point. Key features of the constitutional setting in which federalism is embedded generally have their genesis in a unitary system of government. This may particularly be so, for example, in relation to the structure and power of the three branches of government, the legislature, executive and judiciary, arrangements for shared rule aside. The relationship between these branches typically is underpinned by historical experience, whether local or derived, given continuing relevance through constitutional theories. The political culture in which they have evolved is not necessarily conducive to the power-sharing and consensus-building that federalism requires. In these circumstances, there is potential for a clash between the two sets of principles on which a federal constitution rests, each of which may be resistant to change. The Australian case study illustrates these dynamics in relation to the concept of executive power in one federation. It also shows how, in those particular conditions, a *modus vivendi* of sorts has been reached.

Third, as a logical corollary, the nature and scope of executive power differs in some respects between all federations, depending both on federal design and the constitutional setting more generally. One aim of this chapter has been to suggest an approach to understanding these differences and evaluating their significance for comparative purposes. The exercise is complex, because some differences run deep. It nevertheless is worthwhile. The conditions in which government operates in the early twenty-first century tend to augment executive power, externally and internally. This phenomenon affects all states but has particular implications for states that also divide governing authority for federal purposes. There are insights to be gained into how such pressures might be both accommodated and resolved from a comparison of federal experiences that is adequately informed.

Part III

Federal Trajectories

7

Woodrow Wilson and the Challenge of Federalism in World War One

DUNCAN KELLY*

THIS CHAPTER EXPLORES some of the ways in which Woodrow Wilson's account of federalism generally, and the experience of American federalism particularly, was pressed into service prior to and then during the Great War. It does so in three ways. First, by exploring Wilson's 'exceptionalist' and even 'nationalist' reading of the American federal past, it is possible to see how historical thinking about the politics of federalism was used to justify an exceptional place for the American nation through war and into the twentieth century, in competition with the concerted powers of old Europe.[1] Second, exploring Wilson's rather general theoretical account of federalism sheds comparative light on the ways in which many non-European writers were able to utilise his ideas either as justification for anti-colonial projects of national self-determination, or in the construction of alternative visions of pan-regional forms of federation. My discussion focuses in particular on the way in which Wilson combined his account of federalism with a vision of pan-American power, which could not only counter non-European pan-regional movements, but also align with the nationalist politics behind his federal vision. To that extent, it focuses on the admittedly rather messy intellectual connections between federalism, nationalism and self-determination in the context of a global war, looking at ways in which the battle for ideas lay behind a battle for global power. What Wilson saw as the historical uniqueness of American federal experiments in constitutional government nevertheless prompted him to think that it offered a model that could be generalised, such that the idea of a community of power in the form of a league of nations, rather than a legalistic framework for a balance of power, could become the conscience of a new world order. Finally, these parallel discussions can be seen as part of Wilson's wider strategy to counteract

* With many thanks to the Editor and the other participants in the original conference where these thoughts were first developed, and particularly to John A Thompson for his expert advice on the political ideas of Woodrow Wilson.

[1] On which see Adam Tooze, *The Deluge: The Great War and the Remaking of Global Order, 1916–1931* (London, Penguin Books, 2014).

the power of pan-German forms of union during the war itself. Such ideas were rendered unsupportable in his eyes because of their excess of nationalism and apparent absence of democratic federalism. While Wilson's ideas about law, government and history have been extensively discussed, my particular focus on his sense of the relationship between federalism, nationalism and pan-nationalism through both intellectual history and political strategy offers a different account of an older series of problems, problems at the heart of any discussion of federalism, nationalism and self-determination, but newly focused on some of the international intellectual contexts that illuminate the political implications of his claims.

I. WOODROW WILSON ON DEMOCRACY AND FEDERALISM

Speaking on 2 November 1917 to the American Federation of Labor in Buffalo, New York, shortly after the outbreak of revolution in Russia but before the tide had turned towards the allies in the Great War, President Woodrow Wilson denounced pan-Germanism as a cancer at the heart of modern Germany. 'Power,' he said, 'cannot be used with concentrated force against free peoples if it is used by free peoples.' The pan-German plan would fail because of this, because of the power of free peoples who will fight for democracy. As part of a talk on 'What Democracy Means,' Wilson held fast to the idea that democracy is self-government; self-government is only possible with self-control; and self-control means doing one's patriotic duty as far as 'common counsel' and 'cooperation' requires.[2]

Democracy gestured to both the coming American future according to Wilson, as well as to its past. In 1918 there appeared a specially revised edition of one of his earliest books, *The State*, first published in 1895. In the new edition, some of the general political theory and institutional history had been excised, in order to explain the developmental trajectory of the particular belligerents in the world war. To that end, his rather dry academic work became a clear piece of political practice. And in it, he was clear that 'if Aristocracy seems about to disappear, Democracy seems about universally to prevail.'[3] That historical as well as conceptual shift, nonetheless, hides as much as it reveals. For Wilson's long-standing view of democracy, understood as a form of popular sovereignty, was quite stentorian. His vision of democracy was resolutely safeguarded from majoritarian tyranny, because 'properly organized democracy is the best government of the few.'[4] Those safeguards were given form both in the political economy that shaped the 'interest' of the state, and its administration which managed those interests in wider society. Equally, it was a premise that could be shelved; by the time he entered politics in 1910, running as a Progressive in defence of 'plain people' against corrupt elites, and

[2] Woodrow Wilson, 'What Democracy Means' [1917] in Christian F Gauss (ed) *Democracy Today: An American Interpretation* (Chicago, Scott Forsman and Co, 1917) 186, 190ff.

[3] Woodrow Wilson, *The State* (Boston, DC Heath & Co, 1918) 35.

[4] Woodrow Wilson, 'The Modern Democratic State' [1898] *Papers of Woodrow Wilson* (Princeton, Princeton University Press, 1968) 5, 80, 85; see the discussion in Niels Aage Thorsen, *The Political Thought of Woodrow Wilson, 1875–1910* (Princeton, Princeton University Press, 1988) 222, 227.

in the most general terms. Both positions had implications for how he came to think about the causes and consequences of the war itself.

Wilson's interest in administration had its own deep roots, which relate to the attempt to Americanise and domesticate, through what has become known as an 'exceptionalist' narrative, European legal and political thought. In relying in part on Johan Kaspar Bluntschli's synthetic state and legal theory, Wilson evoked a singular genealogy that was already becoming part of the mainstream of modern American political science. If American political science was, early in the nineteenth century, a 'scattered and diffuse body of knowledge', it seemed not to achieve a new synthesis until the work of the émigré Prussian scholar, Francis Lieber, provided it with his combination of Germanic state theory and antebellum Whiggery.[5] On this account, the origins of American social and political science expressed a continuous attempt to naturalise American historical development, and construct 'models of the world that embody the values and follow the logic of the national ideology of American exceptionalism.'[6] Its theoretical framework was derived from German *Staatstheorie*, which most of the leading American scholars learned whilst doing their graduate work in Germany before returning home to teach it to the next generation.[7] And it routinely focused on debates about the nature of the relationship between state and nation in a federal constitutional system, the administrative arrangements between these branches, and the representative qualities of the statesman or monarch at the apex of the system.

Wilson knew this background very well and it mattered for his own construction of federalism and American democracy, for he was taught by one of Bluntschli's own pupils, the unloved Herbert Baxter Adams, at Johns Hopkins. Bluntschli (alongside Lorenz von Stein) influenced the theory of the separation between politics and administration that Wilson proposed in *The State*. In that work, he devoted two massive chapters to governmental reform in Germany and Switzerland, and the nature of international wars between and surrounding those states, both matters extensively considered by Bluntschli.[8] For Bluntschli was a figure, alongside Lieber, who developed arguments about international law and the laws of war between civilised, cosmopolitan states that would be hugely influential in both Europe and America.[9]

This link between Bluntschli and Lieber is discernible in what is, indisputably, Lieber's most influential intervention, his codification of the treatment of enemy

[5] Dorothy Ross, *The Origins of American Social Science* (Cambridge, Cambridge University Press, 1991) 38ff.

[6] ibid 471.

[7] Sylvia Fries, '*Staatstheorie* and the New American Science of Politics' (1973) 34 *Journal of the History of Ideas* 391–404. More broadly, this sections builds on Duncan Kelly, 'Nationalism and Cosmopolitan Humanity in Mid-Nineteenth-Century American Political Science' in J Isaac, J Kloppenberg, M O'Brien, and J Ratner-Rosenhagen (eds) *Worlds of American Intellectual History* (Oxford, Oxford University Press, 2016) 115–32.

[8] Wilson, *The State* chs 7–8; Christian Rosser, 'Woodrow Wilson's Administrative Thought and German Political Theory' (2010) 70 *Public Administration Review* 551ff; *cf* John A Thompson, 'Woodrow Wilson and a World Governed by Evolving Law' (2008) 20 *Journal of Policy History* 119ff.

[9] Johan Kaspar Bluntschli, *Das Moderne Kriegsrecht der Civilisierten Staaten* 2nd edn (Nordlingen, CH Beck, 1874).

combatants, known as *General Orders 100*. These have exercised a profound influence, informing both twentieth-century field manuals for the United States military, and the four Geneva conventions defining the modern laws of war.[10] Like Bluntschli, Lieber was also an anti-Napoleonic writer, having fought at Waterloo, and when he wrote the Codes he was self-consciously contributing to what he saw as the common project of racially and culturally connecting the American to the wider European and Anglo-Saxon concept of a shared 'civilisation', explicitly governed by the law of nations. This project linked easily to claims about the unconstitutionality of secession.[11] For Lieber, there was a standard of civilisation against which uncivilised or barbarian states were to be judged, and a standard that authorised discrete laws of war when military conflict took place between states of equal levels of civilisation. These were partners who disagreed but who shared a commitment to civilisation, and who acknowledged that conflict resolution had rules. More broadly, there was a distinction between constrained or regulated war between civilised states, and unconstrained warfare with or between uncivilised states. Such a distinction mattered when considering the practicalities of a civil war within a national representative republic.

Wilson agreed with both Bluntschli and Lieber, in presuming a practical difference between Anglo-Saxon and French (and therefore revolutionary) liberty, holding the latter guilty of activity based on a misapprehension of the truth of his Burkean-inspired and evolutionary sense of the relationship between law and society.[12] The constitution was the 'taproot' of American political life, but that life was an evolving, organic body of experience and institutional form with a federal structure.[13] In Wilson's case, too, this had deeply religious familial roots. He felt his life and work determined by 'an over-ruling providence.'[14]

Having re-described popular sovereignty as a problem requiring political leadership as its solution, the transition from a politics based on the 'people' to a politics based on 'nationality' required, he thought, a form of strong, national political leadership. This circular claim was less about the evacuation of democracy from a strongly nationalist program, rather more an argument that popular sovereignty just is, in effect, national sovereignty (the nineteenth century lesson) and that national sovereignty could be given democratic form only through capable, representative political elites.[15] National history, and the history of national government, was the necessary prerequisite to

[10] Francis Lieber, 'Instructions for Armies in the Field: General Orders No. 100' (1863) in Daniel C Gilman (ed) *Miscellaneous Writings of Francis Lieber* (Philadelphia, JB Lippincott, 1881) 2, pp 245–74.

[11] Francis Lieber, letter of 2 May 1863 in Thomas Sergeant Perry (ed), *The Life and Letters of Francis Lieber* (Boston, James R Osgood, 1882) 333ff; Charles Sumner, 'Resolutions on the Theory of Secession and Reconstruction' (11 February 1862) in Henry Steele Commager (ed), *Documents in American History* (New York, Appleton-Century-Crofts, 1963) 406ff.

[12] Thompson, 'Woodrow Wilson and a World Governed by Evolving Law' 117, 119.

[13] Woodrow Wilson, *Congressional Government: A Study in American Politics* (Boston, Houghton Mifflin, 1901) 7ff.

[14] Andrew Scott Berg, *Wilson* (New York, Simon and Schuster, 2013) 223.

[15] On this point, see Duncan Kelly, 'Popular Sovereignty as State Theory in the nineteenth century' in Richard Bourke and Quentin Skinner (eds) *Popular Sovereignty in Historical Perspective* (Cambridge, Cambridge University Press, 2016) 270–296.

understanding and explaining the 'plain evidence' that the 'expansion of federal power is set to continue', as well as the 'radical defect' in American federalism, which was a confusion resulting from an original provision to divide power between the different branches of government.[16] Leadership required an organic, rather than legally formalist (presumably also a reference to adherents of some form of constitutional originalism) or Lockean-individualist, interpretation. The statesman was an organic and embodied representative of the nation, a view that provided ready clues to the combination of Burkean and nineteenth-century German-inspired sources of his academic political theory.[17] In his own practical rendition, that process was also, and again just as Lieber had suggested, a racial project. For Lieber, the anachronism of slavery would be overcome by the transition towards a new union, even if that did not mean racial equality. Alexis de Tocqueville had argued in the 1830s that three things—popular sovereignty, national self-determination, and the rise of democracy—were now part of a wider human drama conceived of as a 'providential fact.'[18] Lieber agreed, not only because he sustained a long correspondence (often about politics) with Tocqueville after an early meeting in Boston, but also because this focus on sentiments was indispensable for understanding the nature of American democracy. Both men concurred that the rootedness of national sentiments was the grounding for general historical prognoses about the future of equality and humanity.[19] The coordinates of Tocqueville's political vision inform the two volumes of Lieber's *Manual of Political Ethics*.[20] There, a comparison of Gallic with Anglican liberty, to the disadvantage of the former, certainly echoed the dichotomy between individualism and centralisation that lay at the heart of Tocqueville's uneasy analysis. Even so, Lieber's rejection of Gallic 'imperatorial' models of sovereignty was clear, and would matter to Wilson.[21] Building upon the classical and conventional foundations offered by Tocqueville and Lieber, Wilson pursued the idea of democracy as long-term fate which, however, required strong, short-term leadership in order to keep it focused. That dilemma, of playing 'for one hundred years hence', as he would put it when defending his position to the Democratic Senator from

[16] Wilson, *Congressional Government* 53, 284. Elsewhere, Wilson talked of the need to render federalism and the constitution into the daily conscience of ordinary people as the task of the constitutional statesman. See Woodrow Wilson, 'The States and the Federal Government' (1908) *North American Review* 701.

[17] Eric Schulzke, 'Wilsonian Crisis Leadership, the Organic State, and the Modern Presidency' (2005) 37 *Polity* 266.

[18] Alexis de Tocqueville, *Democracy in America* (New York, Anchor Books, 1969) 12.

[19] David Clinton, *Tocqueville, Lieber, Bagehot: Liberalism Confronts the World* (Basingstoke, Macmillan, 2003); *cf* Merle Curti, 'Francis Lieber and Nationalism' (1941) 4 *Huntington Library Quarterly* 275ff.

[20] Francis Lieber, *Manual of Political Ethics* (Boston, Charles C Little and James Brown, 1838–39); *cf* Francis Lieber's letter to Alexis de Tocqueville of 4 September 1854 in Jeremy Jennings and Aurelian Craiutu (eds), *Tocqueville on America after 1840: Letters and Other Writings* (Cambridge, Cambridge University Press, 2009) 162.

[21] Francis Lieber, 'Anglican and Gallic Liberty' [1849] in Daniel C Gilman (ed), *Miscellaneous Writings of Francis Lieber* (Philadelphia, JB Lippincott, 1881) 2, p 385; *On Civil Liberty and Self-Government* (Philadelphia, JB Lippincott, 1859) 394–97, 404.

Arizona, Henry Ashurst at the White House on 14 October 1918, would come into conflict with the short-term electoral demands of representative democracy both in America, as well as in those other states with whom Wilson had to deal with afterwards at Versailles. The 'cyclone of the people's wrath' against Germany that Ashurst warned him of was more powerful than any long-term commitment to peace and a new world order.[22]

Nevertheless, it became increasingly obvious throughout the Great War that just as conventional claims about Anglo-Saxon racial superiority from a Southern perspective had been crucial for his sense of politics since the American civil war, Wilson's presumption of racial hierarchy continued to put some broad view of Anglo-Saxon superiority at the current historical apex of civilisation during the Great War, even if its explicit dimensions became more muted in his public utterances. Its background signalling nevertheless structured Wilson's sense of how American politics should deal with revolutionary problems both on its own borders, in Mexico particularly, as well as with the wider challenges of Russian Bolshevism and German militarism.[23] While America during the Great War would be an 'associated power,' not an ally, and while the level of political censorship and campaigning for liberty bonds and victory loans was more pervasive than anything undertaken during the Civil War, this racial connection remained. And as Adam Tooze has recently shown, it transformed the force of Wilson's plea to make the world safe for democracy under American leadership into a clearly nationalist political project.[24]

If the contours of what would become an ideological opposition between democracy and autocracy began to emerge during the war, as a scholar, Woodrow Wilson had earlier thought the nineteenth century a truly 'democratic' century, but only because his sense of democracy meant rough and ready debate. Democracy was 'rebellious,' and America, with its Civil War, was exemplary in its rebelliousness but also exemplary in its exceptional status; the civil war had clarified America's world-historical significance, forging through war a newly-united nation whose exceptionalism nevertheless originated in the particularities of its federal founding. Making a federal nation suggested the route, while forging it in war defeated the alternative confederal model, institutionalising the American 'experiment' anew. That Madison's reports of the 'federal convention' of 1787, rather than the latterly re-described 'constitutional convention,' were reprinted by the Carnegie Foundation at the end of the Great War signalled once again the case of a reading of American history as unique in its federal democracy, a claim that mirrored Wilson's sensibility.[25] Such a federal past made it possible to delineate a distinctively American model of democratic

[22] Arthur S Link (ed), *Papers of Woodrow Wilson* (Princeton, Princeton University Press, 1985) 51, pp 338ff. From many possible discussions, see Thomas J Knock, *To End all Wars: Woodrow Wilson and the Quest for a New World Order* (Princeton, Princeton University Press, 1992) 172f.

[23] Robert Boyce, *The Great Interwar Crisis and the Collapse of Globalization* (Basingstoke, Macmillan, 2012) 18–21, 428–30. Such racial considerations continued to structure modern American international relations. See Robert Vitalis, *White World Order, Black Power Politics: The Birth of American International Relations* (Ithaca, Cornell University Press, 2015).

[24] Tooze, *Deluge* 44f, 61–64, 223ff.

[25] Galliard Hunt and James Brown Scott (eds) *The Debates in the Federal Convention of 1787 which Framed the Constitution of the United States of America* (New York, Oxford University Press, 1920).

union that combined Hamiltonian 'centralism' and Madisonian 'constitutionalism' in its origins, but which advanced new institutional arrangements (particularly in terms of the enhanced role of the judiciary) that could also be aligned to Wilson's ideological requirements.[26] Indeed, for Wilson the Civil War made possible the realisation of this American experiment in federalism in terms that others in the mid nineteenth-century had begun to think of as 'humanitarian' democracy. However, by its end the Civil War had been re-described by many in the North as an anti-revolutionary moment, notable more for playing a role in the exceptional development of the 'true idea' of the modern American state than being about the quest for freedom. The Civil War, as Orestes Brownson insisted, had not been about humanitarianism or even 'the realization of liberty', but instead 'the realization of the true idea of the state' alongside the 'twilight of humanitarianism.'[27] During the Great War, this political and intellectual history of American federalism was largely discussed in terms of its colonial background and origins.[28] So as Wilson tried to stress the modernity and uniqueness of American federal democracy, he was simultaneously making a rhetorical and political statement against the contemporary dominance of the old world empires of Britain and Europe.

The twentieth century and its first global war in turn made possible the rise to pre-eminence of this particular exceptionalist vision of America as the world's preeminent democracy. Wilson also quickly learned to be a 'good hater' in politics, and that cut across his own cabinet as much as it did across a global colour line. Nevertheless, Tooze shows him to have been the strategist behind the rise of an American century in global perspective. For Wilson ended the war years as he had begun them; antipathetic to British imperial hubris (all imperial hubris in fact) and the old-world order, but recognising the enormous importance of allied help in moving towards the League of Nations. Indeed, he claimed in 1918 that rather than short-term gain he was thinking far into the future, only now with the knowledge of what could be done when Washington-style 'politics was adjourned.'[29] And at home, the dramatic administrative re-organisation of the American state on a war footing, allied to Wilson's absolute authority and presence, seemingly made plausible the possibility of realising his vision of a League of Nations. Once again, the American federal experiment in democracy was only going to be judged in the long term in his eyes. However, in the short term Wilson's apparent neglect of domestic constraints and Washington-style politics ruined his chances of getting the treaty accepted in the US Senate, and made him the 'lamest duck ever to inhabit the White House' at the tail end of his presidency.[30]

[26] *cf* Tooze, *Deluge* 41, 61f; Samuel Beer, *To Make a Nation: The Rediscovery of American Federalism* (Cambridge, Mass, Harvard University Press, 1993) esp 20–25, 379–92; Alison LaCroix, 'The Authority for Federalism: Madison's Negative and the Origins of Federal Ideology' (2010) 28 *Law and History Review* 456.

[27] George M Frederickson, *The Inner Civil War: Northern Intellectuals and the Crisis of the Union* (New York, Harper & Row, 1968) 187, 192ff (quotation on p 187).

[28] Andrew C McGlaughlin, 'The Background of American Federalism' (1918) 12 *American Political Science Review* 215–40; *cf* the slightly later developments by Charles H McIlwain, *The American Revolution: A Constitutional Interpretation* (Ithaca, Cornell University Press, 1923); Charles M Andrews, *The Colonial Background of the American Revolution* (New Haven, Yale University Press, 1923).

[29] Tooze, *Deluge* 44f, 61, 218, 221, 223; Berg, *Wilson* 478.

[30] Berg, *Wilson* 679.

Of course, American political leadership would have to deal with American political problems and would, almost by definition, be unique. But that was a general position that Wilson, and Lieber before him, had held to be self-evident. Unsurprisingly it fostered a great deal of justifiable resentment among the wave of anti-colonial, internationalist nationalism that found in Wilson's proclamations about self-determination and the natural development towards international solidarity a defence of the long-run process of democracy across the globe.[31] But there were structural limitations too, determined both by the substantive differences between ancient and modern ideas about politics as well as the transformation of the institutions of contemporary government. As he wrote, limited, modern, and representative forms of government had to temper the 'rhetorical grandeur' of traditional statesmanship, clarifying that active leadership needs to direct the large and diverse population of a large and diverse state, but in a context in which there are clearly-defined structural limits to the power of presidential leadership imposed by federal political institutions locally, nationally and internationally.[32] Indeed, 'leadership, for the statesman, is interpretation': interpretation of the materials and ideas, the people, and the structures of government, and it is therefore historically conditioned but also transcends those limitations when appropriately geared towards action.[33] The practicalities of wartime statecraft seemed therefore to mirror the analysis of federal nationalism and its limits that Wilson had been thinking about as a political scientist. In fact, during that crisis, the organic understanding of politics and political leadership that had informed Wilson's academic studies of American politics also hardened into a practical guide to action. Building on his critique of the fixity of certain interpretations of American political thought, particularly the hypostatised vision of Madison and Hamilton as the dispensers of eternal wisdom rather than merely the best of contemporary thinking, Wilson came to see himself as the representative of a factious people whose 'agitation' for leadership appropriate to the economic and political crises facing American life would justify his soaring rhetoric as a junior politician. By the time of the war, this defensive and defensible combination of presidential demagoguery and a lack of rigidity in federal structures, would make decisive and acclaimed political action entirely possible, and entirely justifiable.[34]

In *The State*, Wilson had offered readers an account of the gradual development of federal systems of government. Such systems were, he suggested, entirely the 'creation of modern politics.' Modern politics really meant the modern state, which was itself a creature of the expropriation of constitutional monarchies and confederations, and a staging post for the development of the 'principle of nationality'; the

[31] Erez Manela, *The Wilsonian Moment: Self-Determination and the International Origins of Anticolonial Nationalism* (New York, Oxford University Press, 2007) 59, 224; Pankaj Mishra, *From the Ruins of Empire: The Revolt Against the West and the Remaking of Asia* (London, Penguin Books, 2014); David Runciman, *The Confidence Trap: A History of Democracy in Crisis from World War I to the Present* (Princeton, Princeton University Press, 2014) 42, 46.

[32] Thorsen, *Wilson's Political Thought* 232, 234.

[33] Woodrow Wilson, 'Leaders of Men: An Address' (17 June 1890) in Arthur S Link (ed) *Papers of Woodrow Wilson* (Princeton, Princeton University Press, 1969) 6, pp 660, 659.

[34] Schulzke, 'Wilsonian Crisis Leadership' 272ff.

federal state was thus 'a single and complete political personality among nations' with three distinctive characteristics.[35] First, a 'permanent surrender on the part of the constituent communities of their right to act independently of each other in matters which touch the common interest ... As regards other states they have merged their individuality into one national whole.' Second, a specifically federal set of laws and jurisprudence. Third, and finally, federalism presupposed a 'new conception of sovereignty. [Here] the functions of political authority are parcelled out,' and all of this was typically agreed and laid out in a written constitution.[36]

When Wilson wrote about federal union, therefore, he was channelling his own sense of American federalism as both a particular form of constitutional government that had developed since the revolutionary foundations of the new American republic, and also as the best hope for humanity in a time of war, one that could counteract the less overtly democratic forms of polity that he found upheld in the states of Germany, the Austro-Hungarian empire and the Balkan states. He was moving towards a different but related confederal idea of a more perfect union between the nations of the civilised world. But what the idea of pan-Germanism was, as opposed to a military German threat, remained less clear and so perhaps even more worrisome. In fact, the manner in which Wilson and others conceived of the relationship between federalism and pan-national ideas is best laid out in the wider orbit of the political and intellectual history of pan-nationalism generally. By 1916 it still was not yet quite clear that the war had become, in Wilson's mind, a war for democracy and against autocracy, delineated in the House-Grey memorandum Wilson approved in February of that year. Yet if pan-Germanism could in theory be associated with autocracy, it would take until his April 1917 war message to entrench that distinction.[37] Autocracy, he argued, could not be the future, because only a confederation or league of nations bound together through friendship and honour would survive the war, and autocratic governments simply cannot have friends, or so Wilson suggested to Congress when he presented them with his war message on 2 April 1917.[38]

II. PAN-NATIONALISM

Pan-regional or pan-national ideas in the nineteenth century very often had clear imperial motivations and frameworks. For instance, in his classic study of the origins of pan-Latinism and the ideological construction of the idea of Latin America, John Leddy-Phelan showed how strongly a French idea of pan-Latinism could be used to further French interest under Napoleon III, and counteract what was perceived as a pan-national and 'virulent' Anglo-Saxon threat from North America, and a

[35] Wilson, *The State* 544.

[36] ibid 545.

[37] Charles Seymour, *Intimate Papers of Colonel House* (Boston, Houghton Mifflin, 1926) 2, pp 101f; see the discussion in Charles E Neu, *Colonel House: A Biography of Woodrow Wilson's Silent Partner* (Oxford, Oxford University Press, 2015) 198ff.

[38] Woodrow Wilson, *War Messages*, 65th Congress, 1st Session, Senate Doc No 5, Serial No 7264 (Washington, DC, 1917) 3–8.

pan-Slavic international threat from the east and Russia.[39] What Wilson, following Lieber and Bluntschli, would cast as Anglo-Saxon versus Gallic and revolutionary liberty was, on the French side, thought of in quite the opposite way. French claims about defending humanity through pan-regional alliances and confederations were pitched against American counter-narratives. These rather fraught geopolitical concerns were grounded in Fourierist and Saint-Simonian ideas about governing the world for the sake of humanity, premised on the legitimacy of the French revolutionary experience.[40] Permeating this half-visionary and half-realistic scheme was a conviction that 'France would be serving the cause of humanity by promoting a more rational development of the resources of America. And for her efforts, France would make a profit in francs.'[41]

Pan-national responses to Western imperial projects in the later nineteenth and earlier twentieth centuries, however, could equally well utilise the global reach of hegemonic projects against themselves. It is well-known, for example, that one of the political consequences of Wilsonian politics, particularly in light of his plans and hopes for a League of Nations abroad that was the source of his downfall at home, saw forms of anti-colonial nationalism develop in which the United States played a leading, or rather guiding, role, so as to further constrain different nationalisms particularly in Europe and in South America.[42] Moreover, non-Western political theorists developed claims about pan-national identities and classifications, in order to put in place anti-imperial unions that were both a symptom and a consequence of an intensely globalising set of predominantly European set of ideas about identity and civilisation. Put more straightforwardly, anti-colonial nationalism prioritised the global and the international sphere, in order to turn an avowedly colonial, liberal nationalism against itself. It was another very sophisticated act of conceptual re-description. As Cemil Aydin has defined the basic parameters of pan-nationalism, it is an attempt to locate the 'nation writ large in a community of nations.'[43] And although the pan-national movements of the earlier twentieth century were politically unrealistic (in the sense that no pan-national agency could enforce their union), they were intellectually and culturally innovative and would over the long run help shape a politics of accommodation and federalism in the aftermath of the Great War. Both imperial proponents of pan-national ideas, as well as anti-imperial pan-nationalisms, often signalled shared assumptions about the spatial and racial division of the globe into

[39] John Leddy Phelan, 'Pan-Latinism, French Intervention in Mexico (1861–1867) and the Genesis of the Idea of Latin America' in Juan Antonio Ortega y Medina (ed), *Conciencia y Autenticidad Históricas. Escritos en Homenaje a Edmundo O'Gorman* (Mexico City, Universidad Nacional Autónoma de México, 1968) 283.

[40] *cf* Mark Mazower, *Governing the World: The History of an Idea* (London, Penguin Books, 2012) 118–28.

[41] Phelan, 'Pan-Latinism' 285.

[42] Lloyd C Gardner, *Safe for Democracy: The Anglo-American Response to Revolution, 1913–1923* (New York, Oxford University Press, 1987) 161; on the strategy that had America and Russia manoeuvering together behind German diplomacy, see Tooze, *Deluge* 76ff, 145. For a further and compelling political rendering of Wilson's thinking, see Knock, *To End all Wars* chs 8–10.

[43] Cemil Aydin, 'Pan-Nationalism' in John Breuilly (ed) *The Oxford Handbook of Nationalism* (Oxford, Oxford University Press, 2013) 675.

discrete groupings. Most obviously, pan-Islamic radical groupings like the Khilifat movement emerged after the perceived harsh treatment of the former Ottoman Empire at diplomatic discussions in Versailles. Established by Indian Muslims and supported by Gandhi among others, their strategy of promoting a rapprochement between Ottoman Turkey and the British Empire as a counterbalance to Bolshevism and German militarism, was 'especially striking.'[44] Such ideas had earlier roots in Ottoman debates about nationalism in the wake of the Balkan Wars and its struggles with the Russian empire.[45]

As war broke out in mainland Europe, numerous writers attempted to define the parameters of this field anew. Emil Deckert, for example, tried to normalise the idea of a pan-German union by illustrating the imperial dimensions of other pan-national movements, whether in England, across the 'East', or in Latin America.[46] He well knew that imperialistic ambition could easily lead to military conflict, having already discussed the ways in which the British Empire had, in his view, conspired with enemies of Germany to destroy it as a principal commercial rival.[47] In fact, the economic drivers of political and military competition as causes of war, a long-standing concern in the history of economic thought, were clearly present in discussions of pan-nationalism in 1914. Robert Buchi, in his contemporary discussion of pan-Latinism, claimed that territorial inequalities between large and small states clearly motivated the rise of pan-nationalism, and therefore that the move towards such union was premised upon questions of economic need which were historically and geographically contingent, rather than possessed of some universal essence.[48] Wilson seemed to sense this, but as students of his political thought have long suggested, the serious philosophical work that was required to bolster his general positions about national character, political development, and institutional design was never concretely detailed; he remained concerned more with political rhetoric than political theory.[49] Consequently, his position on these matters seem to have failed to influence modern American political science to any great degree, even though Wilson's personal focus on education for national leadership through the mechanisms of congressional government has remained an attractive starting point for liberal political writers.[50] His analysis of federalism in *Constitutional Government*, nonetheless, recognised the necessarily historical nature of his quarry.

To Wilson, federalism was not an absolute good per se, but rather the contingent outcome of a set of historical and cultural processes. Because of this, it must and

[44] Aydin, 'Pan-Nationalism' 674f, 682; see also Cemil Aydin, *The Politics of Anti-Westernism in Asia: Visions of World Order in Pan-Islamic and Pan-Asian Thought* (New York, Columbia University Press, 2007) 133–36 (quotation on p 133).

[45] See Michael A Reynolds, *Shattering Empires: The Clash and Collapse of the Ottoman and Russian Empires 1908–1918* (Cambridge, Cambridge University Press, 2011).

[46] Emil Deckert, *Pan-Latinismus, Pan-Slawismus und Panteutonismus* (Frankfurt, Heinrich Keller, 1914) 8, 26.

[47] Emil Deckert, *Das Britische Weltreich: Ein politisch und wirtschaftsgeographisches Charakterbild* (Frankfurt, Heinrich Keller, 1916) 153ff.

[48] Robert Büchi, *Die Geschichte der Pan-Amerikanischen Bewegung* (Breslau, JU Kern, 1914) 14: 'der ökonomischen Bedürfnisse dieser Staatengruppen ... nicht von universeller Natur sein können.'

[49] John Milton Cooper, Jr , *Woodrow Wilson: A Biography* (New York, Vintage Books, 2011) 77f.

[50] Thorsen, *Political Thought of Woodrow Wilson* 225, 62ff.

should be open to change over generations, so that federal structures align with constitutional provisions and challenges as they emerge.[51] It is part of the broadest sense in which he understood the long-term process of democracy. This meant that even canonical and conventional terms and arguments were up for revision as time moved on. As he wrote, the constitution is a 'vehicle of life,' and therefore 'as the life of the nation changes so must the interpretation of the document that contains its change.'[52] The development of the United States and its constitution was, therefore, both open-ended and historically determined; it was a system of states whose legacy demanded continual upkeep and preparedness for change. The organic historical account he defended was abruptly set out in his claim that constitutional and hence federal 'moralization is by life, not by statute.'[53] Constitutional 'adaptation' therefore required both the wise and prudential actions of statesmen, alongside the serious interpretation of the courts, and this too was a historical-developmental story.[54] It is more than merely ironic, then, that of all things Wilson (quite like Lieber before him) was ambiguous as the extent to which racial difference was understood as a natural or contingently historical issue open to adaptation. He remained very much a Southern partisan as he reached the apex of world power, even when this civilisational worldview clearly jarred with the rhetorical support in his famous 14 points for colonial emancipation after the war. He would even help to introduce racial segregation into some executive departments, having earlier maintained that the abolition of slavery through war was a 'natural' human resolution to the problem, if not yet a direct result of legal and Congressional power.[55]

This sort of paradoxical pre-commitment both to racial segregation and strongly historical path-dependency at home, sat awkwardly in theory but favourably in practice for the anti-colonial nationalists who sought to use Wilson's fervour for a League of Nations to their own advantage at Versailles, and who saw, albeit for a brief moment, a beacon for the future in the politics of the West.[56] It was painfully ironic though, for as Wilson and the idea of the League of Nations was popularised and supported in Europe and beyond, domestically, Wilson was under threat; a society that had suffered comparably less in the war than mainland Europe was not yet as committed to a vision of a new and necessary world order, and he could not get American legislative support for American entry into the League. Thus, its institutional arrangements ended up undergirding the demands of old-world imperial post-war reconstruction, even as its rhetoric promised more.[57] Only occasionally

[51] Ronald Pestritto, *Woodrow Wilson and the Roots of Modern Liberalism* (Lanham, MD, Rowman and Littlefield, 2005) 114ff.

[52] Woodrow Wilson, *Constitutional Government in the United States* (New York, Columbia University Press, 1908) 192.

[53] ibid 197; in general, see pp 41, 182–96; for Wilson's historicist appreciation of federalism as a 'stage' in American development. See also Woodrow Wilson, 'The Meaning of the Declaration of Independence' in Gauss (ed), *Democracy Today* 64f.

[54] Wilson, *Constitutional Government* 193.

[55] ibid 176.

[56] See Tooze, *Deluge* ch 18.

[57] See Thrygve Throntveit, 'The Fable of the Fourteen Points: Woodrow Wilson and National Self-Determination' (2011) 35 *Diplomatic History* 445–81.

did offices like the Permanent Mandates Commission of the League shed a brighter light on this ambivalent relationship between empire and internationalism.[58] But the commitment to international politics and great power statesmanship as guiding the world towards its best interests was part and parcel of Wilson's general, evolutionary approach to politics itself, and just as with his rather loose account of federalism, so too did his understanding of the League do without strict legal formulations to propose instead a form of prudential adaptation to circumstance.

The choices Wilson made helped make the American century possible, but the hiatus between his exit and the Great Depression was not a time when this outcome looked entirely obvious. It also led to some unintended consequences for thinking about politics. As Erez Manela argues, even though the cataclysm of war had done more than enough to dint hyperbolic claims to the superiority of a Western civilisation, its draw remained powerful so that it was the 'disappointments of the peace, rather than the devastations of the war as such, that 'sealed the post-war indictment of Asian intellectuals against the West.'[59] If those pan-national imagined futures would necessarily lead elsewhere after the war, Wilson's focus during the war and in its immediate aftermath was, of course, with countering the pan-German threat to America and American federalism. What he did to cement his approach, though, was to assert an effective 15th point into his famous 14-point speech, just prior to the Carthaginian peace settlement at Brest-Litovsk. It suggested that there was no American 'jealousy of German greatness,' which only wanted a form of 'equality' both within and between Germany and the rest of the world rather than 'mastery.'[60] To do this, he would seek to 'mutualise' the Monroe Doctrine while America kept on producing armaments and shipping, in a form of pan-American counter-history that could motivate his current politics.[61] The Monroe Doctrine also quickly became central to Wilson's vision of a future League of Nations, though the support among anti-colonial nationalists who cheered Wilson's focus on self-determination would be stymied by the routine demands of electoral and power politics.[62] 'I am proposing,' he said before the Senate in January 1917 during his famous peroration to 'Peace without Victory,' 'that the nations should with one accord adopt the doctrine of President Monroe as the doctrine of the world.' An American federal tradition of a 'community' rather than a 'balance' of power might therefore become that new conscience for peaceful world order.[63] It would be the counter to all other pan-regional visions,

[58] Susan Pedersen, *The Guardians: The League of Nations and the Crisis of Empire* (New York, Oxford University Press, 2015).

[59] Erez Manela, 'Imagining Woodrow Wilson in Asia: Dreams of East-West Harmony and the Revolt against Empire in 1919' (2006) 111 *American Historical Review* 1330.

[60] For a discussion, see Arthur S Link, *Woodrow Wilson: Revolution, War, and Peace* (Arlington Heights, Harlon Davidson Inc, 1979) 83ff; on Wilson's skepticism about the democratisation process in Germany, see Tooze, *Deluge* 223.

[61] Link, *Wilson* 77ff; Cooper, Jr, *Woodrow Wilson* 246f.

[62] A brief sense of the Wilsonian update of this broader history can be found in Jay Sexton, *The Monroe Doctrine: Empire and Nation in Nineteenth-Century America* (New York, Hill and Wang, 2011) 241ff; see also, Cooper, Jr, *Woodrow Wilson* 478f.

[63] Woodrow Wilson, 'Address to the Senate' [22 January 1917] in Link (ed), *Papers of Woodrow Wilson* (Princeton, Princeton University Press, 1982) 40, pp 533–39; for a wider discussion, see Mark T Gilderhus, *Pan American Visions: Woodrow Wilson in the Western Hemisphere, 1913–1921* (Tucson, University of Arizona Press, 1986) 54, 93; Knock, *To End all Wars* 111–15.

particularly the militaristic vision of pan-Germany. Yet in stretching the limits of the Monroe Doctrine from a century past into a vision of the democratic future he was playing for, he was also, as were the anti-colonial nationalists, stretching the temporal boundaries of the war, filtering them through a much broader, imperial imagination.[64]

For writers like Charles Andler, whose work on pan-Germanism was readily translated into English during the war, pan-Germanism was effectively an all-encompassing ideology of intellectual, cultural, economic and military-territorial conquest and predominance. It represented an almost 'natural' tendency of the German character according to Andler, who cites chapter and verse from contemporary theorists of war, culture, and geopolitics.[65] Of course, such naturalised tendencies towards aggression and domination sit uneasily with contemporary historiography, but that is certainly how many intellectuals presented their case against Germany during the Great War. It was on this intellectual battlefield that Treitschke, Nietzsche, and something called the 'German theory of the state' came to the forefront.[66] It became almost a cliché for many intellectuals that the war was a war of ideas and 'principles,' making it both about the 'vindication of international right' as well as 'for liberty.'[67] But even if there is no direct link between German intellectuals and the actions of German politicians, Andler was keen to claim a degree of common cause. Much as Wilson might have said, 'the men who govern are the sons of their nation, and the ideas which guide the government are those which nourish that nation and circulate in its books.'[68]

If pan-German and other pan-national ideologies constructed their own visions of federal or confederal unions prior to and during the war, it is also important to see that Wilson himself was forced to think about the currency of pan-Americanism at the same time. The force of political Anglophobia in later nineteenth and early twentieth-century America, often filtered through Anglo-Irish émigrés and farmers, seems to have prompted both republican and democrat unease about English old-world imperialism. It surely contributed to Wilson's undoubted desire to build a fleet to match old-world power and so consolidate a hemispheric sphere of influence that international competition could not easily disrupt, as much as constructing a

[64] For a useful general account of this sort of extension into a global First World War, see Eric Gerwarth and Erez Manela, 'The Great War as Global War' (2014) 38 *Diplomatic History* 786–800.

[65] Charles Andler, *Pan-Germanism: Its Plans for German expansion in the World* (Paris, Armand Colin, 1915) 54f; *cf Le pangermanisme philosophique, 1800 à 1914* (Paris, Louis Counard, 1917). A broader discussion of the pan-German league can be found in Roger Chickering, *We Men who feel most German: A Cultural Study of the Pan-German League, 1886–1914* (London, Harper Collins, 1986).

[66] See Ernest Barker, *Nietzsche and Treitschke: The Worship of Power in Modern Germany* (Oxford, Oxford University Press, 1914), where Nietzsche and Treitschke are the malevolent modern usurpers of Kant and Hegel. Barker was also a major contributor to the volume published by the Oxford History Faculty, *Why We are at War* (Oxford, Oxford University Press, 1914), chapter 6 of which dealt with the 'New German Theory of the State.' Here, the Anglo-German antagonism is rendered as a conflict between the rule of law and raison d'état.

[67] See, eg, James Bryce, 'Foreword' in *The War of Democracy: The Allies' Statement* (New York, Doubleday Page & Co, 1915) xxiii; generally, Daniel Pick, *War Machine: The Rationalisation of Slaughter in the Modern Age* (New Haven, Yale University Press, 1996) 156.

[68] Andler, *Pan-Germanism* 56.

claim about the causes of the war in his mind in the first place.[69] And if foreign policy had not been a major component of Wilson's early political career, it was crucial to his re-election campaign during the conflict as the figure who had kept America out of the war, even if that turned out to be nearly coterminous with American entry into it. Indeed, his foreign policy might be thought a triumph of the particular sort of 'radicalism' he preached.[70] The contrast between Wilson's avowedly liberal 'internationalism' here comes up sharply against his robust and imperialist policies of engagement in Latin America and the Caribbean, something noted by his contemporary critics like Roosevelt, and which pivoted around Roosevelt's antipathy towards Wilson's 'closed' diplomacy.[71] Such closed diplomacy easily became part of Wilson's wartime strategy, particularly when dealing with the Russians prior to Brest-Litovsk.[72] The diplomacy of both Wilson and Lenin had something of a competitive utopianism (*Utopiekonkurrenz*) about it.[73] Moreover, because secret diplomacy had been key to Wilson's colonial policy in an American sphere of interest, neither his proposals for a confederated League of Nations nor Roosevelt's less well remarked upon but similarly ambitious international 'legal-sanctionist' league, look particularly democratic. That is, until we remember the specific limitations placed upon what democracy meant to both, and therefore for Wilson particularly, what might be inferred from the proposal to make a world safe for it.[74]

Making the world safe for democracy required the making safe of a pan-American vision. For Wilson, that seemed first to require the abolition of jealousies of state. In his address to the 1916 Pan-American Scientific Congress, he argued that the Americas existed together in common friendship, that the 'statesmen of the two American continents had come into more candid, trustful, mutual conference,' and that one 'cannot have real intercourse amidst political jealousies.'[75] The connection to the 'mutual suspicion' of arms races, exemplified in Wilson's mind by balance of power politics, seems clear enough.[76] For most historians, the broad transition from continental expansion to lonely or insular American empire under the banner of

[69] On the background, see Marc-William Palen, 'The Imperialism of Economic Nationalism, 1890–1913' (2015) 39 *Diplomatic History* 157.

[70] Woodrow Wilson, *The New Freedom* (New York, Doubleday Page & Co, 1919) 242f; also Thompson, 'Woodrow Wilson and a World Governed by Evolving Law' 119.

[71] Emily Rosenberg, 'World War 1, Wilsonianism and Challenges to US Empire' (2014) 38 *Diplomatic History* 855ff.

[72] Gardner, *Safe for Democracy* 161; *cf* Lloyd C Gardner, 'The Geopolitics of Revolution' (2014) 38 *Diplomatic History* 740.

[73] Jörn Leonhard, *Die Büchse der Pandora: Geschichte des Ersten Weltkrieges* (München, CH Beck, 2014) 1008f.

[74] On Roosevelt's internationalist vision, see Stephen Wertheim, 'The League that Wasn't: American Designs for a Legal-Sanctionist League of Nations and the Intellectual Origins of International Organization, 1914–1920' (2011) 35 *Diplomatic History* 797.

[75] Woodrow Wilson, 'What is Pan-Americanism?' [1916] in Albert B Hart (ed) *Selected Addresses and Public Papers of Woodrow Wilson* (New York, Boni and Liveright, 1918) 96, 98.

[76] See the Diary of Colonel House, 30 August 1914 in Link (ed), *Papers of Woodrow Wilson* (Princeton, Princeton University Press, 1979) 30, p 462. This would, of course, make it difficult for Wilson to deal with the renewed security demands of France after the Armistice, which hoped precisely for a 'revolution in the balance of power' in Europe (see Peter Jackson, *Beyond the Balance of Power* (Cambridge, Cambridge University Press, 2013) 136).

pan-Americanism has remained murky. As Benjamin Coates has recently shown, pre-war pan-Americanism was quite clearly bound up with economic nationalism, mired in petty corruption, and certainly designed to secure access to non-European markets. This would be a huge and beneficial boon to the American economy when European exports were otherwise thwarted. But as with the anti-colonial nationalism that Wilson's wartime rhetoric brought forth, here too it was often the case that Latin American preference was for trade with Europe, rather than with America at its imperialist centre.[77]

Small wonder, then, that writers like the contemporary American historian Roland Usher attempted to redefine pan-Americanism as an idea of the future, rather than a contemporary reality. Recognising the existence of a pan-American union, Usher noted that the form of such union could not be racial, or even equal; instead, it would have to become a confederation based on shared interest. And that shared interest would be motivated by both hemispheric proximity on the one hand, and geopolitical self-awareness on the other. To wit, there would be the 'inevitable clash' between the United States and the 'victor' in the European war, and if the United States were to benefit and win in that clash, it would have to be bound already in a union of 'independence and equality' with the rest of the Americas.[78] From the perspective of 1915, Usher carried on to consider the fact that such a pan-American union was likely to come about through the force of economic development and convergence, itself a consequence of economic competition. He presumably thought this was the most likely mechanism by which the economic backwardness of parts of Latin America, pilloried by many later nineteenth-century writers on pan-Americanism, would be overcome.[79] For him, it was the rational strategy to follow because 'the cause of the present struggle for markets in Europe is the attempt to replace the market which the US once afforded their produce but which provides it no longer.' Usher concluded that this was the 'root of Pan-Germanism, the secret of the interest in Morocco, in China, [and] in South America. Europe has always depended upon selling to a rapidly developing market.'[80]

Copying European examples prioritised economic competition: 'They see clearly in Europe that the most vital interest of the state is economic, for without economic prosperity there can be no national independence or "international status"'. However, Usher then moved towards a more general point about principles. Economic competition is not, he says, 'ethical'; ethical values are 'comparative and relative,' but the values of the nation trump contingency in general. If 'international ethics therefore is a subtle and most peculiar mixture of the law of individual self-defence, the ethics of business, and the ethics of the crusader,' then the only justification for direct intervention and compelled economic engagement can come from the 'actual conduct of nations in the past.'[81] European expansion in the past used might to

[77] Benjamin Coates, 'The Pan-American Lobbyist, William Eleroy Curtis and US Empire, 1884–1899 (2014) 38 *Diplomatic History* 32.

[78] Roland Usher, *Pan-Americanism* (New York, The Century, 1915) 204f, 209, 211. Usher also wrote *Pan-Germanism* 2nd edn (New York, Groset and Dunlop, 1913).

[79] Coates, 'Pan-American Lobbyist' 40–43.

[80] Usher, *Pan-Americanism* 346, 359.

[81] ibid 370, 373, 387, 388.

justify right, and so too can contemporary America. That seems to be the message, although Usher is quick to say that there is no interest on the part of the United States in conquering Latin America; though if not conquest, then certainly forced compliance, should conflict with Europe continue in the aftermath of the Great War.[82] Paradoxically, though, this attempt to legalise or legislate for a new future required a legal as well as a moral commitment to new mechanisms of intervention and justification, which in turn only mirrored the ramping up of legal justification for total war that can be seen both in Germany and in England through continuously improvised judicial thinking in the wake of the allied economic blockade.[83]

By contrast, Rómulu S Naón, an Argentinian ambassador considering the question of 'The War in Europe and true pan-Americanism', tried to overcome the obvious fact that European civilisation was a 'product of national individualistic organization' and that the international system of which it was a part was based on 'antagonism.'[84] In order to transcend it, Naón based his case on the claim that 'human solidarity is the final end of social evolution', and that 'to America is reserved the honourable task of exercising an influence in the transformation of the old organization of the world by the example of its organization of solidarity.'[85] For Wilson, that language was resonant. In 1919, he was on the stump against European-style militarism and armaments, suggesting that they were fundamentally anti-democratic; in practice, however, he was still building up armies and navies so as to avoid being beholden to the Old World.[86] Earlier, he had been (at least in private) apoplectic about German untrustworthiness and militarism, but even while he preached neutrality, and as one recent scholar notes, 'however angrily he protested British violations of American neutral rights, he never characterised the allies in such terms.'[87]

III. FEDERATION AND FEDERALISM

In most discussions of federalism and political union, there are at least two classical problems. One concerns the relationship between federation and confederation (*Bundesstaat* and *Staatenbund*), while another concerns the question of the whether federalism is best understood as a legal or political structure. Because of

[82] Usher, *Pan-Americanism* 406; *cf* Boyce, *The Great Interwar Crisis* 28, 45ff, 424.

[83] See Isabel Hull, *A Scrap of Paper: Breaking and Making International Law During the Great War* (Ithaca, Cornell University Press, 2014) 84, 88, 183ff, 198, 206, 326; *cf* Stefano Recchia, 'The Origins of Liberal Wilsonianism: Giuseppe Mazzini on Regime Change and Humanitarian Intervention' in Stefano Recchia and Jennifer M Welsh (eds), *Just and Unjust Military Intervention* (Cambridge, Cambridge University Press, 2013) 237–62.

[84] Rómulu S Naón, 'The War in Europe and True Pan-Americanism' (1916) 7 *Journal of Race Development* 152.

[85] ibid.

[86] Woodrow Wilson, 'Address in Omaha' [8 September 1919] in Arthur S Link and JE Little (eds) *Papers of Woodrow Wilson* (Princeton, Princeton University Press, 1990) 63, p 101. For a discussion, see Ross A Kennedy, 'Woodrow Wilson, World War I, and an American Conception of National Security' (2001) 25 *Diplomatic History* 4–6.

[87] ibid 7.

this, there has typically been a difference in the way that legal historians or constitutional lawyers approach the problem, as compared with political scientists. Political scientists might consider the infrastructural power and capacity of independent nation states first, as a prerequisite for the formation of confederations or federal structures, typically in the face of some common enemy or threat. Here, wars and revolutions bring about union, but whether those unions look (crudely put) more like Italy, or more like Germany, will determine different national histories.[88] Equally, federalism might well be seen as the result of security crises and violence, violence that leads to new forms of union as a practical and self-interested strategy, where politicians must be willing to give up certain aspects of their previous powers in order to move peacefully into a new and rewarding federal union.[89] Indeed, according to the mid-century émigré political scientist Franz Neumann, although the history of federal arrangements was primarily a form of anti-democratic practice in both Germany and America (with Constantin Frantz and JC Calhoun as representative figures), it should only be judged by empirical results.[90] Conversely, lawyers and legal scholars are more likely to consider the particular administrative structures of federal or confederal arrangements, linking them to questions of representation and democracy, as witnessed in several chapters of this volume.

As Olivier Beaud has suggested, federalism has at its core a 'profound ambivalence,' being both a legal or juridical technique and a political idea simultaneously. As a community of communities, federalism attempts to reconcile unity and diversity into a plural structure.[91] Yet combining the twin elements of law and politics into a general theory of the state and its development is precisely what unites the particular strand of the study of federalism in nineteenth-century Europe that writers like Bluntschli proposed, with the sorts of federalist visions propounded by Wilson both prior to and then during the First World War. Both sets of ideas were predicated on a general developmental claim about civilised and liberal or republican states moving towards a shared, cosmopolitan humanity, but that cosmopolitan humanity was structured around the relationships between federally organised nation-states, or federations of states acting in concert. There was little more specific than that for both. For example, just as debates about the parameters of a new pan-American union were considered within the wider teleological framework of the cultivation of human solidarity between nations, so too had Bluntschli's hard-nosed liberal vision of constitutional monarchies united across Europe been part of an historical vision of the advance of 'humanity' spreading out from a newly-enlightened Europe, whose development was outlined in and through the theory and practice of Immanuel Kant and Frederick the Great.

[88] Daniel Ziblatt, 'Rethinking the Origins of Federalism: Puzzle, Theory and Evidence from Nineteenth-Century Europe' (2004) 57 *World Politics* 77ff.

[89] Classically, William Riker, *Federalism: Origin, Operation, Significance* (Boston, Little Brown, 1964) 10; 'Federalism' in Fred Greenstein and Nelson Polsby (eds) *Handbook of Political Science* (Boston, Mass, Addison-Wesley Educational Publishers Inc, 1975) 5, pp 93–172; updated in Joseph M Parent, *Uniting States: Voluntary Union in World Politics* (New York, Oxford University Press, 2011) 8f, 14.

[90] Franz L Neumann, *The Democratic and Authoritarian State* (New York, Harper Torchbooks, 1964) 227.

[91] Olivier Beaud, *Théorie de la Féderation* (Paris, Presses Universitaires de France, 2009).

So if the Enlightenment origins of the modern state were a significant part in motivating Bluntschli's narrative, his account of its modern politics was simultaneously part of a much wider rejection of natural law in German-speaking legal and state theory as scientifically irrelevant to the subject. The history of natural law between Grotius and Kant was from a different age, intellectually as well as politically, and had been overtaken by new, more 'scientific' theories of politics and sociability after Kant. Here, Bluntschli was in line with other writers interested in federalism such as the émigré Austrian legal scholar Georg Jellinek, who, during a long career at Heidelberg, decided to rewrite the history of modern state-legal theory (*Staatsrechtslehre*), taking Kant's 'modern' theory of natural law as a starting point.[92] In Jellinek's case, this led to the famous development of a 'two-sided' theory of law and the state as both an historical as well as a juridical construction, analytically separable but unified through the culturally specific historical development of the state and its people on the one hand, and the contemporary political leadership of that state in the figure of a representative constitutional monarch on the other. This complicated mixture also presumed the existence of a civilisational standard of judgment when measuring the advanced or retrograde character of different state forms. It could then be brought to bear on pressing political questions, for example, through the justification of political and military intervention by the multi-ethnic federal empire of Austria-Hungary towards its rebellious Bosnian neighbour, or the extrusion of China from the principles of an allegedly enlightened international society.[93] Jellinek also considered the *Staatenbund* of the United States of America, and his late nineteenth-century study of the legal relations both within and between states critically developed the idea of a 'real' union, which again had to be considered as a special form of the federation of states. Its motivating dynamics were historical, but its conceptually separate juristic and contractual qualities derived from that history.[94] Its legacy was profound, however, given that the nineteenth and early twentieth century updating of Kantian autonomy and Fichtean self-determination as universalisable, seem to have readily become secularised foundations for territorially limited national self-determination.[95]

Similarly, if the humanist idiom of natural law from Grotius to Kant had been concerned to reconcile the good and the expedient (*honestum* and *utile*) through a

[92] Johann Kaspar Bluntschli, *Lehre vom modernen Staat* (Stuttgart, JG Cotta, 1876) 3, p 547; *cf* Richard Tuck, 'The "Modern" Theory of Natural Law' in Anthony Pagden (ed), *Languages of Political Theory in Early-Modern Europe* (Cambridge, Cambridge University Press, 1987) 116–19.

[93] See Duncan Kelly, 'Revisiting the Rights of Man: Georg Jellinek on Rights and the State' (2004) 22 *Law and History Review* 493–529; Peter Ghosh, 'Max Weber and Georg Jellinek: Two Divergent Conceptions of Law' (2008) 59 *Saeculum* 299–347.

[94] Georg Jellinek, *Die Lehre der Staatenverbindungen* (Vienna, Alfred Hölder, 1882) 197–202, 211ff, esp 215: 'Die Realunion ist daher nur ein Spezialfall des Staatenbundes.' See also Peter Stirk, 'The Westphalian Model, Sovereignty and Law in *Fin-de-siècle* German International Theory' (2005) 19 *International Relations* 163ff.

[95] See Eric D Weitz, 'Self-Determination: How a German Enlightenment Idea Became the Slogan of National Liberation and a Human Right' (2015) 12 *American Historical Review* 483: 'self-determination fully lost its anchor in the universalist individualism of Kant and the early Fichte'; Ian Hunter, 'Secularization: The Birth of a Modern Combat Concept' (2015) 12 *Modern Intellectual History* 18–20, 23f, 26–29, stresses in turn the artificial construction of the concept of 'secularization' through Kant.

refutation of scepticism and the development of a science of morality, the principal use made of Kant by modern legal and political writers is as a theorist of the possibilities of peace and Enlightenment in an era of international economic and political competition, whose argument frames their complex historical and juridical admixtures. On this reading of the history at least, the *utile* and *honestum* of classical natural law are thought once more to be capable of combination, but that combination might now be understood as a Kantian regulative ideal, indeed a regulative ideal that could incorporate a broader cosmopolitan claim about the direction of human history towards its ideal end. That end, literally of a cosmopolitan humanity for Bluntschli, was the possible consequence of a move that based a politics of representative nationalism on a federal system of civilised states, and which emerged from a series of debates about whether European federalism and political union was best understood as the transition from a federation of states (*Staatenbund*) towards a union of federal states (*Bundesstaat*). These unions were entered into for various reasons of force or *fortuna*.[96] Their intellectual history, however, shows how certain ideas about the relationship between commercial society and modern history and politics helped to transform the ways in which the possible futures of such national unions were imagined.[97] In this, Wilson truly was his heir.

For Bluntschli, the answer was to see future political union through the lens of a loose international arrangement of federally organised nation states, where popular sovereignty was indirect and national in each. The nation was primary, so the form of union Bluntschli proposed was designed to incorporate elements of liberalism and republicanism and thus avoid the twin extremes of pure (radical) democracy and Hobbesian (absolutist) unity.[98] That was the sort of flexible federalism he was after, with a form of political union rather less than Hobbesian artificial unity, but more than merely economic or commercial concord. Bluntschli wrote that a 'union is always imperfect when it is merely personal', but a 'higher unity is to be found in the so-called Real Union, which is related to Federation, as Personal Union is to Confederation.'[99] Paying attention to such problems of real union (*Bund*), the Swiss background to his argument was clear. In autobiographical statements he noted that the civil war years of 1847 in Switzerland and of revolution in 1848 in Germany had convinced him (as they had convinced Tocqueville) that out of civil war a new and democratic form of politics could emerge.[100] It also convinced him both that Switzerland could survive within a new European system of states, which had been a pressing question at least since Rousseau's consideration of the politics of the Genevan *représentants* if not before, and, perhaps most importantly here, that

[96] Murray Forsyth, *Unions of States: Theory and Practice of Confederation* (Leicester, Leicester University Press, 1981) chs 4–6; Parent, *Uniting States* chs 4–5.

[97] See, eg, Bruno Hildebrand, *Die Nationalökonomie der Gegewart und Zukunft* (Frankfurt, J Rütten, 1848). For an excellent related discussion, see Mark Hewitson, '"The Old Forms are Breaking Up … Our New Germany is Rebuilding Itself": Constitutionalism, Nationalism and the Creation of a German Polity during the Revolutions of 1848–49' (2010) 75 *English Historical Review* 1173, see especially 1183–90.

[98] Bluntschli, *Lehre vom Modernen Staat* 3, p 382.

[99] Johann Kaspar Bluntschli, *The Theory of the State* (Oxford, The Clarendon Press, 1901) 271, 272.

[100] Johan Kaspar Bluntschli, *Bemerkungen über die neuesten Vorschläge zur deutschen Verfassung* (Munich, Chr Kaster, 1848) 9.

federal union could structure modern political theory based on popular and national sovereignty.[101] There is a case to be made here too, that such earlier insights were on Woodrow Wilson's mind during the war, when the issue of alliances and unions between large and small states was front and centre of discussion. He had already engaged lengthily with the puzzles of Swiss and German federalism in his own work, given the importance of the former in particular, to the development of American federalist thinking.[102]

When German soldiers violated Belgian neutrality, however, the questions this raised about the possibility of confederal alliances against corrosive imperial governments (whether British or otherwise) quickly formed a staple of critical political discourse, one that could in theory unite pan-regional visions of anti-colonial nationalism towards a peace settlement at Versailles, and later Genevan updates to the League of Nations.[103] Even HAL Fisher declared that the threat to small states from not being part of a 'great union' (in this case with the Empire) was that continental Europe would slip not into 'revolution, but servitude.'[104] Bluntschli's own anti-Napoleonic 'mediation' of these intensely political moments in Europe's federal past had focused his attention on the coming question of national sovereignty in an age of international conflict. Furthermore and in line with Tocqueville's insights into the radical difficulties of judging the successes and failures of a democratic politics based on popular sovereignty in the short as opposed to the long term, Bluntschli suggested that such initial disappointments had ultimately made national unification possible.[105] Wilson concurred, transposing the terminology from federalism to democracy, and grounding the national politics of America on a war footing in ways that would have been inconceivable for the Swiss. This new challenge was being met by a new sense of national purpose, with an account of American federalism as both a unique past and a powerful future at its heart.

If this European vision of politics as federation that was on offer in the nineteenth century allowed both for the reconceptualisation of the history that made it possible,

[101] Carl Welcker, 'Bund' in Carl Rotteck and Carl Theodor von Welcker (eds), *Staats-Lexikon, oder Encyklopaedie der Staatswissenschaften* (Altona, Hammerlich, 1839–1848) 3, pp 76, 79. On the wider dynamics of Swiss debates about federation, war and eighteenth-century commercial society, see Richard Whatmore, *Against War and Empire: Geneva, Britain, and France in the Eighteenth Century* (New Haven, Yale University Press, 2013).

[102] Wilson, *The State* especially chs 7–8; see also Horst Dippel, 'The Changing Idea of Popular Sovereignty in Early American Constitutionalism: Breaking Away from European Patterns' (1996) 16 *Journal of the History of the Early Republic* 21–45; Abigail Green, 'The Federal Alternative? A New View of Modern German History' (2003) 46 *Historical Review* 187–202.

[103] Zara Steiner, *The Lights that Failed: European International history, 1919–1933* (Oxford, Oxford University Press, 2007) especially ch 7; for a detailed exploration of the relationship between ideas of world government and the practices of a small state with a large impact, see George Egerton, *Great Britain and the Creation of the League of Nations: Strategy, Political Organization and International Organization, 1914–1919* (Chapel Hill, University of North Carolina Press, 1978).

[104] Herbert AL Fisher, *The Value of Small States* (Oxford, Oxford University Press, 1916) 22, 25. See also p 17, where he noted their value as 'laboratories for social experiment.' The essay was reprinted in *The War of Democracy*.

[105] *cf* Reinhart Koselleck, *Futures Past* (New York, Columbia University Press, 2004) 61, 64ff; Betsy Baker Röben, 'The Method Behind Bluntschli's "Modern" International Law' (2002) 4 *Journal of the History of International Law* 270.

as well as pointing imaginatively to an open-ended political future, it maps on in quite striking ways, it seems to me, to the sort of vision of federalism that Wilson was effectively operating with during the fraught politics of wartime America. Seen in retrospect, he argued that the Civil War was the making of modern America, nineteenth-century democracy was violent and irresolute, but modern representative government with its limited democracy and exceptional history as well as institutional structures, could secure new advantages for a new world under American hegemony. That was the gambit of Wilson's power play against the old-world of Europe generally, and the British Empire particularly, that mirrored in its own virulence the sort of antipathy towards absolutism and ultramontanism found in Bluntschli's defence of a vigorous and masculine constitutional (and Protestant) monarch in the face of old-regime absolutism. They would require and receive quite new and radical rethinking during the interwar years, however, and then again after the Second World War for a brief but powerful moment when economic and political restructuring on a global scale again seemed possible.[106] That rethinking has generated an extensive body of scholarship, but just as the possibilities of mandate politics after the Great War could only function because of, rather than in spite of, the maintenance of a crumbling imperial order, the decline of empire, the rise of nationalism and the triumph of the nation-state model after the Second World War emptied the hopeful alternative promise of federalism and European federation of immediate practical possibility.[107] A different sort of European union did obviously emerge, largely driven by Franco-German commitment and the demands of a powerful American state.[108] The precursors to these alternative visions of union and federation, however, seem to have their roots in the Great War and its intellectual history, just as Wilson recognised. And that may well have deep implications for our sense of the political origins of European federal integration and its continuing possibilities.[109]

[106] See, eg, Walter Lipgens, 'European Federation in the Political Thought of Resistance Movements during World War Two' (1968) 1 *Central European History* 11, 13, 16, 18; Holly Case, 'The Strange Politics of Federative Ideas in East-Central Europe' (2013) 85 *Journal of Modern History* 833f, 839f, 847; Cornelia Navari, 'The Origins of the Briand Plan' (1992) 3 *Diplomacy and Statecraft* 74ff.

[107] For one account, see Hannah Arendt, 'Parties, Movements, and Classes' (1945) 12 *Partisan Review* 504–13; for a discussion, see William Selinger, 'The Politics of Arendtian Historiography: European Federation and *The Origins of Totalitarianism*' (2015) *Modern Intellectual History*, First View Article, DOI: 10.1017/S1479244314000560. See also Or Rosenboim, 'Barbara Wootton, Friedrich Hayek and the Debate on Democratic Federalism in the 1940s' (2014) 36 *International History Review* 894–918.

[108] Alan S Milward, *The European Rescue of the Nation State* (London, Routledge, 1994); *cf* Charles F Delzell, 'The European Federalist Movement in Italy, 1918–1947' (1960) 32 *Journal of Modern History* 241–50.

[109] See, eg, Carl Strikwerda, 'The Troubled Origins of European Integration' (1993) 98 *American Historical Review* 1106–29.

8

Federalism and the Ends of Europe

AMNON LEV*

Cupiditas, quæ ex Lætitiâ oritur, cæteris paribus, fortior est Cupiditate, quæ ex Tristitiâ oritur.

Spinoza, *Ethica*

TO EUROPE'S FEDERALISTS, federalism is not only about distributing power across different levels of government; it is also, and perhaps primarily, about exorcising the demons of the last century. A strong sense of moral imperative underpins the federal integration of Europe. This has left a profound imprint on scholarship that rarely, if ever, looks further back than the crisis that formed the backdrop to the first treaties of what would become the European Union. As a result, centuries of public law theory have been lost from view. This truncation of perspective has stood in the way of efforts to assess how Europe's federalisation fits into a broader history of public law theory. As we shall see, it also has important implications for the claim that the project of federalising Europe makes on us. It is thus with a double purpose in mind that we turn our attention to the public law dimension of modern European history: on the one hand, we want to determine how the ongoing federalisation of public powers in Europe differs from, and carries forward, earlier forms of federalism. On the other hand, we want to identify the intellectual sources on which this federal integration draws.

The exposition falls in three parts. The partition is dialectical and loosely historiographical. Each part sets forth a specific moment in the conceptual reconstruction of European federalism. At the same time, it acts as a prism through which to view the salient problems of interstate relations in Europe in each of the three centuries our account spans, from the eighteenth to the twentieth century. In the first part, the problem is that of devising a system to contain the tension that is inherent in the co-existence of sovereign states (I). The point of our analysis is to show that the structure of the European state system fostered specific strategies of federation and how these strategies made use of the idea of Europe as a quasi-constitutional order. In the second part, we consider how theorists of public law—Constantin Frantz and Georg Jellinek—tried to come to terms with the emergence of a grand federal polity in Europe in the nineteenth century (II). This is likely to be both the least familiar and the most

* I would like to thank Professor Paul Kahn and a group of his postgraduate students for their valuable comments to an earlier draft of this chapter that was presented at a small-group seminar at Yale University in the winter of 2015. All translations in this chapter are by the author.

abstract part. Our exposition is negative in that we are trying to understand why their attempts at theorising the federation ultimately failed, and how that failure was linked to the persistence of sovereignty in their thinking. If we have chosen to focus on these two theories, one of which is only rarely considered in federalism scholarship, it is because federalism's semantic dependence on sovereignty holds the key to understanding what obstacles had to be overcome and what resources had to be mobilised for a process of federalisation to get underway in Europe. The inability of public law theory to theorise the federation is indissociably linked to its ambition of justifying public authority. The persistent pull of foundationalism is central to understanding how public power in European has been federalised in the twentieth century (III). The focus of our analysis is not on changes in the allocation of competencies between the EU and the member states, nor is it on the functional integration of legal orders. Instead, we focus on the conceptions that inform the convergence between legal orders and make it possible; what we might call the ideology of Europe's federal integration. We shall show how a fundamental rupture of European public law theory combined with a sense of existential crisis to bracket the operation of sovereignty, enabling the process of federalisation to get underway.

Taking a longer view of European federalism allows us to understand why the process of European integration, despite being predicated on a rupture with history, has, in so many respects, been continuous with the institutional forms of that history. This makes sense of why states could be brought on board. It also sheds new light on the singular sense of destiny that attaches to European federalism, the belief that its success will mean the realisation of what Europe, as an idea, was always about.[1] In a sense, we are vindicating key aspects of a federalism that has been often found to be wanting in comparison with its more assertive American counterpart because, unlike the latter, it has never managed to capture the hearts of the people(s) it governs. As we shall see, the vindication is not without ambivalence.

I. FEDERALISM IN THE EUROPEAN STATE SYSTEM

The basic categories of federalism were elaborated within the European state system and reflect its structure.[2] From the sixteenth century, at the latest, the continent was seen to constitute a separate system, the public law of which revolved around the idea of a self-correcting mechanism that perpetuated a precarious state

[1] Incompletion has been seen by some as a defining characteristic of Europe, an essential indeterminacy that finds its expression in European philosophy and science. For this reading, see Rémi Brague, *Europe, la voie romaine* (Paris, Éditions Gallimard, 1992) 35, 119, 186–88; Massimo Cacciari, *Geofilosofia dell'Europa* (Milan, Adelphi Edizioni, 1994) 156–58; Edmund Husserl, *The Crisis of European Sciences and Transcendental Phenomenology* (Evanston, Northwestern University Press, 1970) 275, 289; Jean-François Mattei, *Le regard vide. Essai sur l'épuisement de la culture européenne* (Paris, Flammarion, 2007) 31, 282; Jan Patočka, *L'Europe après l'Europe* (Paris, Éditions Verdier, 2007) 68, 225, 236. On the reading we present, the sense of moral imperative that propels the construction of Europe does refer back to what we might, for convenience's sake, call the occidental tradition. But where the above readings posit the existence of a unitary tradition as a trans-historical given, we inquire how this tradition or, rather, specific elements drawn from it, came to have currency within public law theory.

[2] For a different acount, see the contribution of Nicholas Aroney to this volume.

of equilibrium between the parts of the system.[3] It was believed that were a state to become too powerful, the imbalance would be met with concerted action by the other states. Without fail, they would act to prevent local domination from developing into global hegemony. States were bound to do so as the territorial integrity of each was predicated on that of the system. Ultimately, the belief that the system would automatically self-correct was based in a metaphysics which taught that, this side of eternity, authority would never again be gathered into a single point. Belief in this tenet sustained early modern public law theorists as they tried to defend the position of their temporal sovereigns against the Holy Roman Emperor, and it is reflected in the confidence with which Montesquieu, in his reflections on universal monarchy, declares that, even if successful, the attempt to unite Europe by conquest would inevitably lead to its fragmentation into an 'infinity of Sovereignties.'[4]

Conflict, that is, the constant overturning of the status quo, was endemic to the European state, but it was not of a nature to overturn the system because the system depended on movement to perpetuate itself. If Europe was in a state of constant agitation, it was at the same time fundamentally immobile.[5] Founding a system of interaction on the propensity to use force is obviously a dangerous game. Even among the champions of the system, there was palpable concern that the remedy might be just as bad as the disease. Several publicists note the problem of how to determine when a 'legitimate' growth in state power becomes a 'dangerous excess of power' that justifies the taking of countermeasures.[6] This problem was, in turn, linked to another, more fundamental conundrum: if the imperative of preserving (relative) equality between states justified the use of force, it offered no guarantee that such countermeasures would not in turn prove disruptive. In fact, there was every reason to expect that they would, given that the system had 'no absolute principle, no fixed goal, [its] essence that of a never-ending oscillation, mutual self-suspension, and boundless disloyalty in the shifting of alliances and breaking of treaties ...'[7]

[3] Heinz Duchhardt, *Gleichgewicht der Kräfte, Convenance, Europäisches Konzert: Friedenskongresse und Friedensschlüsse vom Zeitalter Ludwigs XIV. bis zum Wiener Kongress* (Darmstadt, Wissenschaftliche Buchgesellschaft, 1976) 68.

[4] Charles-Louis de Secondat Montesquieu, *Réflexions sur la monarchie universelle en Europe* (Geneva, Libraire Droz, 2000) x, 84: 'Les Français ayant subjugué plusieurs Nations barbares établis avant eux, Charlemagne fonda un grand Empire; mais cela même redivisa Europe en une infinité de Souverainetés.' See Maurizio Bazzoli, 'L'idea d'ordine internazionale nell'Europa di Montesquieu' in Alberto Postigliola and Maria Grazia Bottaro Palumbo (eds), *L'Europe de Montesquieu* (Naples, Liguori Editore, 1995) 62–63.

[5] This analysis is echoed by Rousseau, for whom Europe had a 'degree of solidity that will keep it in a state of perpetual unrest without ever overturning it completely ... [such that] henceforth great revolutions are impossible' (Jean-Jacques Rousseau, *Paix perpétuelle* in Jean-Jacques Rousseau, *Œuvres completes* (Paris, Éditions Gallimard, 1964) III, 570).

[6] See August Wilhelm Heffter, *Das Europäische Völkerrecht der Gegenwart* (Berlin, Verlag von HW Müller, 1882) § 6, p 13; Theodore AH Schmalz, *Das europäische Völkerrecht* (Berlin, Duncker & Humblot, 1817) V, iv, p 207.

[7] Heinrich Bernhard Oppenheim, *System des Völkerrechts* (Stuttgart, Kröner Verlag, 1866) I, iii, § 4, p 32. This is reflected by de Mably who in his study of the strategic dealings of European states notes that 'in relation to a state of which one is not a natural ally, there is, and can only be, fleeting alliances' (Gabriel Bonnot de Mably, *Principes des Négociations*, (London, 1789) x, p 91). This would seem to leave the alliances between natural allies, by which Mably understands powers that cannot, because of the position of their respective domains, harm each other and are furthermore united by a common enmity towards a third power (ix, p 79). But even the bond between such natural allies is precarious and can be overturned by 'accidents ... in a hundred different ways' (ix, p 81).

Not surprisingly, there was an acute sense that what the principle of equilibrium delivered was not, strictly speaking, law. However, by introducing laws of movement into a system that was constituted by the free play of forces, the principle of equilibrium held out the promise of something resembling law. The ambivalence that attached to the principle are reflected in von Marten's remark that even if the system invited abuse, it could not be 'dismissed as superfluous, condemned as illegitimate, or effaced from the law of peoples.'[8] Basing the law of peoples on a principle of equilibrium had the effect of suspending law on decisions that would be taken as a function of particular interests. But the principle of equilibrium was, nonetheless, indispensable because it, and it alone, offered a means of aligning law on the actual distribution of power and therefore made it more likely that those capable of re-establishing equilibrium would do so. This is why the great powers were all committed to the principle:

> [Even if none of the great powers] have laboured in earnest and with consistency to uphold or re-establish equilibrium, with the exception of Great Britain from the end of the seventeenth century, or later Prussia, to this day most of Europe's great powers believe that they are entitled to monitor the equilibrium as if it were a principle of the law of peoples.[9]

On this understanding of international life according to which there is no law among states, just rational force, only two strategies of federalism were available: (1) a utopian federalism that aimed at changing the mode of state interaction and was therefore universal in scope; and (2) a federalism *a minima* that situated itself at the most basic level of political life in order to obtain purchase on state action. We see the former strategy exemplified in the work of Rousseau; the latter in the work of Montesquieu.

From the structure of the state system, Rousseau would draw an argument to dissuade sovereigns from engaging in hostilities. The impossibility of hegemony meant that they could not hope to consolidate gains obtained by force. Seeing that an attempt to alter the status quo by force was doomed to fail, the most they could hope for was to consolidate whatever position they presently held:

> As we have shown, under the present system, everyone will be met by a resistance superior to his efforts from which it follows that, the strongest having no reason to risk anything and the weakest no hope of success, it would be beneficial for all if they were to renounce that which they desire in order to safeguard that which they possess.[10]

Rousseau's hope is that this intuition could constitute the basis of a European federation in which recourse to arms would not be an aspect of state interaction. This would leave an invasion from the outside as the only eventuality that would need to be defended against.[11] For that to happen, the intuition would, however, need to be shared by all states, which would require each future member of the federation to renounce

[8] Georg Friedrich von Martens, *Précis du Droit des Gens Moderne de l'Europe* (hereinafter *Droit des Gens*) (Paris, Guillaumin et Cie, 1838 (1796)), IV, I, p 328.

[9] ibid, IV, I, p 334.

[10] Rousseau, *Paix perpétuelle* 581.

[11] Rousseau assures us that, at present, no power on Earth is in a position to threaten Europe as a whole and were one to arise, its emergence would be preceded by signs that would leave ample time to make the necessary preparations (ibid 586).

force in its dealings with other states, without any assurance that they would do the same. Rousseau did not find a solution to the problem. In the fragment 'A judgement on perpetual peace,' he no longer appealed to the self-interest, properly understood, of each prince. What would make the project of perpetual peace, at present an 'absurd' idea, reasonable was not a change in the mode of state interaction but the emergence of a military commander who was capable of uniting Europe's nations.[12]

If Rousseau's federalism is predicated on the hope that force might, one day, come to be governed by reason, Montesquieu's federalism rests on the acknowledgement that ties between the members of a federation extend no further than relations of force allow. To Montesquieu, federalism is a means whereby a small republic can avert otherwise inevitable defeat and destruction. By federating a small republic can make up its military weakness.[13] Federalism gives a small republic the best of both worlds, allowing it to enjoy 'the goodness of internal government …; and, with regard to the exterior, it has, by the force of the association, all the advantages of large monarchies.'[14] As the qualification of internal government indicates, federation was seen merely as a means to ensure the survival of what was good about the republic, namely its internal life in which federalism played no part. This is federalism as an auxiliary to 'real,' political government, a federalism that, if it ensures the survival of the polity, adds nothing to it.

Within the state system, federalism, in both of its forms, is without substantive content, its meaning fully and wholly determined by the modality of interaction in a system based on the formal equality of sovereigns and the material inequality of power. But this is not the full picture. The European state system did not operate in isolation. It was set within an over-arching cultural context that referred the exercise of sovereign power to an idea of Europe that cut across the divide between inner and outer, reaching to where federation could not go. It repays the effort to consider this nexus as it illustrates the role the idea of Europe played in efforts to theorise state relations within Europe.

To this end we turn our attention to the chapters from *Spirit of the Laws* where Montesquieu treats of Alexander the Great's conquest of Asia. Here, we learn that the nature of government is a function of its material preconditions, the importance of which is brought home to us by the striking difference that the comparison reveals. Europe's mountainous lay-out and temperate climate allow for, indeed predispose to, the institution of medium-sized kingdoms that are apt to be ruled by law. In contrast, the endless plains and extreme weather of Asia means that the continent is divided into vast empires fit only for despotic rule because nothing short of total domination could induce public officials to obey the commands of a distant ruler.[15]

In political terms Europe and Asia are thus polar opposites. They are, however, connected as the end points of a sliding scale of material conditions (climate, topography) that determine how power is exercised. Asian despotism is correlated with an

[12] Jean-Jacques Rousseau, *Jugement sur le projet de paix* in Jean-Jacques Rousseau, *Œuvres completes* (Paris, Éditions Gallimard, 1964) III, p 600.

[13] Charles-Luis de Secondat Montesquieu, *Spirit of the Laws* (Cambridge, Cambridge University Press, 1989) II, ix, 1, p 131. See also Emer de Vattel, *The Law of Nations* (Indianapolis, Liberty Fund, 2008) III, §§ 47–49, pp 496–498.

[14] ibid, II, ix, 1, p 132.

[15] ibid, III, xvii, 6, p 283–84. On Montesquieu's use of the topos of Alexander the Great, see Pierre Briant, *Alexandre des Lumières. Fragments d'histoire européenne* (Paris, Éditions Gallimard, 2012) 330–32, 348–58.

absence of that which renders Europe apt to be ruled by law.[16] Much rides on this correlation. The significance of the absence of mountains in Asia appears only when seen in contrast to the nature of government in Europe. Conversely, the significance of the fragmentation of Europe's territory appears only when seen in contrast to Asia's despotism which it casts as an immutable fact of nature. The symmetry of the relation creates a nexus of reciprocal reinforcement between its terms. Their implication/opposition confirms each as a destinal trajectory. In the case of Europe, this reflects and confirms a belief that political liberty is tied to the continent, not by some accident of history but because it has its locus there. In telling us that 'liberty is never strengthened in Asia, whereas in Europe liberty is strengthened or weakened according to circumstances,' Montesquieu is not reserving judgment on the future trajectory of republican government in Europe.[17] That liberty varies according to circumstance in a world where this is not so is a sign of moderation. The possibility of moderation implies moderation. It warrants that in Europe, political liberty *is* or *is already*, in spite of having never been claimed or exercised by its subjects.

It is in this light that we should view Montesquieu's insistence that moderation constitutes the primary virtue of the legislator.[18] This is, first and foremost, a prudential maxim for the sovereign to remember. But the reference to Europe also has the effect of naturalising a mode of government that, if it does not give rise to rights that could be asserted against the sovereign, does entail a strong supposition that he will exercise his power so as to accommodate individual liberty. Anything else would be contrary to the nature of government in Europe—and to the nature of Europe itself.

The idea of Europe operates within the polity to maintain the equilibrium between the ruler and the ruled, but it also brings the polities of Europe together around a specific practice of power. The force of the idea of Europe depends upon the fact that it is not tied to the particulars of one polity. As an idea, Europe is doubly transversal. In relation to each polity, it cuts across the boundary lines marking off the inner from the outer just as it cuts across the boundaries between the polities whose government it informs. The effect of this double mediation is to integrate Europe to the point where it (almost) constitutes a polity of peoples, which is exactly how it is defined in what is perhaps the most influential manual of public international law of the eighteenth century, Georg Friedrich von Martens's *Droit de Gens Moderne de l'Europe*, first published in 1789 with multiple subsequent editions. In spite of growing discord between its states, we should, he tells us, look at Europe

> as a whole that is separate from the rest of the universe, not only in terms of geography but as a specific assembly of states that, without having entered into actual society, has its own laws, its own mores, and its own customs and which can, in some respects, be seen as a people that has not yet given itself a constitution.[19]

[16] For this view, see Catherine Larrère, 'L'empire, entre fédération et république' (2005–2006) 8 *Revue Montesquieu* 130; Marco Platania, 'Dynamiques des empires et dynamiques du commerce: inflexions de la pensée de Montesquieu (1734–1802)' (2005–2006) 8 *Revue Montesquieu* 47, 52 n 40.

[17] Montesquieu, *Spirit of the Laws*, III, xvii, 6, p 283–84; I, xvii, 3, p 428.

[18] ibid, VI, xxix, 1, p 601.

[19] von Martens, *Droit de Gens* I, p 84.

When held up against this idea of European community, the absence of substantive federalism in the state system takes on a different allure. If there was no substantive federalism in European publicism, it was perhaps because there was no need for one. In a system where force constitutes the basic modality of interaction, the idea of Europe already operated as quasi-federalism that moderated the exercise of sovereign power within polities and brought them together around a specific form of government. Seen in this perspective, which posits an idea of cultural unity as the telos and pivot of state relations, sovereignty and federalism are not in opposition. On the contrary, the fact that the idea of Europe was already federating its states made it all the more mysterious that they had not formalised the community between them. The perplexity to which the absence of federation gives rise comes through very clearly in the work of von Martens:

> By continuing to live side by side in the state of nature, [Europe's states remain] heir to all the inconveniences that flow from the uncertainty and fear of the position they occupy and which are a thousand times worse for them than they would be for individuals. On certain points of law, they have reached a general consensus. Could they not settle more points? Could they not *federalise*, in whole or in part, so as to secure for themselves the peaceful enjoyment of their rights?[20]

II. THEORISING THE FEDERATION

We might say that the federalism of the European state system was impossible in form but almost realised in fact. Clearly, this paradox is intimately bound up with the principle of sovereign equality but the challenge is to understand how exactly sovereignty informs federalism theory. It is this question we shall attempt to answer as we turn our attention to the theories of federation of Constantin Frantz and Georg Jellinek. It bears saying that they were chosen not for their impact on subsequent federalism theory, which, in Frantz's case, was negligible, but because they are illustrative of the concerns of a century that had to come to terms with a reconfiguration of international life that saw states, thought to be the only real form of political organisation, integrated into greater entities. Frantz and Jellinek dismissed the idea that the form of the state could be stretched to fit the federation, but in the end, both aligned their theory of federation on the sovereign state. The analysis reveals that the implication of sovereignty in federalism goes deeper than the question of how power should be distributed; that it extends to the work that public law theory sees itself as doing. This insight shall prove essential when we consider European integration in the twentieth century. On that topic, it bears saying that both Frantz and Jellinek took Europe as the natural locus, and semantic horizon, of their theory of federation.

[20] ibid, I, pp 84–85.

Arguably, one could not give a broader definition to federalism than Frantz. Federalism is not only about distribution of constitutional authority; it is a universal principle of social and institutional development, a new world-view.[21] As it had been in Montesquieu's work, Germany is the fulcrum of the federal system Frantz proposes. Its constitution makes it uniquely qualified to play that role. It is naturally federal. Its territories extend through the non-German dominions of Austria and Prussia into Europe and its regional differences keep in place the political equality of its parts, unlike France the homogeneity of which has favoured, indeed rendered all but inevitable, the advent of despotism.[22] The integration of Germany's regional differences illustrates the 'synthetic nature' of federalism that integrates all the realms man belongs to: nature, history, and divine grace.[23] As the locus of synthetic federalism, Germany is thus destined to be the 'real basis of the federative development of Europe.'[24]

Federalism, Frantz tells us, represents the only hope of securing the freedom of the people against the illusory promises of, on the one hand, political liberty through representation and, on the other hand, a revolutionary institution of complete equality. Alone amongst political doctrines, federalism is capable of rising to the challenges of the age, both the challenges that face Germany, whose third way between parliamentary rule and democracy it reflects, and the challenges that are specific to political modernity. Frantz's theory of federalism recalls aspects of Montesquieu's theory, but it also entails a movement beyond it inasmuch as his ambitions for the federation go beyond the protection of life and property. On his analysis, the German Confederation, the most recent attempt at organising Europe along federal lines, failed because it did not propose an ideal of political life around which people could rally. He acknowledges that the confederation played an important role in organising European politics, but it did so in a merely 'passive manner,' as a 'guarantor of the status quo,' which meant that it could not outgrow its initial state of powerlessness (*Ohnmacht*).[25]

Frantz attributes the impotence of the German Confederation to the expansionist ambitions of Austria and Prussia that led them to pursue their interests in isolation from, and at the expense of, their confederates. But the ill-fate of the confederation is not fully explained by the prevarication of others. More troubling still is the 'incomprehensible' disinterest of non-hegemonic German states in federalising.

[21] Constantin Frantz, *Der Föderalismus als das leitende Prinzip für die sociale, staatliche und internationale Organisation unter besonderer Bezugnahme auf Deutschland* (hereinafter *Föderalismus*) (Mainz, Verlag von Franz Kirchheim, 1879) v, 416. Frantz's theory of federalism builds on his earlier critique of political philosophy in which he argues that the principles on which it would found civil authority—popular sovereignty, reason, and divine revelation—are all without foundation (*bodenlos*) (Constantin Frantz, *Die Naturlehre des Staates als Grundlage aller Staatswissenschaft* (Leipzig, CF Winter'sche Verlagshandlung, 1870) ix, 195).

[22] Frantz, *Föderalismus* 242, *cf* 221.

[23] ibid 198, 424.

[24] ibid vii, 223–24. This idea is a recurrent topos in Enlightenment liberalism. For another example, see Karl Heinrich Ludwig Pölitz, *Die Staatswissenschaften im Lichte unsrer Zeit* (Leipzig, JC Hinricsche Buchhandlung, 1823) III, pp 17–18, 126, 429–430.

[25] Frantz, *Föderalismus* 304.

Despite having the most to gain from federalism, they saw the defunct confederation only as a means of securing their security and individual glory.[26] We would therefore expect Frantz to develop a conception of life in a federative mode, especially as he is acutely aware that the small German states on whose participation the success of his project depended were being swept up in process of unification under Prussian dominance.[27] But Frantz does not deliver. No attempt is made to flesh out the federal world-view, to articulate what it has to offer. Instead, other doctrines, most notably nationalism, are pressed into service to advance the cause. Despite his scathing critique of the nationalism that propelled the creation of the German Empire, he argued that federalism could not afford to turn its back on nationalism. Nationalism was necessary because it 'creates an instinctual community founded on language and a certain commonality in how people feel, think, and in what they strive for.' In other words, nationalism could deliver all the things federalism needed in order to move beyond its passive mode.[28]

The appeal to nationalism might be a stopgap solution, but Frantz's willingness to tether his 'real' federalism to a doctrine with which it is, at first blush, incompatible is highly significant. It reveals that ultimately, his concern was with the alignment of community and constitutional order, which refers us back to the tradition of public law theory. Connecting community and constitutional order was exactly what sovereignty promised. If federalism, to Frantz, is the only ideology capable of meeting the challenges of political modernity, it is because he expects life in the federal mode to release pent-up existential energies that will allow Germany to make good on sovereignty's promise. The exit from the tradition that Frantz is looking for is therefore a complex matter. In repudiating the form to which public law theory had tied its fortunes—the state—Frantz is committing to the ideal that guided public law theory. In fact, it is by reference to this commitment that he liquidates the idea of the state.[29]

The analysis of Frantz's federalism reveals how the idea of sovereignty continued to inform public law theory even as it dissociated itself from the tradition. Turning to Georg Jellinek's theory of federation, we find that it too is caught up in a complex exchange with the tradition of public law theory that revolves around the idea of sovereignty. As with Frantz, Jellinek's theory of federation must be seen in the context of the creation of the German Empire, but we would be wrong to think that this burning political question exhausted his concerns.[30] He was also looking to elevate the federation to the status of a public law form, claiming it for public law theory. To Jellinek, it was in fact not given that the federation was a legitimate object of scientific public law inquiry as it did not belong within any of the existing sciences of public law. Inasmuch as it straddled the divide between state law and international

[26] ibid 311.

[27] ibid 313, *cf* 233.

[28] ibid 347, *cf* 340, 345.

[29] The semantic dependence of his theory on sovereignty extends even further. In tethering his theory of federalism to nationalism Frantz is repeating a mode of operation that was constitutive of sovereign power. Sovereignty made its claim to allegiance precisely by dissociating form and content. It required the subject to commit fully and unconditionally but it did not require anything in particular.

[30] On Jellinek and the context of his work, see the contribution of Duncan Kelly to this volume.

law, it threatened to destabilise both disciplines, which prompted Jellinek to warn that if the concepts of state law and international law could not be as neatly delineated as the concepts of private law, neither state law nor international law would qualify as sciences.[31]

Jellinek's argument for why the federation should be seen as a legitimate object of public law theory is that it meets all the requirements public law theory habitually makes in relation to its objects. This involved him in a reinterpretation of the foundations of public law, more precisely, the belief that public law authority would have to rest on consent, express or tacit. This belief justified excluding the federation from the remit of public law. As a federation was only an aggregation of already constituted polities, it could not, it was thought, become the object of consent for the simple reason that there was no federal people to give consent. To elevate the federation to the status of an object of public law theory, Jellinek had to disaggregate the conception of authority that public law theory had inherited from natural law and for that, he relied on international law. It was by adopting its external perspective on the state that he was able to underwrite the claim that a federation could legitimately be seen as a self-standing entity. International law was right to view a plurality of states that federate as a collective power (*Gesamtmacht*), not as a mere aggregate power. More than anything else, international law is concerned with impact and, seen from the outside, 'long-lasting community and internal unity give rise to the same effect.'[32]

But if international law was right to hold that a federation can constitute a collective, it was wrong in supposing that its status as a collective was founded in its internal unity. Looking beyond the question of impact, we find, Jellinek tells us, that external community and internal unity do not map onto each other. External community, however long-lasting, is not necessarily reflective of internal unity, and only the latter warrants the ascription of legal personality. Whether a plurality counts as a collective or not is a question that international law simply cannot answer. It depends on a determination international law cannot make because the terms of determination lie beyond its remit. The point of Jellinek's critique is double: on the one hand, he refers the theory of federation back to the state as its point of reference and, on the other hand, he dissociates that theory from the internal perspective of the state, the adoption of which invariably ties the unity of community to a form of political agency. This operation leaves open the possibility that while some unions of states are not genuine objects of public law, others might be and should be placed on a par with the state.[33]

This is the background against which Jellinek theorises the 'federal' state, a federation that is 'in and of itself' a state. His partial assimilation of federation and state pushes the question of what a federation is back to the question of what it is that constitutes a state as a subject. The conventional answer of public law theory was representation. Crucially, this is not the answer Jellinek gives. What sets the state

[31] Georg Jellinek, *Die Lehre von den Staatenverbindungen* (Vienna, Alfred Hölder, 1882) 15.

[32] ibid 182.

[33] Jellinek is careful not to advertise that he is breaking new ground. When we read that a union of states that is not 'in and of itself' a state does not, for the purposes of law, count as a subject (*Rechtssubjekt*) but as a relation (*Rechtsverhältniss*), the emphasis is not on the assimilation of federation and state but on the uncontroversial denial of personality to non-state federations (ibid 178).

apart from other institutions is that its power is concerned with 'furthering the common ends of men (*menschlichen Gemeinzwecke*).'[34] This determination of the specific difference of the state leaves much unanswered but, for our purposes, that is not essential. In tying legal personality to the substantive objectives of action, Jellinek is making the point that the state is not, in principle, better placed to exercise the powers of a subject than is a federation.

This rehabilitation of the federation comes at the cost of throwing into doubt how precisely a state, unitary or federal, differs from non-state federations. Jellinek does not address this question directly, but his text identifies two ways in which a non-state federation, a confederation, comes up short: (1) it is too dependent on its component parts that retain the power to unmake the union at their discretion; and (2) it does not command the existential commitment of its subjects. Jellinek takes for granted that states will meet both requirements; not on account of some inherent quality of statehood that might be arrived at through conceptual analysis, but because that is *in fact* what states do. Public law theory should build on this basic fact. In assessing the status of a federation, it should not look to its constitutional characteristics (which would collapse the difference between forms of federation that Jellinek is working to establish) but to how closely the federation in question approximates the reality of the state. This explains why, as he tries to indicate the difference between a federal state and a confederation, he should warn of the danger for public law that lies in detaching the idea of the state from its 'natural foundations.'[35]

But if a federation should aspire to the reality of the state, for no other reason than to exist *in law*, federalism theory must find a way to reference that reality. Sovereignty is that way. Jellinek tells us that sovereignty is what defines a federal state and sets it apart from a confederation. This is quite remarkable, for a number of reasons. For one, outside the context of federations, Jellinek avoids the concept altogether. It is absent from his earlier work on international law as it shall be from his later theory of state. His theory of international law proceeds from an analysis of the requirements for the self-determination of will, with no consideration of sovereignty, and in his theory of state he denies that sovereignty constitutes an essential aspect of state power.[36] However, sovereignty is needed for the purposes of theorising the federation because, unlike state law and international law, federalism theory is not predicated on the existence of an already-formed body politic in which a unitary will is rendered manifest and real. The reality of a federation must inhere in something other than a body politic. That something is sovereignty. Sovereignty delivers on both the counts that Jellinek identified in relation to the confederation. It marks the point at which the power of society detaches itself from the plurality that brought it into being and becomes self-standing. At the same time, the detachment of a sovereign power requires the commitment of each individual within the plurality.

[34] ibid 180.

[35] ibid 181 n 17.

[36] Georg Jellinek, *Die rechtliche Natur der Staatenverträge* (Vienna, Alfred Hölder, 1880) 15–18, 43–45; *Allgemeine Staatslehre* (Berlin, Verlag von O Häring, 1900) 420, 445. We find the same oscillation around the link between sovereignty and federation in Raymond Carré de Malberg's theory of state (see Raymond Carré de Malberg, *Contribution à la Théorie Générale de l'État* (Paris, Librairie de la Société du Recuil Siery, 1920) I, 123–47).

Seen in this light, attributing sovereignty to the federation is simply another way of saying that it is a genuine form of public law, a genuine object of public law theory.

Given the challenges that federations pose to theory, it is not hard to see why the idea of sovereignty should hold such attraction for Jellinek. But invoking it is not without problems. It is not clear that Jellinek can in fact accommodate sovereignty within his theory of federation. As he introduces the idea of sovereignty, Jellinek dismisses the mechanism by which Hobbes first brought it into being. A federation, in this respect no different from any other polity, cannot be founded in contract because the power to command cannot rest on the assent of those that are subject to this power:

> One cannot, by means of a contract, bring forth a higher will to sit above or an independent will to sit next to one. [...] A public authority that had been created in this way would not have the most prominent characteristic of state power: it could not rule or command unconditionally but would at all times depend on the good will of the members of society.[37]

At first glance the problem seems to be that of finding a means of tying sovereignty to the federation, indicating how it arises out of the workings of a federal polity. A closer reading reveals that the problem goes deeper. Ultimately, it is not with the form in which the creative agency of the people is exercised but with popular agency itself. As it had been in Hobbes, the idea of sovereignty is tied to the political impotence of the people, but because Jellinek rejects as a fiction the idea of representation by which Hobbes implicated the people in constitutional order, he is left with an alternative of which both terms are unacceptable. If the involvement of the people in the federal polity is not mediated through an original but extraordinary constitutional agency—the corollary to representation—either the people is implicated through ordinary political agency or it is not implicated at all, which would mean that the federation would be in name only. It would be a structure, not a subject. Without stating it, Jellinek tries to keep open the possibility that the German Empire could take a path that would steer clear of both alternatives. This is why he undertakes a tortured comparison between the German Empire and the United States of America, the aim of which is to show that agency on the part of the people is not a requirement for the reality of a federal polity. It does not invalidate the claim of the German Empire to be a genuine public law form that it was created from above, not by an act of the people. No federation ever is, not even the vibrant American federation that was created on the battlefields of Antietam, Vicksburg and Gettysburg. Its creation might have involved the people, but ultimately, the federation was the work of forces of history that transcended the people's capacity for agency.

The implication of Jellinek's argument is that a federal people will always find its federation already made, which shifts focus from what constitutes a federation to the mode in which a federal people appropriates its polity. Not only does Jellinek's argument leave open the possibility that a people might commit fully and wholly to a federation; through the elision of the intermediary stages of its being, he posits that commitment as an imperative, and a structural necessity. To exist at all,

[37] Jellinek, *Die Lehre von den Staatenverbindungen* 257–58.

a federation must exist in full. To be, it must be real. This, we would argue, is the sense of Jellinek's reference to this untethered sovereignty which he is, for want of conceptual means, unable to connect to the federation.[38] Indeed, there is no other sense we can ascribe to it. Referencing sovereignty serves no systematic purpose. It does not pick out a form of treaty-based interstate relations, nor does it shed light on the way federal constitutions operate. It is a speech act that posits a determined collective subject, a people for whom the German Empire is the fulfilment of its national aspirations, which, Jellinek tells us, is what allows a confederation to become a federal state.[39]

The oscillation between supposition and conjuration is congenital to sovereignty. We see it already in Hobbes' theory of commonwealth. What changes from Hobbes to Jellinek is the way that sovereignty relates to the polity, and what it picks out. In Hobbes' work, it serves as a *symbol* of the polity's existence, in Jellinek's theory of federation, as a *metaphor* of its reality. The change, in both mode and object, reflects a movement beyond the abstraction of modern natural law. It is not surprising that Jellinek would enter into this movement. His work as a theorist rests on the rejection of representation and popular sovereignty, the two key elements of natural law. That he nevertheless brought sovereignty back indicates the depth to which public law theory was implicated in modern natural law. No longer a conscious reference, natural law continued to influence public law theory indirectly, by shaping the expectations it had to meet. Federalism remained in thrall of sovereignty because it carried forward the ambition of justifying power. This ambition had been the lodestar of European political philosophy and public law theory.[40] Europe's federalisation has only begun in earnest with its fading-away.

III. CRISIS AND POST-HUMANISM: FEDERALISING EUROPE

The work of Frantz and Jellinek illustrates what is perhaps the most important way in which the idea of sovereignty continued to inform federalism theory even as sovereignty was eclipsed within public law theory. The federalist critique of sovereignty proceeded by reference to the promise of political life that sovereignty held out. In claiming that sovereignty had not delivered on its promise, federalist theory accepted

[38] In later work Jellinek continues to struggle with the question of how to connect public authority to those it governs, given that they are not seen as having political agency. See the analysis in Amnon Lev, *Sovereignty and Liberty: A Study of the Foundations of Power* (Abingdon, Routledge, 2014) 170–73.

[39] Jellinek, *Die Lehre von den Staatenverbindungen* 257. Jellinek's analysis suggests a reason to be wary of post-modern readings of the European Union that see the dialectic of identity and alterity as constitutive of its being (see, eg, Hans Lindahl, 'Sovereignty and Representation in the EU' in Neil Walker (ed), *Sovereignty in Transition* (Oxford, Hart Publishing, 2003) 113). Such readings overlook the fact that this dialectic does not get off the ground in theories of federation that are not, or only weakly, predicated on agency, and they mistake the inarticulation of the self for the implication of otherness.

[40] For a similar view, see Guiseppe Duso, 'Pensare il federalismo: tra categorie e costituzione' in Guiseppe Duso and Antonino Scalone (eds), *Come pensare il federalismo? Nouve categorie e trasformazioni costituzionali* (Monza, Polimetria, 2010) 73–77, 107–110.

that promise as the yardstick by which it would itself be measured. This placed a heavy onus on theorists of federation. They would have to show that a federation could deliver what the state could and what it could not; that, like the state, a federation could command the commitment of those it governed, and that, unlike the state, it would make good on sovereignty's promise of political life. The inability of Frantz to articulate a positive mode of federalism reflects his inability to do the latter; the alignment of the federation on the state in Jellinek's work reflects an awareness that the state, and it alone, carries the symbolic power to do the former.

It would be too simple to say that European public law theory of the twentieth century gave up on the promise of political life, but the public law theory of the twentieth century was born under the sign of the dissocation of legal order and political life. It is worth noting that if the federation did not pose a problem for Kelsen, whose legal theory would, more than any other, define the public law theory of the century, it is because he did not predicate the compelling force of civil authority on its capacity to span all the dimensions of human life. To Kelsen, the idea of justifying civil authority through authorisation involved a misconception about the ontology of the state inasmuch as it presupposed that a state could be justified in the absolute. What can be justified to Kelsen are the social objectives a state pursues, and such justification is always only relative. On this view, the existence of a hierarchy between central and non-central public law organs is of no significance. Rules issued by these types of organs differ only in the territorial extent of the domain to which they apply; their political valence is identical. It would be a 'gross misunderstanding' to equate rules that emanate from the centre with heteronomy and rules that have local origin with democratic autonomy.[41] The difference between federation and state is only a difference of degree, and a trivial one at that.

In a sense, the exorcising of the idea of political life from public law theory is already a fact before Kelsen, as we can see in Jellinek's work where it is not at all clear that public law maps onto human life as there are no conduits to connect the sphere of existence and the sphere of public authority. But the disaggregation of the format of political power was contained within theory. The crisis of political power was brought about by the cataclysm of the First World War.[42] Thinkers like Ernst Jünger and Carl Schmitt intuited that the war had swept away the traditional, humanist underpinnings of power. On the supposition that human agency is the

[41] Hans Kelsen, *Allgemeine Staatslehre* (Berlin, Franz Steiner Verlag, 1925) 185–86, *cf* 38. See the analysis in Antonino Scalone, 'Federalismo e decentramento fra Schmitt et Kelsen' in Duso and Scalone (eds), *Come pensare il federalismo?* 251. On Kelsen's apolitical conception of liberty, see Carlos Miguel Herrera, 'Kelsen et le libéralisme' in Carlos Miguel Herrera (ed), *Le droit, le politique: autour de Max Weber, Hans Kelsen, Carl Schmitt* (Paris, Éditions L'Harmattan, 1995) 62–67; Oliver Lepsius, 'Kelsen, théoricien de la démocratie' in Olivier Jouanjan (ed), *Hans Kelsen. Forme du droit et politique de l'autonomie* (Paris, Presses Universitaires de France, 2010) 163–68.

[42] Ernst Jünger, *Der Arbeiter. Herrschaft und Gestalt* (Stuttgart, Klett-Cotta, 1982) 165, *cf* 55; Carl Schmitt, *The Concept of the Political* (Chicago, University of Chicago Press, 2007) 29–30, 37. The analysis is prefigured in the work of Georg Lukács who in 1920 credits the most progressive elements of the bourgeoisie with having realised, from the experience of the war and the crises of the postwar period, the need for a planned economy (Georg Lukács, *Geschichte und Klassenbewußtsein* (Darmstadt, Herman Luchterhand Verlag, 1968) 150).

source of all power, political conflict had revolved around the question of the identity of the agent: was man an individual, as liberalism would have it, or a generic being, as communism taught? The war had shown the irrelevance of the question, and of the configuration of conflict that attended on it. In modern society, pursuing a war required the deployment of resources in excess of what man, however conceived, could marshal. In this sense, the war superseded the conceptual opposition of liberalism and communism around which nineteenth century political thought had revolved. What it ushered in was a social configuration in which the questions of property and ownership, and the humanism that these questions implied, were eclipsed by the question of how to mobilise all available resources in society.

Jünger will at times lapse into the language of the nineteenth century, its metaphysics and politics.[43] However, his insistence that the worker—the emblem of the new configuration—should be seen not as a new estate, a new form of society, or a new mode of production, but as a new way of appropriating the space of power,[44] clearly conveys the intention of breaking with the humanist foundations of power. What replaces humanism is an ontology of the social that indexes the being of all things on their capacity to contribute to the general mobilisation of society. Seen in this light, man no longer occupies a special place; he is not an end but a resource, one among many, and by no means the most important one.

The opprobrium that attaches to Jünger and Schmitt has glossed over the fact that this shift away from humanism is replicated in one of the most important texts of twentieth century European federalism, the Ventotene Manifesto of Altiero Spinelli and Ernesto Rossi. Much has been made of its repudiation of democracy, but for our purposes, what matters are the reasons Spinelli and Rossi give for it, and the conception of polity they advance by repudiating not only democracy but also communism. It bears saying that in situating political action between democracy and communism, they are taking up position on the same territory that Jünger explores in his work, which, by the way, makes sense of why they can look to fascism as having paved the way for the federal reorganisation of Europe.[45] Like Jünger, they are convinced that the forms of governance associated with the ideologies of the nineteenth century are inadequate to the challenges facing Europe; democracy because it is driven by an indistinct raging of passion (*torbido tumultuare di passioni*), communism because it is sectarian and conceives of society only in terms of class opposition.

What Spinelli and Rossi outline in the manifesto is a form of governance that is concerned, above all, with the rational and comprehensive organisation of society which entails that human resources should be put to the best possible use. If the manifesto recognises that the state becomes totalitarian once it ceases to be the

[43] The reference to a 'heroic realism' where life is not only experienced as a domain of necessity but of freedom (Jünger, *Der Arbeiter* 66) reflects the persistence of thematics formerly set within the philosophical tradition. As such, it marks a regression from the standpoint at which Jünger situates his theory. Influence does not only go one way, however. Jünger projects the totalitarian state whose emergence he chronicles back onto the 'genuine state tradition' of absolutism (p 268) which was in fact a much less absolute and much more precarious undertaking than he supposes.

[44] ibid 67, 77–78.

[45] Altiero Spinelli and Ernesto Rossi, *Il Manifesto di Ventotene* (Milan, Mondadori, 2006) 23–24.

guardian of the citizens' liberty, and decries the fact that, in a totalitarian state, mothers are seen only as breeders of soldiers, we look in vain for references to individual liberty or political rights that would reflect the idea of man as an end in himself. Where the manifesto addresses the question of how to safeguard the individual, it does so by ensuring that the young have access to education to acquire the skills needed to assert themselves in the 'struggle of life,' in which connection schools should take care that their output of students within any professional field correspond to the demand of the market in order to align average salaries between professions, whatever the spread might be within a particular profession.[46]

The institutional trajectory of the European Union reflects the post-humanist tendency of Spinelli and Rossi's federalism. This is perhaps most obvious in relation to the decision to place coal and steel, then the primary resources of war, under the control of a supra-statal organ composed of civil servants. On this view, war is emptied of all political significance. It does not engage questions of existential commitment or political identity; war is simply the deployment of a productive capacity that cannot be coded in the terms of traditional political philosophy or ideology.

Perhaps more importantly, the post-humanism of European federalism is also reflected in the way its economies have been integrated. In this process the individual has been doubly eclipsed, not only by the worker but also by goods. Integration has been driven by the freedom of movement of goods, the movement of workers being seen as an aspect thereof. The treaties of Paris and Rome both state the freedom of movement of workers but not before the mid-1970s did rights relating to this freedom develop in the practice of the European Court of Justice, and then only as a condition for the optimal functioning of the free movement of goods.[47] As for a proper doctrine of individual rights, it emerged only in response to pressure from especially German courts that were concerned with upholding higher levels of national protection against the claim of the supremacy of EU law.[48]

[46] ibid 28, *cf* 12.

[47] Case 48/75 *Royer* [1976] ECR 497; Case 118/75 *Watson and Belmann* [1976] ECR 1185; Case 362/88 *GB-INNO-BM* [1990] ECR 686.

[48] Case 29/69 *Stauder* [1969] ECR 419; Case 11/70 *Internationale Handelsgesellschaft* [1970] ECR 1125; Case 4/73 *Nold* [1974] ECR 491. Our account seem to be contradicted by the work Gráinne de Búrca has done on the European Political Community in which she argues that a firm commitment to human rights, unequalled since, presided over this first attempt to establish a constitution for Europe (see Gráinne de Búrca, 'The Road not Taken: The European Union as a Global Human Rights Actor' (2011) 105 *The American Journal of International Law* 651, 690–692). It is not clear, however, that the use of human rights in the draft treaties of the European Political Community reflected humanist considerations. We have good reason to doubt that it did. For one, the fact that the project of establishing a European political community was borne out of a French proposal for a common European army, the aim of which was to prevent the re-armament of West Germany proposed by the United States of America, and that it died with the failure of the European Defence Community, indicates that other concerns were primary (on this point, see R Dwan, 'Jean Monnet and the European Defence Community, 1950–1954' (2001) 1 *Cold War History* 144–49; Richard T Griffiths, 'Europe's First Constitution: The European Political Community 1952–1954' in Stephen Martin (ed), *The Construction of Europe* (Berlin, Springer Verlag, 1994) 23–24, 29). As for the 'strong' enforcement mechanism of the European Political Community human rights regime that, to de Búrca, is indicative of the strength of commitment to human rights of the prospective member states, she herself notes that it was chiefly directed at preventing member states from sliding back into totalitarianism (656–657).

Post-humanist forms of governance do not require consent, authorisation, or commitment. As Jünger intuited, they do, however, require crisis; more precisely, a mindset of crisis. Only on the assumption of imminent existential danger can the normative expectations that attach to sovereignty be rendered inoperative. Crisis, or catastrophe, is needed to put paid to foundationalism. One of the legacies of the Great War was precisely to have introduced catastrophe as the basic mode of social life, 'the a priori of a changed way of thinking.'[49] This a priori has been the backdrop to Europe's federalisation. It is no coincidence that institutional Europe gives as its own raison d'être the need to prevent another slaughter of millions, and that it grew into maturity while under the threat of total annihilation. Europe is at risk, always; that is how Europe *is*. This is perhaps the deeper sense of Jean Monnet's famous remark that Europe is the sum of its crises: Europe needs crisis to generate convergence between its members, but it also needs crisis to suspend the ambition of founding civil authority that sends us back to the traditional formats of public law theory, looking for ways to channel a commitment Europe was neither designed to solicit nor to process. It is not without irony that those who contest institutional Europe in the name of a Europe to come, a Europe of social harmony and justice,[50] confirm, more often than not, the fundamental presupposition of Europe's integration: that Europe is in peril.

Circumstances combined to keep from view the radical novelty of the mode of governance that was developing in Europe. The first decades of European integration took place in a context that recalled that of early modern public law theory and thus did not put into question traditional modes of governance. Welfare and survival were the basic, and non-contradictory, public concerns, as they had been in Hobbes' theory of commonwealth, where the constant threat of a return of the state of nature co-existed with the image of a life dedicated to properly human endeavours: 'industry, culture of the earth, commerce, navigation, arts, letters, and society.'[51] The difference was that where Hobbes departed from the notion of man as an individual, a composite, yet self-standing entity the rights and interests of which had to be accommodated in the practice of power, European law had to piece together something like an individual from the various aspects of the work relationship it extended its protection to,[52] in the process reversing capitalism's reduction of man to his quantum of force without, however, changing the distribution of rights of ownership to the means of production.

The change of register from man to worker imbued community law with an abstract quality but then the order of European law was abstract, which explains that it could

[49] Jünger, *Der Arbeiter* 57.

[50] See Etienne Balibar, 'Un nouvel élan, mais pour quelle Europe?', *Le Monde Diplomatique* (May, 2014).

[51] Hobbes, *Leviathan* (Indianapolis, Hackett Publishing Company, 1994) I, xiii, 9, 76.

[52] This accounts, at least in part, for the oft-noted lack of internal coherence in the jurisprudence of the European Court of Justice, which developed individual rights before the institution of a community citizenship. See Paul Magnette, *La citoyenneté européenne* (Brussels, Éditions de l'Université de Bruxelles, 1999) 111; Siofra O'Leary, *The Evolving Concept of Community Citizenship. From the Free Movement of Persons to Union Citizenship* (Hague, Kluwer Law International, 1996) 18; Christoph Schönberger. *Unionsbürger: Europas föderales Bürgerrecht in vergleichender Sicht* (Tübinger, Mohr Siebeck, 2005) 16.

supervene on aspects of state power. Given their non-political nature, the rights that EU law conferred on individuals did not fundamentally call into question the position of the state because the piecemeal construction of the individual did not create new identity relationships to challenge existing ones.[53] In spite of being an independent source of rights, whether in legislation or in judicial practice, the institutions of the European Community did not compete with member states because they did not look to solicit allegiance from the beneficiaries of their action. The lack of political presence mediated the transfer of power between member states and the European Community, taking the sting out of the claim that such transfer was irrevocable. In contrast to American federalism, where the relationship between levels of government was always potentially conflictual, which is why the non-identity of tasks that devolved on each level was such an important consideration,[54] this mode of federalisation offered assurance that the European Community would serve as a medium of state power and, at the same time, a support-system of the European state.[55]

Effort to bring the community closer to the peoples of Europe did not, at first, disrupt this mode of governance. Leo Tindeman, in whose report on European Union the idea of a Europe of citizens was introduced, suggested that the union take steps to render visible its contributions to the daily lives of people. The notion that Europe should be reconfigured as a Europe of citizens carries a republican air, but Tindeman's *Europe du quotidien* did not live up to that expectation. The concerns it addressed were fundamentally apolitical: the union was to prove its worth to citizens, on the one hand, by protecting them against fraud and other 'real dangers' to the enjoyment of their consumer rights where member states were unable to do so because of the free movement of goods, and, on the other hand, by setting up a common body to regulate and control nuclear power stations.[56] Slim pickings, considering that the report bears testimony to a strongly-felt need to affirm the real, tangible existence

[53] The separation of market and society is all the more remarkable as it represents a break with a specifically European tradition of state involvement in the construction of markets (see Sergio Fabbrini, 'Building a market without a state: the EU in an American perspective' in Sergio Fabbrini (ed), *Democracy and Federalism in the European Union and the United States: Exploring Post-National Governance* (Abingdon, Routledge, 2005) 120–22).

[54] See *The Federalist* (London, Penguin, 1987) XVII, p 156 (Hamilton); XLVI, p 297 (Madison).

[55] On this point, see Corrado Malandrino, 'Sviluppo di un nuovo paradigm federalista-comunicativo nella prospettiva di un'Europa federale' in Duso and Scalone (eds), *Come pensare il federalismo?* 134–35. In this connection it is worth noting that the idea of the 'market citizen,' from which the idea of a European citizenship would develop, was, from the very beginning, mediated through the relationship between individual and member state (Hans Peter Ipsen and Gert Nicolaysen, 'Haager Kongreβ für Europarecht und Bericht über die aktuelle Entwicklung des Gemeinschaftsrechts' (1964) 17 *Neue Juristische Wochenschrift* 340 n 2). The non-conflictual nature of the relationship between community institutions and member states enables the interpenetration of levels of government, as a result of which federalisation proceeds by cooperation as Robert Schütze has shown so convincingly (see Robert Schütze, *From Dual to Cooperative Federalism: The Changing Structure of European Law* (Oxford, Oxford University Press, 2009) 213–14, 235–37). However, if the cooperative element of European federalism is undisputed, it is not clear that the move towards it is best described as a move from a 'dual' federalism, rather than a gradual articulation and filling out of a skeletal structure.

[56] Bull EC (8) 1975 II, p 27. Tindeman goes on to indicate a series of measures by which the union could render itself useful to the citizens of Europe, including the gradual removal of frontier controls, improving the means of transportation and communication between states, and fostering student exchanges.

of Europe as reflected in the wealth of references to its identity. The implication of focusing community action on the apolitical (consumption) and the pre-political (environment) was that the European Union had no *political* identity separate from that of its member states. It acted as a complement to the state, and only to do what the state would have done, had it been able to.

It is an open question whether the need for self-affirmation would in time have led the European Union to dis-align with its member states. It did not come to that. External events moved the question of Europe's identity to the forefront of preoccupations. As the Cold War began to thaw, the European Community, in a flurry of activity that lasted from 1985 to 1988, adopted many of the symbolic trimmings of a state, including a flag and a hymn. These changes can only be understood as attempts to step out of the shadow of the states, not only in the sense of relating directly to the citizens of Europe, which the European Community had done in law for decades, but also in the sense of being seen to posses a capacity for agency that would elevate it above the status of a mere auxiliary to the state. This explains a series of developments that took place in the aftermath of the Cold War, both in law and in theory. Of the former, two examples come to mind: the fleshing-out of the idea of citizenship in the Maastricht Treaty and the affirmation of a more aggressive stance on how far national courts should go to give effect to directives.[57] Of the latter, the most telling example is perhaps the turn, in the scholarly literature on European integration, to federalist terminology to capture the specific identity of the EU legal order.[58]

With the end of the Cold War, the edifice that had been built in Europe during that time came into full view, its seeming novelty a marked contrast to the long years of its construction. This paradox of Europe's integration was intuited by one of its most prominent theorists who noted, some years later, the dissociation of constitution and constitutionalism in the European Union, adding that what the union needed was 'an ethos and a *telos* to justify ... the constitutional order it has already embraced.'[59] But Europe's crisis was not a crisis of ideals, as Joseph Weiler thought. Europe was in crisis because it had reached a point where, for the first time, the question of what its ideals were had become a real question.

[57] The Court developed this obligation from the mid-1980s (see Case 286/85 *McDermott and Cotter v The Minister for Social Welfare* [1987] ECR 1453) but only affirmed it aggressively in the following decade (see Case C-106/89 *Marleasing SA v La Comercial Internacional de Alimentacion SA* [1991] 1 ECR 4135). Stripping away the latitude left to states as to how directives should be implemented would, in the words of a contemporary scholar, '[invest] the notion of Community citizenship with concrete meaning' (Deidre Curtin, 'Directives: The Effectiveness of Judicial Protection of Individual Rights' (1990) 27 *Common Market Law Review* 712).

[58] See Christoph Schönberger, 'Die Europäische Union als Bund. Zugleich ein Beitrag zur Verabschiedung des Staatenbund-Bundesstaat-Schemas' (2004) 129 *Archiv des öffentlichen Rechts* 82 n 3 with references.

[59] Joseph Weiler, 'European Neo-constitutionalism: In Search of Foundations for the European Constitutional Order' (1996) XLIV *Political Studies* 518. Weiler does not query the disconnect between constitution and constitutionalism but displaces it. From the imperative of cohesion, which is, of course, the imperative of Europe, he argues to the existence of a practice of 'critical citizenship'by which we, Europeans, would resolve that which law cannot: 'A Demos which coheres around values must live those values' (at 528). This move is completely standard in public law theory. It also marks the point at which theory abdicates its vocation as critique.

This was the moment federalists across Europe had been waiting for, the moment when the European Union would finally come alive. But the conditions that lent such urgency to the question of Europe also rendered inoperative its particular brand of federalism, not by throwing the policies of Europe open to contestation, but because the determination of identity raised the question of foundations. We would argue that this, and not the jealousy of states or community institutions, is why the campaign to democratise the European Union has remained a dead letter, indeed, why it gave way to attempts to dissociate popular will from the European project altogether by painting will, and thus sovereignty, as the source of the ills that befell Europe in the twentieth century.[60]

It is an irony of history that out of the impasse in which the European Union found itself at the end of the Cold War would grow a stronger sense of its identity as a *European* project. If the detachment of the European Union from the peoples of Europe was cause for concern, indeed fear, it also lent added urgency to the project. As federalisation did not refer back to a political struggle, the idea of Europe as a realm of a liberty that was pure and exalted because it had not been won or claimed by anyone could be projected onto the legal order that had arisen in Europe. As history overlaid recent history, the construction of Europe took on the allure of a destinal trajectory, the continent's journey towards its final, original destination. Institutional Europe became, for the first time, an incantation, if only to some.

At the same time, the fact that the European Union had not come about as a result of struggles that were reflective, and generative, of political identity meant that the institutions that now had to embody the idea of a European liberty were not seen also as embodiments of a history in relation to which the peoples of Europe could situate them. If Europe now had a destination, it did not have a direction. This is the predicament in which Europe now finds itself, when there is no crisis to allow it to bracket the question of where it is going and focus instead on what it does best, viz to survive. Fortunately, one might say, crises have not been in short supply in recent years: Eurozone, refugees, and Brexit. Even if we allow for the part the European Union leadership has had in creating and perpetuating an ongoing state of crisis, we might feel that Europe, like any other polity, should be able to chart its own course. In requiring direction we might, however, be committing a category mistake. Direction might be one thing post-humanist orders do not have. We should perhaps begin to think differently of European federalism. Rather than wait for it to develop into a

[60] See, eg, Ulrich Haltern, *Europarecht und das Politische* (Tübingen, Mohr Siebeck, 2005) 264; Neil MacCormick, *Questioning Sovereignty: Law, State, and Nation in the European Commonwealth* (Oxford, Oxford University Press, 1999); Joseph HH Weiler, 'Federalism without Constitutionalism: Europe's *Sonderweg*' in Kalypso Nicolaidis and Robert Howse (eds), *The Federal Vision: Legitimacy and Levels of Governance in the United States and the European Union* (Oxford, Oxford University Press, 2001) 65–66. Pitting federalisation against sovereignty gave Europe a polemical, and political, content. It was also a source of obfuscation. It meant positing the existence of sovereign power where it had been on the wane for some time or was not operative anymore. Furthermore, it has had the effect of dissociating the ideology of European integration from the actual governance of the union, riveting discourse on institutional Europe to the moment of eclipse of a supposedly monolithic sovereign power.

full-fledged, real federalism, we should accept that this, our federalism, is as real as it is ever going to get, as much a reflection of Europe as the federalisms we look to are reflections of their communities of reference. This would be a vindication of European federalism. It is another question whether it is the federalism Europe's federalists have been waiting for.

9

Federalism and Democracy: The Far-Reaching Dynamism of Democratic Federations

DWIGHT NEWMAN*

IT IS NOT every final appellate court decision—indeed, not even every final appellate court—that encounters the opportunity to engage theoretically with the relationship between federalism and democracy. The Supreme Court of Canada, however, had precisely such an opportunity in its famed 1998 *Secession Reference*,[1] a case in which it was called upon to examine the constitutional rules that would apply if a Canadian province were to hold a provincial vote showing a majority vote for secession from Canada. In the course of pronouncing upon this purportedly hypothetical question (albeit one framed after a razor-thin 1995 Quebec vote to stay in Canada), the Court drew out of Canadian constitutional text and history a set of four unwritten constitutional principles, which included those of federalism and of democracy, and it spoke to the historical and constitutional interactions between these principles. In particular, the Court suggested that the interaction of these two principles of federalism and democracy had certain characteristics that helped to shape the legal consequences of a democratic vote within one federal unit to seek to end the federation.

As a matter of law, the mode of reasoning involved in drawing out various seemingly justiciable unwritten principles from constitutional text and history is, of course, subject to critiques, but the Court's pronouncements arising from its discussion of federalism and democracy actually speak to a broader question of interest within federalism theory both in Canada and internationally. The relationship between federalism and democracy has been the subject of past scholarship of several sorts. Some scholarship has focused on federalism as being a sort of collective parallel of individual rights constraints on democratic majoritarianism within an otherwise unitary demos, with varying perspectives then arising for whether federal

* I thank Julia Kindrachuk for research assistance.

[1] *Reference re Secession of Quebec* [1998] 2 SCR 217. For a further discussion of the *Secession Reference* contextualised within the topic of constitutional amendment, see generally Guy Régimbald and Dwight Newman, *The Law of the Canadian Constitution* (Toronto, LexisNexis Canada, 2013) 35–39.

states are thereby inherently undemocratic.[2] Other scholarship has seen the federal sharing of power as a key means of promoting noncentralised and/or multi-party popular democratic governance.[3] And yet other scholarship attempts to explore the connection between these concepts through various empirical schema that suggest various kinds of nuance.[4]

However, this extant political science scholarship has largely not tended to focus on what constitutional law ends up highlighting. Namely, federalism both responds to and constructs divisions within democratic identities. Federalism responds to but also reshapes the demos. It is in some ways difficult for citizens to take their bearings—where they might have assumed that federal structures were a response to their community identities, federal structures may actually also alter their community identities in a variety of ways. That complex reality about the nature of political communities is the fundamental claim of this chapter, aided by but not limited to the legal reasoning within the Canadian constitutional law discussion with which this chapter commences.

The first part of this chapter further draws out just what the Supreme Court of Canada did in its *Secession Reference* in its discussion of the interaction of federalism and democracy, first describing what the Court did and then attempting to reach for a broader significance to that. Given the constitutional context of the *Secession Reference*, the chapter then engages further with Canadian constitutional history to instantiate two more general claims. The second part turns to flesh out the

[2] See, eg, William H Riker, *Liberalism Against Populism: A Confrontation Between the Theory of Democracy and the Theory of Social Choice* (San Francisco, WH Freeman and Co, 1982) (seeing federation as a bargain involving a surrender of some part of democratic sovereignty); Preston King, *Federalism and Federation* (Baltimore, Johns Hopkins University Press, 1982) (focusing on inequalities resulting to citizens of different regions); Robert A Dahl, 'Federalism and the Democratic Process' in Robert A Dahl, *Democracy, Liberty, and Equality* (Oslo, Norwegian University Press, 1986) 114 (identifying the constitutional privileging of regional majorities inherent in federalism); Michael Burgess, '*Federalism as Political Ideology: Interests, Benefits, and Beneficiaries in Federalism and Federation*' in Michael Burgess and Alain-G Gagnon (eds), *Comparative Federalism and Federation: Competing Traditions and Future Directions* (Toronto, University of Toronto Press, 1993) 102 (suggesting a more nuanced read on the political ideology of federalism); Alfred Stepan, *Arguing Comparative Politics* (Oxford, Oxford University Press, 2001) 191, 318–19 (discussing necessary links between democracy and federalism to satisfy certain conditions of definitions of these systems of government).

[3] See, eg, Daniel Elazar, *Exploring Federalism* (Tuscaloosa, University of Alabama Press, 1987) 108, 146 (distinguishing federal democracy from Jacobin democracy); Daniel J Elazar (ed), *Federal Systems of the World: A Handbook of Federal, Confederal and Autonomy Arrangements* (Harlow, Longman Group, 1991) ix–xxiii (showing federalism as liberating global movement); Donald L Horowitz, *A Democratic South Africa? Constitutional Engineering in a Divided Society* (Berkeley, University of California Press, 1991) 217 (showing role of multiple regional governments in facilitating multiparty democracy); Arend Lijphart, *Democracy in Plural Societies: A Comparative Exploration* (New Haven, Yale University Press, 1977) 25 (seeing federalism as a special form of consociational democracy); Seymour M Lipset, 'Some Social Requisites of Democracy: Economic Development and Political Legitimacy' (1959) 53 *American Political Science Review* 69 (federalism strengthening democracy by increasing opportunity for multiple interests to be considered).

[4] See, eg, Edward L Gibson (ed), *Federalism and Democracy in Latin America* (Baltimore, Johns Hopkins University Press, 2004); Axel Hadenius, 'The Duration of Democracy: Institutional vs Socio-Economic Factors' in David Beetham (ed), *Defining and Measuring Democracy* (London, Sage Books, 1994) 63; Ursula K Hicks, *Federalism: Failure and Success. A Comparative Study* (Oxford, Oxford University Press, 1978).

claim that federalism arises partly as a response to pre-existing democratic cleavages. The third part develops the claim that, once present, federalism has the ongoing effect of entrenching or constructing demos-identities, thus reshaping the conditions that had purportedly been the pre-existing conditions giving rise to the need for federalism or for federalism in a specific form. For example, the scope of powers held by subfederal units may appear to be in response to the types of diverse identities within a particular state, but it also reshapes those identities, whether by further entrenching them or whether through more complex impacts on them. Indeed, it may also have the effect of entrenching vicissitudes of history in certain ways, without predetermining them but simply by entrenching their effects differently in different parts of a state and thus amplifying specific types of path dependence. The ultimate conclusion is that any federal democratic state has an additional dynamic dimension in the ongoing interaction of federalism and democracy, with the last section seeking to distinguish several possible ways in which that dynamism can play out.

I. FEDERALISM AND DEMOCRACY IN THE *SECESSION REFERENCE*

The *Secession Reference* saw the Supreme Court of Canada asked to tackle a question about constitutional change not specifically addressed within the Canadian constitutional amending formulae.[5] To answer the question, the Court tried to turn to broader principles it saw within the Canadian constitutional order. Four points from the case stand out in terms of the Court's discussion of the unwritten principles of federalism and democracy.

First, the Court, interpreting the history of Canadian Confederation, suggested that the constitutional implementation of an institutional system of federalism was an attempt to respond to historical, pre-existing diversity. In the Court's words:

> [federalism] was a legal response to the underlying political and cultural realities that existed at Confederation and continue to exist today. At Confederation, political leaders told their respective communities that the Canadian union would be able to reconcile diversity with unity.[6]

Confederation thus becomes a coming together of different demoi, with these having previously existed in different imperial colonies, with federalism a natural response to the differences between the communities coming together.

Second, the Court articulated the notion that federalism defines the scope within which democracy operates insofar as it provides for the scope of the democratically

[5] For a recent exploration of the idea of having constitutional provisions on secession, see David Haljan, *Constitutionalising Secession* (Oxford, Hart Publishing, 2014).

[6] *Reference re Secession of Quebec* at para 43. See also ibid at para 59: 'The principle of federalism facilitates the pursuit of collective goals by cultural and linguistic minorities which form the majority within a particular province. This is the case in Quebec, where the majority of the population is French-speaking, and which possesses a distinct culture. This is not merely the result of chance. The social and demographic reality of Quebec explains the existence of the province of Quebec as a political unit and indeed, was one of the essential reasons for establishing a federal structure for the Canadian union in 1867.'

pertinent community in relation to various decisions expressing democratic popular sovereignty. The Court notes as follows:

> It is, of course, true that democracy expresses the sovereign will of the people. Yet this expression, too, must be taken in the context of the other institutional values we have identified as pertinent to this Reference. The relationship between democracy and federalism means, for example, that in Canada there may be different and equally legitimate majorities in different provinces and territories and at the federal level. No one majority is more or less 'legitimate' than the others as an expression of democratic opinion, although, of course, the consequences will vary with the subject matter. A federal system of government enables different provinces to pursue policies responsive to the particular concerns and interests of people in that province. At the same time, Canada as a whole is also a democratic community in which citizens construct and achieve goals on a national scale through a federal government acting within the limits of its jurisdiction. The function of federalism is to enable citizens to participate concurrently in different collectivities and to pursue goals at both a provincial and a federal level.[7]

Third, the Court held that the two principles together imply that a federal unit can pose challenges to the existing constitutional order and expect some responsiveness to these challenges:

> The federalism principle, in conjunction with the democratic principle, dictates that the clear repudiation of the existing constitutional order and the clear expression of the desire to pursue secession by the population of a province would give rise to a reciprocal obligation on all parties to Confederation to negotiate constitutional changes to respond to that desire.[8]

Fourth, however, the Court also held that the two principles have the potential to limit one another:

> The democracy principle, as we have emphasized, cannot be invoked to trump the principles of federalism and rule of law, the rights of individuals and minorities, or the operation of democracy in the other provinces or in Canada as a whole. No negotiations could be effective if their ultimate outcome, secession, is cast as an absolute legal entitlement based upon an obligation to give effect to that act of secession in the Constitution.[9]

That these principles had the legal effects they did was a significant novelty. In a previous decision in the leadup to Canada's 1982 patriation, the Supreme Court of Canada was asked whether the principle of federalism amounted to a legal principle that constrained the federal government's approach to the United Kingdom Parliament for a constitutional amendment under the amending procedure required at the time. This decision, the *Patriation Reference*,[10] saw only two of nine justices taking the view that the principle of federalism was a legal principle. A majority were ready to identify a constitutional convention of substantial provincial consent for constitutional amendments, but a convention did not amount to a justiciable legal rule.

[7] ibid para 66.
[8] ibid para 88.
[9] ibid para 90.
[10] *Reference Re Resolution to Amend the Constitution* [1981] 1 SCR 753.

In a significant move from the reasoning in the *Patriation Reference*, the *Secession Reference* saw the Court ready to apply legal force directly to principles like federalism and democracy. In doing so, it operates within Canada's new post-1982 constitutional context established after the *Patriation Reference*. The 1982 constitutional amendments that followed the *Patriation Reference* involved a fundamental change in Canadian constitutionalism from purer parliamentary sovereignty to constitutional supremacy.[11] To simply impose the supremacy of a constitutional text, though, would not be legitimate. The Court must elaborate the structural values underpinning it. There is a distinguishing contextual factor that has changed between the *Patriation Reference* and the *Secession Reference*, with the result that the Court is now ready to give legal force to the principles of federalism and democracy. However, in recognising their legal force, the Court must pursue a more elaborated discussion of these principles' relationship.

The Supreme Court of Canada's *Secession Reference*, historic in its legal reasoning, begins with a particular historical narrative about the naturally pre-existing identities to which federalism responded. Building from this, the Court also reasons that there are a mix of different legitimate majorities within the identity units of the federal system, with different units or demoi thus reasonably able to make different policy choices on an ongoing basis. Where the choices of one demos would call into question the overall constitutional structure, that demos's view calls for a response from other demoi. At the same time, the existence of other demoi means that one demos's view does not trump those of others. Different demoi thus become locked together in a complex relationship, with the Court's articulation of an obligation to negotiate striking a balance between any claim that secession is either impermissible or achievable on a unilateral basis. In a context where the principles of federalism and democracy take on actual legal or constitutional force, then, the Court comes to articulate key concepts related to these principles and their relation. Reflecting further on its reasoning and some of the constitutional historical context from which it stems allows us to flesh out some of the key ideas concerning the relationship of federalism and democracy.

II. FEDERALISM AS A RESPONSE TO DIVIDED DEMOI

Constitutional history is, of course, inherently particular rather than universal. The particular history of Canadian constitutionalism saw the 1867 constitutional Confederation bringing together, initially, four colonies in what would become Canada, albeit with others soon to join. The British North America Act, later renamed the Constitution Act, 1867, purported in its preamble to be a 'Constitution similar in principle to that of the United Kingdom.'[12] However, it rapidly diverged from the centralised governmental system of the United Kingdom and, indeed, modelled

[11] *Secession Reference* at para 72 (noting the shift from a system of parliamentary sovereignty to one of constitutional supremacy).

[12] Constitution Act 1867, preamble.

itself partly after American federalism, albeit with careful responses to American constitutional experience to that point which some saw as having enabled the civil war that immediately preceded Canadian Confederation.[13] The resulting choice was a particular system of federalism that ensured significant ongoing jurisdictional control particularly for the province of Quebec, with the initial Confederation arrangement showing even some asymmetries in terms of stronger protections of Quebec civil law than of the distinctive common law systems of the other provinces.[14]

At the same time, particular constitutional choices are responses to more general considerations, to broader constitutional values. Although this phenomenon does not arise so much in respect of American federalism, there is sometimes an anachronistic tendency to read Canadian constitutional history as if based around negotiated bargains rather than principled constitutional formulations. However, the constitutional discussions leading up to 1867 can actually be recognised as having encompassed a rich discussion of fundamental rights and principles, within which constitutional design choices responded to a full consideration of rights, principles, and values.[15] In this context, the choice of a system of federalism responded to principled reasons for jurisdictional control at a sub-state level, with principled consideration of the effects of federalism giving rise to a balanced system of federal units and minority rights of various sorts.

Contrary to extant scholarly suspicion of federalism as interfering with majoritarian democracy,[16] there is a manner in which federalism actually responds very directly to the principle of democracy by responding to overlapping normative concerns. Obviously, it is not within the scope of this chapter to make an effort at fully elaborating all underlying normative values of federalism and/or democracy; within the limited scope of this chapter, then, there remains a necessary agnosticism as between different analyses of their underlying values. However, on two broad approaches to the notion of democratic legitimacy, it is possible to see the overlap with the normative concerns of federalism.

[13] Garth Stevenson, *Unfulfilled Union: Canadian Federalism and National Unity* (Toronto, Gage, 1989) 22–33. On the broader linkages of American, Canadian, and Australian federalism, see Michelle Biddulph and Dwight Newman, 'Comparativist-Structural Approaches to Interpretation of the Post-Obamacare Spending Power' (2012) 21 *Cardozo Journal of International Law & Comparative Law* 24–28, 45–47, 69–73.

[14] At the outset, provision was made for the federal government to choose to unify common law in the three provinces other than Quebec, with s 94 of the Constitution Act, 1867 providing that '[n]otwithstanding anything in this Act, the Parliament of Canada may make Provision for the Uniformity of all or any of the Laws relative to Property and Civil Rights in Ontario, Nova Scotia, and New Brunswick, and of the Procedure of all or any of the Courts in those Three Provinces, and from and after the passing of any Act in that Behalf the Power of the Parliament of Canada to make Laws in relation to any Matter comprised in any such Act shall, notwithstanding anything in this Act, be unrestricted; but any Act of the Parliament of Canada making Provision for such Uniformity shall not have effect in any Province unless and until it is adopted and enacted as Law by the Legislature thereof.' There was no contemplation of uniformity of private law with Quebec, which could maintain its civil law system, but there was such contemplation in respect of the common law provinces.

[15] For discussion, see generally Janet Ajzenstat, *The Canadian Founding* (Montreal, McGill-Queen's University Press, 2007).

[16] See, eg, Riker, *Liberalism Against Populism*. For a more positive view analogous to the present one, see Lipset, 'Social Requisites of Democracy'.

First, one broad set of approaches to why democracy is a particularly legitimate form of government are concerned with what may be thought of as 'democracy as autonomy',[17] with this broad concept encompassing different traditions ranging from republicanism to liberalism to populism that are all concerned with the ability of democracy to be particularly supportive of ideals of autonomy. Second, and in what will read to some as a highly attenuated form of democracy, some may look more simply from a social choice point of view to preference satisfaction as a consequentialist-based social choice analysis of what democracy attempts to achieve.[18]

On either of these sorts of broad accounts of what makes democracy legitimate, there is a link to federalism. That will be easier in practical terms to set out primarily in terms of preference satisfaction. However, that greater preference satisfaction would also, in general terms, track autonomy enhancement for those for whom the different strands of 'democracy as autonomy' serve as the markers of democratic legitimacy. In simple terms, where division of the demoi makes accurate preference satisfaction simpler, that also enhances the responsiveness of democracy to autonomy-enhancing factors. So, the chapter proceeds in terms of that simpler analysis, but with full respect for deeper accounts of democratic legitimacy as potentially underlying it.

Considered abstractly, division of jurisdiction through federalism has the potential to respond very effectively to any significant democratic cleavage, thus promoting greater preference satisfaction, so long as two conditions are met: (1) policy choices on a matter over which there is a democratic cleavage can be made independently by different units, without external effects on other units; and (2) units can be defined in a manner corresponding to the democratic cleavage.

Note the generality of this account. Federalism need not, of course, be territorial but can be based on non-territorial means of dividing jurisdiction (or a combination of territorial and non-territorial means) if those means are practicable and better respond to these conditions; there can even be complex overlapping layers of federalism.[19] For example, very significant ongoing discussions of powers to be held by indigenous governments within Canada sometimes think of those indigenous governments as exercising powers on a territorial basis and sometimes think of them as exercising some powers in relation to their own members (or 'citizens') on a non-territorial basis, even as many of their members move to off-reserve urban contexts for employment.

Whether federalism is territorial or non-territorial in its basis, the key point is that the division of jurisdiction into units can provide for choices better corresponding to

[17] See, eg, Henry S Richardson, *Democratic Autonomy: Public Reasoning About the Ends of Policy* (New York, Oxford University Press, 2002).

[18] This tradition is found in the likes of Amartya Sen, *Collective Choice and Social Welfare* (San Francisco, Holden-Day, 1970) and many other economics-minded thinkers.

[19] On non-territorial federalism and the possibilities of overlapping layers of federalism, see generally Roderick A Macdonald, 'Kaleidoscopic Federalism' in Jean-François Gaudreault-DesBiens and Fabien Gélinas (eds), *Le fédéralisme dans tous ses états. Gouvernance, identité et méthodologie/The States and Moods of Federalism: Governance, Identity and Methodology* (Brussels, Bruylant & Éditions Yvon Blais, 2005) 261.

democratic choices if the conditions are met. For example, if part A of the population homogeneously and consistently prefers policy X on a particular issue and part B of the population homogeneously and consistently prefers policy Y on that issue, so long as the differing policies do not externally affect one another, there would be a consistently greater preference satisfaction if it is possible for each part of the population to have its preferred policy, and there would thus arise a democratic reason to separate the two parts of the population into separate legal jurisdictions on this issue.

Admittedly, non-territorial federalism may well struggle relatively more so to avoid the problem of external effects from policy choices or may be impracticable for any of a variety of other issues, including costs of administration when governance is territorially dispersed. Territorial federalism will often avoid external effects, at least on a range of issues, but homogeneity of the population will of course become less likely than in the context of a non-territorial, identity-based definition of jurisdictional units. Indeed, it will become common to see the presence of minority populations within territorial federal units. If their preferences on the policies in issue diverge from the majorities within the federal units, a federal system may no longer as effectively provide for democratic preference satisfaction, unless it provides for rights for those minority populations to diverge on some issues from the choices that would be made by the majorities in the pertinent federal units.

Full-fledged federal systems are, of course, not based around jurisdictional divisions based on each particular issue, with different units diverging randomly on different issues. Rather, units with a range of powers will be established on the basis of perceptions about larger democratic identities (perhaps 'cultural' identities) that lead to more consistent divisions across a range of issues, potentially with opt-out rights for minorities within those units to offset consistent effects against them. In many respects, federalism is designed precisely as a fulfilment of the democratic principle.

Nonetheless, the simpler model conceived around one policy issue can already find some instantiations in the Canadian example at play. Consider, for instance, the matter of the language in which provincial governments operate in a country where most Canadians are anglophone but both English and French are major languages. The language spoken by Canadians tracks geography closely, with the vast majority of francophone Canadians being in Quebec or immediately adjacent parts of neighbouring provinces. Quebec ends up having a strong francophone majority but significant anglophone minority, New Brunswick a relatively close division between languages, Ontario a numerically significant francophone minority near the Quebec border albeit one less significant as a proportion of the overall population, and other provinces relatively smaller francophone minorities ranging through to very small proportions of the population. A territorial division of units then works reasonably, with Quebec functioning primarily in French but with English-language provision, New Brunswick operating with full bilingualism, and other provinces with English-language operations but with varying francophone rights corresponding to the circumstances of the minority populations. On the preference satisfaction analysis, these different arrangements likely fit with democratic preference satisfaction better than any alternative arrangement would—and they certainly fit better than a unitary majoritarian decision of English unilingualism would. Federalism allows a better fit with democratic preferences on a particular issue.

The significance of language groupings, and their correspondence to broader cultural factors, means that it is unsurprising that the same federal units actually have a range of different powers to make differing policies at a provincial level. The opportunity to do so, combined with some protections for minorities within the different provinces, allows a better fit with the democratic majorities in the different provinces across a range of issues. Thus, for example, a provincial power over education[20] allows different provinces with different cultural identities to make choices about educational systems that would have major effects, ultimately, on culture. At the time of the early federal arrangements when religion had a clear interaction with education, then in several provinces, guaranteed denominational school rights assured the Catholic or Protestant minority in a district the chance to have a separate system. So, a broader power that encompassed a range of issues could be divided by unit, with identifiable sub-units within being empowered with minority rights to offset what would otherwise be negative effects on them.

To some extent, this discussion merely puts a more analytic terminology on Canadian constitutional history while also recognising the more general application of that history. As put by the Supreme Court of Canada in respect of the history but in a statement which could be reframed more abstractly:

> The principle of federalism facilitates the pursuit of collective goals by cultural and linguistic minorities which form the majority within a particular province. This is the case in Quebec, where the majority of the population is French-speaking, and which possesses a distinct culture. This is not merely the result of chance. The social and demographic reality of Quebec explains the existence of the province of Quebec as a political unit and indeed, was one of the essential reasons for establishing a federal structure for the Canadian union in 1867.[21]

As a matter of Canadian constitutional history, then, federalism responded to diversity within the state-level demos, with this response being merely to extended forms of the sort of analysis that could apply to one issue over which there would be a division. Based on the conditions that differing policies do not have external effects on one another and that there are ways to carve out units with differing views on policies within particular spheres of authority (and to align them in more intricate ways through minority rights, if needed), a federal division of powers aligns political power with democratic choices.

In a forward-looking theme to which the last part will return, it bears noting that constitutional design need not have been simply something entrenched at some past moment with no possibility of future change. Indeed, Canadian constitutional history witnesses a more recent creation of a federal unit in light of increased awareness that the unit in question might wish to make a variety of different policy choices than the unit from which it was separated. The relatively recent 1993 creation of

[20] Constitution Act 1867, s 93.

[21] *Secession Reference* at para 59.

Nunavut as a territory in Canada's Eastern Arctic responded to differences between it and the rest of the Northwest Territories (from which it was separated), and it established a territory with a significant Inuit majority.[22] That the large majority of its population is Inuit then facilitates the use of Inuktitut as a language of government and a variety of policy choices that respond to Inuit cultural values in a larger sense than would have been possible while that population remained part of another territorial unit. The process of federalism is ongoing.

III. FEDERALISM AND THE CONSTRUCTION OF DIVIDED DEMOS-IDENTITIES

In a history-regarding sense, however, it is appropriate to begin to complicate the story that federalism simply responds to pre-ordained differences. Federalism also shapes those differences, both in more foreseeable and less foreseeable ways. In 1867, the design of Canadian federalism responded to the realities of Quebec being very different from the other provinces. The existence of those differences arose in meaningful part from its history as having been separate as a colony and having its distinctive language, religion, law, and culture guaranteed to it following the 1763 settlement between England and France. Notably, following rebellions that arose from a variety of reasons in Upper Canada (Ontario) and Lower Canada (Quebec) in 1837, the report of Lord Durham recommended unification of these two colonies, which was pursued for a time,[23] albeit without assimilative 'success' over a relatively short time period. Had a unified government persisted over a lengthy period of time, it is imaginable that differences might have lessened, with the result that negotiations at the time of a subsequent constitutional design might not have been based on the same democratic cleavages.

A later decision in Canadian constitutional history may illustrate the point even better. In 1905, the prairie provinces of Alberta and Saskatchewan were carved out of what was then the southern part of the Northwest Territories. Although some raised the possibility of just one province being created that would occupy the full land mass of what became two provinces, others feared the potential future power of what could become a very populous province. The division into two political units of what was a reasonably undivided area in terms of geography and culture would turn out to be a fateful one. Beginning with diverging populist movements in the 1930s, these two very similar locales developed in very different political directions and, ultimately, quite differently as provinces. Based on beginnings in the 1930s, Saskatchewan elected North America's first democratic socialist government in 1944, and that party remained the province's dominant political force over a number of decades, with only recent years suggesting a longer-term conservative shift. Alberta elected a right-wing populist party, the Social Credit Party, in 1935, and it governed in Alberta until the 1970s before being replaced by a new right-wing dynasty.

[22] This was done through the Nunavut Act, SC 1993, c 28.

[23] Union Act 1840 (3 & 4 Vict c 35) (UK).

Even the renowned sociologist Seymour Lipset became intrigued by this little story from a far-flung corner of Canada, and he wrote in 1968 about the different political development of these provinces after the Depression, noting the lack of any 'adequate explanation, or even a detailed descriptive account, of the factors involved that resulted in such different reactions from two quite similar social units.'[24] Immediately thereafter, political scientist David Smith offered an explanation in terms of federalism,[25] albeit in peculiarly expansive terms. Federalism cannot offer any complete explanation for the different paths of different units if those units are in fact 'quite similar social units.'[26] But it opens the possibility for various factors, including even random shocks, to set different political units on different paths and thus ultimately for those political units to diverge as social units. Even the random division of political peoples opens the possibility of different peoples developing. Federalism thus becomes potentially *demos*-shaping.

Apart from the rather singular example just referenced, in the Canadian constitutional context, this dynamic has played out more generally in the development of strong provincial identities in provinces other than those for whom the federal system was possibly envisioned in the official, Quebec-oriented history often repeated, including by the Supreme Court in the *Secession Reference*.[27] The constitutional design of 1867 was not at the time for the sake of distinctive Western Canadian provinces, which did not exist at the time. However, the allocation of significant areas of jurisdiction to provinces has had longer-term effects in permitting the articulation of regional differences that have emerged within the federation's development. As put by one prominent political scientist, '[t]he very substantial jurisdictional powers of provincial governments—from social policy to economic development to constitutional politics—have helped western provincial governments, and the parties and elites that drive them, to shape, mould, and reinforce regional protest.'[28]

The emergence of strong regional identity in Western Canada is in part a feature of the emergence of provincial identities as enabled by the federal system. In turn, the political forces these provincial identities have supported have pushed for strong versions of federalism that precisely do not fit the official Quebec-oriented asymmetric federalism origin myth. A major concept of the equality of the provinces took firm root in Western Canada and has had various political consequences over time. And the 1982 constitutional patriation and reconfigurations (in many stories,

[24] Seymour M Lipset, *Agrarian Socialism: The Cooperative Commonwealth Federation in Saskatchewan. A Study in Political Sociology* (New York, Anchor Books, 1968) xxii.

[25] David E Smith, 'A Comparison of Prairie Political Developments in Saskatchewan and Alberta' (1969) 4 *Journal of Canadian Studies* 17.

[26] See Peter R Sinclair, 'Class Structure and Populist Protest: The Case of Western Canada' (1975) 1 *Canadian Journal of Sociology* 1 (stating that federalism 'did indeed make separate political development possible, but in itself is no explanation of the nature of that development'); Sinclair's is an example of an ongoing literature trying to explain the example in different terms. On the facts of the example, there has arguably been some re-convergence in recent decades, but the point nonetheless stands that there was a significant divergence as between two socially similar units, which had been enabled by a federal division of political unit.

[27] *Secession Reference* at para 217.

[28] Nelson Wiseman, 'The West as a Political Region' in George Melnyk (ed), *Riel to Reform: A History of Protest in Western Canada* (Saskatoon, Fifth House, 1992) 287.

most famously a constitutional Charter of Rights and constitutionalised aboriginal rights) had to take account of the emergence of strong provincial identities, including through the reinforcement of provincial powers in the context of natural resources as a necessity of there being any constitutional deal.[29]

By definition, the constitutional creation of federal political units opens the legal possibility that these units will adopt different policy choices. If some policy choices affect future policy choices through any of a variety of mechanisms—whether simply by shifting something about the future calculus on particular choices or by having effects on the unit that in some manner alter features of its population—then the constitutional creation of federal political units opens the possibility of larger future differences. If some of these are more entrenched, such as if there are resulting changes to the nature of the population in particular units, then the future effects of the present creation of federal political units may ultimately speak back in some manner to the democratic cleavage reasons that may have been behind the creation of some units. Things that were exogenous before may become endogenous to the system. Insofar as it opens the room for different units to develop separately from one another, federalism can provide a necessary condition for developments that raise future questions about the shape of federal units as they have developed, thus providing the seeds for its own dynamism.

IV. FEDERALISM, DEMOCRACY, AND DYNAMISM

This chapter has kept tying itself to particular features of Canadian constitutional history. But those particular historical developments are just one instantiation of general themes and an analytic calculus that arises. Federalism and democracy can interact in complex ways over time, but there are underlying factors that can partly explicate that interaction in particular circumstances.

Pre-existing social differences can thus create circumstances in which the implementation of federalism is actually a democratic constitutional policy through which democratic preference satisfaction is maximised. Federalism's ability to increase democratic preference satisfaction hinges on an ability to create federal units that correspond to democratic cleavages and a relative absence of external effects from one federal unit's choices on another. Federalism's ability to improve democratic preference satisfaction may be augmented by the addition of other sorts of constitutional policies, including policies that extend federalism at various levels and/or create countervailing rights for those who end up within minorities within federal units. Nonetheless, the degree to which federalism responds to and thus overcomes effects that would otherwise arise from democratic differences has some circumstantial components based on the ways in which pre-existing democratic cleavages run, as well as the institutional technology for following these cleavages, and the nature of particular policy areas and their susceptibility to policy-making that avoids effects running across political units.

[29] On the natural resources provision in the 1982 negotiations, see Dwight Newman, *Natural Resource Jurisdiction in Canada* (Toronto, LexisNexis Canada, 2013) 4–5, 20–23.

Insofar as federal units may be constructed in some countries in response to deeper cultural divisions as between some units, approaches to federalism that seek to meet democratic aspirations may well allocate to a sub-state level policy areas that have broader culture-shaping possibilities and effects. In so doing, the allocation of such powers may have unexpected effects as between jurisdictional units that may have been divided for other reasons. Where asymmetric conditions lie behind the creation of federal units that are nonetheless constructed symmetrically, the ultimate effects may result in federal units that did not initially diverge becoming more divergent over time. The creation of political units can end up affecting future social units, particularly if those political units are jurisdictionally empowered in ways that may shape sociocultural identity.

At an analytic descriptive level, then, federalism may respond to differing democratic *demoi*, but it may also be *demos*-shaping. Federalism may respond to democratic considerations, but it can ultimately then alter the democratic unit in which decisions are made, with potential effects back onto the way in which federalism should logically respond to the now-differently differing democratic *demoi*. Are there ways to predict, or even better understand, this dynamic aspect of federalism and its interaction with democracy?

The ongoing interaction of federalism and democracy has, ultimately, a dynamic aspect that can play out in several different ways. Indeed, the narrative of the last part of this chapter has perhaps taken a tone that will surprise some, in envisioning how federalism can enable larger divergence as between different political units. That possibility arises, perhaps, from a federalism with stronger sub-state power, such as in Canada, and a federalism that simply enables some different policy choices on less consequential matters may play out quite differently. Justice Brandeis's famous suggestion that American states could serve as 'laboratories of democracy'[30] trying out novel policies that might then be adopted by other states rests, perhaps, more on a vision of experimentation on limited policy issues that will not then fundamentally change the identity of states in divergent ways.

Constitutional design elements may affect aspects of how these possibilities play out, or so may the actual democratic choices made within the possibilities that federalism enables. That is to say that the divergence resulting from federalism arises both from what is possible within a particular system of federalism and from the choices actually made within the range of what is possible. The shape of the federal system is not necessarily the determinative point, depending on in what directions democratic forces will go within the range of options they have within the federal system. The shape of the federal system determines what democratic majorities will be recognised on what issues, but it does not necessarily determine what those democratic majorities will decide on those issues.

To restate and build upon what seemed to be a limiting point, though, the shape of a federal system does, however, determine what spheres of jurisdiction have their policy choices endogenised to a particular political unit or particular demos.

[30] *New State Ice Co v Liebmann* 285 US 262, 311 (1932).

Where democratic majorities differ within a state, at least potentially, an issue that is defined by the federal system to be at a national level is essentially exogenously determined relative to the democratic majority within any particular sub-state political unit, so long as that sub-state political unit is 'small.' This 'smallness' qualification is necessary but need not be read in literal numerical terms. If a particular political unit influences the national choice in a major way, then the determination on that issue is not as fully exogenous so far as the democratic majority in that unit is concerned. Such influence can stem from a particular political unit itself containing a significant portion of the national population or from it being in ready coalitions with other political units around particular issues. However, for a sub-state political unit without that influence, national policy choices could essentially be thought of as exogenous political shocks, with the provincial democratic majority able to consider only particular endogenously-determined policy choices.

The dynamics of federalism will rest, in part, on to what extent earlier sets of choices about federal constitutional design have endogenised the federal system itself, either through federal provincial endogenisation of identity-forming policies that affect longer-term federal aspirations and/or provincial endogenisation of abilities to amend features of the federal system. To the extent that these matters are endogenised formally or informally to provincial democratic control, the federal system becomes inherently oriented toward ongoing change and takes on a change-oriented dynamic that is in contrast to the possibility of a simple, stable federal division that exists around certain specific issues.

To return to the particular example that has been at play within the chapter, Canada's 1982 constitutional patriation established constitutional amending formulae located in Canada but largely requiring significant cooperation between provinces for the formal use of these formulae. What the Supreme Court of Canada did in the *Secession Reference*, however, was to recognise that a strong democratic call from a particular federal unit for fundamental change evoked the need for discussions under these amending formulae, and the larger pattern of Canadian constitutional history permits ongoing informal transition in the federal structure. Canada has endogenised at the provincial level both a range of significant policy choices and the ability to pursue further amendment of the federal system. In doing so, it has embodied a different choice than in some other federal systems and has entrenched the long-term potential for a particular dynamism in its federalism.

The scope of spheres of jurisdiction within a federal system, then, bears strongly on the longer-term nature of that particular federal system. It bears noting that the significance of particular areas of jurisdiction has the potential to shift over time, in light of historical developments, though the long-term significance of some would have been more stable and is arguably more foreseeable.

Whether any normative conclusions arise depends, of course, partly on whether one adds any particular normative values. However, even if one does, matters remain immensely complex. If one added a value of maximal constitutional stability over time, that value might appear to speak, in some ways, toward limits on the spheres of jurisdiction to be allocated through a federal system to the sub-state level. Someone of such a mindset might think that constraining the locally endogenised choices would help to prevent divergence and what the chapter has spoken of as the dynamism present in some federations. However, there would be reasons to question the underlying analytical descriptive claims behind this argument. First, to the extent that federal division does respond to democratic preference satisfaction, there is even a matter of democratic legitimacy at issue under which a federal system with significant divergence may permit a more satisfactory and thus more legitimate and thus more stable set of democratic choices. Second, to the extent that the significance of some areas of jurisdiction shifts over time, there is a complicating factor. Third, to the extent that there are genuinely exogenous shocks to a system, a federal system may be more supple in dealing with these, precisely if they are better dealt with at a more local level. The value of subsidiarity sometimes enables flexibility, with flexibility enabling stability if it lets a system bend without breaking.

A further interesting dimension arises from the reality that both the principle of federalism and the principle of democracy have inherently normative value in themselves. The point will be taken as obvious with respect to the principle of democracy. However, the principle of federalism arguably takes on some of the exact same value. In circumstances where federalism enables a more closely attuned democracy—those in which federally defined democratic units can respond more precisely to the aspirations of social units and individuals within—federalism is the fulfilment of a greater democracy.

Moreover, it now bears noting that this analysis, thus far, has thought of democracy in relatively static terms associated with social choice at a moment in time. If one is concerned with democratic dialogue, or other more discursive practices necessary to forms of deliberative democracy or democratic republicanism, federalism may also enable democratic dialogue in ways that further enrich its connection with democracy, dynamically understood. Insofar as some forms of federalism enable a dynamism about more matters, they are implicitly enabling a broader set of democratic dialogues and expanding the scope of democratic decision-making.

This chapter commenced with what appeared to be defences of federalism in terms of its responses to pre-existing democratic differences. It has added on the complexities of the ways in which federalism can lead to reshaping of those democratic differences over time. There are many different analytic dimensions to how those concepts play out, with complexities in how to relate them to any normative conclusions. But the federal idea may well embody a more dynamic form of democracy than anyone has thus far assumed. If the federal idea enables democratic dialogues across a broader range of matters, it may actually sustain democracy in richer possible senses. Suggestions that principles of federalism and democracy must constrain one another, as in the *Secession Reference*,[31] are not incorrect, but they are incomplete. Federalism and democracy do not only constrain one another; they also have the very real potential to dynamically sustain one another. The federal idea is a democratic idea in larger senses than often appreciated by extant scholarship. Hopefully the rich understandings of the federal idea within this collection help to contribute to a new wave of scholarship that further enriches our broad appreciation for the federal idea.

[31] *Secession Reference* at para 217.

10

Federalism and the Plurinational Challenge

STEPHEN TIERNEY

IT HAS BEEN remarked that federalism is under-theorised.[1] This is certainly true and this book offers a welcome opportunity to expand the study of federalism to take account of recent developments in political and constitutional theory. There are many ways in which theory can intervene to help us understand the conception, institutionalisation and practice of federal systems. In line with the book's focus on the place of federalism in public law theory, I attempt to connect federalism to political and constitutional theory, situating federalism as a form of constitutional practice that has developed against the backdrop of wider trends in political theory.

Federalism as a concept, as an ideal, and as a system of government, is intimately connected to, and informed by, the surrounding ideological environment within which it has been shaped, and therefore to understand federalism properly we must locate it more broadly as part of the wider development of liberal democracy. Of course, during the twentieth century instances of federalism emerged from other ideological or even theological backgrounds such as state socialism and Islam, but the origins of modern federalism, from its first instantiation in the foundation of the United States to the present day, are tied inextricably to the birth and development of the liberal model of government.

Despite this historical legacy and the ideological framework liberalism has provided for the construction of federal states, federalism's close connection with this one particular political philosophy is rarely discussed and indeed is generally taken for granted. This is so even though liberalism as a political philosophy is inherently normative and imbues federalism with many of its foundational assumptions about the nature of man and society, as well as with the normative commitments which flow from these assumptions.

But the task in which we are engaged here is to consider not only what federalism is but also how we think about the federal model and the types of values which have been super-imposed upon it. A broad re-evaluation of the liberal model of federalism is itself a huge challenge, and if undertaken in anything like a comprehensive way

[1] Malcolm M Feeley and Edward L Rubin, *Federalism: Political Identity and Tragic Compromise* (Ann Arbor, University of Michigan Press, 2008).

would take us in a number of different directions. The issue I will focus upon in this chapter is 'the demos question.' Liberal democracy's principal normative commitments—to liberty and equality—have largely taken for granted the nature of the demos as the setting within which these values play out. In particular, it is assumed that in each state there functions one unified national community from which the rights and duties of citizenship flow among individuals who are in turn largely undifferentiated, at least for the purpose of how these values apply, by key markers such as territorially-based identity or ethnic origin.

This has two relevant and immediately notable implications. The first is that federalism rarely—if ever—features in the work of key liberal theorists as a factor that might impact upon their notions of justice. This is so even for theorists such as John Rawls or Jürgen Habermas who grew up and worked within federal states.[2] A second is that federal theory (informed greatly as it is by the ideological underpinnings of liberal democratic thought) has, somewhat paradoxically, also adopted a monistic conception of the demos. I say paradoxically because one of the oft-stated purposes and benefits of federalism is its purported capacity to accommodate territorial diversity. It may be argued, of course, that federalism, with its division of powers between centre and territorial government, a notion of shared or divided sovereignty etc, does implicitly acknowledge at least the possibility of multiple demoi within the state. In due course, therefore, I will defend my claim that these facets of federalism do not, of themselves, amount to a pluralisation of the concept of the demos within either the federal state or the federal idea.

I. FEDERALISM: WHY DOES IT MATTER, WHAT IS IT?

I do not propose to catalogue or categorise federal systems; this is the staple of much federal scholarship and while this is interesting and valuable groundwork to which I will refer, I will not review it in detail. I do, however, want to make one or two preparatory comments concerning the nature of the phenomenon we are discussing. The first is a note about relevance. Federalism clearly does matter. In the world today there are many federal states, each functioning in its own particular way. A precise figure is difficult to arrive at because of the range of definitions of 'federal system.' For example, in 1994 Daniel Elazar estimated that of the world's 180 odd states, over half were federal or had some kind of federal arrangement.[3] In 1996, using a narrower definition, Ronald Watts estimated there were merely 23 federations in the world.[4] This seems like a stark contrast of course, but in fact it is a figure with which

[2] John Rawls, *A Theory of Justice* (Oxford, Oxford University Press, 1972) 102, 357; John Rawls, *The Law of Peoples* (Cambridge, Mass, Cambridge University Press, 1999). On Habermas, see Margaret Canovan, 'Sleeping Dogs, Prowling Cats and Soaring Doves: Three Paradoxes in the Political Theory of Nationhood' (2001) 49 *Political Studies* 205–206.

[3] Daniel J Elazar, *Federal Systems of the World: A Handbook of Federal, Confederal and Autonomy Arrangements* (Harlow, Longman, 1994) xvi–xvii.

[4] Ronald L Watts, *Comparing Federal Systems* (Montreal, McGill-Queens University Press, 1999).

in some sense Elazar agreed.[5] These differences are accounted for by a different approach to categorising what a federal system is. And this in itself illustrates just how contested the terrain of definition is in the area of federalism.

Indeed, we find a highly-developed literature on terminological or conceptual differences, for example on the distinction between federalism and federation. An increasingly prominent school of thought sees the former as a largely normative concept, in contract to the descriptive properties of 'federation,' a distinction first made by Preston King.[6] Burgess also adopts this distinction in much of his work exploring the boundaries of federalism. For him a federation 'is a particular kind of state,' while he takes 'federalism to mean the recommendation (and sometimes) the active promotion of support for federation.'[7]

Notably Ronald Watts went further in the search for clarity, introducing a three type distinction: federalism, federal political systems, and federations. For him federalism

> is basically not a descriptive but a normative term and refers to the advocacy of multi-tiered government combining elements of shared rule and regional self-rule ... The essence of federalism as a normative principle is the perpetuation of both union and non-centralisation at the same time.[8]

This identifies the same normative approach to federalism adopted by King, Burgess and others.[9]

Federal political systems and federations, by contrast, are for Watts 'descriptive terms applying to particular forms of political organisation.' The former is broader and more inclusive than the latter, which is a 'particular species' of the former.[10] By the term 'federal political system' Watts refers

> to a broad category of political systems in which, by contrast to the single central source of authority in unitary systems, there are two (or more) levels of government which combine elements of *shared-rule* through common institutions and *regional self-rule* for the governments of constituent units.[11]

This 'broad genus' embraces many of the species ranging from 'quasi-federations' and 'federations' to 'confederacies' and beyond.

[5] Notably, Elazar also arrived at this number using the more narrow species of 'formally federal systems in the world today' (Elazar, *Federal Systems of the World* xvii).

[6] Preston King, *Federalism and Federation* (London, Croom Helm, 1982).

[7] Michael Burgess, *Comparative Federalism: Theory and Practice* (Abingdon, Routledge, 2006) 2, 47–48. See also Ronald L Watts, *Comparing Federal Systems in the 1990s* (Kingston, Institute of Intergovernmental Relations, 1996) 6–7.

[8] ibid 6.

[9] See, eg, Nicholas Aroney: 'I use the term "federalism" to designate a certain body of ideas, while I reserve the term "federation" to refer to a particular form of political organization influenced by those ideas.' (Nicholas Aroney, 'Before Federalism? Thomas Aquinas, Jean Quidort and Nicola Casanus' in Ann Ward and Lee Ward (eds), *The Ashgate Research Companion to Federalism* (Farnham, Ashgate, 2009) 31, 32).

[10] Watts, *Comparing Federal Systems in the 1990s* 7.

[11] ibid 6–7.

In such an open-textured approach, and in his reference to shared-rule and self-rule, Watts embraces Daniel Elazar's expansion of the very concept of federalism, to which I will return shortly. Watts goes on

> [furthermore], other political systems outside the general category of federal systems may incorporate some federal arrangements because political leaders and nation-builders are less bound by considerations of theoretical purity than by the pragmatic search for workable political arrangements. Such considerations may also lead to hybrids such as the European Union which, although originally a purely confederal arrangement, has in recent years been moving towards incorporating some features of a federation.[12]

He therefore reserves the term 'federation' for a particular, specific category within the genus of federal political systems:

> Federations represent a particular species in which neither the federal nor the constituent units of government are constitutionally subordinate to the other, ie each has sovereign powers derived from the constitution rather than another level of government, each is empowered to deal directly with its citizens in the exercise of its legislative, executive and taxing powers and each is directly elected by its citizens.[13]

This expansive approach to definitions adopted by Watts, King, Burgess and others tends also to be coupled with a more flexible approach to looking for federal forms in a variety of different political arrangements. In this regard Watts is not alone in being influenced by the open-textured approach taken by Daniel Elazar and his idea that a federation is a particular form of union the essence of which is 'self-rule plus shared rule.'[14] This broader, functional notion of federalism can also embrace devolved models of government that do not satisfy classical definitions of federalism offered, for example, by Kenneth C Wheare.[15] Instead both Elazar and, as we have seen, Watts reserve the term federation for the classical model. This remains a notable category but it certainly is not a conclusive account of all of those polities today which embrace self-rule and shared rule in all its diversity across the world.

The new wave of federal scholars has therefore brought within the federal conceptual fold those polities which demonstrate some of the classical characteristics of federalism but not all, with the term quasi-federal system becoming commonly used. And it does seem that this more fluid approach is better suited to describing the complex and changing face of federalism today. For example, when analysing plurinational states in the context of federal theory it allows us to engage with a number of states which are not federations in Wheare's sense, such as the United Kingdom or Spain, but which have some of the characteristics of a federal system, most notably

[12] ibid 7.

[13] ibid.

[14] Daniel J Elazar, *Exploring Federalism* (Tuscaloosa, University of Alabama Press, 1987) 12.

[15] Wheare described the federal principle as 'the method of dividing powers so that the general and regional governments are each within a sphere co-ordinate and independent' (Kenneth C Wheare, *Federal Government* (Oxford, Oxford University Press, 1963) 11). Wheare's approach has been described as a 'somewhat static and legalistic interpretation of federation' (see Michael Burgess, 'Federalism and Federation' in Michael Burgess and Alain-G Gagnon (eds), *Comparative Federalism and Federation: Competing Traditions and Future Directions* (Hemel Hempstead, Harvester Wheatsheaf, 1993) 3.

multiple systems of government, the rationale for which is at least in part the existence of territorial diversity within the state.

In taking on board the more expansive empirical account of federalism offered by Elazar and others, it is also important to remember the other dimension in the revisionist account of federalism offered by King and Burgess, namely that federalism is more than simply a descriptive term. If, as I suggest, liberalism has provided the intellectual background through which it developed, then the overtly normative nature of liberal thought has surely left its mark, imbuing federalism implicitly with many of liberalism's values. The new wave of scholarship allows us to view federalism as a term bearing both a descriptive/empirical dimension and a normative under-current—not unlike liberal democracy itself, we might say.

It is in the context of the three key insights we have so far attempted to draw out—that federalism is an idea rather than merely an empirical manifestation of a system of government, that this idea has an inherently normative dimension, and that its normativity has been shaped by its close elision in terms of historical development and subsequent empirical instantiation from place to place—that we must locate the plurinational challenge to traditional conceptions of federalism. It is this challenge which I attempt to outline in the remainder of this chapter.

As I embark upon this task, another important question that stems from the efforts to catalogue and categorise federal systems, and indeed to pin down the federal idea, is whether a general account of this model of government is even possible. Is there one general theory that can define a multi-level government structure that is of sufficient breadth to encompass the great diversity of systems we think of as federal, and still be of sufficient specificity to constitute a meaningful genus? This raises ancillary questions such as, are there certain core characteristics and certain values shared by every instance of the federal model (bearing in mind the normative as well as empirical dimensions that must be encapsulated by such a model)? Such an account should be able to set out some common purpose or set of purposes shared in whole or in part by any federal system, some common system for the distribution of powers, some common institutional characteristics etc.

When we do turn to the standard purposes that are often offered for federalism, we see the normative dimension of the concept emerge very clearly. These purposes attribute goods that flow from federalism, or dangers that can be avoided or lessened by it, in this way presenting federalism as a subset of that other normatively-laden idea—liberal democracy. It is beyond the scope of this chapter to try to offer a comprehensive account of the main purposes of federalism and a full-blown account of these goods etc, but by way of illustration I will mention briefly a few of the key purposes that it is often claimed are served by federalism since the intimate conception to liberalism is illustrated thereby:

(1) the control of public power by dividing or sharing it among more than one level of government (the security argument): this is clearly informed by a liberal approach to government, for example in the Madisonian tradition that views public power as a threat to private liberty and consequently values constitutionalism as a device with which to delimit the extent and potency of government;

(2) maximisation of economic/public policy efficiency (the effectiveness argument): again this is informed by a liberal approach to rational individual decision-making, embracing values such as free market determination, the benefits of competition etc;
(3) maximisation of individual preferences (the rational choice argument): this relates closely to the second argument but is more overtly informed by the liberal commitment that individual choice is better reflected through more localised levels of government.

Two other rationales are less obviously liberal in nature, since they seem to recognise that collective attachments also matter to people:

(1) maintenance of democracy in a diverse polity (the stability argument): this recognises that territorial and other differences do exist within certain states, and that the federal state is more stable if it accommodates multiple polities in a way that offers a governmental outlet for the discrete preferences of these respective territories;
(2) accommodation of different identities across a polity (the diversity argument): this relates to the stability argument but is different in being more clearly normative. Territorial or ethnic/cultural diversity is advanced as something worthy of protection. A system of government should be designed to reflect and accommodate the identities of different groups of people. As the rise of liberal multiculturalism has demonstrated, this goal is also fully consistent with liberal values, although this relationship is a highly tense one, as I will discuss.

II. INHERENT TENSIONS IN THE FEDERAL IDEA

I have offered the view that the term federalism performs both descriptive and theoretical (normative) functions. As a normative category it offers an ideal form of a particular model of government, and this form is imbued with a liberal set of presuppositions, which is itself a useful starting point from which to explore its relationship to the nation-state. But it is also notable that at the empirical level, federalism as a model of multi-level government brings with it certain inherent, immanent tensions, since it also embraces incongruous, and perhaps even mutually contradictory, components.

The federal model is an ideal form of a particular system of government; but that system is by definition made up of multiple levels. There is a foundational conceptual strain here between the singular and plural forms of government that the federal model encompasses, since, by definition, the very model of federalism seems to create the conditions for competition between these different levels of government. In the constitutional foundations of the federal state there is a tension, and hence a balance to be struck, between singularity and plurality, and hence between unity and diversity. We have seen how Elazar describes federalism as the combination of self-rule and shared rule in a contractual power-sharing relationship. This can manifest itself in particular constitutional arrangements, eg where should the residual power lie? How can the constitution be amended? We tend to take for granted these inherent tensions in the federal idea, but to do so is perhaps to overlook the incongruous nature of such an idea, particularly when it is itself a normative proposal, not only describing but also prescribing precisely such an arrangement.

III. THE PLURINATIONAL STATE AND FEDERALISM

I would now like to explore how these various components—federalism as both a descriptive and normative term, the close synergy between liberalism and the normative dimension of federalism, and the very tension that attends the notion of federalism as in some sense, and at least in certain situations, an ideal model of government—play out in the context of plurinational states, in particular as these have been explored and analysed in the recent theoretical turn addressing 'plurinational federalism.'

What is the plurinational state? Over the past 40 years, sub-state national societies in a number of developed liberal democracies including Canada, Spain and the United Kingdom have both reasserted their national distinctiveness and demanded recognition of it in political and legal terms.[16] Of course, these are not the only plurinational states but they are ones I have concentrated on in my research,[17] and they serve as good examples, albeit that they are each Western states with all of the specificities which attend this type of state.[18]

The turn in constitutional theory that has accompanied this phenomenon contends that the democratic plurinational state that has reached constitutional maturity within industrialised states, and is characterised by the presence of more than one national group within the state, is a particular type of multi-level polity. The term 'nation' has been widely applied to define sub-state territorial polities such as Catalonia, Quebec and Scotland, not only because many in these territories adopt this term by way of self-description, but also because it captures how these societies represent discrete *demoi* within the plurinational state. In this way the plurinational state is distinct from other institutional models of diversity; in particular, multiculturalism.[19]

One key characteristic of these states is a common but also pluralised historical development whereby in processes of state-led nation-building different national groups within the state retained, and today continue to retain, their individuality. In other words, the state built for itself a nation, which became the dominant cultural reference point, marker of identity and focus of loyalty. But at the same time sub-state nations also underwent processes of nation-building and consolidation often

[16] Michael Keating, *Plurinational Democracy: Stateless Nations in a Post-Sovereignty Era* (Oxford, Oxford University Press, 2001).

[17] Stephen Tierney, *Constitutional Law and National Pluralism* (Oxford, Oxford University Press, 2004).

[18] I have in recent years supervised doctoral theses on China, Sri Lanka and Nigeria as plurinational states, and these raise very different issues, which are beyond the scope of this chapter.

[19] Will Kymlicka, *Multicultural Citizenship: A Liberal Theory of Minority Rights* (Oxford, Oxford University Press, 1995).

supported by pre-existing institutions of cultural and, in some cases, governmental life. This led to an ongoing reality of national distinctiveness even within the state.

The significance of this distinctiveness does not depend necessarily upon points of cultural demarcation; indeed, the extent to which national societies, whether substatal or statal, are in reality culturally, as opposed to societally, distinctive is now an issue of some dispute.[20] It stems rather from their role as societies that are territorially concentrated, potentially self-governing and possessed of the desire for specific constitutional recognition.[21] In other words, these societies position themselves in a relational way to the state not as internal 'minorities,' but rather as polities that are in fact comparable to the state in the way they offer, or have the potential to offer, an effective site for many—if not all—of those functional and identificatory roles that the state plays in the life of the citizen. The particularity of these societies is such that we must therefore disaggregate the terms 'state' and 'nation'; the term 'nation-state', which stands for one politico-constitutional territory encapsulating one national society, simply will not serve; instead, the plurinational state must be understood in the context of its essential societal plurality.

Plurinational states certainly have been criticised in recent years for not giving adequate constitutional articulation to the reality of their multinational composition.[22] But this is symptomatic of a deeper philosophical problem, namely a general failure of liberalism not only to accommodate, but even to recognise, the empirical reality of multiple nations within certain states that are either federal or federal-like in nature, and the normative challenge presented by this multinational reality and articulated by the political agents it has produced. If this critique is valid, then liberalism's failure is also federalism's failure, not only in its particular practice from state to state, but also conceptually as a normative project; namely a failure to offer the resources needed for an articulation of the plurinational federation as a particular type of polity demarcated by the plural patterns of nation-building to which it has played host, and of the issues of justice that attend the constitutional construction and development of such a polity.

The default conception of federalism, however, as the term is overwhelmingly understood today, is built upon the terrain of mainstream liberal democracy, and as such it implicitly embraces a unitary conception of the demos. This may seem like an odd assertion to make. As has been noted, the very project of federalism, and a source of tension within this project, is an attempt to recognise, in the constitution of the state, the plurality of territories and the communities they contain. Indeed, in terms of classical categorisations, the federal state stands in contrast with the unitary state. It is also the case that one of the purposes of federalism outlined above is to recognise and accommodate territorial and ethnic diversity within the state.

But it is a mistake to assume that the concept of the demos is somehow obviously pluralised simply through the existence of a federal state. It is certainly not the case

[20] Margaret Moore, 'Globalization, Cosmopolitanism, and Minority Nationalism' in Michael Keating and John McGarry (eds), *Minority Nationalism and the Changing International Order* (Oxford, Oxford University Press, 2001) 44–60.

[21] Kymlicka, *Multicultural Citizenship*.

[22] ibid; Moore, 'Globalization, Cosmopolitanism, and Minority Nationalism'.

that 'unitary state' implies and instantiates recognition of a unitary demos, while 'federal state' implies and instantiates recognition of a plurality of demoi. First, we must distinguish the institutional design of the federal state from the demotic premise upon which this institutional design is constructed and which it is designed to serve. Yes, the federal state has a plurality of territories, each of which has its own institutions, each of which is constitutionally recognised, and among which power within the state is dispersed. However, in the classical conception of federalism, the 'peoples' of each of these states are conceived in a categorically different way from 'the people' of the state as a whole. The default position of liberal federalism conceives the people of the state in a unitary way—embracing and including within it any territorially-concentrated groups of citizens within the state not just in jurisdictional but also in demotic terms—and this in turn is crucial to the constitutional self-understanding of the state.

This demotic premise is implicit and until recently was rarely explored in theoretical accounts of federalism. In this respect it is part of a broader story of liberal democratic theory that, in characterising the state, has generally taken for granted the demos question. Liberal democracy in its theoretical underpinnings brings with it, implicitly, a unitary conceptualisation of the people of the state, whether that state be unitary or federal. What is remarkable about many of the classical accounts of liberalism is the way in which they have not entertained the possibility of a plurality of *demoi* within the plurinational state.[23]

The idea that the terms state and nation are in effect synonyms has also led to an assumption that the liberal democratic state is neutral in cultural or societal terms. But again this is mistaken. As Requejo puts it, 'practically speaking, all liberal democracies have acted as nationalising agencies for specific cultural particularisms.'[24] And crucially, in Requejo's critique, this is the case in federal and decentralised states no less than in straightforwardly unitary ones.

IV. WHY DOES THIS MATTER?

The problem in all of this is that many of the normative prescriptions emerging from traditional liberal accounts have been built upon this monist presupposition. Notions of justice, equality and fairness have been formulated in relation to a unitary national society. But in fact this has served to overlook the existence of one dominant national group within plurinational states. Since rights and duties of citizenship are formulated in the context of a unified *demos*, this can serve to overlook deeply imbalanced relations of power between communities, territories and nations within the state.[25] In the context of these imbalances, individuals from place to place

[23] Ferran Requejo, 'Introduction' in Ferran Requejo (ed), *Democracy and National Pluralism* (London, Routledge, 2001) 4.

[24] ibid. See also Ferran Requejo, 'Democratic Legitimacy and National Pluralism' in Requejo (ed), *Democracy and National Pluralism* 167–69.

[25] Alain-G Gagnon, André Lecours and Genevieve Nootens (eds), *Dominant Nationalisms* (Montreal, University of Montreal Press, 2008).

and community to community may be affected very differently by state policies, but traditional liberalism offers no remedy for this sense of injustice, since justice is itself conceptualised in a demotically unitary context and hence applied in an individualised and homogenising way. We see this, for example, in the protracted efforts by sub-state nations within countries such as Canada and Spain to achieve asymmetrical arrangements, and the strong predisposition within the federal model to resist these.

The school of 'liberal nationalist' or 'ethno-cultural pluralist' scholars working over the past two decades has challenged traditional liberalism from within as it were, asserting that liberalism has failed to meet its own normative standards in the context of the plurinational state. Liberalism has failed properly to take account of the fact that in the plurinational state the individual citizen relates to the state through the strong and often primary attachments—in terms of identity and loyalty—that are felt towards a sub-state national society. In this sense, the person fulfils the right of *individual* self-determination within a broader condition of *collective* self-determination for the particular primary *demos*. The full recognition of the sub-state national society as an equal partner in the state is a prerequisite for individual members of such a society to play a full role in the plurinational polity.

V. PLURINATIONAL SCHOLARSHIP AND THE LIBERAL THEORY OF THE STATE

The emergence of a new wave of scholarship has served to confront the liberal theory of the state. This has occurred most notably in political theory but new theoretical insights have themselves been constructed upon the empirical evidence provided by sociology and political science.

A number of sociologists have, since the 1960s, demonstrated the multinational origins of certain states, the resilience of multiple patterns of national identity within some of these, such as Belgium, Canada, Spain and the United Kingdom, and indeed the strengthening of sub-state national attachments from the 1960s onwards within these states. Notably, national identity remains strong even as cultural distinctions within multinational states and around the world seem to diminish in an era of cosmopolitanism.[26]

Following upon this work, political scientists from the 1970s onwards addressed the political mobilisation of these sub-state nations, and the political and constitutional programmes they were advancing. This resulted in a number of important implications for federalism and federal theory. The first finding was that, contrary to many expectations, political actors adopting the nationalist mantle were—for the most part—not backward-looking or reactionary, but espoused values wholly

[26] Stephane Dion has referred to the ever-closer alignment of values among nations within states at the same time as nationalist sentiment within these nations grows as 'de Tocqueville's paradox' (see Stephane Dion, 'Le nationalisme dans la convergence culturelle: le Québec contemporain et le paradoxe de Tocqueville' in Raymond Hudon and Réjean Pelletier (eds) *L'engagement intellectuel: Mélanges en l'honneur de Léon Dion* (Quebec, Presses de l'Université Laval, 1991)).

consistent with the plurality of opinion in modern, Western societies, for example on issues such as social welfare, citizenship and human rights.[27] Furthermore, these nationalist movements have advanced political programmes that run largely with the grain of changing state power, supra-state integration, and internationalisation of previously monopolistic state functions; nationalists in Scotland, Catalonia and Quebec, for example, situate themselves within the context of their respective integrating continents in ways similar to state nationalists, and in some respects are in fact more pro-integrationist.[28] In other words, the new nationalism was found to fit wholly consistently within the 'progressive' trend of modern politics, weakening the negative stereotype with which nationalism has been tarnished.

Another key point for a theory of federalism is that these nationalists were not always separatist in intention. Overtly nationalist parties often sought constitutional change, and in particular a move towards greater autonomy and representation at the centre; in other words a federalising trajectory. This created the impetus towards constitutional change that was destined to take polities like Spain and the United Kingdom in a federal direction, and cause constitutional upheaval in already federal states like Canada and Belgium. This in fact was the most radical nature of the challenge. Secession was obviously bitterly opposed by the state, but conceptually it is something the traditional liberal state can understand—a sub-state polity seeking to become a state itself. But a reform agenda that seeks to reorientate the very meaning of statehood itself by pluralising the monistic assumptions that underpin the traditional statism, assaulting the very implicit normative self-understanding of the state, is something else altogether.

VI. IMPLICATIONS FOR FEDERAL THEORY AND PRACTICE

With liberal nationalist political philosophers demonstrating how the monistic demos thesis is deeply problematised by the existence of more than one societal demos within the same polity, constitutional theorists have begun to address the implications of this theory for constitutional practice.[29] In particular, we need to re-align how we categorise federal states in light of the plurinational/uninational distinction. Some states are plurinational, some are uninational. Some federal or quasi-federal states are plurinational in composition, for example, Canada, Belgium, Nigeria, Spain and the United Kingdom (if the latter two can indeed be characterised as quasi-federal), while some federations are unitary in demotic composition, eg the USA, Australia, Germany. We also need to distinguish the sociological fact of plurinational states from their government structure. Models of plurinational federalism are now being discussed, but it goes without saying that simply because a plurinational state is federal in government structure, that does not mean the federal

[27] Michael Keating, *Nations Against the State: The New Politics of Nationalism in Quebec, Catalonia and Scotland* (New York, Palgrave Macmillan, 2001); Alain-G Gagnon and James Tully (eds), *Multinational Democracies* (Cambridge, Cambridge University Press, 2001).

[28] Keating, *Plurinational Democracy*.

[29] Tierney, *Constitutional Law and National Pluralism* (Oxford, Oxford University Press, 2004).

system in question is designed to take account of this demotic structure. One clear consequence of the general acceptance that each state contains only one demos across states whether federal or otherwise is that a federal state can be plurinational in sociological terms, without being a plurinational federation in governmental or constitutional terms.

VII. E PLURIBUS UNUM: THE PLURINATIONAL CHALLENGE

I suggested that federalism as an idea brings with it a condition of tension in seeking to combine one state system of government with multiple sub-state systems—one state territory and a number of sub-state territories. This challenge is magnified in the plurinational scenario. By the 'monistic demos' thesis there may be considerable diversity in cultural and ethnic terms within the state, and federalism is one response to this, designing institutions to reflect diversity, but there remains a foundational understanding that the federation is composed of only one statal people. Sub-state national societies are not viewed as national societies co-equal to the dominant or statal national society. Instead, if recognised at all as a salient community, they are categorised as 'minorities,' comprising a 'second order' type of group, categorically different from that of the national society of the state; hence the classical federal distinction between the federal level and the *sub*-state level. And so in the federal context we find a category distinction between one statal or federal people, which embodies the federal nation, and those sub-state communities, which make up the federal state's constituent territorial units.

Plurinational federalism questions this very categorical distinction between state and sub-state national societies, and the notion that only one national society is entitled to engage in nation-building and consolidation. The radical claims of sub-state nationalists seek a conceptual reorientation of the nature of the state. This involves first the recognition of the state's demotic plurality and that the different nations of the state form a partnership of equals. The powerful normative claims to be found in the narratives of sub-state national societies are rooted, therefore, not in the politics of difference but rather what we might call the politics of similarity. This alludes to the processes of nation-building and consolidation that remain ongoing within sub-state nations, which run in parallel to the equivalent processes at state level. These principles of union and equality therefore offer foundational principles for the construction of a plurinational federal idea, and it is in these ideas of union and equality that sub-state national societies call for partnership *with* the dominant society rather than accommodation *by* it.[30]

Two other elements are important. One is history, or more pertinently, historiography. There is the argument that alternative and therefore multiple nation-building projects have occurred within the state, resulting in multiple historically-based stories cataloguing different understandings of the origin and nature of the state and its

[30] The agenda of sovereignty and partnership advanced by Quebec nationalists at the time of the 1995 referendum on sovereignty is one example.

constitution, with those presented by sub-state nationalists often varying substantially from the dominant historical narrative embodied in the orthodox constitutionalism of the state.[31] History and how it is told combines then with the sociological reality of different national societies functioning today, to present an argument that the state, be it federal or otherwise, must take account of this reality.

Another issue is, of course, constitutionalism. The real challenge of plurinational federalism is to be found in sub-state nationalist demands for a radical reconfiguration of the state, a reconfiguration that has at its root a call to reconceive how sovereignty itself is understood within the state.[32] And central to the argument for constitutional reconstruction are the historically-informed narratives of union and equality. The notion that the sub-state territory entered the state either as a fully-formed, or at least as an incipient, national society, is often central to the construction of constitutional claims presented by sub-state nationalists. This has tended to create a vision among sub-state national societies that the larger polities to which they belong are in some sense 'union states.'[33] From this plurinational reconfiguration of some of constitutionalism's most basic self-understandings, federalism is challenged to be a system that can forge a single state but in doing so give recognition to this level of deep societal diversity.

VIII. PLURINATIONAL FEDERATION AND SOVEREIGNTY

The plurinational challenge extends to how sovereignty is conceived within the liberal democratic state, including in its federal manifestations; and this presents one of the sternest challenges to classical federalism. The challenge to traditional constitutionalism is both methodological and substantive. In methodological terms, the 'conceptual' challenge often critiques also the narrow positivism that supports a unitary model of supreme legal power and the artificial distinction it attempts to draw between the legal and the political. One foundational theoretical presupposition of narrow legal positivism is that sovereignty can be understood hermeneutically or internally. This overlooks the extent to which this idea is conditioned by the political environment within which it has developed. As MacCormick notes: 'A doctrinal understanding of the rules and principles of a system so understood gives a genuine though partial picture of a social reality.'[34] The challenge presented by sub-state national societies to federal states and to federalism as an idea is one of a

[31] Eugénie Brouillet, *La négation de la nation. L'identité culturelle québécoise et le fédéralisme canadien* (Sillery, Les Éditions du Septentrion, 2005).

[32] Stephen Tierney, 'We the Peoples: Balancing Constituent Power and Constitutionalism in Plurinational States' in Martin Loughlin and Neil Walker (eds), *The Paradox of Constitutionalism* (Oxford, Oxford University Press 2007) 229.

[33] Stein Rokkan and Derek Urwin, 'Introduction: Centres Peripheries in Western Europe' in Stein Rokkan and Derek Urwin (eds), *The Politics of Territorial Identity: Studies in European Regionalism* (London, Sage Books 1982) 11; James Mitchell, 'Evolution and Devolution: Citizenship, Institutions, and Public Policy' (2006) 36 *Publius: The Journal of Federalism* 153.

[34] Neil MacCormick, *Questioning Sovereignty: Law, State, and Nation in the European Commonwealth* (Oxford, Oxford University Press, 1999) 106.

number that call both for a fuller picture of the social reality that conditions legal form, and with it a better understanding of the nature of legal sovereignty and of its inherent and deeply symbiotic relationship with political power.[35] As Loughlin reminds us, sovereignty has both a legal and political dimension. Through this duality, sovereignty is itself a relational concept, 'devised for the purpose of giving expression to the distinctively political bond between a group of people and its mode of governance.'[36]

Sub-state nationalists call for the expression of this political bond through the constitution, but they do so in a radical way by suggesting that within the plurinational state the 'people' are plural and so, concomitantly, are the political bonds between these peoples and the different levels of governance that affect their lives, and to which they relate through variegated pathways of identity and loyalty.[37]

In substantive terms, and flowing from this methodological/historicist critique, sub-state nationalists challenge the particular constitutional manifestations of the unitary concept of legal sovereignty that arise so prevalently in plurinational states, including federal states. Here they observe that the notion of 'sovereignty' or 'fundamental law' is itself a product of extra-legal sources. This notion of legal sovereignty has been a central ideological device in legitimising the dominant, monistic vision by which the plurinational state has masqueraded as *the* nation of the state.[38] The new constitutional challenge presented by sub-state nationalists is, therefore, one that calls not simply for substantive constitutional reform; it is one that in a broader way seeks a new constitutional culture within deeply diverse liberal democracies; it challenges these states to pluralise their conception both of the *demos* and hence, through a recognition of the historical foundations of the constitution, of the sources of supreme legal authority that underpin the origins and continuing legitimacy of the state. If sovereignty does indeed give expression to the distinctively political bond between a group of people and its mode of governance[39] then, when the conceptualisation of 'the people' within the state is pluralised, a pluralisation of the very concept of sovereignty seems logically, and normatively, to be required.

IX. CONCLUSION

Will Kymlicka noted:

> A fundamental challenge facing liberal theorists … is to identify the sources of unity in a democratic multination state … A.V. Dicey once said that a stable multination federation

[35] Marc E Gold, 'The Mask of Objectivity: Politics and Rhetoric in the Supreme Court of Canada' (1985) *Supreme Court Law Review* 455; Carol Harlow, 'Discarding Dicey. Legitimating Legal Politics' in Rodney Barker (ed), *Political Ideas and Political Action* (London, Blackwell, 2000); Trevor RS Allen, 'Constitutional Dialogue and the Justification of Judicial Review' (2003) 23 *Oxford Journal of Legal Studies* 563.

[36] Martin Loughlin, 'Ten Tenets of Sovereignty' (conference paper, Corpus Christi College, Oxford, 4 October 2002) p 2. See also pp 15, 26–27.

[37] Tierney, 'We the Peoples' 229–46.

[38] Heather Rae, *State Identities and the Homogenisation of Peoples* (Cambridge, Cambridge University Press, 2002).

[39] Loughlin, 'Ten Tenets of Sovereignty'.

> requires 'a very peculiar sentiment' among its citizens, since 'they must desire union, and must not desire unity'... Liberal theory has not yet succeeded in clarifying the nature of this 'peculiar sentiment.'[40]

So the plurinational challenge is a considerable one but it also challenges sub-state nationalists to be imaginative too. Many sub-state nationalists, such as those in Scotland and Catalonia, have been looking for independence but this in the Scottish case did not attract the support of a majority of voters in the 2014 referendum, while the Catalan authorities face a very difficult task in pursuing their goal of a constitutional referendum. It is also the case that when we look at the detail of the constitutional aspirations of nationalists in these territories, they often do not look like Westphalian statehood. Even when independence proposals are advanced they often look more like radical federal proposals as with Quebec in 1995 and as with the proposal for a currency and social union advanced by Scottish nationalists in September 2014. In the end some form of federalism seems to be the aspiration. But the form that is envisaged is very different from the classical models built upon a monistic approach to the demos. The challenge, then, is to construct genuine multinational federalism. It is not easy, but the very survival of plurinational states may well depend upon the success of the project.

[40] Kymlicka, *Multicultural Citizenship* 192.

Index

T